THE COMPLETE GUIDE
INTEGRATED MEDICINE

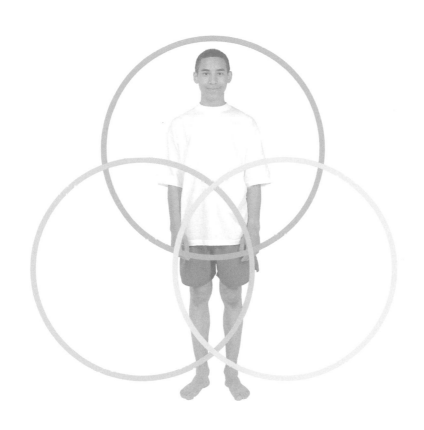

THE COMPLETE GUIDE

INTEGRATED MEDICINE

The Best of Complementary and Conventional Care

DR. DAVID PETERS & ANNE WOODHAM

A Dorling Kindersley Book

Dorling Kindersley

LONDON, NEW YORK, SYDNEY, DELHI, PARIS,
MUNICH AND JOHANNESBURG

Project Editor David Summers

Art Editor Emy Manby

Designer David Ball

Senior Editor Penny Warren

Managing Editor Susannah Marriott

Managing Art Editors Clare Shedden, Tracey Ward

DTP Designer Conrad van Dyk

Production Controllers Martin Croshaw

For Ben, Theo, Sam and Lilah, Tamsin and Jonty

AUTHORS' NOTE
The authors strongly recommend that you consult
a conventional medical practitioner before following any
complementary therapies if you have any symptoms of illness,
any diagnosed ailment or are receiving conventional treatment
or medication for any condition. Do not cease conventional
treatment or medication without first consulting your doctor.
Always inform your doctor and your complementary
practitioner of any treatments, medication or remedies that
you are taking or intend to take. See also page 21.

First published in Great Britain in 2000
by Dorling Kindersley Limited
8–9 Henrietta Street,
London WC2E 8PS

A CIP catalogue record for this book is available from
the British Library.

ISBN 0 7513 0602 9

Reproduced in Italy by GRB Editrice, Verona
Printed in China by Sun Fung Offset Binding Co. Ltd.

See our complete catalogue at
www.dk.com

CONTENTS

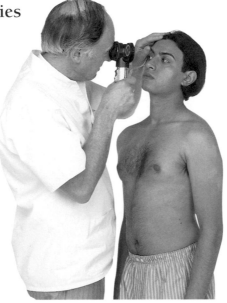

INTRODUCTION

As fast as medical science forges ahead into a future of on-line diagnosis, gene therapy and laser surgery, older, gentle modes of healing are acquiring renewed appeal. In many countries that boast state-of-the-art medicine, for example, nearly half the population claims to be using some form of non-conventional therapy, such as acupuncture, herbal medicine or massage – healing techniques that are hundreds or even thousands of years old.

HOLISTIC HEALTH

Many reasons are suggested for the popularity of non-conventional therapies. Most persuasive, perhaps, is the desire in a computerized, impersonal world to exert a measure of control over well-being. At the same time, researchers are confirming what traditional healers have always known: there is a constant interplay between our emotions, thoughts and actions and our body systems. It seems that the food we eat, the air we breathe, the exercise we take, how much we laugh or cry, and our feelings about family, friends and colleagues all have a direct bearing on health. This interaction is played out at every level of our being and affects all biochemical, structural and psycho-social systems. Clearly more is involved in healthcare than practitioners of high-tech medicine could possibly hope to deliver on their own.

BEST OF BOTH WORLDS

Of course it would be foolish to ignore the life-saving achievements of modern medicine, and many of us have cause to be grateful for the latest drugs and skills of medical specialists. But the future of healthcare involves practitioners of all approaches working hand in hand. While the surgeon repairs organs and tissues and the physician prescribes lifesaving drugs, the naturopath, herbalist and

homeopath can offer remedies to stimulate
natural healing processes, the osteopath
can realign the body, the hypnotherapist can
teach us calm and the healer can soothe the spirit.
This new approach, known as integrated medicine, is
beginning to gain cautious acceptance among some doctors and
other health professionals. Meanwhile, with a little knowledge,
an intelligent curiosity, an insightful mind and a seasoning of
common sense, you can adopt a more integrated approach
to your own healthcare, drawing on both complementary and
conventional methods. It's the aim of this book to show you how.

INTEGRATED MEDICINE IN PRACTICE

Here we explore concepts of well-being and healing and reveal
how modern medical science and traditional health systems may
have more in common than was once thought. We describe how
the causes of ailments can be tackled with both complementary
and conventional medicine on a biochemical, structural and
psycho-social level, and explain how these three "realms"
of the body interact. We show how scientific evidence is
accumulating to support non-conventional approaches,
and describe the therapies most likely to play a part in
integrated healthcare. Since prevention of disease is
as important as treatment, we explain how to make
necessary lifestyle changes for optimum health and
well-being, from eating a healthy diet to adopting a
positive attitude. These steps may help us harness
the best of both worlds: surely the way forward
for medicine in the 21st century.

chapter

Integrated medicine draws on the lifesaving drugs

and procedures of medical science and on

complementary therapies that relieve stress, stimulate

natural healing processes and nourish the spirit. It

INTEGRATED MEDICINE

addresses the needs of the *whole* person, taking into

account the astonishing subtleties of mind–body

interaction, and seeks to show how structural,

biochemical and psycho-social health are intimately

entwined. Above all, integrated medicine encourages

patients, doctors and complementary practitioners

to work as a team for the best possible outcome.

THE INTEGRATED APPROACH

Many people already combine conventional and complementary medicine on a self-help basis, in an effort to take the best from both worlds. For example, if you have a cold, you might ease the symptoms with a drug like paracetamol and take the herb echinacea to boost the immune system. Integrated medicine, however, involves more than just adding together conventional medicine and complementary therapies. It entails thinking about why you might be ill and seeking the kind of treatment – whether conventional, complementary or both – that is appropriate for your condition, given your situation, beliefs and temperament. It is also a question of taking charge of your health and, in particular, of making lifestyle changes to promote well-being.

Integrated medicine involves doctors and patients working in partnership to improve health

INTEGRATED MEDICINE IN ACTION

A small but growing number of conventional health practitioners and complementary therapists are beginning to explore ways of working together. Such teams offer treatment based on a variety of conventional and complementary options, including psychological care, with an overall emphasis on health education and active self-help. Their aim is to encourage well-being, even in the face of established disease. In this kind of partnership, a doctor might treat migraine, for example, by prescribing medication, but would also look for underlying factors, such as how you cope with stress, or foods that might be causing or perpetuating the condition. An integrated therapeutic package agreed with the patient could include acupuncture to reduce the frequency of attacks and induce relaxation; dietary advice and the keeping of a food diary; the use of a herbal remedy as a preventive measure (if the patient was reluctant to rely on the usual drugs); biofeedback to help defuse an attack; and yoga, relaxation and stress-management techniques.

HOLISTIC HEALTHCARE

Since the integrated approach is based on an understanding of the whole person, not just of his or her physical diseases or symptoms, it has come to be known as "holistic" medicine. This approach is not the exclusive preserve of complementary practitioners. Indeed, some medical doctors have been practising holistically for years and it is the accepted aim of family medicine, paediatrics and psychiatry. Conversely, some complementary therapists stick rigidly to

treating physical symptoms, ignoring the psychological dimension of disease. Others attribute even the symptoms of serious conditions such as coronary heart disease exclusively to "blocked energy", rather than to something that is in urgent need of conventional medical attention. Nor do complementary therapists usually have experience of acute disease or necessarily understand the psychological dimension of chronic disease and the often excellent resources afforded by conventional healthcare. All the more reason, therefore, to bring together the best in every discipline.

At the heart of traditional health systems such as naturopathy and Chinese and Ayurvedic (Indian) medicine is the belief that the body has a natural tendency towards equilibrium. Modern medical science calls this "homeostasis" (*see pages 12–13*), and is increasingly aware that maintaining this internal balance and boosting the body's self-healing powers are crucial to long-term good health and well-being.

Major physical injury, deficiency diseases, severe infection and even extreme mental illness can overwhelm homeostatic processes, and in these instances modern medicine does its most critical work. In the past, medical science's triumphs have tended to overshadow traditional ideas of homeostasis, but today many doctors agree that it takes more than drugs or surgery to cope with persistent disease or stress-related ailments, and the notion of holistic health is becoming popular once more.

Keeping fit helps the body's self-healing processes to work efficiently

THE MIND-BODY CONNECTION

There is increasing scientific understanding of how mind and body are inextricably intertwined, and evidence to show that the health of one influences the other. Research, for example, reveals that emotional states such as loneliness and grief can depress the immune system, leaving people susceptible to disease. When psychologists, immunologists and endocrinologists (those who study glands and hormones) began to pool information in the 1980s, they found they could track chemical pathways linking brain activity to physiological processes in the body. It had long been understood that the stress hormones adrenaline and cortisol suppressed the production of antibodies, the body's defence against disease. But studies in 1977 and 1983 showed precisely how white blood cells (which kill viruses) were temporarily paralysed in bereaved men: possibly accounting for deaths from so-called "broken-heart syndrome".

In the US, Dr. Candace Pert found that emotions trigger waves of messenger chemicals called neuropeptides, which reach all parts of the body, prompting physical changes that disturb or support homeostasis. Dr. Pert even suggests that these neuropeptides enable different body systems to communicate with each other. Key evidence came in the 1980s when endorphins, which are brain chemicals that enhance mood, were found not only in the brain, but throughout the body, even in the gut and immune system. Even more remarkably, it has now been discovered that messenger chemicals produced in the body, such as hormones, directly affect the workings of the brain.

So in the new scientific view, not only are mind and body one system, but it seems the body may influence the brain as much as the brain affects the body. The body is not just a collection of tissues and cells in a chemical soup, carrying round a detached mind. Rather, it is a moving, pulsing structure that emerges from an ever-changing flow of matter and information. The challenge of integrated medicine is to apply this idea to healthcare in an intelligent and practical way.

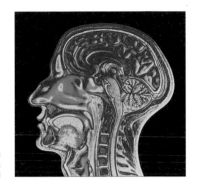

Studying the brain reveals the complex link between body and mind

---

THREE-CIRCLE APPROACH TO WELL-BEING

WELL-BEING IS COMPLEX. It depends on body chemistry, on the health of physical structures (for example, blood vessels and muscles) and on how well adjusted you are psychologically. Challenges to health affect all three spheres. On an emotional level, stress can make you anxious, irritable and depressed, but it does not just have psychological effects. Structurally, stress causes muscle tension, congested circulation, irregular breathing and raised blood pressure, while biochemically, it has an adverse effect on the messenger molecules in the bloodstream, it disturbs the way the gut, circulation and skin function, and it undermines the body's repair processes. Unrelenting stress can cause you to succumb to a host of conditions, such as irritable bowel syndrome, eczema and recurrent viral infections. As homeostasis fails, over a long period of continuing biochemical, structural and psycho-social strain, the stage is set for chronic inflammatory diseases, coronary heart disease and even cancer.

The three factors that determine an individual's state of health – biochemical, structural and psycho-social – are fundamental to homeostasis, disease prevention and health promotion. How the three realms of the body interact, the reasons why you might become ill, what conventional and complementary treatments you could consider, and how you might prevent illness, maintain well-being or cope better with established disease are the subjects of this book.

THE THREE REALMS OF THE BODY-MIND

Health depends on the state of three interdependent "realms", which are underpinned by "vital force" or "energy"

BIOCHEMICAL REALM
This is made up of:
- cells
- hormones
- enzymes
- chemical processes
- digestion and respiration
- the chemical environment
- pollution

STRUCTURAL REALM
This is made up of:
- muscles
- bones
- blood vessels and nerves
- movement
- the physical environment

PSYCHO-SOCIAL REALM
This is made up of:
- thoughts
- feelings
- relationships
- the social environment
- culture
- family
- community
- workplace

HEALTH IN THE BALANCE

W e ought to be more amazed by ourselves. Countless cells in the body, each a miraculous tiny cauldron of chemical processes, perform the intricate chain reactions on which life depends – yet the body does not overheat from the sheer energy involved and copes seamlessly with outside pressures. The body maintains a state of balance, or equilibrium, called *homeostasis*, in which all systems function smoothly. The term implies a stable internal environment, but the very nature of being alive – the continuous generation, growth and breaking down of cells, and the ever-changing environment and flux of feelings and thoughts – means that homeostasis is a dynamic state.

Well-being of people of all ages depends on staying in healthy homeostasis (balance)

MAINTAINING HOMEOSTASIS

The body is equipped to deal with everyday challenges, perpetually making the adjustments necessary to maintain equilibrium. In order to do this, it draws on resources in each of the three realms of the body and mind: the biochemical realm that fuels body processes; the structural realm that supports the organs and body systems; and the psycho-social realm that governs thoughts, desires, actions and emotions. For example, after an exhausting and stressful day, a good night's sleep allows the biochemical furnace to cool down, the body's structures to rest and relax, and the mind to assimilate the day's events.

WHEN THINGS GO WRONG

If challenges become intense, unrelenting or too frequent, the body and mind's extraordinary capacity to adapt can be overwhelmed. Coping relies on energy and order, but if a person's resources are depleted then the ability to maintain balance is undermined. Defence and repair systems may begin to fail if the integrity of cell chemistry, body structures and mind are threatened.

So entwined and so intimate is the relationship between the three realms of the body that if a problem develops in one, it can affect the working of the other two. For example, a biochemical disorder such as a nutritional deficiency or food sensitivity may have psychological consequences such as depression. Loneliness, depression, bereavement and inner conflicts can undermine immune defences, while a structural injury might cause pain that then leads to relationship problems.

The underlying factor upsetting homeostasis might be obvious – a bereavement triggering depression, or a spell of rushed working lunches resulting in bouts of indigestion. But sometimes the key cause is more difficult to pinpoint. It may be a combination of daily hassles and unhealthy diet, or the strain may lie in one realm but the effect may manifest in another, seemingly unconnected, quarter. Eczema, for example, can be provoked by emotional factors.

THE BALANCED BODY

HOMEOSTASIS IS LIKE A GYROSCOPE, which keeps spinning in the right conditions. Our bodies and minds can cope with change and adapt to challenges if they get what they need and are not pushed too far.

What builds up our power to cope and adapt?
• A balanced diet
• Relaxation
• Fresh air
• Regular exercise
• A balance of rest and activity
• Optimism
• Positive relationships
• Knowledge and access to information.

THE BODY OUT OF BALANCE

LIKE THE SPINNING GYROSCOPE, which if tilted too far will slow down and fall, homeostasis can be knocked off balance. Susceptibility increases when our needs are not met or if challenges are too great.

What undermines our resilience?
• Poor diet • Unremitting stress
• Environmental pollution and toxins
• Inertia and lack of stimulation
• Low levels of physical activity
• Lack of rest
• Persistent psychological conflicts
• Pessimism and hostility
• Isolation and loneliness.

THE RESPONSE TO STRESS

Well-being depends on maintaining a balance in the biochemical, structural and psycho-social realms of the body, and on the adaptations that each realm must make in order to deal with the stressful demands placed on it. In the 1950s, Dr. Hans Selye first described the effects of stress and explained the three stages of adaptation as follows:

Stage One: The alarm stage, or the "fight or flight" response (*see page 168*). Biochemically, the stress hormones adrenaline and cortisol pour into the body. Structurally, muscles tense, especially around the head, neck, lower back, chest and abdomen; blood flows to the muscles and away from the gut. Psycho-socially, thoughts and feelings focus on escape or attack: the impulse is to fight, take flight or freeze. If the cause of stress is removed, the body returns to normal functioning.

Stage Two: If people remain under stress, their bodies compensate by maintaining these responses. At first this "adaptation" may feel normal, but energy is drained by the continual biochemical, structural and psycho-social demands. They may get minor infections, experience discomfort, or become psychologically uneasy.

Stage Three: Long term biochemical, structural or psycho-social stress leads to a deeper kind of exhaustion as reserves are depleted. It is harder to recover from even small demands, and severe health problems can develop. Whether this is expressed biochemically, for example, a chronic inflammatory disease, structurally (persistent pain), or psycho-socially (depression or panic attacks), depends more on the individual than on the stressors.

PREVENTING ILLNESS

The idea that homeostasis, or our ability to maintain it, depends on how we react to external influences is relatively new to Western medicine. It implies that internal factors may determine an individual's response to external demands. While illness may be triggered by factors such as infections, toxins and work crises, its outcome is determined by internal resources. These include biochemical factors (diet, genetic constitution), structural factors (fitness, flexibility) and perhaps especially by psycho-social factors (temperament and coping style). Traditional holistic medical systems, such as Traditional Chinese Medicine, have always recognized the interplay between our inner nature and the world we inhabit, which may account for the renewed interest in these medical systems. The key to preventing health problems, increasing the ability to cope with life's demands, and recovering from illness lies in mobilizing the body and mind's natural resources. Irrespective of how or where a health problem first manifested, it helps to tackle it in all three realms: for example, recovery from an infectious illness demands a positive outlook as well as a nutritious diet and plenty of rest.

Homeostasis involves adapting to extremes, such as vigorous exercise and periods of rest

CHALLENGES TO HOMEOSTASIS

In a healthy person, the body's internal resources can cope with external threats. But if homeostasis is undermined, illness may result.

	BIOCHEMICAL	STRUCTURAL	PSYCHO-SOCIAL
External Threats	Infections, pollution, toxins	Physical strain	Work overload, strife and adversity
Internal Resources	Genetic constitution; good diet	Fitness; grace, flexibilty, strength	Temperament; communication skills; coping style, beliefs
External Threats			
Small (can be beneficial, helping to strengthen ways of coping, but in time can have cumulative effects)	Infections; environmental pollution	Minor injuries; physical demands and exercise	Deadlines at work; disputes with neighbours or relatives
Moderate (can impair the body's ability to cope if internal resources are weak)	Inadequate diet	Persistent poor posture; repetitive occupational strain	Bad relationship; bereavement
Severe (can overwhelm body and mind's ability to cope, causing permanent damage or even death)	Poisoning; radiation	Severe injury from an accident or car crash	Suicidal depression; psychosis

TREATING ILLNESS

Illness is not the same as disease. Someone with a headache may feel ill, for example, without having a diagnosable disease. A doctor makes a diagnosis on the basis of the patient's story and clinical signs and then prescribes treatment. Complementary practitioners look differently at the symptoms and may suggest treatments to stimulate the patient's self-healing processes. The integrated approach seeks to use conventional treatments if a clear diagnosis and safe, effective treatments are available, and to negotiate complementary treatments with the patient depending on their appropriateness and availability.

Stimulating the body's self-healing powers is an important part of integrated medicine

CONVENTIONAL DIAGNOSIS AND TREATMENT

Moments of pain, discomfort, tension, nausea, breathlessness or weakness are something most of us experience. If they are severe, persistent or worrying, we might report them to a doctor, who will ask questions – how long have we had these feelings, perhaps, and what makes them worse or better? – and make an examination to find clinical signs that could indicate the body is working abnormally, such as a raised temperature, rash, lumps, enlarged liver or abnormal heart beat. Once the doctor has made an examination, he might order blood or urine tests, X-rays or even scans if a problem is potentially serious. These tests provide clues to the inner workings of the body. Some diseases, like high blood pressure, are detected with tests alone, before feelings of illness become apparent. Others, like depression, are diagnosed by symptoms because there are no relevant physiological tests. Once a diagnosis is made, the doctor can proceed with suitable treatment. In life-threatening situations, such as appendicitis or a heart attack, medical science's hi-tech interventions can be wonderfully effective. Magnetic resonance imaging, laser surgery, computer-targeted radiotherapy, organ transplants and powerful drugs that fight infection are some of the leading-edge techniques that save lives every day. Gene therapy, with its exciting potential for so-far hard-to-treat diseases, lies just over the horizon.

DIFFICULT CONDITIONS

Doctors who practise integrated medicine aim not to focus solely on symptoms to the exclusion of other relevant aspects of the person's life. The approach comes into its own for a number of conditions, including recurring disorders such as arthritis or eczema. For

CONVENTIONAL DIAGNOSIS

- A doctor asks you about symptoms.
- He examines you for clinical signs of disease, such as a raised temperature, a rash, lumps, enlarged liver, or abnormal heart beat.
- You may have blood and urine tests and X-rays.
- Only if there is doubt about the possibility of serious illness would you be referred for tests, such as magnetic resonance imaging.
- Depending on the diagnosis, treatment might include laser surgery, computer-targeted radiotherapy, organ transplants and a wide range of drugs.

COMPLEMENTARY DIAGNOSIS

- A practitioner takes a full case history and asks about your lifestyle.
- Depending on the type of therapy, the practitioner might run diagnostic tests.
- The explanation given may bear no relationship to conventional diagnosis.
- The diagnosis will usually imply certain biochemical, structural or psycho-social causes.
- Treatment is likely to be tailored to suit the individual.

In integrated medicine, diagnosis is approached from both conventional and complementary points of view

DIFFERENT METHODS OF DIAGNOSIS AND TREATMENT			
	CONVENTIONAL MEDICINE	TRADITIONAL CHINESE MEDICINE	INTEGRATED MEDICINE
Illness	Recurring headaches	Recurring headaches	Recurring headaches
Physical symptoms	One-sided with visual disturbance and nausea	ALSO patient looks florid and has a bad taste in the mouth	ALSO patient is eating erratically and over-working
Method of diagnosis	As onset was recent, full neurological examination to exclude tumour	Note appearance of face and tongue; take pulses	ALSO discuss psychological factors and ways of coping
Diagnosis	Migraine headaches	Stagnant Liver *qi*	Stress-related migraine and poor ways of coping
Treatment	Painkillers and anti-nausea drugs	Acupuncture and herbal remedy	Possibly medication and acupuncture, and definitely advice about diet, relaxation and stress-management

these, conventional medicine on its own has no "magic bullet" to offer, and existing pharmaceutical treatments may be unsatisfactory or cause unwanted side effects. Not only are these conditions difficult and uncomfortable to live with, but they frequently require drugs such as anti-inflammatories, painkillers or antibiotics that patients are reluctant to take for long periods. For these conditions, other approaches and improving lifestyle can greatly help to improve well-being.

In chronic fatigue or persistent pain syndromes, a biochemical approach may be unable to offer any effective treatment, since tests will not usually indicate any changes in body tissues. The absence of a specific detectable cause on which to target treatment can be frustrating. Such cases of "undifferentiated" illness pose difficulties for doctors, but those who take a more holistic approach will probe for any factors, such as overwork or poor diet, that might contribute to feelings of illness and suggest complementary approaches.

Painful, stress-related illnesses that have not responded well to mainstream medicine are also conditions for which integrated medicine is likely to be most relevant. Such an approach might make use of traditional systems, such as herbal medicine or Chinese medicine, when the lack of a set of symptoms or clinical signs recognizable to Western medicine presents a problem. Language and concepts can be a stumbling block to co-operation, however. Complementary therapies base diagnosis on a different interpretation of information about the patient's body and experiences and express ideas about causes which are incomprehensible to a conventional doctor. For example, an acupuncturist might attribute a certain type of headache to "stagnant Liver *qi*".

WHY TRY INTEGRATED MEDICINE?

Surveys show that between one-third and one-half of people in industrialized countries are using complementary therapies, which is perhaps evidence of the gap between people's expectations of conventional medicine and what it can actually provide. In particular, mainstream medicine's poor track record with chronic disorders (*see Glossary, pages 177–78*) and stress-related illnesses could be one of the

reasons for the growing popularity of non-conventional medicine. Even where conventional medicine is successful, the hope of avoiding unpleasant side-effects has led to a growing public scepticism and even suspicion of the medical profession. Ironically, orthodox medicine could be a victim of its own success. Better housing, nutrition and public health

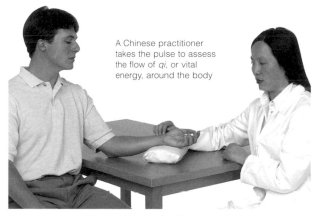

A Chinese practitioner takes the pulse to assess the flow of *qi*, or vital energy, around the body

have overcome the much-feared infectious diseases of the 19th century, and in wealthy countries, child mortality has fallen and people live longer than ever before. As our expectations of well-being have risen, so it is perhaps inevitable that we hope for too much from medical science.

However unrealistic these expectations, disappointed people are now also less inclined to accept that "doctor knows best" and we all are less prepared to tolerate paternalistic or authoritarian attitudes.

The integrated approach to health with its emphasis on active self-help and on making use of complementary approaches is especially relevant for chronic illnesses and stress-related conditions. If a doctor or a complementary therapist spends an hour or more asking detailed questions about our lifestyle, feelings and experiences, we are likely to find this personally validating. It may also give us room to consider the emotional aspects of illness and even to explore a spiritual dimension. On a more mundane level, time spent working out how to become more healthy is time well spent.

IMPROVING RESILIENCE

Practising yoga regularly helps to improve resilience to disease

Health and well-being are too important and too complex to be simply a medical matter. Ultimately they depend on the ability to adapt to challenges and to maintain homeostasis (*see pages 12–13*). In all three realms of the "body-mind" there are aspects of life that build us up and break us down. If we are under strain in one realm, it may be possible to compensate by strengthening the others. For example, playing tennis releases "feel-good" chemicals that can offset the damaging effects of emotional stress. The likelihood of becoming ill, which increases if the body and mind fail to adapt to outside pressures, depends on factors that influence *susceptiblity* and *resilience*.

ADAPTING TO PRESSURES

Some aspects of life are more controllable than others. It is possible to modify our diet, the amount of exercise we take and our ways of coping with stress, for example, more readily than our workload or environment, whereas our genetic inheritance and past medical history are totally beyond our control. Optimum well-being involves learning to minimize factors that increase susceptibility to challenges and increase resilience.

"Susceptibility" is determined by factors that undermine well-being and make us more likely to fall ill. Factors can be biochemical (inadequate diet, a genetic tendency to certain diseases), structural (lack of exercise, insanitary living conditions) or psycho-social (job loss, hostility). They may be one-off traumatic structural events, such as deprivation of oxygen at birth, or a major, hurtful psychological event in childhood. Alternatively they may be cumulative negative influences, for example, an over-critical parent or a scoliotic (curved) spine.

Resilience in one realm can be undermined by weakness in another. Even the sturdiest genetic constitution can be sabotaged by childhood malnutrition, for example, or by a disabling injury. However, it is often possible to learn to cope with factors that could sabotage health, and sometimes susceptibility can even be a spur for personal growth. Fortunately human beings are remarkably resilient. Factors that promote health can be biochemical (good diet, protective genes), structural (regular exercise, clean airy accommodation) and psycho-social (high self-esteem, community, supportive friends and family, a culture of openness). We are creative and responsive by nature, and given the chance will naturally move towards well-being.

PROMOTING GOOD HEALTH

There is a direct relationship between susceptibility and disease: low susceptibility implies a high resilience. This equation varies enormously according to an individual's ability to cope, and obviously most people have more to work on in some areas than in others. Health promotion means building up what is good rather than only changing what is bad. It is important to aim for optimum health in all realms: biochemical, structural and psycho-social (*see pages 138–75*). The great majority of diseases may be preventable if resilience is improved. In the early stages, if mind and body are not functioning well, but there are no obvious signs of disease, improving diet, lifestyle and outlook will allow the body's natural health-restoring processes to get on with their work.

Eating antioxidant fruit and vegetables protects against cell damage

SUSCEPTIBILITY AND RESILIENCE

	CAUSES OF SUSCEPTIBILITY	AIDS TO RESILIENCE
Biochemical	Hereditary tendencies	Antioxidant and fibre-rich, low-fat diet
Structural	Poor environment (overcrowding, pollution)	Appropriate exercise
Psycho-social	Poor coping skills Pessimism and hostility Poverty	Social support Humour Self-esteem

BECOMING INVOLVED IN YOUR CARE

We have a lot to thank modern medicine for: drugs or surgery can be life-saving, even life-enhancing. At the same time, if you are ill, you should try to become involved in your care, building yourself up as much as possible to counteract any side-effects of orthodox treatment or to maximize post-operative recovery, as well as to help the body's self-healing powers to do their work. You may need drugs for high blood pressure, for instance, but a healthy diet that includes foods high in potassium, such as fresh fruit and vegetables, combined with appropriate exercise and relaxation and stress-management techniques, could forestall an increase in the dosage.

Becoming involved in your healthcare leads to a greater sense of control – what some experts have called "health empowerment". In an international programme known as the Arthritis Self-Help Course, people with arthritis are offered a course in the self-

management of their disease. They learn how to design their own exercise regimes, improve their nutrition and master pain-management techniques such as relaxation, as well as how to fight depression and fatigue, how to solve problems created by their condition and how to communicate better with their doctors. The result is that participants report a dramatic decrease in pain, experience less disability than other people with arthritis and need fewer visits to the doctor.

The trend to consult people as experts about their condition is part of a welcome move towards doctor-patient partnerships. It promises a new science of well-being in which people help to shape the healthcare system to meet their real needs.

Learning how to relax can help the body's self-healing powers

---

BENEFITS OF EXERCISE

AEROBIC EXERCISE CAN HELP people to cope with stress, depression and other types of psychological strain.

It releases "feel-good" chemicals (endorphins) and improves resilience in other ways (see pages 152–53).

STRUCTURAL
- Stretches soft tissues
- Improves muscle tone
- Makes the heart work harder
- Expands lung capacity
- Helps muscles to relax (after exercise)

BIOCHEMICAL
- Produces feel-good chemicals
- Boosts metabolic rate
- Burns off stress chemicals

PSYCHO-SOCIAL
- Source of companionship
- Releases aggression
- Encourages pride in sporting skills
- Promotes calmness (after exercise)

STEPS TO IMPROVE RESILIENCE

Efforts to improve resilience and maintain homeostasis should be made in all three realms of body and mind.

Biochemical Good nutrition (see pages 158–59) helps build and nourish cells and tissues, protects against disease and counters premature ageing. Avoiding pesticides, additives and environmental chemicals may help counter cell damage.

Structural Exercise has far-reaching effects (see left) and generates a sense of well-being (see pages 152–53). Massage and other touch therapies, yoga and qigong induce the "relaxation response" (see pages 170–71) that reverses the "fight or flight" response (see page 168).

Psycho-social Helpful techniques include behavioural methods (biofeedback, relaxation and breathing) and cognitive approaches (meditation, guided imagery). These also induce the relaxation response (see pages 170–71). Psychotherapy may counteract a tendency to anxiety or depression. Positive thinking can help to raise self-esteem and increase a sense of control, enabling people to communicate better and develop social support networks.

INTEGRATED CARE IN ACTION

Combining conventional and complementary medicine is more common than most people realize. In many European countries, including the UK, an estimated 30–40 per cent of family doctors use complementary therapies themselves or refer patients to practitioners. When properly organized, the integrated approach benefits all those involved – practitioners as well as patients. Most frequently integrated into family practices are those therapies with which doctors are most comfortable. These tend to be manipulation, acupuncture, stress-management techniques, dietary advice and counselling. Herbal medicine and meditation are sanctioned, though less frequently provided. Massage therapy, aromatherapy and reflexology have been widely introduced into hospitals by nurses.

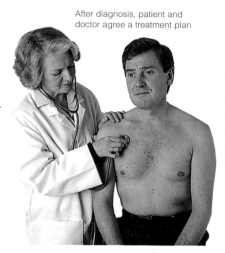

After diagnosis, patient and doctor agree a treatment plan

PIONEERING INITIATIVES

A number of programmes around the world have pioneered the use of integrated medicine. In the US, for example, Dr. Dean Ornish has devised a programme to reverse coronary heart disease without recourse to surgery or drugs. Patients follow a high-fibre diet, of which only 10 per cent of daily calories come from fat. They exercise regularly, practise yoga and other stress-management techniques and attend group therapy sessions. It's an exacting regime – but it gets results.

The benefits of innovative programmes are far-reaching. A Californian psychiatrist, Dr. David Spiegel, found that women with advanced breast cancer who attended weekly support groups, coupled with relaxation techniques and self-hypnosis, survived twice as long as those who did not. His study, published in *The Lancet* in 1989, has encouraged thousands of similar support groups around the world – not only for breast cancer patients but for those with other life-threatening diseases, adding immeasurably to their quality of life.

INTEGRATED CARE IN HOSPITALS

Hospital pain clinics, cancer treatment centres and hospices are at the forefront of integrated healthcare in which therapists and doctors co-operate to provide all-round care. Cancer patients at London's Hammersmith and Charing Cross hospitals are routinely offered massage, aromatherapy, reflexology and relaxation, as well as art therapy for those who prefer an alternative to "touch and talk" therapies. The service has the enthusiastic support of doctors, radiotherapists and nurses; one noticeable effect is that head and neck cancer patients require less Valium when undergoing claustrophobic radiotherapy.

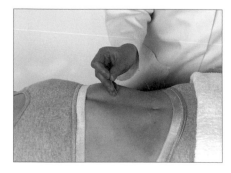

INTEGRATED MEDICINE CENTRES

Marylebone Health Centre in London, which opened in 1987, was the first National Health Service practice to employ complementary therapists, and it is the subject of a long-term research study into the effectiveness of integrated medicine. The team comprises three full-time and two part-time family doctors, an osteopath, homeopath, naturopath, acupuncturist, massage therapist and a counsellor. Conventional medicine is still the foundation of the practice but doctors have the option of suggesting a therapy if they consider it appropriate for the patient's condition.

Dr. Sue Morrison, who is in charge of the practice, says that she could not now imagine working without complementary therapies. "We have found we can contain problems – emotional as well as physical – that are usually difficult to look after in normal practice." Integrated medicine may also be part of the reason why the Marylebone Health Centre has a low referral rate to specialists and a drug-prescribing rate that is half the national average.

Centres for integrated medicine are also flowering in the US. In Lyme, New Hampshire, for example, Dr. Robert Rufsvold, a holistic family doctor, merged practices with naturopath Maureen Williams to found the New England Center for Integrative Health, Inc. The two practitioners have regular case conferences to discuss shared patients and to tap into each other's expertise. Also working at the Center are a nutritionist, massage therapist and other bodyworkers, two counsellors, a chiropractor and a Traditional Chinese Medicine practitioner as well as yoga and t'ai chi instructors.

Acupuncturists increasingly work in tandem with conventional doctors

Patient care is "relationship-centred", meaning that the alliance of patient and practitioner is central to all treatment and healing – a key element in integrated medicine.

THE FUTURE OF INTEGRATED MEDICINE

Integrated medicine centres sometimes come under the umbrella of a hospital or university, where they have a strong research element. Dr. Herbert Benson's Mind-Body Medical Institute at New England's Deaconess Hospital and Harvard University Medical School is an example, as is Dr. Jon Kabat-Zinn's Center for Mindfulness in Medicine, Health and Society at the University of Massachusetts Medical Center. "What are the common elements that allow a healing interaction to take place?" is a question that the newly established Osher Center for Integrative Medicine at the University of California is seeking to answer. It is pledged to offer patients complementary approaches of proven value and to provide information about integrated medicine to both public and medical communities.

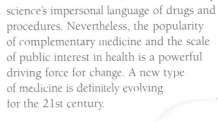

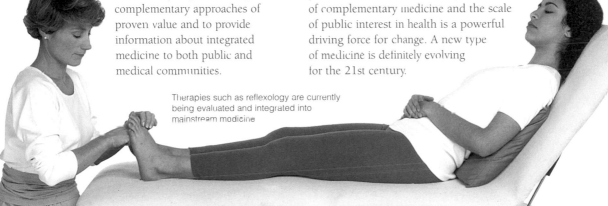

Therapies such as reflexology are currently being evaluated and integrated into mainstream medicine

It would be foolish to deny that there are many difficulties in the path of integration. More research is needed to prove complementary therapies are safe and effective. Safety and efficacy themselves depend on a practitioner's skills which is why education and training need to be improved and regulation introduced. In the UK, The Foundation for Integrated Medicine, whose President is HRH The Prince of Wales, is dedicated to resolving these issues. In the US, the National Institute of Health Advisory Council for Complementary and Alternative Medicine now spends many million dollars a year on research and disseminating information.

Communication between doctors and therapists can still be difficult. Even finding a common language is problematic. "Energy", "vital force" and "*qi*" are concepts that conventional medicine stumbles over, while some therapists abhor medical science's impersonal language of drugs and procedures. Nevertheless, the popularity of complementary medicine and the scale of public interest in health is a powerful driving force for change. A new type of medicine is definitely evolving for the 21st century.

THE POWER OF THE THERAPEUTIC RELATIONSHIP

THE RELATIONSHIP BETWEEN PATIENT and practitioner is a powerful force for healing, as demonstrated in the so-called "placebo response". (A placebo is a chemically inert substance given in place of a drug.) It shows the power of relationships and expectations, and is one explanation for why a drug or treatment that should have no effect can actually make someone feel better.

If a group of people is given a placebo treatment, 30 per cent – and, according to some researchers, as many as 90 per cent – will report improvements. In clinical research trials, one half of a patient group is given placebo pills, while the other receives the active drug. Any treatment must out-perform the placebo to be considered effective. Researchers have shown that expectation can actually change immune responses, even in animals. Some experts say this shows that the mind can trigger our natural healing processes.

PATIENT-PRACTITIONER TRUST

According to Professor Herbert Benson of Harvard Medical School, the essence of healing depends on three elements:

• The patient's belief or expectancy of a good outcome
• The caregiver's belief and expectancy of a good outcome
• A relationship between the patient and the caregiver that generates positive belief and expectancies.

Perhaps the special relationship between the patient and the practitioner is the most important fuel for this expectation of healing. In a famous study at Massachusetts General Hospital, Boston, in 1964, patients undergoing surgery who received a pre-operative visit from a warm and sympathetic anaesthetist recovered more quickly than other patients undergoing similar surgery who did not.

It also seems that the patient has responsibilities to cultivate a good relationship with caregivers. In another Boston study, patients with chronic illnesses such as diabetes, rheumatoid arthritis and high blood pressure were coached to ask relevant questions of their doctor. Afterwards they reported more satisfaction with their visit and even enjoyed better health than those who were not coached.

However, expectation can also work against healing. People experiencing insensitive treatment from practitioners often complain of feeling worse. This is known as the "nocebo" effect – the opposite of the placebo.

YOUR HEALTHCARE STRATEGY

Health is defined as the ability to adapt to change. The capacity to adapt depends on three inter-dependent realms: biochemical, structural and psycho-social (*see right*). Disease, or simply feeling unwell, is more likely if the body or mind is under strain. While factors that make illness more likely are found in all three realms, so too are the means of healing. In Treating Ailments (*pages 22–113*), various conditions and the different options for treatment, both conventional and complementary, are described, while Your Healthcare Plan (*pages 138–75*) explains health skills that help you maintain well-being and build up resilience in all realms of body and mind.

BIOCHEMICAL REALM
Consists of: cells, hormones and enzymes; body systems such as digestion and respiration; the chemical environment and pollution; nutritional factors

STRUCTURAL REALM
Consists of: muscles, bones, blood vessels and nerves, organs and tissues; movement and posture; the physical environment

PSYCHO-SOCIAL REALM
Consists of: thoughts, feelings and relationships; the social environment, culture, family, the community and the workplace

TAKING CHARGE OF HEALTH

Becoming involved in your own healthcare, working with your practitioners and caregivers, and taking charge of your health destiny is empowering. Research shows that when people take responsibility for their healthcare, symptoms often improve and quality of life is enhanced. Responsibility, however, depends on knowledge and resources, so it is important to learn as much as possible about all the factors that influence your health. If you are prone to, or already have, a health problem, understanding that you need to compensate for this susceptibility is a necessary start. Knowing about causes, symptoms and the range of available treatment options is obviously empowering. Knowledge about healthy eating, exercise, relaxation and stress-

management techniques is essential for everyone who wants to build good health.

Certain attitudes of mind improve your chances of well-being, while others, such as poor self-esteem, high anxiety, not feeling in control of your life, pessimism and hostility can make you more susceptible to illness. The relationship you have with health professionals, including complementary therapists, may determine whether you forge a "therapeutic alliance" (*see page 19*), potentially a key to unlocking the healing process. As in any good partnership, trust, communication and mutual respect are vital (*see Working With Your Doctor, pages 146–47 and Finding a Practitioner, pages 180–81*). To make best use of this book, follow the route below.

THE ROUTE TO BETTER HEALTH

1 SELF-ASSESSMENT
Which approaches best suit your personality, situation and lifestyle?
• Fill out the questionnaire (*pages 140–43*) and see Finding the Right Therapy (*pages 144–45*).

4 MAKING PROGRESS
• Keep a symptom diary (*page 147*) to monitor the success of your integrated health programme.
• Fill out the questionnaire (*pages 140–43*) again to compare your progress.

2 ASSESSING YOUR PROBLEM
• Find out about particular health problems in Treating Ailments (*pages 22–113*).
• Any treatment should be safe and effective. Although research on complementary therapies is limited, it is growing. The "evidence of efficacy" ratings for each therapy in Treating Ailments indicates how effective the therapy is likely to be for that specific ailment.
• Research your ailment using the Bibliography (*pages 182–85*) and Finding Out More (*page 181*).

3 FINDING INFORMATION AND SUPPORT
• To find out how to improve your health, see Your Structural Health (*page 148–57*); Your Biochemical Health (*pages 158–67*) and Your Psychological Health (*pages 168–75*).
• To access the help you need, see Working With Your Doctor (*pages 146–47*); Finding a Practitioner (*pages 180–81*), Finding Out More (*page 181*) and Useful Addresses (*pages 186–87*).

PRECAUTIONS

- Do not attempt to diagnose any sort of health problem yourself. Always consult your doctor.
- Consult a doctor immediately if you have any of the red flag symptoms (*see page 147*).
- Check with a doctor if there is no improvement within 2–3 weeks (48 hours in children under five) or if symptoms get worse.
- Do not stop taking any prescribed medication without first consulting your doctor.
- Tell your complementary practitioner about any prescribed medication you are taking, and any other complementary remedies you are taking.
- Tell your doctor about any complementary treatments you are taking.
- Always check with a doctor before embarking on any type of complementary treatment if you have

a serious medical condition.
- Do not embark on vigorous exercise without first consulting a doctor if you are pregnant or if you have have serious back pain, high blood pressure or heart disease.
- People with persistent mental illness may be disturbed by hypnosis, visualization and meditation.
- Tell your practitioner if you have any sexually transmitted disease.
- Do not begin a course of complementary therapy without first consulting your doctor if you are pregnant or trying to conceive.
- Do not take or use any herbal or aromatherapy products or nutritional supplements (except folic acid) during the first three months of pregnancy or if breast-feeding unless supervised by an experienced practitioner.
- Consult your doctor before allowing babies or toddlers to receive long-term complementary treatments.

- Enemas and certain herbal remedies, are unsuitable for small children.
- Children under 12 should only follow complementary treatments with professional supervision and a doctor's consent.
- Children under 16 should not fast.
- Do not take iron or vitamin A supplements without first consulting your doctor. Do not exceed the recommended dosage of other supplements unless directed by a qualified practitioner.
- Do not take high doses of nutritional supplements without professional supervision.
- Do not embark on fasts lasting longer than two days without professional advice.

HERBAL REMEDY CAUTIONS

SOME HERBAL REMEDIES can interfere with the action of conventional drugs or heighten their effect. Consult a pharmacist, doctor or medical herbalist.

Echinacea can affect the liver if used for more than eight weeks, especially if taken with liver-toxic drugs, e.g. anabolic steroids.

Evening primrose oil and **borage oil** can lower the seizure threshold if taken with anticonvulsants.

Feverfew, ginkgo biloba, garlic and **Chinese angelica** (dong quai) can interfere with warfarin.

Ginseng can interfere with digoxin, increase the effect of oestrogens and corticosteroids, and cause manic side effects with antidepressants.

Liquorice can increase side-effects of corticosteroids.

St John's wort can increase

side effects of antidepressants. Do not take without medical advice if prescribed cyclosporin, warfarin, digoxin, theophylline or oral contraceptives.

Senna, cascara and **psyllium** can decrease drug absorption.

Valerian may increase the sedative effects of barbiturates.

Yohimbe can increase hypertension if taken with tricyclic antidepressants.

A partnership of trust between patient and practitioner is key for the success of integrated healthcare

POINTS TO REMEMBER

- Sharing ideas and working together to address different aspects of a patient's health is a bold new step for many practitioners, both conventional and complementary. If you are not fortunate enough to be in an integrated practice, expect to find that YOU are the one orchestrating any integration of healthcare approaches.
- Not all orthodox practitioners are knowledgeable about non-conventional therapies and few can offer expert advice about procedures, benefits or even risks.
- Many complementary practitioners know little about other therapies and tend to believe that the one they practise will suit you best.
- Find out as much as you can about
  (a) your illness,
  (b) your practitioner and/or therapist,
  (c) the treatments they offer.

chapter

Drugs and surgery are essential in life-threatening

conditions and can ease many symptoms, while

complementary therapies may alleviate some of their

side-effects and tackle underlying causes of illness.

TREATING AILMENTS

Here we describe over 40 ailments that especially

benefit from integrated medicine. We explain the best

treatment options, suggest self-help strategies and

offer case studies showing the integrated approach in

action. To help you evaluate the efficacy of a therapy

in relation to a particular ailment, we give ratings

based on the available evidence (*see page 182*).

HEADACHES

Most adults suffer from tension-type headaches at some time, and about 2–3 per cent of adults get chronic tension or muscle contraction headaches for more than 15 days a month. "Tension headache" is the conventional diagnosis when there is no vascular cause, as in migraine (*see page 26*).

The exact cause is poorly understood, but factors include disorders of the joints and muscles of the neck and jaw, and psychological strain. The site of the pain may vary and it can range in intensity from a dull thudding to intense pain. A doctor will try to identify and treat the root cause of a severe, unusual non-tension headache.

CASE STUDY

Mark, an osteopath, saw Simon, 32, a journalist who often suffered from neck pain and headaches. Mark found tender points in the back of Simon's neck and restricted upper-neck movement. "Simon is a tall guy and, as I discovered, he often sat hunched over his keyboard. His screen was set to one side of his desk, with glare from a window, and his office chair was difficult to readjust." After stretching and manipulating Simon's neck joints, Mark gave him advice about posture and a booklet explaining how to position his workstation correctly. Simon also persuaded his employer to buy him a better chair. After three sessions, his neck pain eased. "The headaches were slow to get better, but moving the computer screen has made a big difference."

BIOCHEMICAL FACTORS

Headaches can be signs of dehydration or too much caffeine or alcohol. They may also be side-effects of a drug or symptoms of a fever. Daily headaches, soon after waking, may be due to low blood-sugar levels. In the long term painkillers may lose their effect and actually cause more headaches. Withdrawal headaches can also result if painkillers are stopped suddenly.

BIOCHEMICAL TRIGGERS

• Low blood-sugar levels (hypoglycaemia) • Mild dehydration • Excess caffeine or sudden withdrawal • Excess alcohol • Food additives • Premenstrual tension and other hormonal changes • Medication such as oral contraceptives or HRT • Overuse of painkillers, especially codeine • Constipation or fever

PSYCHO-SOCIAL FACTORS

Stress, fatigue and depression account for the tension that produces most headaches, especially those located in the back of the head or behind the forehead.

PSYCHO-SOCIAL TRIGGERS

• Anxiety • Lack of sleep • Overwork • Emotional trauma • Depression • Personality traits (e.g. difficulty in expressing anger)

STRUCTURAL FACTORS

Conditions such as high blood pressure and sinusitis can give rise to headaches. However, tension in the muscles of the shoulders, neck and around the eyes and jaw is probably the most usual cause. This structural tension builds up gradually and eventually becomes persistent with the muscles prone to irritability and spasm.

STRUCTURAL TRIGGERS

• Poor posture • Working too long at a computer • Neck injury (such as whiplash) • Wear and tear of neck joints • Bright sunlight, wind, or changes in atmospheric pressure • Sinusitis • High blood pressure

PRECAUTIONS

Consult a doctor about any unusual, severe, one-sided or persistent headache, in particular if it is accompanied by drowsiness, nausea, vomiting, intolerance to light, stiff neck or a rash. See a doctor also after a head injury and if self-help treatments for minor headaches do not work within 3–7 days.

Realms of the Body *(see page 20)*

⬤ **BIOCHEMICAL**
Body systems,
such as digestion.

⬤ **STRUCTURAL**
Muscles, bones,
joints and nerves.

PSYCHO-SOCIAL
Thoughts, feelings
and relationships.

Key: Evidence of Efficacy *(see page 182)*

❶ ❷ ❸ ❹ ❺

least evidence ◄────────► most evidence

BIOCHEMICAL TREATMENT OPTIONS

CONVENTIONAL MEDICINE
Painkillers such as paracetamol, aspirin or ibuprofen *(see Drugs Glossary, page 179)* help relieve occasional headaches. Some preparations include a muscle relaxant. Amitriptyline can help chronic tension headaches.

COMPLEMENTARY THERAPIES
Western Herbalism ❷ *(see page 127)*
A practitioner may recommend a calming herb such as valerian or chamomile. These help to calm the mind, reduce stress and encourage sleep.
Caution: do not take valerian with sleep-inducing drugs.
Nutritional Therapies ❷ *(see pages 128–29)*
Practitioners seek to address the cause, for example a tendency to constipation or low blood sugar, and try to boost general health. This might involve detoxification to support the liver, short fasts and antioxidant vitamins.

Valerian

Homeopathy ❷ *(see page 130)*
Nux vomica 6c may be worth trying for chronic tension headaches, although there is little research to support its use.

SELF-HELP TECHNIQUES
• Eat sensibly and make time for regular meals and snacks if you are prone to low blood-sugar levels • Drink plenty of fluids but limit tea, coffee, cocoa and cola, which contain caffeine
• Do not smoke or drink excess alcohol
• Avoid excessive use of painkillers.

STRUCTURAL TREATMENT OPTIONS

CONVENTIONAL MEDICINE
If headaches are severe, unusual or persistent, a blood test, X-rays and even a brain scan may be advised. Physio-therapy can help to ease muscle tension.

COMPLEMENTARY THERAPIES
Chiropractic ❸ *(see page 118)* and
Osteopathy ❸ *(see page 119)*
Treatment aims to help the muscles relax and the joints to move more freely. Cranial osteopathy uses delicate manipulation to ease tension.

Alexander Technique ❷ *(see page 121)*
This can help prevent tension headaches by correcting poor posture.
Hydrotherapy ❷ *(see page 126)*

Cold water relieves symptoms

Splashing your face with cold water before lying down for an hour eases a headache. Alternate hot and cold showers dilate then constrict blood vessels, stimulating the circulation. An ice pack to the back of the head may help.

Caution: Avoid alternate hot and cold showers if you have a heart condition.

SELF-HELP TECHNIQUES
• Take regular exercise • With your fingertips, massage up the back of your neck, around the base of your skull, over your scalp and around your ears
• Pressing acupressure points Colon 4 and Liver 3 may help *(see page 125)*
• Check that your office chair is correctly adjusted, and always sit correctly facing your computer screen.

PSYCHO-SOCIAL TREATMENT OPTIONS

CONVENTIONAL MEDICINE
Clinical depression should be treated. Cognitive behavioural therapy might be advised if headaches are persistent and severe.

COMPLEMENTARY THERAPIES
Visualization ❸ *(see page 134)*
Learning this technique, which shows you how to harness the power of your imagination, can enable you to relax tense muscles and calm your mind at will, so relieving stress.

Biofeedback ❹ *(see page 136)*
Techniques that train you to control muscle tension may relieve headaches.

SELF-HELP TECHNIQUES
• Keep a symptom- and stress-trigger diary *(see pages 147 and 175)* • Examine the causes of stress in your life and be prepared to make some changes • Make sure you get adequate sleep
• Practise relaxation and breathing techniques *(see pages 170–71)* and use stress-management techniques *(see pages 168–69)* • If you feel a headache coming on, a therapy such as meditation *(see page 137)* or autogenic training *(see page 136)* may help to prevent it. Alternatively, follow the self-help relaxation sequence on page 171.

Autogenic training can allow you to relax at will

MIGRAINE

About 10 per cent of people suffer from migraine, with three times as many women affected as men. An intense, throbbing pain is felt, usually on one side of the head, with nausea, vomiting and sensitivity to sound, light and smells. Before an attack, about 25 per cent of sufferers have visual disturbances such as zigzag lines, blind spots and flashing lights, known as an aura. Migraine is caused by a spasm of large blood vessels in the brain. Blood vessels constrict, which can bring about the hallucinatory aura, and then dilate, causing the throbbing pain. Attacks vary in severity and frequency and can last for up to 72 hours.

CASE STUDY

John, who runs a hatha yoga class, helped Angie control the migraines that had plagued her for years. Angie, a 40-year-old manager with two children had suffered a major migraine almost every week. After trying painkillers and other treatments, she was recommended the yoga class by her doctor. John suggested that Angie do a series of neck-stretching exercises, the Cobra, the Pose of the Child and alternate nostril breathing. After her first class, Angie had her best night's sleep for a long time. Angie now practises yoga daily. She concludes, "Calm, deep breathing helps me to recognize when I am tense; I can relax my mind and body, and I feel in control. Now months go by without a migraine."

BIOCHEMICAL FACTORS

Migraine tends to run in families, so there may be a genetic predisposition. Certain chemicals found in food or made by the body raise levels of the chemical serotonin, which constricts blood vessels in the brain. When these vessels widen again, they release prostaglandins, causing pain, nausea and vomiting.

BIOCHEMICAL TRIGGERS

• Intolerance of certain foods, especially of tyrosine-rich foods, such as mature cheese, red wine and pickled herrings, and of preservative nitrates, found in processed meats • Chemicals such as caffeine and alcohol • Hormonal swings caused by the Pill, menstruation, pregnancy or the menopause

STRUCTURAL FACTORS

Musculo-skeletal disorders sometimes cause migraines, possibly because a spasm in the arteries that supply the brain is triggered by misalignment of the neck vertebrae. This seems more likely to happen if there are tender points in the upper back or the neck. Tension in the muscles of the neck and shoulders makes the problem worse.

STRUCTURAL TRIGGERS

• Physical tension caused by emotional stress such as anxiety or overwork • Poor posture • Injury to the neck • Lack of exercise and fitness • Hyperventilation (overbreathing)

PSYCHO-SOCIAL FACTORS

Lifestyle and stress can contribute to migraine attacks. Personality is also a factor: ambitious, intelligent, extroverted or obsessional people are more likely to be sufferers. Even childhood experiences and relationships can influence a person's reaction to emotional or environmental triggers.

PSYCHO-SOCIAL TRIGGERS

• Emotional stress such as anxiety, excitement, anger or shock • Loud noises, strong smells, bright or flickering lights • Travel, weather changes • Lack of, or too much sleep

Realms of the Body (*see page 20*)

● BIOCHEMICAL
Body systems,
such as digestion

● STRUCTURAL
Muscles, bones,
joints and nerves

● PSYCHO-SOCIAL
Thoughts, feelings
and relationships

Key: Evidence of Efficacy (*see page 182*)

least evidence ◄──────────► most evidence

BIOCHEMICAL TREATMENT OPTIONS

CONVENTIONAL MEDICINE
A doctor might prescribe painkillers such as paracetamol, aspirin or codeine; anti-nausea drugs such as domperidone or ergotamine (these are now used less as they can cause side-effects); or serotonin-inhibiting drugs such as sumatriptan, zolmitriptan or naratriptan (*see Drugs Glossary, page 179*). Severe migraine attacks can be halted with injectable medicines.

COMPLEMENTARY THERAPIES
Western Herbalism ❹ (*see page 127*)
Regular intake of fresh feverfew leaves may prevent attacks: parthenolide, the key ingredient in feverfew, can inhibit the release of serotonin. Feverfew tablets are available over the counter, but check that the parthenolide content in them is high.
Caution: Do not take feverfew if you are pregnant or if mouth ulcers appear.

Fresh feverfew

Nutritional Therapies ❹
(*see pages 128–29*)
Short fasts are recommended to clear toxins, and elimination and rotation diets to avoid trigger foods. Nutritional supplements such as evening primrose oil and bioflavin (vitamin B^2) may be recommended.

SELF-HELP TECHNIQUES
• Avoid foods high in tyrosine (*see opposite*) and preservatives • Do not skip meals.

STRUCTURAL TREATMENT OPTIONS

CONVENTIONAL MEDICINE
You may be prescribed beta-blockers or a serotonin blocker to prevent the dilation of blood vessels (*see Drugs Glossary, page 179*).

COMPLEMENTARY THERAPIES
Chiropractic ❸ (*see page 118*) and **Osteopathy** ❸ (*see page 119*)
Manipulation of the neck or cranial osteopathy may be used to correct misalignments of the vertebrae that can cause migraines.

Shiatsu ❷ (*see page 125*)
A combination of massage and pressure aims to restore "energy balance" and induce relaxation.
Acupuncture ❹ (*see page 125*)
Practitioners seek to restore "energy balance". Stimulating acupoints may ease pain by encouraging production of endorphins (natural painkillers).

SELF-HELP TECHNIQUES
• Massage your neck, scalp and face (*see page 116*) • Soothing aromatherapy

oils include lavender, peppermint, eucalyptus and chamomile essential oils (*see page 117*) • Apply pressure to acupressure points Liver 3, Liver 4, Gallbladder 14 and Gallbladder 20 (*see page 125*) • Try yoga breathing exercises and postures such as neck stretches (*see page 123*).

Massage away the pain of a migraine

PSYCHO-SOCIAL TREATMENT OPTIONS

CONVENTIONAL MEDICINE
Your doctor may advise you to learn to recognize and avoid potentially stressful situations.

COMPLEMENTARY THERAPIES
Hypnotherapy ❸ (*see page 134*)
Experiencing trance-induced relaxation during hypnosis may help you to relax at will.
Meditation ❸ (*see page 135*)
Relaxation techniques such as meditation can help you recognize

signs of stress in your body, and let you calm the mind and relax muscles.
Biofeedback ❹ (*see page 136*)
By using a sensory device, you can learn to control spasms in the arteries that supply the brain.

Biofeedback can aid relaxation

SELF-HELP TECHNIQUES
• Keep a diary of your migraine attacks, noting any triggers to avoid
• Techniques that lower stress can be learnt as part of a therapy such as autogenic training (*see page 136*)
• Learn relaxation and breathing techniques by following the self-help sequences on pages 170–71. The diaphragmatic breathing and relaxation these techniques encourage can ease muscle tension, and may help prevent a migraine attack in its early stages.

ACNE

For a number of reasons, the sebaceous (oil) glands at the base of hair follicles in the skin can become blocked, resulting in acne – an unsightly skin disorder that includes spots, blackheads, whiteheads and, if the oil gland becomes inflamed, pustules and cysts. The most common form, *Acne vulgaris*, affects the areas of the body with high concentrations of sebaceous glands: the face, neck, upper chest, shoulders and upper back. A tendency to acne may be hereditary and the condition is definitely linked to hormonal activity – some women are prone to outbreaks in the few days before their periods, for example, and outbreaks commonly occur at puberty, affecting as many as seven out of ten adolescents.

CASE STUDY

Karen, a nutritional therapist, treated Matt, 13, for acne. A fast-growing boy, he ate a typical teenage diet of junk food and sugary drinks. His doctor had prescribed low-level antibiotics and Karen suggested "live" yoghurt and *lactobacillus* supplements to restore 'friendly' gut bacteria. Matt agreed to reduce his intake of sweet and fatty foods, to eat three pieces of fruit and a green vegetable every day, and to drink a litre of water. "Zinc is a vital nutrient for skin health and is often depleted as the body's demand increases during growth spurts," said Karen. She recommended a daily 15mg zinc supplement and advised Matt to wash only with natural, unperfumed soap. Six months later Matt's acne had diminished and his skin looked better.

BIOCHEMICAL FACTORS

At puberty, testosterone production increases in both sexes, which stimulates overproduction of sebum (the skin's natural oil) in some people. Most doctors say there is no evidence that diet and stress play a part, but many complementary therapists think that a high-fat, sugary diet can aggravate acne.

BIOCHEMICAL TRIGGERS

• Increase in testosterone production at puberty • Mid-cycle female hormonal fluctuations • Family history • Certain drugs such as corticosteroids, androgens, barbiturates and anticonvulsants • Oral contraceptives • Contact with cooking oils, greasy cosmetics and industrial pollutants • High intake of junk food and fizzy drinks

STRUCTURAL FACTORS

A plug of sebum can form in a hair follicle, creating a blackhead. If the opening to the hair follicle is blocked, the sebaceous gland enlarges, turning into a whitehead. Bacteria multiply, infecting the blocked follicle which becomes inflamed, forming a pimple. This fills with pus and eventually bursts. Infection can spread, particularly if hygiene is poor, so that as one spot heals, others appear.

STRUCTURAL TRIGGERS

• Poor skin hygiene • Irritation from backpack or helmet straps

PSYCHO-SOCIAL FACTORS

Although acne is not a serious complaint, and certainly not infectious, the emotional impact can be considerable, particularly on self-conscious teenagers. Some practitioners believe that the stress resulting from the psychological effects of acne, which can include embarrassment, lack of confidence, anxiety and even depression, make the condition worse.

PSYCHO-SOCIAL TRIGGERS

• Stress and fatigue

Realms of the Body (see page 20)

● **BIOCHEMICAL**
Body systems,
such as digestion.

● **STRUCTURAL**
Muscles, bones,
joints and nerves.

PSYCHO-SOCIAL
Thoughts, feelings
and relationships.

Key: Evidence of Efficacy (see page 182)

❶ ❷ ❸ ❹ ❺

least evidence ◄————————► most evidence

BIOCHEMICAL TREATMENT OPTIONS

CONVENTIONAL MEDICINE

If topical preparations (see below) do not clear up acne, a doctor might prescribe long-term courses of antibiotics, usually tetracycline or erythromycin (see Drugs Glossary, page 179), to kill bacteria and reduce inflammation. Your doctor might also suggest retinoid drugs to reduce production of sebum and to promote skin regrowth. Hormones might be prescribed to treat women with cyclical acne.

COMPLEMENTARY THERAPIES

Western Herbalism ❷ (see page 127)
Practitioners may recommend blood-cleansing herbs such as red clover and dandelion, and immunity enhancing remedies, including echinacea.
Nutritional Therapies ❸
(see pages 128–29)
Practitioners see acne as a sign that the digestion and/or hormonal system are unbalanced. They may recommend an elimination diet and a short fast or a raw food diet, with supplements of zinc,

evening primrose oil, betacarotene and other antioxidants including selenium and vitamin E, and, for menstrual-related acne, vitamin B6. Long-term use of antibiotics can affect well-being, and in such cases, a therapist might treat for dysbiosis (see page 93).

SELF-HELP TECHNIQUES

• Eat a high-fibre diet and avoid saturated fat (see page 158).

Antioxidant fruit
and vegetables

STRUCTURAL TREATMENT OPTIONS

CONVENTIONAL MEDICINE

Your doctor might prescribe topical creams and lotions that contain benzoyl peroxide and retinoic acid (see Drugs Glossary, page 179) to reduce sebum and loosen blackheads, and antibiotics to kill bacteria. Controlled exposure to ultraviolet light, in the form of natural sunlight or artificial UVA light, may be recommended. In severe cases, dermabrasion (removal of the top layer of skin) can improve the appearance of the skin.

COMPLEMENTARY THERAPIES

Aromatherapy ❸ (see page 117)
A 1990 Australian study found antiseptic essential oil of tea tree to be as effective for acne as benzoyl peroxide. Dab a spot with one drop, or add 3–4 drops to one teaspoon (5ml) of witch hazel and use as a lotion. A steam inhalation with 3–4 drops of lavender or

Cleansing steam
helps acne

chamomile oil can help open pores, reduce inflammation and aid healing. **Caution:** use steam inhalations with care if you have asthma.

SELF-HELP TECHNIQUES

• Do not squeeze spots, which can make them worse and lead to scarring
• Keep affected areas clean by washing daily with soap or cleansing bars and hot water • Take regular exercise, which stimulates the circulation to the skin and improves immune defences.

PSYCHO-SOCIAL TREATMENT OPTIONS

CONVENTIONAL MEDICINE

A doctor may suggest psychotherapy if lack of confidence and depression are severe.

COMPLEMENTARY THERAPIES

Psychotherapy & Counselling ❷
(see pages 132–33)
If the skin condition is severe enough to cause lack of confidence and emotional or relationship difficulties, talking about your feelings with a trained counsellor can be useful.

This will help put things in perspective, and restore dented self-esteem and confidence.
Visualization ❷ (see page 134)
Biofeedback ❷ (see page 136)
Relaxation & Breathing ❷
(see pages 170–71)
In a research study a combination of these therapies was

found effective in helping to relieve chronic acne.

SELF-HELP TECHNIQUES

• Ensure you have plenty of sleep to help promote skin cell regeneration • Stress-management techniques, including regular exercise and relaxation, combined with limiting alcohol may give your immune system a necessary boost.

PSORIASIS

In psoriasis, raised, rough reddened patches covered with silvery-grey scales appear on the skin, accompanied by itching in some cases. Caused by over-production of new skin, they can occur all over the body but are most likely to be found around the elbows, knees, scalp, trunk, back and nails. About one person in 50 is prone to psoriasis, which usually appears in late childhood or early adulthood, but can develop at any age. It is hereditary in 30 per cent of cases and is not contagious. Psoriasis is a persistent condition, but fluctuates in intensity, tending to be more severe when people are run-down or ill, and during the winter.

CASE STUDY

Ling, a herbalist practising Traditional Chinese Medicine (TCM), treated Alison, 39, who had developed widespread psoriasis following a car accident 11 years previously. Recently the condition had worsened, spreading to her arms, legs, back and abdomen, and itching intensely at night. Alison had discussed TCM with her doctor because she found conventional ointments messy. He agreed to monitor her progress. Ling examined Alison's skin, tongue and pulse according to TCM diagnostic methods and, based on the results, prescribed a herbal remedy with nine ingredients, including rehmannia, red peony root and liquorice. She also recommended a ta'i chi class to help Alison feel calmer and suggested she cut down on animal fats. A month later, Alison's itching had begun to subside, and within four months her skin was much better.

BIOCHEMICAL FACTORS

The cause of psoriasis is unknown, although it tends to run in families. It is thought that an inherited skin defect that allows skin cells to proliferate at many times the normal rate causes psoriasis to develop under certain conditions. Hormonal factors may be involved, as the condition often appears around puberty.

BIOCHEMICAL TRIGGERS

• Family history • Infections, especially streptococcal sore throat • Certain drugs (chloroquine, lithium, indomethacin, some beta-blockers – *see Drugs Glossary, page 179*) • Severe sunburn or irritation • Acute urticaria (allergic skin rash), especially in children

STRUCTURAL FACTORS

There are three types: discoid or plaque psoriasis with red scaly patches; pustular psoriasis with tiny yellow blisters; and guttate psoriasis in which many small patches develop rapidly. In each case, new skin cells are produced about ten times faster than usual. Live cells pile up forming thickened patches, covered with dead, scaly, flaking skin. One in 20 people develop a painful complication – inflammation of the joints known as psoriatic arthropathy.

STRUCTURAL TRIGGERS

• Skin injury or surgery

PSYCHO-SOCIAL FACTORS

Emotional stress and anxiety at home or in the workplace can trigger and aggravate psoriasis. Worry about the appearance may also be a contributing factor.

PSYCHO-SOCIAL TRIGGERS

• Emotional stress • Embarrassment and lack of confidence if patches are visible and shedding scales • Stress caused by pain and irritation from sore, itchy skin • Interference with work and social life if psoriasis leads to psoriatic arthropathy (*see left*), which can restrict movement • Stress caused by loss of earnings if employers object to time off work for treatment

Realms of the Body *(see page 20)*

● **BIOCHEMICAL**
Body systems,
such as digestion.

● **STRUCTURAL**
Muscles, bones,
joints and nerves.

● **PSYCHO-SOCIAL**
Thoughts, feelings
and relationships.

Key: Evidence of Efficacy *(see page 182)*

❶ ❷ ❸ ❹ ❺

least evidence ◀——————————▶ most evidence

BIOCHEMICAL TREATMENT OPTIONS

CONVENTIONAL MEDICINE
Cancer-therapy drugs methotrexate and cyclosporin *(see Drugs Glossary, page 179)* stop cell growth in severe cases but can have unpleasant side-effects. Acitretin, derived from vitamin A, reduces the thickness of patches and helps pustular psoriasis, but must not be taken in pregnancy.

Aloe vera

COMPLEMENTARY THERAPIES
Western Herbalism ❸ *(see page 127)*

Natural creams containing beeswax or banana peel extract may help.

In German studies, extract of *Mahonia aquifolium* tree bark relieved patients' symptoms. Medical herbalists may give sarsaparilla to improve elimination of waste products, and chamomile, liquorice and aloe vera to calm the nervous system and soothe the skin.

Nutritional Therapies ❸
(see pages 128–29)
Practitioners link psoriasis with bowel

toxins and impaired liver function, so may advise detoxification and immune-enhancing or elimination diets *(see page 166)*. Supplements of vitamin C, zinc and vitamin A (betacarotene) may be suggested to inhibit excessive skin-cell growth. Evidence for benefits of essential fatty acids (fish oils and evening primrose oil) is conflicting.

SELF-HELP TECHNIQUES
• Follow a healthy wholemeal diet with plenty of fruit and vegetables.

STRUCTURAL TREATMENT OPTIONS

CONVENTIONAL MEDICINE
Greasy preparations for the skin, such as soft paraffin, ease dryness. Coal-tar and dithranol creams *(see Drugs Glossary, page 179)* are helpful but are smelly, messy and leave stains. Topical retinoid gels inhibit skin-cell production and inflammation. Steroid creams are very effective but can thin the skin and are prescribed sparingly. In PUVA (psoralen-ultraviolet A) light treatment, patients take oral psoralen which sensitizes skin cells to UVA radiation.

Relaxing in a hot bath for 15 minutes each day will help to remove skin scales

COMPLEMENTARY THERAPIES
Hydrotherapy ❷ *(see page 122)*
A hot Epsom Salts bath may help to eliminate toxins through the skin and stimulate circulation.

SELF-HELP TECHNIQUES
• Avoid nylon, leather and wool
• Moisturize your skin and do not use strong soaps, detergents, shampoos, perfumes and bubble baths • Controlled exposure to sunlight (for limited periods and with sun protection) may help.

PSYCHO-SOCIAL TREATMENT OPTIONS

CONVENTIONAL MEDICINE
Doctors may suggest learning stress-management skills *(see pages 168–69)*.

COMPLEMENTARY THERAPIES
Psychotherapy & Counselling ❶
(see page 132–33)
Cognitive behavioural therapy and hypnotherapy can help to prevent scratching and improve coping skills.
Meditation ❷ *(see page 135)*
Recent studies have found that meditating "mindfully" while

undergoing controlled exposure to UVA light treatment improved results; patients were asked to become aware of their breathing, and to visualize the light slowing down skin-cell growth.
Biofeedback ❸ *(see page 136)*
Learning to lower skin temperature through biofeedback training, plus relaxation techniques, may help.
Relaxation & Breathing ❸
(see pages 170–71)
Patients who, while undergoing conventional treatment, learn

relaxation techniques in group therapy, improve faster and need fewer drugs.

SELF-HELP TECHNIQUES
• Recording your feelings in a diary *(see page 175)* helps to identify and avoid stress triggers
• Avoid overwork: psoriasis often improves during holidays with plenty of sunshine and relaxation.

ECZEMA

Also known as dermatitis, eczema is a chronic inflammation of the skin causing itching, blistering, weeping and scaling. It affects about one in eight children and one in 12 adults. Eczema can occur anywhere, but most commonly appears on the hands, arms and face, or in skin folds and creases. The most widespread type, *atopic eczema*, runs in families and is associated with asthma and hay fever. *Seborrhoeic eczema* occurs on the face and head, and is the most common cause of dandruff. It is caused by the overproduction of skin cells and a yeast organism on the skin. *Contact eczema*, as the name suggests, is a localized reaction to irritants.

CASE STUDY

Charles, a homeopath, treated Maria, a hairdresser aged 25, for eczema. Maria also complained of lack of energy, backache and pains in her hips. "She was charming, quiet, overweight, slightly sweaty and anxious," said Charles. "When particularly worried – as she was with her wedding coming up – eczema broke out on her face." He concluded that Maria was a typical *Calc. carb.* homeopathic type and prescribed a one-off, potent dose of the remedy *Calc.carb. 200c*. For about a month, Maria reported very vivid, anxious dreams, but then her skin improved by "about 70 per cent", her backache eased and her energy increased. "Once or twice a year she relapses with an outbreak of eczema," said Charles, "but another *200c* dose of *Calc.carb.* clears it up."

BIOCHEMICAL FACTORS

Eczema is an allergic skin reaction to a wide range of external and internal irritants. In many cases, it can be difficult to identify the exact cause. For some reason, the immune system reacts to an innocuous substance as if it were harmful, triggering inflammation in the skin cells. Food sensitivities can often trigger eczema. Many children with eczema are also allergic to house dust.

BIOCHEMICAL TRIGGERS

• Cow's milk • Wheat • Eggs • Peanuts • Citrus fruit • Food additives and preservatives • Lack of protective proteins acquired during breastfeeding • Premature weaning on to dairy products and wheat

STRUCTURAL FACTORS

External irritants provoke contact eczema and can work in tandem with internal causes to aggravate atopic eczema. It is possible for some people to become allergic to things they have used for years.

STRUCTURAL TRIGGERS

• Chemicals found in detergents, soaps, cosmetics and perfumes • Environmental chemicals and pollutants • Nickel and chrome (found in jewellery and wrist watches) • Sticking plaster • Wool, leather and synthetic fibres • Chemicals in rubber • Heat

PSYCHO-SOCIAL FACTORS

Stress and emotional tension of any sort can provoke and aggravate eczema. Studies show that people with chronic eczema have higher levels of anxiety, hostility and neurosis than others.

PSYCHO-SOCIAL TRIGGERS

• Unacknowledged stress • Bereavement • Bullying • Embarrassment and lack of confidence

Realms of the Body (*see page 20*)

BIOCHEMICAL
Body systems,
such as digestion.

STRUCTURAL
Muscles, bones,
joints and nerves.

PSYCHO-SOCIAL
Thoughts, feelings
and relationships.

Key: Evidence of Efficacy (*see page 182*)

❶ ❷ ❸ ❹ ❺

least evidence ◄———————————► most evidence

BIOCHEMICAL TREATMENT OPTIONS

CONVENTIONAL MEDICINE

Antibiotics

A doctor will try to identify and remove the cause and may carry out allergy tests. Antibiotics (*see Drugs Glossary, page 179*) will be prescribed for infection and antihistamines to reduce itching. Corticosteroid creams reduce inflammation: hydrocortisone is the weakest and safest. Antifungals help relieve seborrhoeic eczema.

COMPLEMENTARY THERAPIES
Traditional Chinese Medicine ❹
(*see pages 124–25*)
Traditional Chinese Medicine practitioners regard the occurrence of skin diseases as a failure of digestion and elimination. They treat cases individually, prescribing diets and herbs that reduce toxic build-up and improve excretion. In a 1992 study a Chinese herbal formula containing liquorice was found effective in treating atopic eczema.

Nutritional Therapies ❹
(*see pages 128–29*)
Treatments include rotation or exclusion diets to identify food allergies and a detoxifying regime. Supplements of zinc and fish oil may be recommended

SELF-HELP TECHNIQUES
• Avoid dairy products, citrus fruit, peanuts, eggs, wheat, alcohol and processed foods • Eat foods rich in essential fatty acids, such as oily fish, plus oats and green leafy vegetables.

STRUCTURAL TREATMENT OPTIONS

CONVENTIONAL MEDICINE
Doctors use patch-testing to help identify contact allergens. Soothing emollients such as petroleum jelly and preservative-free, unscented moisturizers, which form a protective film over dry, flaky skin, can help In severe atopic eczema, wet wraps of cotton tubular bandages are soothing and seal in moisture. Tar formulations containing zinc oxide and zinc carbonate soothe the skin, but are messy.

COMPLEMENTARY THERAPIES
Environmental Medicine ❷
(*see page 131*)
A practitioner will run tests to identify irritants so that exposure to them may be avoided or desensitization achieved.

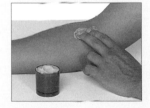
Plenty of emollient cream is soothing

SELF-HELP TECHNIQUES
Give up smoking and avoid smoky atmospheres • Minimize contact with known allergens such as animal dander, house-dust mites and pollen • Switch to non-biological washing powder
• Bathe frequently and wear cotton
• Avoid fragranced detergents, soaps and shampoos • Only use hypoallergenic cosmetics and skincare products
• Use emollients continually • Exercise regularly • Consider changing your job if conditions cause contact eczema.

PSYCHO-SOCIAL TREATMENT OPTIONS

CONVENTIONAL MEDICINE
Patients are encouraged to learn how to resist the urge to scratch – a habit that makes eczema worse. The itch-scratch-itch cycle is exacerbated by stress and anxiety. Techniques include aversive conditioning, methods of relaxation and stress-management, and training in social skills to boost self-esteem.

Stress and anxiety can be relieved by counselling

COMPLEMENTARY THERAPIES
Psychotherapy & Counselling ❸
(*see pages 132–33*)
Ways are found to express unacknowledged anxiety and emotional tension. Cognitive behavioural therapy and autogenic training (*see page 136*) can relieve symptoms and lessen the need for steroid creams.
Hypnotherapy ❸ (*see page 134*)
Studies have shown that hypnotherapy can be effective in controlling itching.

SELF-HELP TECHNIQUES
• Keep a stress-trigger diary (*see page 175*) • Practise relaxation and breathing techniques (*see pages 170–71*) and stress-management skills such as time management and prioritizing.

HERPES

The herpes viruses cause several conditions characterized by small, painful blisters on the skin and mucous membranes. There are two kinds of *herpes simplex* virus: type 1 (HSV1) usually causes cold sores (blisters on the lips and mouth) and type 2 (HSV2) causes genital herpes. However, both types can lead to either problem.

The virus lives in the nerves and can also inflame the eyes and even the brain. The related *herpes zoster* virus causes chickenpox. This can re-emerge as shingles, causing mild, flu-like symptoms, a localized rash and blisters and pain that settles in one place. Intense pain, known as post-herpetic neuralgia can persist long-term.

CASE STUDY

Christine, a homeopath, saw George, 23, who had genital herpes and was anxious about infecting his fiancée. Conventional drugs seemed to clear it up, but after a few days he felt run down. "From answers to my questions, I identified his constitutional type as *Sulphur*," said Christine, who prescribed a single dose of the "nosode" *Medorrhinum 200c*. She suggested a high-lysine, low arginine diet (*see Nutritional Therapies, opposite*) and they talked about stress management. George was advised to avoid sex at the first inkling of an attack. He says, "In the first four months I had a couple of mild outbreaks but for the last nine months I've been completely free. Occasionally Christine prescribes a one-off dose of *Sulphur 200c*, which makes me feel better all round."

BIOCHEMICAL FACTORS

By adulthood, most people have been exposed to HSV1, which is transmitted by touching and kissing. Most either become immune or prone just to cold sores. HSV2 is sexually transmitted. The first attack of HSV2 may pass unnoticed or seem like a mild dose of flu, while further bouts cause genital blisters. The *herpes zoster* virus remains dormant in the nerve cells after chickenpox. Once in the body, all the herpes viruses remain for life and can be activated by a number of different triggers.

BIOCHEMICAL TRIGGERS
• Other infections • Lowered immunity
• Inadequate diet • Hormonal changes, such as those during menstruation

STRUCTURAL FACTORS

It is not clear why some people get recurring severe episodes of herpes. A patient is infectious just before the blisters appear, when the tell-tale tingling in the lips or genitals heralds the appearance of a sore. In genital herpes, there may be some local pain. Swollen and painful lymph nodes disappear along with the blisters after about a week. A shingles rash lasts about 2–3 weeks, but in a third of cases, pain continues for months or even years due to damage to the nerves. In general, the older you are, the more badly shingles affects you.

STRUCTURAL TRIGGERS
• Heat, fever, sun and cold winds (cold sores)

PSYCHO-SOCIAL FACTORS

Stress is linked to an increased susceptibility to viral infections because it depresses the immune system. One of the triggers below may be responsible for a herpes outbreak.

PSYCHO-SOCIAL TRIGGERS
• Anxiety • Overwork and lack of adequate sleep • Depression • Traumatic events, such as bereavement or divorce

Realms of the Body (*see page 20*)

● **BIOCHEMICAL**
Body systems,
such as digestion.

● **STRUCTURAL**
Muscles, bones,
joints and nerves.

PSYCHO-SOCIAL
Thoughts, feelings
and relationships.

Key: Evidence of Efficacy (*see page 182*)

❶ ❷ ❸ ❹ ❺

least evidence ◄————————► most evidence

BIOCHEMICAL TREATMENT OPTIONS

CONVENTIONAL MEDICINE
Antiviral tablets such as aciclovir (*see Drugs Glossary, page 179*), if taken early on, can shorten attacks. Over-the-counter painkillers help ease mild discomfort, but stronger analgesics may be necessary, especially for post-herpetic pain. If sores become infected, doctors may prescribe antibiotics.

COMPLEMENTARY THERAPIES
Western Herbalism ❸
(*see page 127*)
A practitioner may suggest the immune-boosting herb echinacea; liquorice gel to ease inflammation; lemon balm cream to promote healing and prevent cold sores; and ointment with capsaicin to relieve the pain of post-herpetic neuralgia.

Nutritional Therapies ❶
(*see pages 128–29*)
Therapists may advise you to eat lamb, chicken, fish, potatoes, milk, beans and eggs, which contain the amino acid lysine that may suppress HSV.

Zinc-rich foods may help to control the growth of the HSV viruses

Zinc, in the form of supplements, ointments and zinc-rich foods, may inhibit the growth of HSV. Some practitioners recommend garlic, which is antiviral, and immunity enhancing supplements such as bioflavonoids, vitamin C and vitamin E. You may be advised to avoid chocolate, peanuts, seeds and cereals, which contain arginine which the herpes viruses need.

SELF-HELP TECHNIQUES
• Avoid sugar, coffee, alcohol and tobacco, all of which can reduce immune resistance.

STRUCTURAL TREATMENT OPTIONS

CONVENTIONAL MEDICINE
Doctors will prescribe ointments containing the antivirals idoxuridine or acyclovir (*see Drugs Glossary, page 179*) to apply to the affected area. Treatment should begin as soon as the first symptoms occur. Atropine ointment may ease shingle pain in the early stages and transcutaneous nerve stimulation (TENS – *see Glossary, pages 177–78*) may help to reduce the pain of post-herpetic neuralgia.

COMPLEMENTARY THERAPIES
Acupuncture ❶ (*see page 125*)
A practitioner may stimulate local acupoints, which sometimes relieves post-herpetic pain.

SELF-HELP TECHNIQUES
• As soon as a cold sore appears, hold an ice cube wrapped in a tea towel to it for at least three-quarters of an hour, removing it for 15 seconds every few minutes to avoid "burning" • To ease the pain of genital herpes, bathe the area in a solution of one teaspoon of salt dissolved in 250ml (½ pint) of warm water • To prevent infection spreading: do not squeeze or touch sores; wash your hands frequently; keep your towels and bed linen separate; avoid touching or kissing (cold sores), oral sex or sexual intercourse (genital herpes) • Exercise regularly to help strengthen the immune system.

PSYCHO-SOCIAL TREATMENT OPTIONS

CONVENTIONAL MEDICINE
Because it is a highly infectious sexually transmitted disease, some people find genital herpes shameful and a cause of anxiety. A doctor may suggest counselling or couples' therapy.

COMPLEMENTARY THERAPIES
Visualization ❸ (*see page 134*)
A practitioner might ask you to imagine post-herpetic pain as something such as a lump of ice that melts or disappears to help alter your perception of it and make you feel more in control.
Biofeedback ❷ (*see page 136*)
This relaxation technique may help with stress-related problems and persistent pain.

SELF-HELP TECHNIQUES
• Keep a stress diary (*see page 175*)
• Practise stress-management and breathing and relaxation techniques (*see pages 168–71*) to help you cope with stressful events
• Get plenty of rest during busy periods at work.

Breathing exercises can help to relieve stress

COLDS & FLU

Colds and flu are viral infections of the respiratory tract (the nose, throat, lungs and bronchial tubes). New strains of the flu virus appear each year and a cold may be the result of any one of 200 viruses. The symptoms they produce indicate that the immune system is fighting the virus. The flu virus produces symptoms similar to a cold, but worse, and, while a cold starts gradually, flu develops rapidly: a fever appears within 24 hours, along with loss of appetite, nausea and aching muscles. The symptoms of colds and flu may be relieved and the duration possibly shortened, but the infection must run its course.

CASE STUDY

Elaine, a medical herbalist, was asked to help Diana, who was having difficulty recovering after flu and needed to improve her resistance to infections. Diana complained that she seemed to catch every virus going and never fully recovered. She told Elaine that for months she had been overworking and feeling tense. Elaine explained how stress affects the immune response and recommended that Diana review her work pattern and rejoin the yoga class she had once belonged to. She also prescribed echinacea tablets to boost Diana's immune system, and gave her a seven-day herbal remedy to use whenever she caught a cold. Diana was strongly advised not to return to work too soon. She quickly got over her bout of flu and had fewer respiratory infections that winter.

BIOCHEMICAL FACTORS

When the immune system is weak, a virus can overcome the body's primary defences, which include the hairs and mucus in the nose and throat and protective proteins called immunoglobulins in the mucous membranes. The virus infects cells lining the respiratory tract and rapidly multiplies. The infected cells secrete histamine, which causes inflammation, and toxins produced by the virus make the muscles ache. Yellow-green mucus results from the death of white blood cells summoned to fight infection.

BIOCHEMICAL TRIGGERS

• An immune system weakened by poor nutrition, stress or exhaustion

PSYCHO-SOCIAL FACTORS

Research shows that white blood cell activity, which helps fight infection, and antibodies are depleted by stress. Emotional stress has been linked to a greater susceptibility to colds and other viral infections.

PSYCHO-SOCIAL TRIGGERS

• Loneliness • Depression • Overwork and lack of adequate sleep • Traumatic life events such as bereavement or divorce

STRUCTURAL FACTORS

A cold or flu virus is spread in tiny airborne droplets, produced when an infected person breathes, coughs or sneezes. Smoking and inhaling polluted air harm the body's defences, increasing susceptibility to infection. Fighting the virus causes inflammation of the membranes that line the nose, sinuses and throat, as well as a blocked or runny nose, sneezing, a sore throat and a cough.

STRUCTURAL TRIGGERS

• Close contact with an infected person

PRECAUTIONS

See a doctor if symptoms persist or worsen, or if you become short of breath or cough up blood or large amounts of yellow or green phlegm. Consult a pharmacist about cold medications, which can interact with one another and affect pre-existing conditions.

Realms of the Body (*see page 20*)

● **BIOCHEMICAL**
Body systems,
such as digestion.

● **STRUCTURAL**
Muscles, bones,
joints and nerves.

● **PSYCHO-SOCIAL**
Thoughts, feelings
and relationships.

Key: Evidence of Efficacy (*see page 182*)

❶ ❷ ❸ ❹ ❺

least evidence ◄――――――――► most evidence

BIOCHEMICAL TREATMENT OPTIONS

CONVENTIONAL MEDICINE

Aspirin tablets

Flu immunization, is useful for the elderly, people with respiratory problems and those with weak immune systems. Over-the-counter drugs such as aspirin, paracetamol and ibuprofen ease symptoms; antibiotics will only be suggested if there is a secondary bacterial infection. New nasal sprays may fight viruses.

COMPLEMENTARY THERAPIES

Naturopathy ❹ (*see page 126*)
For flu, a 48-hour fast will be advised to eliminate toxins, as well as plenty of fluids, rest and warm baths. A naturopath will not suppress a fever unless it reaches 40°C (104°F).
Western Herbalism ❺ (*see page 127*)
Echinacea, which helps the immune system to fight infection, may be recommended. Garlic has antibiotic, antiviral properties: eat two crushed raw cloves when symptoms first

appear, then one a day until they subside. Black elderberry extract is claimed to shorten the duration of flu.
Homeopathy ❹ (*see page 130*)
Oscillococcinum (a remedy made from duck heart and liver), which reduced flu symptoms in one study, may be given.

SELF-HELP TECHNIQUES

• At the first sign of cold and flu symptoms take a daily dose of both vitamin C (1000–1500mg) and zinc gluconate (10–15mg).

STRUCTURAL TREATMENT OPTIONS

CONVENTIONAL MEDICINE

Pastilles or lozenges with local anaesthetic soothe sore throats; decongestants and inhalants relieve runny or stuffy noses and blocked sinuses; cough suppressants ease dry tickly coughs, and expectorants help moist chesty coughs.

COMPLEMENTARY THERAPIES

Aromatherapy ❸ (*see page 117*)
A steam inhalation using chamomile essential oil has been shown to reduce

cold symptoms. Practitioners advise adding 4 drops of chamomile, eucalyptus, lavender or tea tree oil to one litre (2 pints) of freshly boiled water, and inhaling the steam for ten minutes. Alternatively, gargle with 1–2 drops in 250ml (½ pint) water. **Caution:** use steam inhalations with care if you have asthma.

Eucalyptus oil and plant

SELF-HELP TECHNIQUES

• Avoid close contact with people who have colds or flu • Avoid environmental pollutants and tobacco smoke, both of which irritate the mucous membranes • Rest, keep warm and drink plenty of fluids, such as fruit juices, while symptoms persist • For a sore throat, gargle several times a day with hot water, honey, lemon juice and crushed garlic • Use menthol products to help clear a stuffy nose and airways.

PSYCHO-SOCIAL TREATMENT OPTIONS

CONVENTIONAL MEDICINE

If you frequently have colds, a doctor might suggest that you consider whether you are prone to stress. He or she may then suggest stress-management techniques (*see pages 168–69*).

COMPLEMENTARY THERAPIES

Visualization ❷ (*see page 134*)
Imagining your white blood cells attacking and destroying the cold and flu viruses in your respiratory tract may boost the immune system. In one

study, it raised levels of immuno-globulins (antibodies produced by the immune system) in the saliva.
Meditation ❷ (*see page 135*)
Regular meditation helps to calm the mind and relax muscles. Long-term meditators seem to get fewer respiratory infections.

SELF-HELP TECHNIQUES

• A bad bout of flu is stressful and can leave you feeling tired and depressed for weeks afterwards. Rest while the

infection is acute, and allow yourself time to recover • Learn relaxation techniques (*see pages 170–71*).

Regular meditation may help ward off frequent colds

CATARRH & SINUSITIS

I f the mucous membranes of the upper respiratory tract become inflamed, they produce excess mucus known as catarrh. This condition, which may be triggered by infections, allergies or environmental irritants, may cause sneezing, a runny nose, and loss of smell and taste. Catarrh can also block the sinuses, which are spaces in the facial bones that form the nasal cavity. Blocked sinuses can lead to infection (*sinusitis*), which causes throbbing pain in the forehead, upper jaw and cheek bones. The eustachian tube, linking the middle ear to the back of the nose, may also become blocked, leading to what is known as *glue ear*.

CASE STUDY

Maria, a homeopath, treated Simon, 35, a college lecturer with persistent sinusitis. His doctor referred him after medication had failed to help and the only alternative was a drainage operation, which Simon was anxious to avoid. Maria observed that Simon was quiet, reserved and self-contained, he generally felt warm and he had a craving for fish and salt. "I concluded his constitutional type was *Natrum mur.* and prescribed a single high-potency 200c dose of this remedy," she said. "I also suggested Simon avoid dairy products and sugar, take multi-vitamins and use steam inhalations with tea tree oil every day." Over the next year the catarrh causing the sinusitis gradually cleared. Every 3–4 months Simon would have a slight relapse and need another dose of *Natrum mur. 200c.*

BIOCHEMICAL FACTORS

The immune system responds to invading viruses, bacteria or allergens in the respiratory tract by sending infection-fighting white blood cells to the site. This reaction is accompanied by inflammation and excessive mucus secretion. Repeated ear infections in children can cause glue ear – constant production of sticky fluid in the middle ear – which can lead to a degree of deafness.

BIOCHEMICAL TRIGGERS

• Cold and flu viruses, or other infections
• Environmental and food allergies
• "Sick-building syndrome" *(see Glossary, pages 177–78)* • Tooth abscess (for sinusitis)

STRUCTURAL FACTORS

If mucus in the upper respiratory tract is unable to drain away, bacterial infections can result. In the middle ear, the accumulation of sticky mucus interferes with the movement of delicate bones and affects hearing. Children are particularly susceptible to middle-ear infection because their eustachian tubes are shorter than those of adults.

STRUCTURAL TRIGGERS

• Irritation and inflammation of the linings of the nose, sinuses and eustachian tubes caused, for example, by pressure, injury, environmental particles or chemicals
• Enlargement of the adenoids

PSYCHO-SOCIAL FACTORS

Stress can result in a disturbed immune system and greater susceptibility to infections that lead to catarrh and sinusitis. Pain from blocked sinuses causes irritability and depression. In children, impaired hearing due to glue ear may lead to behavioural and educational problems; the condition may be undetected until a routine hearing test is given.

PSYCHO-SOCIAL TRIGGERS

• Anxiety • Overwork and lack of adequate sleep • Traumatic life events
• Depression

BIOCHEMICAL TREATMENT OPTIONS

CONVENTIONAL MEDICINE

If catarrh is persistent, a doctor may suggest decongestants. Antibiotics are often prescribed for catarrh of the sinuses and middle ear, but can be ineffective. There is concern that over-prescribing antibiotics can lead to antibiotic-resistant bacteria.

COMPLEMENTARY THERAPIES

Naturopathy ❷ (*see page 126*)
For sinusitis, holding a hot water bottle or a menthol or eucalyptus compress to the area may be suggested.

Western Herbalism ❷ (*see page 127*)
Echinacea may be recommended to help boost the immune system, and eucalyptus to ease breathing.

Nutritional Therapies ❷
(*see pages 128–29*)
Therapists may suspect food sensitivities, for example to milk, wheat, eggs, citrus fruits and sugar, and suggest you eliminate them from your diet.

Homeopathy ❷ (*see page 130*)
Various remedies may be recommended for symptoms including *Kali bich.* 6c for thick stringy discharge, *Sticta pulmonaria* 6c for chronic sinusitis and *Pulsatilla* 6c for creamy discharge.

SELF-HELP TECHNIQUES

• Avoid dairy foods, which can increase mucus • Drink lots of water and fruit juice to expel toxins and eat a raw food diet (*see page 129*).

A diet rich in vitamin C helps fight infection

STRUCTURAL TREATMENT OPTIONS

CONVENTIONAL MEDICINE

If decongestants do not help glue ear, a doctor can improve hearing by inserting a tiny drainage tube (grommet) through the eardrum. However, some specialists believe the ear should clear of its own accord. Surgery or sinus wash-outs can help persistent sinusitis.

COMPLEMENTARY THERAPIES

Aromatherapy ❷ (*see page 117*)
To ease nasal congestion, you may be advised to add lemon, eucalyptus or cedarwood essential oils to bathwater. For sinusitis, a steam inhalation with eucalyptus, lavender or tea tree oil can be very effective. **Caution:** avoid inhalations if you have asthma.

Osteopathy ❷ (*see page 119*)
Cranial osteopaths will gently manipulate the skull of a child with glue ear to improve fluid drainage through the middle ear.

Hydrotherapy ❷ (*see page 126*)
A practitioner may suggest hot showers, mustard baths, saunas and steam baths to help clear catarrh.

SELF-HELP TECHNIQUES

• Children who are breast-fed seem to be less prone to glue ear (the shorter nipples on bottles may not exercise a muscle that opens the ear tubes, allowing mucus to drain) • Ask for a hearing test from your doctor if you or teachers at school suspect your child has a mild hearing problem.

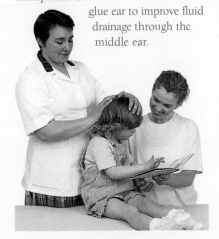

Cranial osteopathy helps fluids drain away from the head

PSYCHO-SOCIAL TREATMENT OPTIONS

CONVENTIONAL MEDICINE

Doctors support the use of stress-management methods (*see pages 168–69*).

COMPLEMENTARY THERAPIES

Visualization ❷ (*see pages 134*)
By helping you to concentrate your mind on positive, sustaining images, visualization skills can aid relaxation.

Relaxation & Breathing ❷
(*see pages 170–71*)
These techniques help you to relax at will, so reducing the stress and tension which can leave you susceptible to viral and bacterial infections that may lead to catarrh and sinusitis.

SELF-HELP TECHNIQUES

• Practise stress-management skills regularly (*see pages 168–69*)
• Ensure that you get plenty of restful sleep • Make time to relax each day, even if only for half an hour, and learn relaxation and deep breathing techniques (*see pages 170–71*).

INDIGESTION

A blanket term for any discomfort in the upper abdomen, indigestion is also known as *dyspepsia* and *acid stomach*. Sometimes caused by over-eating or rushed meals, its symptoms include belching, hiccups, heartburn (a burning acidic sensation behind the breast bone and at the same level in the mid-line of the back), nausea and flatulence. Persistent indigestion may be a sign of a peptic ulcer, gallstones, or *oesophagitis* – inflammation of the oesophagus or gullet. Indigestion can cause severe chest pain similar to angina and is occasionally mistaken for heart disease. To rule these out, it may need to be investigated.

CASE STUDY

Hannah, a nutritional therapist, treated Barbara, 44, for indigestion, flatulence and bloating. Medical tests had shown nothing wrong and Barbara was reluctant to continue her prescribed ranitidine (*see Drugs Glossary, page 179*), as it seemed to make no difference. "Acid production can go down or up if you are stressed," said Hannah. Tests confirmed that Barbara had low levels of stomach acid. "The enzymes that digest protein need an acid environment, and poorly digested proteins in the lower bowel can create flatulence and bloating," Hannah explained. She advised a stomach acid supplement with each meal, a daily 15mg zinc supplement to increase stomach acid production and a diet rich in fruit and vegetables. Several weeks later Barbara said her indigestion had begun to ease.

BIOCHEMICAL FACTORS

Chewed food passes down the oesophagus into the stomach where gastric acids and enzymes break it down further. Excessive gas and acid can flow back (reflux) into the oesophagus. Since, unlike the stomach, the oesophagus does not have a protective lining, when it is exposed to stomach acid it can become inflamed and painful.

BIOCHEMICAL TRIGGERS

• Eating too much rich, spicy, fatty or fried food, especially near bedtime • Drinking excess alcohol • Rushing meals • Chewing food insufficiently • Swallowing air • Eating unripe fruit, which is high in indigestible pectin

STRUCTURAL FACTORS

Reflux (*see right*) and heartburn occur when the muscle at the bottom of the oesophagus fails to keep gastric acid in the stomach. It is not clear why this happens, but increased pressure on the digestive tract may be a factor. Smoking relaxes this muscle with the same effect. A hiatus hernia may cause frequent heartburn. This results when a small part of the stomach rises above the diaphragm (the muscle sheet that separates the stomach from the chest).

STRUCTURAL TRIGGERS

• Pregnancy • Being very overweight
• Hiatus hernia • Lying down after a meal
• Straining to lift or if constipated • Wearing tight clothing around the waist

PSYCHO-SOCIAL FACTORS

Stress can lower or increase stomach-acid production. It can also affect the secretion of enzymes, digestive juices and hormones in the gut. Tension can make gut movement irregular and reduce the flow of blood to the stomach and intestines (*see page 158*).

PSYCHO-SOCIAL TRIGGERS

• Anxiety • Fear • Impatience

PRECAUTIONS

Consult a doctor if symptoms last more than a few days, if you are regularly taking antacids, or if you are over 40 and suddenly experience indigestion.

Realms of the Body (*see page 20*)

● **BIOCHEMICAL**
Body systems,
such as digestion.

● **STRUCTURAL**
Muscles, bones,
joints and nerves.

PSYCHO-SOCIAL
Thoughts, feelings
and relationships.

Key: Evidence of Efficacy (*see page 182*)

❶ ❷ ❸ ❹ ❺

least evidence ◄————————► most evidence

BIOCHEMICAL TREATMENT OPTIONS

CONVENTIONAL MEDICINE
Antacids reduce the acidity of digestive juices. H2 blockers (*see Drugs Glossary, page 179*) such as ranitidine limit the amount of acid released.

COMPLEMENTARY THERAPIES
Western Herbalism ❷ (*see page 127*)
Herbalists may suggest slippery elm to protect the digestive tract lining,

Burdock and dandelion can help to improve digestion

peppermint and chamomile to settle the stomach, and dandelion and burdock before eating to enhance digestion and prevent indigestion.

Nutritional Therapies ❷
(*see pages 128–29*)
Hydrochloric acid deficiency is thought to cause indigestion, so a therapist may suggest a short course of Betain capsules. Dysbiosis and food sensitivities may also be suspected (*see pages 92–95*) and an exclusion diet recommended to identify offending foods. "Live" yoghurt, which contains beneficial bacteria, is thought to help. Food combining, or the Hay Diet (*see page 129*), in which proteins and

carbohydrates are eaten separately, may be advised. Vitamin C, zinc and betacarotene supplements may help to repair the stomach lining.

SELF-HELP TECHNIQUES
• Eat regular small meals and follow a healthy, fibre-rich diet • Keep a food diary (*see page 147*) if you suspect a sensitivity • Avoid highly spiced, rich or fatty foods and steam, grill or bake, rather than fry • Avoid raw foods and acidic foods such as vinegar and pickles • Cut down on tobacco and alcohol which increase stomach acidity, strong coffee which irritates the stomach lining, and fizzy drinks which cause gas.

STRUCTURAL TREATMENT OPTIONS

CONVENTIONAL MEDICINE
Swallowing antacid gels can help prevent reflux.

COMPLEMENTARY THERAPIES
Chiropractic ❷ (*see page 118*) and **Osteopathy** ❷ (*see page 119*)
Practitioners may manipulate the area of the spine where nerve and blood supplies to the digestive organs arise.
Acupuncture ❸ (*see page 125*)
Some research suggests that stimulating acupoints can reduce high levels of acid production and relieve tension.

SELF-HELP TECHNIQUES
• Relax before and during meals and chew food thoroughly • If you get reflux or heartburn, avoid activities that involve bending from the waist or stooping straight after meals • Eat at a table sitting upright rather than slumped in front of the TV • Take regular exercise to help the circulation and induce relaxation • Raise the head of the bed by 15cm (6in) so gravity can help keep digestive acids in the stomach • Refrain from eating just before going to bed.

Take time to chew and to digest your food, and maintain an upright posture when eating

PSYCHO-SOCIAL TREATMENT OPTIONS

CONVENTIONAL MEDICINE
Stress-management techniques may be suggested (*see pages 168–69*).

COMPLEMENTARY THERAPIES
Psychotherapy & Counselling ❷
(*see pages 132–33*)
Talking through problems may help

identify areas of anxiety and a practitioner will suggest ways of dealing with them.
Meditation & Hypnotherapy ❷
(*see pages 134–35*)
Focusing the mind may help induce relaxation and relieve the stress that can lead to "nervous" indigestion.

SELF-HELP TECHNIQUES
• Keep a symptom- and stress-trigger diary (*see pages 147 and 175*) • Practise relaxation and breathing techniques (*see pages 170–71*) to help deal with stress and anxiety.

IRRITABLE BOWEL SYNDROME

One of the most common gastrointestinal complaints, irritable bowel syndrome (IBS) may affect up to two people in ten. It is particularly prevalent among women aged between 20 and 45. IBS, also known as spastic colon, may come and go for years, with no infection or other apparent cause. The wave-like motion of the gut (peristalsis) becomes irregular, causing erratic bowel movements with constipation, diarrhoea, or both, as well as wind and intermittent abdominal pain. Although IBS is not life-threatening, symptoms can cause distress and be difficult to control. Treatment can bring relief but does not always offer a cure.

CASE STUDY

Jane, an acupuncturist, treated Alison, 41, a divorcee with a teenage daughter. For two years, Alison had complained of insomnia, abdominal pains, diarrhoea and constipation, but medical tests had found nothing wrong. Jane diagnosed her pattern of disharmony as Liver *qi* stagnation: "This is commonly associated with stress-related problems," she said. "I worked on acupuncture points between the knee and foot to release the blocked energy of the Liver. Meanwhile, Alison would relax deeply and often fall asleep." After six treatments, most of Alison's symptoms had gone.

BIOCHEMICAL FACTORS

Various nutritional factors can interfere with contractions of the colon, the release of digestive enzymes and the absorption of food through the wall of the gut.

BIOCHEMICAL TRIGGERS

• Chemicals released by the body in response to stress • Intolerance to foods, especially to dairy products and to grains such as wheat, barley, oats, rye and millet • Dysbiosis (*see page 93*), when poorly digested food in the gut encourages the growth of unfriendly gut bacteria • "Leaky gut" (*see page 93*) which is especially likely after gastroenteritis or after a course of broad-spectrum antibiotics (*see Drugs Glossary, pages 179*)

PSYCHO-SOCIAL FACTORS

The stress response affects digestion and absorption by changing peristalsic rhythm, altering the secretion of juices and enzymes, and by affecting blood circulation. Over 50 per cent of people with IBS report a history of emotional problems, and evidence indicates that people with anxiety or depression may be more likely to develop IBS after a gut infection. Poor sleep also seems to trigger IBS symptoms.

PSYCHO-SOCIAL TRIGGERS

• Continual, low-level stress • Anxiety • Inadequate sleep • Depression • Hostility

STRUCTURAL FACTORS

Peristalsis, the wave-like action of the gut that propels faeces towards the rectum, becomes irregular with IBS. Symptoms can include mucus in the faeces, an urgent need to open the bowels, and a feeling of incomplete evacuation.

STRUCTURAL TRIGGERS

• Muscles in the wall of the colon pushing its contents either too quickly, causing diarrhoea, or too slowly, causing constipation • Muscular overactivity or spasm causing cramps • Bloating, rumbling and flatulence caused by irregular peristalsis, fermentation processes or by swallowing air – a nervous habit sometimes linked with hyperventilation (overbreathing) and eating too quickly

PRECAUTIONS

Consult a doctor if you are over 40 years old and your bowel habits have recently changed. Check with a doctor if there is blood in your stools. See a doctor if you are over 60 and have symptoms for the first time.

Realms of the Body (*see page 20*)

● BIOCHEMICAL
Body systems,
such as digestion.

● STRUCTURAL
Muscles, bones,
joints and nerves.

PSYCHO-SOCIAL
Thoughts, feelings
and relationships.

Key: Evidence of Efficacy (*see page 182*)

❶ ❷ ❸ ❹ ❺

least evidence ◄──────► most evidence

BIOCHEMICAL TREATMENT OPTIONS

CONVENTIONAL MEDICINE
A diet high in soluble fibre or bulking agents, such as methylcellulose, may be advised to soften stools.

COMPLEMENTARY THERAPIES
Naturopathy ❹ (*see page 126*)
Exclusion and rotation diets (*see page 129*) may identify a food intolerance. Citrus fruits, tea,

Elimination diet has "neutral" foods

coffee and alcohol are often suspects as well as dairy products and wheat. A high-fibre diet may be advised, especially if you have constipation. Live yogurt or supplements such as *lactobacillus* help normalize levels of bacteria in the gut.
Chinese Herbalism ❹ (*see page 125*)
A study reported in 1998 showed that herbal formulas were effective in relieving symptoms.
Western Herbalism ❸ (*see page 127*)
Peppermint oil capsules may help to reduce muscular gut contractions.

SELF-HELP TECHNIQUES
• Keep a record of episodes of IBS. do they coincide with certain foods or situations? • Check ingredients on food labels • Reduce fat intake • Avoid refined carbohydrates, which encourage muscle spasm • For constipation, increase water-soluble fibre (in leafy vegetables, fruit and oat bran), which is easier to digest than insoluble fibre (in wheat bran and rice), which can irritate the gut • Drink at least 2 litres (3½ pints) of water a day.

STRUCTURAL TREATMENT OPTIONS

CONVENTIONAL MEDICINE
A doctor may prescribe antispasmodic drugs to relieve muscular spasm and cramping pain. A short course of antidiarrhoeal drugs may be suggested.

COMPLEMENTARY THERAPIES
Massage ❷ (*see page 116*)
Gentle massage of the lower abdomen may relax muscular tension in the colon wall and help regulate the bowels. It is best demonstrated by a practitioner before you practise on yourself.

Yoga ❷ (*see page 123*)
Postures such as the Half Shoulderstand and the Cobra can stimulate digestion. Calming breathing exercises, or *pranayama*, help relieve stress.

Cobra pose aids digestion

Acupuncture ❷ (*see page 125*)
An acupuncturist usually links IBS to one of the following: "stagnant Liver *qi*" (stress or hostility); "deficient Kidney or

Spleen" (poor digestion and food absorption) or "damp heat" (such as a disturbance in gut bacteria). Western acupuncturists believe that stimulating acupoints can positively affect the nerve system controlling the gut's contractions.

SELF-HELP TECHNIQUES
• At the first sign of pain, squeeze acupoints Colon 4 or Liver 3 (*see page 125*) • Take plenty of gentle exercise • Leave adequate time for meals • Ensure that you get enough sleep.

PSYCHO-SOCIAL TREATMENT OPTIONS

CONVENTIONAL MEDICINE
Those with IBS are advised to learn stress-management techniques (*see pages 168–69*).

COMPLEMENTARY THERAPIES
Psychotherapy & Counselling ❹
(*see pages 132–33*)
Cognitive behavioural therapy may help you change ways of thinking and behaving in response to stress. Counselling may help identify sources of stress and ways of coping.

Hypnotherapy ❹ (*see page 134*)
In a study by Dr. Peter Whorwell of the Withington Hospital, Manchester, reported in *The Lancet* (1989), hypnotherapy proved successful in relieving symptoms of IBS. Practitioners explain the gut's anatomy and function, then induce a state

Hypnotherapy may reduce symptoms

of deep relaxation and a sensation of abdominal warmth before asking patients to try to imagine their gut working normally.

SELF-HELP TECHNIQUES
• Relaxation and breathing techniques (*see pages 170–71*) are important in reducing muscle tension and stress responses • Keep a diary of symptoms and stress triggers (*see pages 147 and 175*) • Meditation (*see page 135*) may also help to reduce stress symptoms.

INFLAMMATORY BOWEL DISEASE

The two main types of inflammatory bowel disease are Crohn's disease and ulcerative colitis. Both are becoming much more common in developed countries, particularly among people aged 15–35. Crohn's disease affects any part of the digestive tract but especially the lower small intestine. Common symptoms include pain, spasms, flatulence, diarrhoea, fever and weight loss. Ulcerative colitis inflames the colon and rectum, then ulcerates the gut lining. It can cause abdominal tenderness, diarrhoea with cramps, mucus and blood in the faeces, weight loss, a general feeling of being unwell, and fever.

CASE STUDY

Tim, 42, an accountant, suffered from mild ulcerative colitis diagnosed by endoscopy (*see Glossary, pages 177–78*). Before going on to anti-inflammatory drugs, Tim and his doctor agreed to try an alternative, and Tim consulted George, a naturopath. A challenge test and stool analysis pointed to a wheat intolerance with dysbiosis (*see page 93*) and yeast overgrowth. Tim's diet lacked vegetable fibre, so George advised him to eat grated apple or carrot before meals, as well as vegetable soups and brown rice. He also advised him not to include starch and protein in the same meal. Tim was given *lactobacillus* supplements to replace the abnormal gut flora, slippery elm gruel to soothe the gut, and liquorice, wild yam and barberry to help repair the intestinal lining. Three months later, his symptoms had improved, although eating out could still cause a bout of diarrhoea.

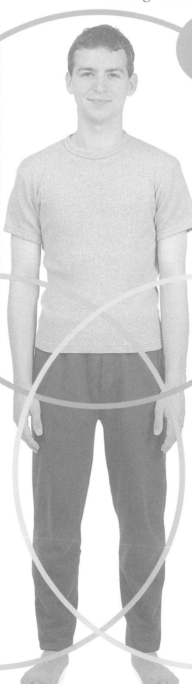

BIOCHEMICAL FACTORS

The exact cause of inflammatory bowel disease is unknown. In some cases it is part of an auto-immune disorder in which the immune system attacks the body's own tissues. Nutritional deficiencies occur if food is not properly absorbed by the gut.

BIOCHEMICAL TRIGGERS

• Family history • Food allergy or intolerance (*see pages 92–95*) • Inflammatory auto-immune diseases such as rheumatoid arthritis • Bacterial or viral infection • Possibly ingesting the bacterium *Mycobacterium paratuberculosis*, found in milk (Crohn's disease) • A diet high in refined sugar and low in raw fruit, vegetables, fibre and omega-3 fatty acids (found in oily fish) • Smoking (Crohn's disease) • Overusing antibiotics

PSYCHO-SOCIAL FACTORS

Although there is little evidence that psychological factors can trigger either type of inflammatory bowel disease, emotional stress is thought to aggravate it. Symptoms of both conditions can often be a source of stress in themselves.

PSYCHO-SOCIAL TRIGGERS

• Anxiety • Overwork and inadequate sleep • Traumatic life events

STRUCTURAL FACTORS

In Crohn's disease, chronic inflammation greatly thickens the intestinal wall and penetrating ulcers may form. The intestine can become so narrow that it becomes blocked. Complications of Crohn's disease include abscesses, fistulas (abnormal openings between loops of the intestines) and inflammation of the joints, spine, eyes and skin. Complications of ulcerative colitis include a dangerously enlarged colon, rashes, mouth ulcers, anaemia, arthritis and conjunctivitis. Both conditions may go into remission for months or years, and so far there are no known structural triggers involved.

PRECAUTIONS

Consult a doctor if you have prolonged or unexplained diarrhoea; any persistent change in bowel habits; blood or mucus in stools; or unexplained severe or persistent abdominal pain.

Realms of the Body (*see page 20*)

● **BIOCHEMICAL**
Body systems,
such as digestion.

● **STRUCTURAL**
Muscles, bones,
joints and nerves.

PSYCHO-SOCIAL
Thoughts, feelings
and relationships.

Key: Evidence of Efficacy (*see page 182*)

❶　❷　❸　❹　❺

least evidence ◄──────────► most evidence

BIOCHEMICAL TREATMENT OPTIONS

CONVENTIONAL MEDICINE
A doctor may prescribe sulphasalazine, corticosteroids and mesalazine to ease inflammation (*see Drugs Glossary, page 179*). A new treatment, infliximab, is being developed. A combination of antibiotics (rifabutin and clarithromycin) is being researched for Crohn's disease.

COMPLEMENTARY THERAPIES
Western Herbalism ❷ (*see page 127*)
Robert's Formula, a traditional herbal remedy, may be recommended.

Nutritional Therapies ❹
(*see pages 128–29*)
Practitioners aim to improve digestion by resting the liver, and may suggest a bowel-cleansing juice fast. Supervised exclusion diets (*see page 129*) may help 50 per cent of Crohn's disease patients – dairy products and wheat are often trigger foods. Oily fish and fish oil

Live yogurt aids digestion

supplements may redress an imbalance of essential fatty acids. A practitioner may suggest "live" yogurt or *lactobacillus* supplements for dysbiosis and a "leaky" gut (*see page 159*). Vitamin and mineral supplements can aid nutrient absorption. Quercetin, a natural anti-inflammatory, may help.

SELF-HELP TECHNIQUES
• Eat a diet high in complex carbohydrates, and take multivitamin and mineral supplements.

STRUCTURAL TREATMENT OPTIONS

CONVENTIONAL MEDICINE
A biopsy, barium X-ray, barium enema, colonoscopy and sigmoidoscopy (*see Glossary, pages 177–78*) are used to make a correct diagnosis, as similar symptoms can make it difficult to differentiate between the two conditions. In severe cases of either disease, damaged portions of intestine may be removed surgically. If the colon is removed, the patient is left with an ileostomy (*see Glossary*). People with ulcerative colitis require regular checks for bowel cancer.

COMPLEMENTARY THERAPIES
Massage ❸ (*see page 116*)
In one study, breathing exercises, combined with massage, encouraged sleep and the feeling of being in control of pain.
Acupuncture ❷ (*see page 125*)
A practitioner will aim to correct disturbances in the flow of qi. For ulcerative colitis, acupoints on the Gallbladder meridian may be stimulated with either needles or moxibustion.

SELF-HELP TECHNIQUES
• Practise yoga regularly. The breathing techniques, methods of mental focus and body postures can all help to relieve stress and improve circulation to the inner organs (*see page 123*).

Practising the Half Shoulder-stand may relieve stress

PSYCHO-SOCIAL TREATMENT OPTIONS

CONVENTIONAL MEDICINE
Your doctor may suggest you try various techniques to manage stress and pain.

COMPLEMENTARY THERAPIES
Hypnotherapy ❷ (*see page 134*)
A practitioner will demonstrate a number of techniques that enable you to calm your mind at will to relieve stress. These may include visualization (*see page 134*), which can help you to use your imagination to overcome stress and relax tense muscles.

Thinking about a restful scene can help to reduce stress levels

Biofeedback ❸ (*see page 136*)
By responding to signals on devices measuring body changes, you can learn to relax muscle tension.

SELF-HELP TECHNIQUES
• Keep a daily diary of diet, symptoms and stress triggers (*see pages 147 and 175*) • Practise relaxation and breathing techniques (*see pages 170–71*) and learn stress-management skills (*see pages 168–69*) to help you deal with the symptoms.

HIGH BLOOD PRESSURE

lood pumped from the heart around the body exerts a constantly fluctuating pressure on the walls of arteries. Pressure levels are lowest early in the morning, and are highest during physical exercise. When blood pressure is consistently raised, it is known as high blood pressure, or hypertension.

This condition is estimated to affect up to 20 per cent of adults in developed countries but, as there are usually no symptoms, it may go undetected until picked up during a medical. Untreated, hypertension can damage blood vessels and increase the risk of stroke, heart and kidney disease, as well as other disorders.

CASE STUDY

James, a psychologist, saw Paul, a 35-year-old teacher with chest pains and borderline high blood pressure. Though Paul was keen to try drug treatment, the medicines had made him feel unwell. James discovered that Paul's father-in-law had died recently and that a tree had crushed the greenhouse in which he used to unwind after work. James suggested Paul buy another greenhouse and taught him autogenic techniques to help him relax.

"Paul's blood pressure came down ten points and a cardiogram showed his heart was fine. In fact the chest pains soon went away," said James. "So far Paul has no need for drugs, but his doctor checks his blood pressure twice a year just in case."

BIOCHEMICAL FACTORS

In 10 per cent of cases, hypertension is attributed to disorders of the kidneys or adrenal glands, congenital abnormality of the aorta (the heart's main artery), pre-eclampsia in pregnancy, and to the use of certain drugs such as oral contraceptives. Oestrogen seems to protect women until the menopause, after which their risk equals and even exceeds that of men. A diet low in potassium and high in sodium is linked to high blood pressure in some people, and nicotine and adrenaline cause the arteries to constrict, resulting in a temporary rise in blood pressure.

BIOCHEMICAL TRIGGERS

- Persistently high levels of "stress" chemicals
- Excessive alcohol and caffeine consumption
- Being male or a post-menopausal woman
- High salt intake • Smoking • Family history

STRUCTURAL FACTORS

In 90 per cent of cases, hypertension is "essential" or "primary", meaning there is no specific cause. Untreated hypertension causes irreversible changes in the blood-vessel walls that increase the risk of fatty plaque deposits forming. These narrow the arteries and encourage blood clots, which can cause a heart attack or stroke (see Heart Disease, pages 48–51). Symptoms of hypertension, which only occur if blood pressure is very high, include dizziness, headaches, fatigue and breathlessness.

STRUCTURAL TRIGGERS

- Race (black people suffer more than other races from hypertension) • Age • Obesity
- Lack of exercise • Environmental factors, such as crowded living conditions

PSYCHO-SOCIAL FACTORS

Under stress, the body undergoes a "fight or flight" response, which provokes a temporary rise in blood pressure. Persistently high stress levels can contribute to hypertension. In the fight or flight response, the heart beats faster and extra reserves of the stress hormones adrenaline, noradrenaline and cortisol flood the system. Arteries constrict so that less blood is lost in case wounds occur, and blood stickiness increases to form clots more easily. "Hostile" personality types and people with high anxiety levels react more strongly to stressful situations (see page 49).

PSYCHO-SOCIAL TRIGGERS

- Hostility and aggression • Work or social stress • Anxiety

Realms of the Body (*see page 20*)

● **BIOCHEMICAL**
Body systems,
such as digestion.

● **STRUCTURAL**
Muscles, bones,
joints and nerves.

PSYCHO-SOCIAL
Thoughts, feelings
and relationships.

Key: Evidence of Efficacy (*see page 182*)

❶ ❷ ❸ ❹ ❺

least evidence ◄──────► most evidence

BIOCHEMICAL TREATMENT OPTIONS

CONVENTIONAL MEDICINE
For mild cases of hypertension, a doctor will suggest dietary and lifestyle changes (*see right*). Beta-blockers, which reduce heart-beat force, and diuretics, which reduce blood volume, are usually prescribed first. (Tiredness and nightmares are fairly common side-effects of beta-blockers.) These may be followed by ACE inhibitors to dilate blood vessels, calcium channel blockers and vasodilators (*see Drugs Glossary, page 179*)

COMPLEMENTARY THERAPIES
Nutritional Therapies ❸
(*see pages 128–29*)
A practitioner may advise a vegetarian diet with plenty of potassium-rich fruit and vegetables, as studies suggest this lowers blood pressure and reduces the incidence of heart disease. Eating plenty of oat bran and psyllium seeds, garlic and onion may be suggested, along with supplements such as omega-3 fatty acids (fish oils), magnesium to relax muscle tissue, vitamin C and Coenzyme Q10.

SELF-HELP TECHNIQUES
• Reduce salt intake to no more than one teaspoon a day • Eat plenty of potassium-rich foods (bananas, celery, prunes, watercress, oranges) • Cut back on processed foods, alcohol and coffee
• Avoid foods high in saturated fats and cholesterol.
• Stop smoking.

Watercress is an excellent
source of potassium

STRUCTURAL TREATMENT OPTIONS

CONVENTIONAL MEDICINE
Doctors recommend regular exercise since it is known to help reduce mild hypertension.

COMPLEMENTARY THERAPIES
Massage ❷ (*see page 116*)
A practitioner may use long, slow strokes to help you unwind. Several studies show gentle, full body massage temporarily lowers blood pressure and helps relaxation, but there is no evidence so far that it controls hypertension.

Aromatherapy ❷ (*see page 117*)
Many essential oils, including lavender and rose, are said to have sedative qualities. Aromatherapy can help if stress and tension are part of the problem, but it has not been shown to reduce hypertension in the long term.

Rose and essential oil

T'ai Chi ❸ (*see page 125*)
The combination of movement, breathing and mental focus in t'ai chi has been shown to lower blood pressure raised by mental and emotional stress.

SELF-HELP TECHNIQUES
• Take regular exercise (consult your doctor first if you have moderate hypertension) • Lose any excess weight.

PSYCHO-SOCIAL TREATMENT OPTIONS

CONVENTIONAL MEDICINE
A doctor may suggest cognitive behavioural therapy which can help people with "hostile" personalities.

COMPLEMENTARY THERAPIES
Hypnotherapy ❸ (*see page 134*)
Recalling the memory of a hypnotically induced state of relaxation may enable you to re-enter it when necessary.
Meditation ❸ (*see page 135*)
A practitioner will show you techniques that quieten and focus the

mind, which can help to generate deep alpha brain-waves that are associated with relaxation.
Biofeedback ❸ (*see page 136*)
Monitoring devices can help you learn how to relax at will. Studies show that

Devices measure
skin temperature

Electrodes monitor
brain-wave activity

biofeedback helps mild hypertension so that medication can be reduced.
Relaxation & Breathing ❸
(*see pages 170–71*)
You will be taught how to breathe diaphragmatically to induce relaxation and combat the body's stress response.

SELF-HELP TECHNIQUES
• Keep a stress diary (*see page 175*) and practise stress-management techniques (*see pages 168–69*) • Listening to music can temporarily lower hypertension.

HEART DISEASE

The heart is a hollow muscular organ at the centre of the network of arteries and veins that circulates blood around the body. The blood supplies the tissues with oxygen and nutrients and removes waste products. Coronary arteries carry oxygenated blood from the lungs directly to the heart; any disease that damages or causes malfunction of these arteries affects the heart's ability to contract effectively. The conditions that result are known as *coronary artery disease* or *coronary heart disease*.

Coronary artery disease is one of the conditions caused by *atherosclerosis*, in which the insides of the coronary artery walls gradually become clogged with fatty plaque deposits,called atheroma. This narrowing restricts blood flow to the heart muscle. Eventually, the arteries become so narrow that the heart gets cramp when it has to work harder during exercise, causing pain known as *angina pectoris*. A *heart attack* (myocardial infarction) can be fatal: part of the heart muscle dies because its blood supply is cut off due to narrowing of arteries, or because a blood clot (thrombus) is blocking a coronary artery.

BIOCHEMICAL FACTORS

HIGH LEVELS OF BLOOD CHOLESTEROL contribute to atherosclerosis and angina (*see above*). Blood cholesterol is one of a group of fat-like substances, known as lipids, and is made by the liver. It is needed for digestion and to build cell membranes and hormones, but excess blood cholesterol is a health risk.

There are two types of cholesterol: high-density lipoprotein (HDL) and low-density lipoprotein (LDL). The latter makes up about two-thirds of cholesterol and is called "bad" cholesterol because its small molecules allow it to slip into the lining of damaged blood vessels and fur them up.

The higher your levels of LDL blood cholesterol, the greater your risk of heart disease. The arteries carry blood rich in oxygen and nutrients, which are vital for the growth, maintenance and repair of cells and tissues. If LDL cholesterol builds up on artery walls, sticky blood-clotting cells (platelets) adhere so that plaque deposits form, impeding the flow of blood. When a coronary artery becomes blocked, the blood supply to the heart muscle is cut off, and the muscle may die (myocardial infarction or heart attack).

BIOCHEMICAL TRIGGERS

• Low levels of antioxidants, obtained from fruit and vegetables, which fight damaging free radicals that attack artery walls • A diet high in saturated fats and trans-fatty acids (*see page 161*) which can raise levels of LDL blood cholesterol (*see left*) • An inherited tendency to high levels of blood cholesterol and a related blood fat, triglyceride • High levels of fibrinogen, a blood-clotting agent that makes blood more sticky and likely to clot • Smoking, which quadruples the risk of heart attack: toxic tobacco smoke chemicals in the bloodstream damage the arteries, increase blood cholesterol and fibrinogen levels, and raise blood pressure • Cortisol and adrenaline, chemicals produced under stress, which inhibit tissue repair and prevent artery walls from healing • Elevated levels of the amino acid homocysteine, a chemical "sandpaper" that damages the arteries and promotes atherosclerosis • The presence in arterial walls of *Chlamydia pneumoniae*, a common bacterium, which may provoke a damaging immune system reaction.

See over for Biochemical Treatment Options

Realms of the Body *(see page 20)*

BIOCHEMICAL
Body systems,
such as digestion.

STRUCTURAL
Muscles, bones,
joints and nerves.

PSYCHO-SOCIAL
Thoughts, feelings
and relationships.

STRUCTURAL FACTORS

DAMAGE TO ARTERY WALLS is exacerbated by high blood pressure, stress and smoking, causing atherosclerosis *(see opposite)*. This occurs when white blood cells cling to damaged areas of artery walls and attract fat, particularly cholesterol, which forms plaque deposits. The higher the cholesterol levels, the faster plaque narrows the arteries. High cholesterol also reduces levels of a muscle-relaxing substance in artery walls that encourages blood flow.

Damage and cracking of plaque deposits attracts platelet blood cells. These rapidly grow into a blood clot (thrombus) which further hinders blood flow through the artery and may even completely block it. The clot may move into the bloodstream to cause harm elsewhere, particularly in the lung (pulmonary embolism) or brain (stroke, caused by a cerebro-embolism).

STRUCTURAL TRIGGERS

• Stress, which raises blood pressure and triggers coronary artery spasm and abnormal heart rhythms. This in turn may lead to palpitations, hyperventilation, chest pain, and can even cause a heart attack
• Obesity, which puts the heart at risk. Overweight, "apple-shaped" people, who carry fat around the middle rather than the hips, are at greater risk of coronary artery disease than others • High blood pressure, placing a strain on the artery walls (*see page 46*) • Lack of exercise, which reduces cardiac efficiency • Smoking, which damages artery walls.

See over for Structural Treatment Options

PSYCHO-SOCIAL FACTORS

IMPATIENT, AGGRESSIVE, WORKAHOLIC "Type A" personalities used to be considered more prone to heart disease. Now only one element of Type A behaviour, "hostility" *(see right)*, is considered a health risk. Hostility is a mixture of cynicism, self-involvement and anger, and is often characteristic of people who feel they have little or no control over their lives.

When hostile, the mind and body are in "battle" mode: the heart works faster, the liver releases sugars and fats for fast energy, and blood-clotting accelerates to seal injuries. If this condition is sustained, stress hormones, cholesterol and fibrinogen (a clotting agent) rise to harmful levels. Hostile people also often tend to have poor health habits, such as overeating, smoking and drinking alcohol to excess.

PSYCHO-SOCIAL TRIGGERS

• Cumulative tiredness • A life or job that is highly demanding and low in autonomy • Poor ability to cope with situations • Loneliness and lack of social support

See over for Psycho-social Treatment Options

ARE YOU HOSTILE?

The more "yes" answers you give to these questions, devised by Dr. Redford Williams, the higher your risk of contracting heart disease. Use the Steps to a Trusting Heart exercise (*see page 51*) to help combat this risk.

• Do you always feel pressed for time?
• Do you hurry when you eat?
• At the end of the day, do you feel stretched to your limits?
• When angry, do you sulk or keep things bottled up inside?
• Do you always like to have the last word in an argument?
• If someone ahead of you in the supermarket express queue has too many items in their basket, do you seethe but say nothing?
• If you see an able-bodied person park in a disabled driver's parking space, do you say nothing but fume inwardly?

HEART DISEASE

Key: Evidence of Efficacy (*see page 182*)

❶ ❷ ❸ ❹ ❺

least evidence ◄─────────► most evidence

BIOCHEMICAL TREATMENT OPTIONS

The Ornish diet

CONVENTIONAL MEDICINE

Patients diagnosed with coronary artery disease may be recommended the following by their doctor: one aspirin (75mg) twice a week to prevent blood clotting; vasodilator drugs to improve blood flow in narrowed arteries; drugs to improve the heart's pumping; beta-blockers to treat high blood pressure, angina and irregular heart rhythms; anti-angina drugs such as nitrates and calcium channel blockers; cholesterol-lowering drugs such as statins; and anti-coagulant drugs (*see Drugs Glossary, page 179*). Post-menopausal women may be offered hormone replacement therapy (HRT),

Gentle exercise improves heart health

particularly if there is a family history of heart disease as it appears to reduce the risk of a heart attack by up to 50 per cent.

COMPLEMENTARY THERAPIES

Naturopathy ❹ (*see page 126*)
Improvements in diet and lifestyle may help people with coronary artery disease. In the US, Dr. Dean Ornish has devised the Ornish Lifestyle Program to reverse heart disease without surgery or drugs. It comprises a rigorous high-fibre vegetarian diet, of which only 10 per cent of calories come from fat (the conventional recommendation for patients with coronary heart disease is 30 per cent), 15–20 per cent from protein and 70–75 per cent from complex carbohydrates. Further to this, patients must exercise for one hour three times a week and attend group therapy classes and daily stress-management exercises adapted from yoga. In one study, arterial blood flow improved and chest pain diminished in 82 per cent of Dr. Ornish's patients, while in 53 per cent of a control group, symptoms grew worse.

Western Herbalism ❸ (*see page 127*)
The following herbs may be recommended by a practitioner: the Chinese herb ginkgo to improve blood circulation in peripheral blood vessels and prevent a second heart attack or stroke; ginger to inhibit blood clotting; and garlic oil – allicin, an active constituent in garlic, has been found to lower blood fats, lower blood pressure, improve circulation to the skin and thin the blood.

Ginkgo

Garlic bulb

Nutritional Therapies ❹

(*see pages 128–29*)
Diet appears to have an important role in preventing and treating heart disease. Antioxidants can reduce damage from LDL cholesterol (*see page 48*). These include vitamin E (a UK study found this could reduce risk of a heart attack in patients with atherosclerosis by 77 per cent), vitamin C, selenium and Coenzyme Q10. Other supplements include: omega-3 fatty acids, such as fish oils and flaxseed oil, to lower blood fats and fibrinogen; omega-6 fatty acids, found in evening primrose and borage oil, to reduce cholesterol and improve heart function; and vitamins B^6, B^{12} and folic acid, to break down homocysteine.

SELF-HELP TECHNIQUES

Eating for a Healthy Heart
• Avoid saturated animal fats from red meats, hard cheese, cream and butter
• Avoid hydrogenated trans-fatty acids, in margarine and biscuits, which may raise "bad" blood cholesterol levels
• Drink less coffee, especially if boiled, infused or made in a cafetière: roasting releases cholesterol-raising substances.
Eat more:
• Vegetable oils rich in mono-unsaturated fatty acids, such as olive and rapeseed oil, to reduce cholesterol. Also use polyunsaturated spreads such as those from sunflower or soya oil
• Oily fish full of omega-3 fatty acids, such as salmon, herring and sardines
• Antioxidant and flavonoid-rich fruit and vegetables (*see page 162*)
• High-fibre foods, especially soluble fibre, found in oats, beans and lentils
• Enjoy one or two glasses of flavonoid-rich red wine each day.

PRECAUTIONS

If you suspect a heart attack, call an ambulance immediately. Symptoms include intense chest pain, possibly spreading down the left arm, or up into the throat or jaw. Sweating, breathlessness, nausea and clammy skin may also occur.

STRUCTURAL TREATMENT OPTIONS

CONVENTIONAL MEDICINE
Surgery for severe cases may include angioplasty to widen arteries, or a coronary artery bypass to improve blood flow past damaged areas.

COMPLEMENTARY THERAPIES
Chiropractic ❺ (*see page 118*) and **Osteopathy** ❸ (*see page 119*) Soft-tissue manipulation may improve the circulation and nerve supply to the chest.
Yoga ❸ (*see page 123*) Exercise involving stretching movements and breathing helps relieve stress and encourages relaxation.
T'ai Chi and **Qigong** ❸ (*see page 125*) In a British study, heart

Qigong

attack patients who practised t'ai chi had lower blood pressure and maintained their exercise programme longer than others, speeding recovery and improving chances of survival.

Acupuncture ❸ (*see page 125*) There is evidence that electro-acupuncture may relieve angina.

SELF-HELP TECHNIQUES
• Exercise can reduce high blood pressure and cholesterol levels, and optimize the efficiency of the heart and circulation. It also provides a means of channelling hostility and burning off stress chemicals. Aim for 20 minutes' aerobic exercise three times a week, but consult your doctor first if you have a heart problem.

PSYCHO-SOCIAL TREATMENT OPTIONS

CONVENTIONAL MEDICINE
Stress-management techniques may be recommended by your doctor.

COMPLEMENTARY THERAPIES
Psychotherapy and **Counselling** ❹ (*see pages 132–33*) Cognitive behavioural therapy may help people with hostile personalities alter their behaviour. The Trusting Heart Program (Dr. Redford Williams of Duke University, US) includes meditation, monitoring cynical, hostile thoughts, learning to listen and forgive, and asserting yourself rather than bottling up anger.

Meditation can bring inner calm

STEPS TO A TRUSTING HEART
• Avoid cynicism
• Be tolerant
• Keep things in proportion
• Practise trusting people
• Listen without interrupting
• Let go of resentful feelings.

In a study at Duke University, results showed that having a spouse or close confidant tripled a heart attack patient's chances of being alive five years later. Religious faith and involvement in a social group seemed to help patients survive and recover from open-heart surgery. Group therapy, self-help and support groups may sustain those lacking a social network.

Meditation ❸ (*see page 135*) Focusing on a particular object or activity to produce a state of "relaxed awareness" has been shown to induce relaxation and relieve stress (*see page 170*). Researchers into transcendental meditation claim it can reduce the major risk factors of heart disease.
Autogenic Training ❸ (*see page 136*) **Biofeedback** ❸ (*see page 136*) These show people how to induce relaxation at will. Autogenic classes teach a series of imagery techniques which most participants can follow and use in daily life.

SELF-HELP TECHNIQUES
• Use relaxation and breathing techniques (*see pages 170–71*) to reverse the heart-damaging effects of stress • Ask yourself if you are hostile (*see page 49*). If you feel you are at risk, try to follow the Steps to a Trusting Heart (*see left*), and let go of hostile feelings, aiming to be more trustful of yourself and others • Examine your lifestyle, and consider which activities and companions you find supportive and which tend to undermine you. Try to spend more time with the former and less with the latter • Relax by spending time listening to soothing music or taking part in music sessions; studies show that music can have a temporarily beneficial effect on blood pressure levels.

Relaxing to music can help lower blood pressure

BACK & NECK PAIN

At least two-thirds of the adult population suffer from back and neck pain at some stage in their lives. In many cases, the cause of pain is unclear, and even severe pain often gets better with little treatment within four to six weeks. However, the problem commonly recurs and one-third of sufferers claim they are prone to long-term episodes. Those most likely to have back pain are manual and office workers, sports men and women, tall or overweight people and the elderly.

Simple back and neck pain is usually caused by injury to strained and tense muscles. Surprisingly, back problems are seldom due to a prolapsed or "slipped" disc, in which the pad that separates two spinal vertebrae splits, putting pressure on a spinal nerve. This results in back stiffness and severe leg pain. Although serious spinal damage or disease is rare, nevertheless correct diagnosis is essential for everyone with acute, severe or persistent back and neck pain to rule out the possibility of inflammatory arthritis, osteomyelitis, a bone fracture or cancer.

BIOCHEMICAL FACTORS

A BONY ARCH on the back of each vertebra forms a protective canal through which runs the spinal cord, the main communication line between the brain and the body. Nerves from the spinal cord branch off between each vertebrae and spread throughout the body to control movement and regulate involuntary processes such as digestion and the immune response. Nerves feeding into the spinal column carry sensory impressions, including pain sensations, to the brain and hormonal system, which orchestrate all body functions.

When strains or injuries to joints, tissues or muscles occur, they trigger a biochemical chain reaction in the body. Injured body tissue releases histamine and other chemicals that cause inflammation and swelling; these inflammatory chemicals also stimulate the nerves that transmit pain. Joints and muscles respond to pain and inflammation by tensing up to prevent further harm, which in turn restricts the circulation so that insufficient nutrients needed for healing can reach the area. Waste products, including lactic acid which irritates the muscles, tend to accumulate in the injured tissue,

exacerbating the problem. This vicious cycle of congested circulation and build-up of inflammatory chemicals and the toxic products of injury makes the muscles more irritable and prone to spasm.

Back and neck pain can be symptoms of more widespread disease, including osteoporosis and other bone conditions, kidney disease, infections and cancer. Also, in some people the spinal discs are genetically predisposed to wear out too quickly. Usually the onset of back and neck pain is gradual. If it is acute and sudden, the problem is probably due to an injury (*see Structural Factors*). If other symptoms are present, a practitioner might suspect acute infection or bone disease.

BIOCHEMICAL TRIGGERS
• Kidney infections and kidney stones • Osteoporosis (brittle bone disease) • Infection or malignancy in the bone • Abdominal conditions such as peptic ulcers and pelvic infections, which can cause pain in the back

See over for Biochemical Treatment Options

Realms of the Body (*see page 20*)

BIOCHEMICAL
Body systems,
such as digestion.

STRUCTURAL
Muscles, bones,
joints and nerves.

PSYCHO-SOCIAL
Thoughts, feelings
and relationships.

STRUCTURAL FACTORS

THE SPINE CONSISTS of 33 girdle-shaped bones, the vertebrae. There are 24 individual, moveable bones; five fused sacral vertebrae; and four fused vertebrae in the coccyx ("tail bone"). The vertebrae are connected to each other by small facet joints, muscles and ligaments that together enable the spine to bend and move in almost any direction. The most mobile areas, and therefore the most prone to problems, are the seven cervical (neck) vertebrae, and the five lumbar (lower back) vertebrae that allow bending sideways, forwards and backwards, and rotation.

The vertebrae are separated by intervertebral discs, thick pads of cartilage which help the spine flex and bend and which act as shock absorbers to prevent the bones rubbing together. The vertebrae are stabilized by interlocking facet joints. Poor posture, overloading, stiffness and old age make problems with these joints and discs more likely. Bodywork and movement therapies counter this tendency, promoting better circulation of nutrient-rich blood and easier movement.

Back and neck pain may result after an injury, such as whiplash. If the pain does not immediately start after an injury, it is usually due to strain on, or wear in one of the small facet joints. Supporting muscles and ligaments can also become tense – even when there is no injury or inflammation. Then constant tension restricts blood circulation in the joints and muscles, so that painful waste products accumulate, resulting in pain and stiffness. As the affected areas weaken, other muscles compensate and in turn come under strain, so that pain and stiffness build up in the large back, buttock, shoulder and neck muscles. These areas can remain tense and irritable long after an acute backache seems to have got better, which may be why so many people find that backache becomes a recurring problem.

STRUCTURAL TRIGGERS
• Injuries, such as whiplash or bone fractures
• Lifting and carrying heavy objects • Poor posture: twisting while bending; sitting badly in one position for long periods of time • Using poorly designed chairs and sagging mattresses • Unaccustomed spells of manual work • Pregnancy and excess weight, both of which put pressure on the back and abdominal muscles
• Osteoarthritis, which results in degenerating cartilage and stiffness • Minor skeletal abnormalities, e.g. legs of unequal length or exaggerated spinal curves; over-flexible (hyper-mobile) joints; stretched ligaments

See over for Structural Treatment Options

PSYCHO-SOCIAL FACTORS

NEGATIVE FEELINGS AND ATTITUDES may contribute to back pain, which in itself is stressful and tiring. Personality and early negative experiences may result in habitual hunching, stooping and other postural problems that encourage the very emotions that started them. Long-term, persistent back pain often has a psychological dimension and may be associated with anxiety and depression. Pain makes us tense and the feeling of wanting to resist the pain may result in restricted breathing and tightening of muscles in the painful area. This response encourages a worsening cycle of pain and tension.

PSYCHO-SOCIAL TRIGGERS
• Emotional upset, stress and anxiety affecting posture and causing muscle tension, especially in the neck and shoulder muscles • Tense or hurried behaviour resulting in sudden movements that risk back or neck strain and injury • Lack of information, motivation or support preventing those with back pain from taking exercise, which could relieve muscle tension and enhance mood
• Fear of worsening persistent pain leading to anxiety and inactivity, which increase existing muscle tension and soreness

See over for Psycho-social Treatment Options

BACK & NECK PAIN

CASE STUDY

David, an osteopath, treated Philip, a storeman in his 50s, who had strained his back handling heavy boxes three years ago, and had suffered a combination of pain, sexual problems and insomnia ever since. Analgesic and inflammatory drugs were some help, but Paul had started to drink heavily. David diagnosed various spasms and stiffness in Philip's back, and over the course of a month used a combination of gentle manipulation and stretch techniques to restore normal function. In discussing Philip's work, David learned that the warehouse that Philip runs was understaffed, and suggested that Philip ask his employers for more physical help so he could concentrate on the managerial side of his job. David also gave advice on posture, especially when handling heavy loads, and sexual positions that would help to lessen the strain on Philip's back. Three months after his consultation, Philip reported that his company had agreed to employ an extra staff member: "That has taken the pressure off me. I've been careful to follow David's instructions on lifting. The pain has pretty much gone, sex with my wife has improved, I'm sleeping much better and I'm less tempted to drown my sorrows in alcohol."

PRECAUTIONS

See a doctor immediately if back pain is accompanied by nausea, vomiting, fever, abdominal pain, weight loss, urinary problems, weakness, pain down one or both arms or legs, or loss of bladder or bowel control.

You should also consult a doctor if the pain worsens over a period of several weeks, does not get better on lying down, or prevents you from sleeping.

BIOCHEMICAL TREATMENT OPTIONS

CONVENTIONAL MEDICINE

Paracetamol relieves pain

A doctor may prescribe painkillers (such as ibuprofen or paracetamol), muscle relaxants and anti-inflammatories (*see Drugs Glossary, page 179*). Local injections of anti-inflammatory medication can help acute inflammatory back pain that results from facet joint disease and acute disc prolapse.

COMPLEMENTARY THERAPIES

Western Herbalism ❷ *(see page 127)*
Herbal remedies may help alleviate pain and muscle tension. St. John's wort, valerian and lavender are calming; cramp bark and devil's claw have anti-inflammatory properties. **Caution:** see page 21 before taking herbal remedies.

St John's wort is relaxing

Valerian has sedative properties

Nutritional Therapies ❸
(see pages 128–29)
Bromelaine enzymes may be prescribed to reduce joint inflammation. For persistent inflammatory joint pain, you may be put on a diet that is low in animal fat and high in fish oil, to reduce levels of arachidonic acid which helps produce inflammatory chemicals. Glucosamine sulphate may be given to help rebuild joint cartilage.

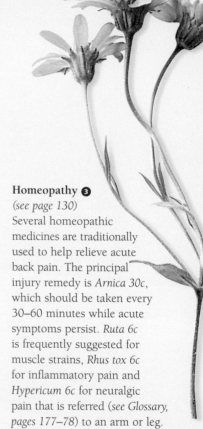

Arnica flowers used in the homeopathic remedy

Homeopathy ❸
(see page 130)
Several homeopathic medicines are traditionally used to help relieve acute back pain. The principal injury remedy is *Arnica 30c*, which should be taken every 30–60 minutes while acute symptoms persist. *Ruta 6c* is frequently suggested for muscle strains, *Rhus tox 6c* for inflammatory pain and *Hypericum 6c* for neuralgic pain that is referred (*see Glossary, pages 177–78*) to an arm or leg.

SELF-HELP TECHNIQUES

• For chronic back and neck pain, consider an anti-inflammatory diet (*see Nutritional Therapies, left*) • Eat oily fish such as sardines, salmon and pilchards twice a week • Reduce your intake of animal fats by substituting low-fat dairy products, limiting red meat, and removing poultry skin.

Eating oily fish such as mackerel and sardines helps to reduce joint inflammation

STRUCTURAL TREATMENT OPTIONS

CONVENTIONAL MEDICINE

X-rays and scans may be used to determine the cause of persistent or severe back pain. Gentle exercise or physiotherapy is recommended early on. Only in severe cases would traction, a collar or a corset be advised. Surgery is reserved for large prolapsed discs, when a nerve is badly compressed.

Protruding disc

A section view of the spine showing a prolapsed disc

COMPLEMENTARY THERAPIES

Massage ❸ *(see page 116)*
Practitioners use massage to reduce muscle tension and stiffness, and to promote better circulation.
Rolfing & Hellerwork ❸
(see page 116)
These therapies involving deep massage and stretching, are helpful in reducing persistent, painful muscle tension.
Chiropractic ❹ *(see page 118)* and
Osteopathy ❹ *(see page 119)*
Manipulation of joints and vertebrae restores mobility. Studies show chiropractic and osteopathy can be effective in relieving acute back pain.

Alexander Technique ❸ *(see page 121)*
An Alexander teacher will show you how to correct your posture to relieve strain on joints and muscles and to ease pressure on nerves in the back and neck. It is very helpful for recurring or persistent pain.
Hydrotherapy ❸
(see page 126)
"Compressing" can help to ease pain that comes on suddenly. Hot and cold compresses are alternately held on the skin – the hot compress for three minutes, followed by the cold compress for one minute. This process, which is repeated every 20 minutes, helps to increase blood flow, relax the muscles and reduce inflammation.
Acupuncture ❺ *(see page 125)*
To relieve pain, practitioners stimulate acupoints on the *yang* channels that flow down the back and legs. Studies suggest acupuncture is valuable for both acute and persistent back and neck pain.
Yoga ❺ *(see page 123)*
Gentle breathing exercises, or *pranayama*, relax back muscles in

The head and neck are aligned to relax the spine

cases of acute pain. Gentle postures like the Child and the Corpse may relax and stretch the back. A full yoga programme taught by a qualified teacher can help to prevent persistent back pain and relapses.

SELF-HELP TECHNIQUES

• If pain is acute, try stimulating acupressure point Colon 4 *(see page 125)* • Use very gentle stretching movements to keep spasm at bay • Wrap a hot-water bottle or a pack of frozen peas in a towel and hold it to the area • Only rest in bed for severe pain, and begin gentle stretching exercises as soon as possible to mobilize the back *(see pages 154–55)* • Improve your overall level of fitness to reduce persistent pain • Pilates exercises *(see Glossary, pages 177–78)* may help to prevent or diminish relapses • Invest in a well-designed chair and a mattress that supports the back • Make sure your computer and other equipment are at appropriate levels *(see page 151)* • Learn correct techniques for lifting and carrying heavy objects *(see page 150)* • Lose any excess weight.

PSYCHO-SOCIAL TREATMENT OPTIONS

CONVENTIONAL MEDICINE

Your doctor may recommend stress-management techniques if your pain is persistent, if it recurs or is stress-related.

COMPLEMENTARY THERAPIES

Psychotherapy & Counselling ❷
(see pages 132–33)
If you have persistent pain, cognitive behavioural therapy can help you to understand how your thoughts and feelings may be involved. The therapy can offer strategies to help change your coping style and behaviour.
Biofeedback ❸ *(see page 136)*
Training can make you aware of habitual muscle contractions that cause long-

term pain. You can then learn to relax the tense area.
Hypnotherapy ❷ *(see page 134)*
A hypnotherapist will help you to recognise sources and signs of tension, and to relax.
Autogenic Training ❸ *(see page 136)*
Effective techniques can be learned to induce relaxation at will through autogenic training.

Autogenic exercises help to relax the neck and shoulders

SELF-HELP TECHNIQUES

• If you have acute pain, allow yourself time out: rest completely for 2–3 days to recover. But don't be afraid to start gentle exercise as soon as possible; remember that remaining immobile means you will take longer to recover • Relaxation and breathing techniques *(see pages 170–71)* can help to ease tension

Exercise eases tension and pain

• Long-term absence from work is associated with pain becoming persistent, so stay at work or return as quickly as possible.

OSTEOARTHRITIS

The most common form of joint disease, osteoarthritis affects up to 80 per cent of people over the age of 50. Three times as many women as men suffer from severe osteoarthritis. Symptoms range from mild pain, stiffness of one or more joints, swelling and "creaking", to total loss of joint function so that walking and dressing become difficult, and even sleep patterns are disrupted. Muscles may waste away around an arthritic joint, and the bones can change shape. Osteoarthritis tends to affect large weight-bearing joints, such as the hips and knees, as well as small joints in the feet, hands, fingers, neck and lower back.

CASE STUDY

Jim, an osteopath, is treating Mary, an active 65-year-old with osteoarthritis in her hip. Mary's orthopaedic surgeon has advised her to delay a hip replacement for as long as possible. For the past year Mary has seen Jim every month. He mobilizes her lower back and hips, and uses acupuncture on trigger points (*see Glossary, pages 177–78*) to release tension in her hip and thigh muscles. On his recommendation, Mary follows a low-sugar, low-fat vegetarian diet for one week every month, and takes glucosamine supplements as well as daily doses of cod liver oil. She practises yoga and has also joined an aqua-aerobics class to strengthen her hips and knees. "The effort has been worthwhile," says Mary. "My arthritis feels manageable, I can walk much further than before, and my surgeon says X-rays show my hip is no worse than it was five years ago."

BIOCHEMICAL FACTORS

Faulty circulation may weaken cartilage, causing inflammation and swelling. Chemicals released when cartilage is damaged trigger the release of enzymes that destroy collagen, an important protein in connective tissue.

BIOCHEMICAL TRIGGERS

• Nutritional deficiencies • Food intolerances (in some forms of osteoarthritis, allergic-type reactions have been found in affected joints) • Family history

STRUCTURAL FACTORS

In osteoarthritis, the cartilage that protects the ends of bones at their points of contact gradually degenerates. Bony outgrowths can distort the joints and cause the misshapen appearance seen in badly arthritic hands. This leads to changes in joint use and posture. Surrounding muscles may become painfully stiff, tighten up or waste away, and blood circulation around the area deteriorates.

STRUCTURAL TRIGGERS

• Ageing • Overuse of joints
• Injury • Obesity

PSYCHO-SOCIAL FACTORS

Persistent pain is stressful and tiring. Feelings of anxiety, anger, denial, depression and helplessness may make the pain feel worse and can affect family relationships.

PSYCHO-SOCIAL TRIGGERS

• Loss of mobility and fitness • Problems in coping with disability • Pain

Realms of the Body *(see page 20)*

● **BIOCHEMICAL**
Body systems,
such as digestion.

● **STRUCTURAL**
Muscles, bones,
joints and nerves.

● **PSYCHO-SOCIAL**
Thoughts, feelings
and relationships.

Key: Evidence of Efficacy *(see page 182)*

❶ ❷ ❸ ❹ ❺

least evidence ◀━━━━━━━▶ most evidence

BIOCHEMICAL TREATMENT OPTIONS

CONVENTIONAL MEDICINE
Aspirin and ibuprofen can relieve both pain and inflammation. Doctors may prescribe stronger non-steroidal anti-inflammatory drugs (NSAIDs) and corticosteroid injections for severe cases *(see Drugs Glossary, page 179)*.

COMPLEMENTARY THERAPIES
Western Herbalism ❸ *(see page 127)*
Ginger, bromelain and curcumin may reduce inflammation. Studies of a herbal remedy containing an avocado

and soya bean compound, known as ASU, have shown promising results.
Nutritional Therapies ❹
(see pages 128–29)
Food avoidance and exclusion diets can identify food intolerances, if these are a suspected factor, and fish oil supplements can help to relieve pain and stiffness. Research supports the use of glucosamine sulphate (a major component of joint fluid) and green-lipped mussel extract to help relieve symptoms of osteoarthritis.

SELF-HELP TECHNIQUES
• Follow an anti-inflammatory diet low in sugar, salt and saturated animal fats and high in wholegrain cereals, fresh fruit, vegetables and oily fish.

An anti-inflammatory diet can help counter symptoms of osteoarthritis

STRUCTURAL TREATMENT OPTIONS

CONVENTIONAL MEDICINE
Physiotherapy, TENS *(see Glossary, pages 177–78)* and heat treatment relieve symptoms. Disability aids may be given to help patients cope at home. Surgery for severe cases includes joint replacement and joint immobilization.

COMPLEMENTARY THERAPIES
Massage ❷ *(see page 116)* and
Osteopathy ❸ *(see page 119)*
Practitioners of both
therapies use massage and

Gentle twists aid flexibility

stretching to improve joint mobility, to increase circulation around joints, and to relieve related muscle tension.
Yoga ❸ *(see page 123)*
Gentle stretching postures can release stiff joints.
Caution: practise exercises with care.
Hydrotherapy ❸
(see page 126)
Mineral and thermal baths relieve joint pain and enhance well-being.

Acupuncture ❸ *(see page 125)*
Research suggests that stimulation of acupoints with needles or moxibustion relieves pain and reduces inflammation.

SELF-HELP TECHNIQUES
• Lose excess weight to relieve pressure on joints • Take gentle exercise such as walking or swimming to strengthen joint-supporting muscles *(see pages 154–55)* • Avoid activities that put pressure on the joints, such as lifting, or walking over rough terrain.

PSYCHO-SOCIAL TREATMENT OPTIONS

CONVENTIONAL MEDICINE
A doctor may recommend one of the following therapies to improve your morale and help you to feel more in control of symptoms.

COMPLEMENTARY THERAPIES
Psychotherapy & Counselling ❸
(see pages 132–33)
Talking through problems and learning cognitive behavioural skills *(see page 133)* may help you to cope with persistent pain.

Visualization ❸ *(see page 134)*
Training can enable you to feel in control of pain, and allow you to combat related stress.
Meditation ❸ *(see page 135)*
Relaxing through meditation can be an important coping skill, and some therapists believe meditation can harness the mind to relieve pain.

Meditating can bring both mental and physical benefits

SELF-HELP TECHNIQUES
• Join a support group, or practise relaxation and breathing exercises *(see pages 170–71)* • Note pain attacks in a diary *(see page 147)* to identify possible triggers • Improve your self-esteem by staying as active as your physical condition permits and becoming involved with hobbies and events.

RHEUMATOID ARTHRITIS

Unlike osteoarthritis (*see pages 56–57*), rheumatoid arthritis is an auto-immune disease, in which the body produces antibodies that attack the membranes lining the joints, which become painfully swollen and stiff. The smaller joints in the hands and toes are most susceptible, but the wrists, ankles, knees, hip and neck may be affected. It usually strikes between the ages of 30 and 50, but can affect children and the elderly. Women are at three times greater risk than men. In severe cases the inflammation can spread to the cartilage and bone, destroying joints and causing deformity. Rheumatoid arthritis may affect other organs including the heart and eyes.

CASE STUDY

Linda, an acupuncturist, treated Susie, 34, a publicist, who had been diagnosed with early rheumatoid arthritis in her hands. Drugs could prevent the condition worsening but, with her doctor's approval, Susie wanted to try acupuncture first. Linda found that Susie led a hectic life and had allowed herself to get run-down. She told her: "Your immune system is impaired. Traditional Chinese Medicine (TCM) sees rheumatoid arthritis as an invasion of Wind, Cold and Damp, which blocks Blood. In TCM, we say that Blood warms the sinews. If it stagnates, its quality becomes impaired." Linda stimulated various points with warming moxibustion to clear Damp and Phlegm, move *qi* in the Blood and correct the underlying imbalance of Liver, Kidney and Spleen. Weekly sessions for two months produced good results; follow-up treatment continued over the next year.

BIOCHEMICAL FACTORS

The blood and joint fluid of people with rheumatoid arthritis contains "rheumatoid factor" antibodies which are not found in other forms of inflammatory arthritis. As in all inflammatory joint diseases, rheumatoid arthritis involves an abnormal over-reaction of the immune system (*see page 67*).

BIOCHEMICAL TRIGGERS

• Genetic predisposition • Food intolerances (*see pages 92–95*) • "Leaky gut" (*see page 159*)

STRUCTURAL FACTORS

Affected joints become warm, swollen and stiff. Ligaments, tendons and surrounding muscles may shorten, stiffen and become weak and painful. Circulation in the area is congested and waste products accumulate. Episodes of pain and stiffness tend to come and go, with gradually worsening joint damage.

ASSOCIATED CONDITIONS

• Raynaud's syndrome (fingers turn white when exposed to cold) • Carpal tunnel syndrome (tingling and pain in the fingers due to pressure on the median nerve in the wrist)• Tenosynovitis (inflamed tendon sheaths in the wrist)

PSYCHO-SOCIAL FACTORS

Feelings of anxiety, anger, denial, depression and helplessness may reduce pain tolerance, undermine the ability to cope (resulting in varying degrees of disability), and affect family relationships. High levels of stress appear to be associated with the onset of the condition and may provoke flare-ups.

PSYCHO-SOCIAL TRIGGERS

• Loss of mobility and fitness • Problems in coping with disability • Pain

Realms of the Body *(see page 20)*

⬤ BIOCHEMICAL
Body systems,
such as digestion.

⬤ STRUCTURAL
Muscles, bones,
joints and nerves.

⬤ PSYCHO-SOCIAL
Thoughts, feelings
and relationships.

Key: Evidence of Efficacy *(see page 182)*

❶ ❷ ❸ ❹ ❺

least evidence ◀──────────▶ most evidence

BIOCHEMICAL TREATMENT OPTIONS

CONVENTIONAL MEDICINE

Aspirin and non-steroidal anti-inflammatories (NSAIDs) ease pain and reduce inflammation. Antirheumatic drugs may slow or halt the condition, but can have

Drugs can ease inflammation

adverse side-effects *(see Drugs Glossary, page 179)*. New drugs are being developed to block the antibody responsible for inflammation.

COMPLEMENTARY THERAPIES

Traditional Chinese Medicine ❷
(see pages 124–25)
An extract (T2) from the "thundergod vine" (*Tripterygium wilfordii*), an ancient

arthritis remedy, may be given as studies of its efficacy are promising.
Western Herbalism ❷ *(see page 127)*
Curcumin and bromelain (extracts of turmeric and pineapple) and ginger are given for their anti-inflammatory effect.
Nutritional Therapies ❷
(see pages 128–29)
Food intolerance is an important factor in some cases of inflammatory arthritis. A therapist may recommend an exclusion diet, probably starting with cutting out wheat and dairy products. Several studies show that short-term supervised fasts and a vegetarian diet can benefit people with rheumatoid arthritis. Omega-3 fatty acids in flaxseed and fish oils can

relieve pain and stiffness, and green-lipped mussel extract may also ease symptoms. Supplements of vitamins A, C, E, B6, and zinc, selenium and pantothenic acid may also be suggested.
Homeopathy ❸ *(see page 130)*
Rhus tox has been found to be effective, and a practitioner will prescribe remedies according to your constitution.

SELF-HELP TECHNIQUES

• Follow a diet low in saturated animal fats to reduce inflammatory arachidonic acid, and in sugar and salt, and rich in wholegrain cereals, fresh fruit, vegetables and cold-water fish • Do not smoke or drink excess alcohol.

STRUCTURAL TREATMENT OPTIONS

CONVENTIONAL MEDICINE

Doctors recommend physiotherapy to relieve muscle spasm and joint stiffness, and occupational therapy to help patients adapt their everyday activities. In severe cases, surgery can replace certain damaged joints.

COMPLEMENTARY THERAPIES

Massage ❸ *(see page 116)*
A therapist aims to stimulate circulation in and around the affected joint to aid flexibility and removal of waste products.

Yoga ❷ *(see page 123)*
Gentle stretching exercises with a yoga teacher may ease stiff joints.
Acupuncture ❸ *(see page 125)*
Therapists stimulate acupoints around the affected area to relieve pain. Traditional acupuncturists treat patients according to their constitution.
Hydrotherapy ❷ *(see page 126)*
Exercising in warm water helps to maintain mobility. Therapy with mineral baths and mud packs can be effective in reducing inflammation and pain.

SELF-HELP TECHNIQUES

• Gentle exercise and stretching can maintain muscle strength, fitness and flexibility.

Practise stretching exercises to ease stiff joints

PSYCHO-SOCIAL TREATMENT OPTIONS

CONVENTIONAL MEDICINE

If clinical depression becomes a problem, antidepressants may be prescribed.

COMPLEMENTARY THERAPIES

Psychotherapy & Counselling ❸
(see pages 132–33)
Talking through problems may help,

and learning cognitive behavioural therapy may be recommended.

SELF-HELP TECHNIQUES

• Self-management programmes in which people take responsibility for their diet, exercise and relaxation increase confidence and encourage

a healthy coping style • Practise relaxation and breathing techniques *(see pages 170–71)* • Hobbies and interests may help maintain activity • Keep a pain diary *(see page 147)* to identify triggers • Being part of a support group may help you deal with psycho-social factors.

PERSISTENT MUSCLE PAIN

There are several causes of persistent muscle pain. When a joint is stiff, as in osteoarthritis, the muscles acting on that joint become inactive and tense. Even though a muscle heals after injury, strain or postural misuse, painful and tender trigger points (TP) may persist (*see Glossary, pages 177–78*). More generalized muscle pain with a characteristic pattern of tender spots around the neck and shoulders, lower back, hips and buttocks, is known as *fibromyalgia syndrome* (FMS). Accompanied by fatigue, sleep disturbance and poor concentration, FMS is linked with other conditions, including chronic fatigue syndrome.

CASE STUDY

Simon, a naturopath, treated Carol, a 39-year-old teacher, for muscle pain and stiffness with tender spots around her neck and lower back, and abdominal pain and bloating. Conventional medical tests were inconclusive, but Simon suspected "leaky gut" (*see page 159*). "This can trigger a release of inflammatory prostaglandins in muscle tissues, causing pain," said Simon. He prescribed slippery elm powder in water to soothe and heal the inflamed gut lining, and a soothing remedy of liquorice, wild yam and marshmallow. Simon used bodywork therapies (*see Glossary, pages 177–78*) to stimulate digestion and lymph drainage, and suggested a diet low in animal fat and a programme of relaxation and exercise. Three months later Carol reported that all symptoms had much improved.

BIOCHEMICAL FACTORS

People with FMS tend to have other mind-body conditions (*see Glossary, pages 177–78*), particularly hyperventilation and irritable bowel syndrome, dysmenorrhoea, PMS and chronic fatigue. These aspects of FMS may be linked to a deficiency of the brain chemical serotonin, which is also a cause of depression. Other factors that may be involved are a build-up of waste products in muscles due to poor circulation in the tissues, as well as food intolerances, infections, nutritional deficiencies and hormone imbalances.

BIOCHEMICAL TRIGGERS
• Food intolerances • Low serotonin levels (*see Glossary, pages 177–78*)

STRUCTURAL FACTORS

Tense, aching muscles are a common sign of poor fitness and loss of well-being and result in a self-perpetuating cycle of pain/muscle spasm/pain. Blood circulation around the area is poor so waste products tend to accumulate, causing aching. Both FMS and trigger points can cause persistent tension and pain in muscles that are structurally normal.

STRUCTURAL TRIGGERS
• Stress and muscle tension • Poor posture • Sleep disturbance • Hyperventilation syndrome (*see pages 170–71*) • Lack of exercise • Cold • Occupational strains from lifting and repetitive movements

PSYCHO-SOCIAL FACTORS

Persistent unexplained pain is depressing, anxiety-provoking and exhausting. It also perpetuates a cycle of inactivity, poor sleep, tension and loss of physical fitness.

PSYCHO-SOCIAL TRIGGERS
• Depression: the majority of people with clinical depression first see a doctor because of pain, often muscle pain • Sleep disturbance • General anxiety • Low pain tolerance

BIOCHEMICAL TREATMENT OPTIONS

CONVENTIONAL MEDICINE
Painkillers such as paracetamol and anti-inflammatories can help in the short term, but are of no benefit for persistent pain. Low-dose amitriptyline may be suggested for FMS (*see Persistent Pain, pages 106–09*).

COMPLEMENTARY THERAPIES
Western Herbalism ❷ *(see page 127)*
You may be recommended to take valerian if sleep is a problem
Caution: Avoid if taking sleeping pills.

Nutritional Therapies ❸
(see pages 128–29)
A nutritionist may recommend an exclusion or rotation diet *(see pages 129)* to identify any food intolerances. To help the body manufacture serotonin, the practitioner may recommend vitamins, magnesium, and the amino acid tryptophan. Calcium and zinc may help to relieve disrupted sleep

Vitamin supplements remedy deficiencies

patterns. Magnesium may be advised as a mild deficiency can cause fatigue and muscle pain.
Homeopathy ❸ *(see page 130)*
Practitioners claim constitutional homeopathy can help.

SELF-HELP TECHNIQUES
• Keep a food diary *(see page 147)* to work out whether certain foods make the pain worse.

STRUCTURAL TREATMENT OPTIONS

CONVENTIONAL MEDICINE
A course of physiotherapy exercises can improve mobility and circulation.

COMPLEMENTARY THERAPIES
Massage ❸ *(see page 116)*
A massage can stimulate the circulation and may ease pain by relaxing trigger points and areas of muscle stiffness.
Aromatherapy ❷ *(see page 117)*
Soothing essential oils such as lavender and rosemary can help relax muscles and promote a feeling of well-being.

Chiropractic ❷ *(see page 118)* and **Osteopathy ❷** *(see page 119)*
A practitioner will aim to relax and lengthen a muscle affected by TP, working around the spine and joints to improve flexibility. You will be advised about factors that cause muscle tension.
Yoga ❸ *(see page 123)*
Gentle stretching postures ease muscle stiffness and improve postural problems that could be causing pain.
Acupuncture ❹ *(see page 125)*
Research suggests that electro-

acupuncture may relieve FMS symptoms. Needle acupuncture also eased fibromyalgia in a 1998 study, in which results were ascribed to the stimulation of the body's natural painkillers.

SELF-HELP TECHNIQUES
• Knead tender areas to relax muscles
• Try acupressure *(see page 125)* on tender spots • Exercise for 20 minutes three times a week to release endorphins and enhance well-being.

PSYCHO-SOCIAL TREATMENT OPTIONS

CONVENTIONAL MEDICINE
A doctor may suggest a cognitive behavioural approach if FMS causes a vicious cycle of pain and inactivity.

COMPLEMENTARY THERAPIES
Psychotherapy & Counselling ❷
(see pages 132–33)
A cognitive behavioural therapist helps those with FMS break cycles of depression and inactivity that reduce tolerance to pain. Brief counselling courses may help if there are

underlying psychological issues contributing to pain.
Hypnotherapy ❸ *(see page 134)*
In a 1991 trial, people with FMS who had not responded to physical therapies reported less pain, fatigue and stiffness and a greater sense of well-being after hypnotherapy.
Visualization ❸ *(see page 134)*, **Meditation ❷** *(see page 135)* and **Biofeedback ❷** *(see page 136)*
These techniques help to relieve stress and release muscle tension.

SELF-HELP TECHNIQUES
• Learn relaxation and breathing techniques *(see pages 170–71)*
• Keep a stress diary *(see page 175)*.

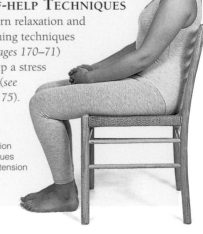

Relaxation techniques relieve tension

61

SPORTS INJURIES

From tennis elbow to swimmer's shoulder, there are many types of sports injuries, and a third are serious enough to need medical attention or to interfere with daily activities. Symptoms may include bruising, bleeding, swelling and pain, and some can take longer to heal than broken bones. Practitioners advise the "RICE" response to hasten recovery: *rest* the injured part; apply *ice* in a towel for ten minutes every two hours for two days; *compress* the injury with a bandage; and *elevate* it above the heart to reduce inflammatory fluids and swelling. Resume gentle movement when it is less painful, but stop if the pain returns.

CASE STUDY

Daniel, an osteopath, treated Graham, a 51-year-old lecturer, who had pulled his shoulder during a vigorous game of tennis. Daniel diagnosed tendonitis: "Tennis was only a trigger," he said, "Graham's shoulder has been turning inwards over a long period. The tendon inflammation would probably respond to a steroid shot, but his posture and the background tension in his neck and upper back make him prone to further injury." Daniel massaged and mobilized the shoulder to release strained, tight muscles and advised about posture and exercises to loosen the shoulders. Graham reported: "It took about nine months before I felt ready for another match, but my upper body feels in much better shape now, and I don't get the headaches I used to."

BIOCHEMICAL FACTORS

A good training regime improves the muscles' capacity to process oxygen and to work harder, but frequent and intensive training can lower immunity and resistance to disease. There may be a connection between diet and the ability to recover.

BIOCHEMICAL TRIGGERS

• A diet high in saturated fats, which produces excess inflammatory chemicals
• Lack of essential fatty acids and antioxidants in the diet, which weakens the body's anti-inflammatory response

STRUCTURAL FACTORS

The most common sports injuries are sprains and strains to the lower limbs. Tendons most susceptible to injury are those in the shoulder, thumb, knee and ankle and the Achilles' tendon on the heel. Half of all tennis players develop tennis elbow, a painful inflammation in the attachments of muscles around the elbow.

STRUCTURAL TRIGGERS

• Overuse of muscles • Lack of fitness
• Inadequate warming-up and cooling-down exercises • Ignoring warning aches and pains
• Cumulative wear and tear from a repetitive movement • Inappropriate style or technique
• Poor footwear

PSYCHO-SOCIAL FACTORS

Too cavalier or too timid an attitude to sports can lead to injury; for example skiing on a run beyond your capability, or tensing up through fear. Lack of proper equipment and ignorance of correct techniques can also result in injury.

PSYCHO-SOCIAL TRIGGERS

• Impatience • Desire to please • Timidity
• Stubbornness • Excessive competitiveness

PRECAUTIONS

Consult a doctor if the pain is severe, persistent, stabbing, radiating or centred on a bone or a joint; if a joint is stiff or immobile; or if there is any numbness or tingling.

Realms of the Body (*see page 20*)

BIOCHEMICAL
Body systems, such as digestion.

STRUCTURAL
Muscles, bones, joints and nerves.

PSYCHO-SOCIAL
Thoughts, feelings and relationships.

Key: Evidence of Efficacy (*see page 182*)

❶ ❷ ❸ ❹ ❺

least evidence ◄——————► most evidence

BIOCHEMICAL TREATMENT OPTIONS

CONVENTIONAL MEDICINE
Painkillers and non-steroidal anti-inflammatory drugs (*see Drugs Glossary, page 179*) help minor strains Steroid injections relieve acute inflammation but can weaken joints if repeated.

COMPLEMENTARY THERAPIES
Western Herbalism ❸ (*see page 127*)
Arnica or St. John's wort, traditional herbs for muscle soreness, may be given.
Nutritional Therapies ❸ (*see page 128*)
Therapists may suggest supplements of

Pineapple speeds repair

flavonoids, especially quercetin and citrus bioflavonoids which can halve recovery times. Antioxidants betacarotene, vitamin C, vitamin E, zinc and selenium may also speed healing, and bromelain, an enzyme in fresh pineapple, is thought to accelerate tissue repair. Essential fatty acids help to produce anti-inflammatory prostaglandins.

Homeopathy ❸ (*see page 130*)
Remedies that a practitioner may advise include *Arnica 6c* for bruising and for muscles aching from overuse in work or sports, or *Ruta 6c* for sprains and strains of muscles, joints and ligaments.

SELF-HELP TECHNIQUES
• Follow a balanced diet high in complex carbohydrates and fruit and vegetables. (There is no evidence that high-protein diets build extra muscle.)

STRUCTURAL TREATMENT OPTIONS

CONVENTIONAL MEDICINE
X-rays can establish if any bones have been broken. A physiotherapist may use ultrasound, which heats the area and improves circulation and drainage.

COMPLEMENTARY THERAPIES
Massage ❸ (*see page 116*)
Many athletes use massage after injury to restore joint mobility and improve local circulation.
Chiropractic ❹ (*see page 118*)
and **Osteopathy ❹**
(*see page 119*)
These therapies can help to mobilize

An ice pack can help to reduce inflammation

stiff joints, loosen tense muscles, rehabilitate muscle weaknesses, and prevent overuse injuries as well as muscular pain.
Acupuncture ❸ (*see page 125*)
A practitioner will stimulate acupoints and trigger points in the muscles to help relax a tense area prone to recurring injury.
Hydrotherapy ❷ (*see page 126*)
Practitioners recommend an ice pack or cold compress to reduce inflammation, and exercise in a warm pool to restore strength and flexibility. Jet showers, jacuzzis and whirlpool baths may ease pain. After swelling has subsided, dry heat from a heating pad or lamp can be used to ease stiffness.

SELF-HELP TECHNIQUES
• Warm up muscles by jogging on the spot, then do some stretches. Stretch again after exercise (*see pages 156–57*)
• Avoid sudden, vigorous or repetitive movements • Get fit before trying any new sport • Allow your body plenty of time to rest following injury.

Massage speeds recovery from sporting injuries by improving circulation and relaxing muscles

PSYCHO-SOCIAL TREATMENT OPTIONS

CONVENTIONAL MEDICINE
Sports psychology is an expanding field that has been incorporated into conventional treatment. Cognitive behavioural therapy may help to identify and change attitudes and behaviour that increase the risk of injury. It can also improve sporting performance.

COMPLEMENTARY THERAPIES
Hypnotherapy ❸ (*see page 134*)
A practitioner may teach self-hypnosis techniques to foster a positive attitude and self-confidence. Hypnotherapy can be used as an adjunct to sports psychology to improve performance in ways that avoid risk of injury.

SELF-HELP TECHNIQUES
• Be patient and allow yourself time to recover from an injury • Make sure you are well prepared before entering into any sport • Do not push your body beyond its limits and avoid over-competitiveness • Learn the correct techniques and practise them.

PREMENSTRUAL SYNDROME

A week or two before menstruation, women often suffer discomfort and distress. The symptoms of premenstrual syndrome (PMS) can be physical or emotional, and some experts categorize them into four types: anxiety (irritability, mood swings and insomnia); craving (increased appetite, headache, palpitations, fatigue and fainting); depression (forgetfulness, confusion and lethargy) and fluid retention (weight gain, bloating and breast tenderness). Symptoms are triggered by hormonal changes, but no single cause has been isolated and no consistent imbalance in progesterone and oestrogen has been identified.

CASE STUDY

Tom, a Traditional Chinese Medicine (TCM) practitioner, was visited by Hannah, who had left her job three years ago to have a baby. Over the last two years her periods had become painful, and recently she found herself becoming irritable and likely to burst into tears in the week before menstruation. Tom explains: "In TCM, menstrual disorders and life events are closely connected, so I asked Hannah how she was coping at home. Painful periods combined with PMS indicate stagnation of Liver *qi*; the fact they started after childbirth suggests deficiency of Blood may be a factor. This, combined with stress from a change in circumstances, may be the cause of discomfort." Tom prescribed a traditional herbal remedy based on dong quai (angelica) taken over three months. Within a month, Hannah's PMS symptoms were greatly reduced.

BIOCHEMICAL FACTORS

Hormones from glands all over the body help orchestrate the menstrual cycle; while one hormone prompts an egg to develop, another triggers ovulation. Various nutritional and hormonal imbalances may cause different symptoms.

BIOCHEMICAL TRIGGERS

• Low levels of vitamin B6, vitamin E, magnesium and essential fatty acids
• Disturbed levels of the hormone prolactin, which affects oestrogen and progesterone levels • Excess oestrogen, which may influence levels of the brain chemical serotonin, affecting mood • Rising levels of the hormone aldosterone, which may cause fluid retention • Fluctuating levels of insulin-regulating hormones, leading to cravings

STRUCTURAL FACTORS

Excessive exercise can disrupt the hormonal cycle and exacerbate PMS symptoms. Poor circulation, fluid retention and too much stress are often factors in PMS, and all can be reduced by moderate exercise, particularly in the two weeks before a period. Gentle exercise also eases aches and pains associated with PMS, as it stimulates the production of endorphins, the body's natural painkillers.

STRUCTURAL TRIGGERS

• Lack of exercise • Sustained, strenuous training

PSYCHO-SOCIAL FACTORS

The hormonal cycle is controlled by those areas of the brain that are also affected by stress. Mild to moderate PMS symptoms may be exacerbated by psychological and lifestyle factors that reflect a general lack of well-being. Raised anxiety and muscle tension in the run-up to menstruation may be due to stress.

PSYCHO-SOCIAL TRIGGERS

• Clinical depression • Relationship problems
• Stress from irregular or painful periods
• A perfectionist personality with a tendency to take on too much • Stressful life events

BIOCHEMICAL TREATMENT OPTIONS

CONVENTIONAL MEDICINE
Prescribed drugs include progestogen, oestrogen and the contraceptive pill to regulate the normal menstrual cycle; bromocriptine, a hormone-suppressing drug; diuretics for fluid retention; tranquillizers; antidepressants and painkillers (*see Drugs Glossary, page 179*).

COMPLEMENTARY THERAPIES
Western Herbalism ❸ (*see page 127*)
German studies show that agnus castus may help to adjust the hormone balance by increasing the amount of progesterone available. If depression is a factor, St. John's wort, which is a traditional nerve tonic, may be suggested.
Nutritional Therapies ❹
(*see pages 128–29*)
Various studies suggest that for all PMS symptoms the following supplements are beneficial: vitamin B^6, vitamin E, magnesium, zinc and evening primrose oil. Nutritionists recommend a diet

Agnus castus

low in fats, caffeine and refined carbohydrates including sugar, and some practitioners test for food intolerances.

SELF-HELP TECHNIQUES
• To combat cravings, eat regularly
• Reduce your intake of salt, sugar, saturated fats, milk and caffeine
• Taking 1200mg of calcium carbonate daily may relieve symptoms • Eat plenty of phytoestrogenic foods – soya, pulses, cereals and fruit and vegetables – which help regulate hormones.

STRUCTURAL TREATMENT OPTIONS

CONVENTIONAL MEDICINE
Your doctor will recommend regular exercise to improve the circulation.

COMPLEMENTARY THERAPIES
Aromatherapy ❷
(*see page 117*)
Essential oils of lavender, clary sage and geranium, especially if used

Lavender has relaxing properties

in massage (*see page 116*), appear to soothe, relieve tension and reduce fluid retention.
Chiropractic ❷ (*see page 118*)
and **Osteopathy ❷** (*see page 119*)
Practitioners may use soft-tissue manipulation to aid relaxation and improve muscle tension and circulation in the pelvis.
Reflexology ❹ (*see page 120*)
A 1991 US study found stimulating certain acupoints in the feet effective in relieving PMS symptoms.

Yoga ❷ (*see page 123*)
The Triangle, Bow, Half Shoulderstand and Butterfly postures are recommended. Caution: Avoid upside-down postures during menstruation.
Acupuncture ❷ (*see page 125*)
Many women report that acupuncture brings relief from symptoms.

SELF-HELP TECHNIQUES
• Warm compresses or a hot-water bottle on the lower abdomen and back may help relieve discomfort.

PSYCHO-SOCIAL TREATMENT OPTIONS

CONVENTIONAL MEDICINE
Some doctors may prescribe antidepressants. Stress-management techniques may be suggested.

COMPLEMENTARY THERAPIES
Psychotherapy & Counselling ❷
(*see pages 132–33*)
Therapy may help those with severe PMS to resolve any emotional problems contributing to anxiety and tension. Relationship counselling may be useful. Cognitive behavioural therapy

can help women change negative attitudes and become more positive.
Autogenic Training ❸ (*see page 136*)
This structured approach to relaxation can induce a calm state of mind and help relieve stress-related symptoms.

SELF-HELP TECHNIQUES
• Keep a diary of daily events and moods to identify problem areas that need particular care before a period (*see page 147*) • Some experts suggest that you should try to regard the mood

swings of PMS not as an illness but as a potential for assertiveness and creativity • Relaxation and breathing techniques (*see pages 170–71*) can relieve stress and reduce muscle tension.

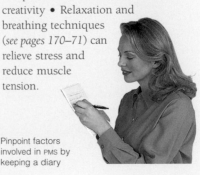

Pinpoint factors involved in PMS by keeping a diary

MENSTRUAL PAIN

At the beginning of a menstrual period, or just before, women commonly experience menstrual pain (dysmenorrhoea), accompanied by dull aches in the lower back and headaches. "Primary" dysmenorrhoea usually starts soon after puberty and tends to disappear between the ages of 25 and 30, or after childbirth. Pain begins shortly before the period and rarely lasts for more than 12 hours. "Secondary" dysmenorrhoea, in which periods suddenly become painful after a number of years without problems, is usually caused by an underlying disorder. Pain starts several days before a period and continues throughout.

CASE STUDY

Gillian, a homeopath, treated Pam, a 45-year-old business administrator who had painful, flooding periods. A surgical biopsy and ultrasound had revealed fibroids and her doctor advised having a hysterectomy if homeopathy did not work. "Pam was hardworking, but could be bad-tempered with her staff," said Gillian, who concluded that Pam's constitutional type (*see page 130*) was *Lachesis*, a remedy derived from snake venom. Gillian prescribed a single dose in a dilution of *1m*. "In three months, the pain and discomfort seemed to ease, and the flooding was less," said Pam. Now 50, she sees Gillian 2–3 times a year and, so far, has avoided surgery. Pam's doctor expects the fibroids to shrink as her menopause approaches, which will resolve the problem.

BIOCHEMICAL FACTORS

Primary dysmenorrhoea may be caused by strong uterine contractions, triggered when progesterone levels decline at the onset of a period. They are due to an excess of, or a sensitivity to, inflammatory prostaglandins, which are hormone-like fatty acids produced in the body (*see Glossary, pages 177–78*).

BIOCHEMICAL TRIGGERS

• Accumulating waste products in uterine and pelvic muscles • Inadequate nutrition

PSYCHO-SOCIAL FACTORS

Stress, emotional upsets and life events can lead to pelvic muscle tension and raise sensitivity to pain. Primary dysmenorrhoea, along with premenstrual syndrome, tends to be associated with chronic fatigue syndrome, irritable bowel syndrome and fibromyalgia syndrome (muscle pain). It can also indicate a general lack of well-being.

PSYCHO-SOCIAL TRIGGERS

• Anxiety and/or depression • Poor posture and breathing • Work or emotional overload • Poor coping skills

STRUCTURAL FACTORS

Secondary dysmenorrhoea is due to uterine congestion, a condition in which blood circulation in the pelvis is restricted and pelvic muscles become tense. It may be accompanied by heavy periods and should be checked by a doctor since it is likely to be caused by an underlying condition. Poor fitness is a factor in both primary and secondary dysmenorrhoea.

STRUCTURAL TRIGGERS

• Fibroids • Endometriosis • Pelvic inflammatory disease (infection of the uterus, fallopian tubes and/or ovaries) • Sensitivity to an IUD (intra-uterine device) • Lack of fitness

PRECAUTIONS

Consult your doctor if you suspect you have secondary dysmenorrhoea.

Realms of the Body *(see page 20)*

● **BIOCHEMICAL**
Body systems,
such as digestion.

● **STRUCTURAL**
Muscles, bones,
joints and nerves.

● **PSYCHO-SOCIAL**
Thoughts, feelings
and relationships.

Key: Evidence of Efficacy *(see page 182)*

❶ ❷ ❸ ❹ ❺
least evidence ◄————————► most evidence

BIOCHEMICAL TREATMENT OPTIONS

CONVENTIONAL MEDICINE
For primary dysmenorrhoea a doctor
will suggest paracetamol, anti-
inflammatories like ibuprofen, aspirin
or mefenamic acid, and/or muscle-
relaxants *(see Drugs Glossary, page 179)*.
Severe pain is treated by suppressing
ovulation with oral contraceptives or
hormonal drugs such as danazol.

COMPLEMENTARY THERAPIES
Western Herbalism ❸ *(see page 127)*
Agnus castus may be recommended
to regulate reproductive hormones.
Nutritional Therapies ❸
(see page 128–29)
Supplements of magnesium, essential
fatty acids, calcium, vitamins B^6 and B
complex and vitamin E may be advised.
A high-fibre or vegan diet may be
suggested, comprising 75 per cent
complex carbohydrates, 15 per cent
protein and 10 per cent fat.

Vegan diet

Homeopathy ❷ *(see page 130)*
Remedies include: *Pulsatilla 6c* for
cramps with nausea, *Sepia 6c* for pains
with depression, *Nux vomica 6c* for
cramps and irritability, and *Magnesia
phos. 6c* for pain eased by pressure.

SELF-HELP TECHNIQUES
• Eat less animal fat and more essential
fatty acids *(see pages 160–61)* • Balance
hormones with natural phytoestrogens
(see Glossary, pages 177–78) from celery,
fennel, parsley and soya.

STRUCTURAL TREATMENT OPTIONS

CONVENTIONAL MEDICINE
Treatment of secondary dysmenorrhoea
will depend on the cause. A doctor
may suggest exercise as it can help both
types of dysmenorrhoea by improving
circulation and fitness.

COMPLEMENTARY THERAPIES
Chiropractic ❹ *(see page 118)* and
Osteopathy ❹ *(see page 119)*
A practitioner will treat the spine,
pelvis and abdominal muscles, aiming
to improve uterine circulation and
relieve muscle tension. Trials show that
chiropractic can relieve period pain
Yoga ❷ *(see page 123)*
Postures that release tension in the
lower abdomen include the Pelvic
Lift, Triangle, Moon, Corpse and
Forward Stretch.
Caution: Experts advise against
upside-down poses during periods.
Acupuncture ❹ *(see page 125)*
A practitioner will suspect "deficiency
of *qi* or Blood", or "weakness of the
Kidney and Liver" and treat
accordingly. In one trial, 91 per cent of
patients improved with acupuncture.

SELF-HELP TECHNIQUES
• Lie on your back with knees bent
and use the palm of your hand
to massage the lower abdomen
with circular motions. This
relieves uterine muscle
spasm and promotes blood
flow • Holding a hot water
bottle to the area helps
boost local circulation.

Hot water bottle
relieves pain

PSYCHO-SOCIAL TREATMENT OPTIONS

CONVENTIONAL MEDICINE
Your doctor may suggest you practise
one of the complementary therapies
listed below.

COMPLEMENTARY THERAPIES
Hypnotherapy ❷ *(see page 134)*
You might be taught simple relaxation
and imagery exercises to improve
pelvic circulation and relieve pain.
Biofeedback ❸ *(see page 136)*
By responding to signals measuring
minute body changes, you can learn
to relieve muscle tension at will. You
will be shown techniques to calm the
mind and relax the muscles. Slow
diaphragmatic breathing improves
blood circulation to the pelvis.

SELF-HELP TECHNIQUES
• Try relaxation and breathing
techniques *(see pages 170–71)* or
meditation *(see page 135)*, which
can relieve muscle tension
and improve circulation
• Regular exercise can
improve circulation, tone muscles
and relieve tension *(see pages 150–53)*

• Keep a stress-trigger diary
(see page 175) to check
which factors make
dysmenorrhoea
symptoms worse.

Regular meditation
is excellent for
relieving stress

INFERTILITY IN WOMEN

Infertility is defined as the inability to conceive after a year or more of trying. In over 10 per cent of cases no obvious reason can be found, but usually there is a specific problem in one or both partners (*see also Infertility In Men, pages 80–81*). Failure to ovulate and blocked fallopian tubes account for 60 per cent of cases of female infertility. Complementary therapies may not trigger ovulation or clear tubes, but they support conventional fertility techniques if they strengthen and regulate body systems. "Mind-body" techniques help in the same way and may counteract the stress that can affect biological factors involved in fertility.

CASE STUDY

James, a psychologist, saw Anne, 33, who had recently got married for the second time. She had been trying to conceive for over a year and the medical investigations had found nothing wrong."I discovered she had had an ectopic pregnancy at 28," said James. "Understandably she was anxious. She wanted a baby, but unconsciously feared disaster. I contacted her family doctor and eventually she saw a second gynaecologist who said there was little chance of another ectopic pregnancy. I asked Anne to forget about trying to conceive and taught her self-hypnosis so she could relax and visualize becoming pregnant and carrying the baby to term." Anne started her "homework" straight away and five months later became pregnant.

BIOCHEMICAL FACTORS

Absent or erratic menstrual periods usually indicate a failure to ovulate regularly. Problems with ovulation, the likely cause in a third of cases of infertility, are often due to hormonal imbalances.

BIOCHEMICAL TRIGGERS

• Coming off the contraceptive pill
• Approaching the menopause • Having inadequate levels of the hormone progesterone which prepares the womb lining for conception • Certain medications (ask your doctor) • Taking excessive exercise • An underactive thyroid gland • Inadequate nutrition • Environmental chemicals

STRUCTURAL FACTORS

Conception is impossible if: the ovaries do not produce eggs; the eggs fail to reach the uterus because the fallopian tubes are blocked; the uterus does not retain the fertilized egg; or the cervical mucus is hostile to sperm and prevents it entering the uterus.

STRUCTURAL TRIGGERS

• Scarring or blocking of the fallopian tubes or ovaries caused by pelvic inflammatory disease (PID), sometimes due to sexually transmitted diseases, for example, chlamydia • Multiple ovarian cysts • Endometriosis (growth of womb lining in tubes and ovaries) • Fibroids • Extreme weight loss or gain • Genetic abnormalities
• Cervical mucus that is too sticky, too acidic or that contains spermicidal antibodies

PSYCHO-SOCIAL FACTORS

Inability to conceive can be distressing, especially if there is no detectable reason. In animals, stress and under-feeding can cause temporary infertility and these factors may have the same effect in humans. There is some scientific evidence that reducing stress may reduce levels of the hormone prolactin (which in excess inhibits fertility). Striving to have a child and the burdens of infertility treatment can be enormously stressful too: in one American study, infertile women were found to be as depressed as people with cancer or heart disease. Curiously, couples with unexplained infertility who eventually reconcile themselves to childlessness or adoption often achieve a successful pregnancy.

PSYCHO-SOCIAL TRIGGERS

• Stress and overwork • Subconscious feelings of fear or anger • Depression

Realms of the Body *(see page 20)*

● BIOCHEMICAL
Body systems,
such as digestion.

● STRUCTURAL
Muscles, bones,
joints and nerves.

● PSYCHO-SOCIAL
Thoughts, feelings
and relationships.

Key: Evidence of Efficacy *(see page 182)*

❶ ❷ ❸ ❹ ❺

least evidence ◄─────────► most evidence

BIOCHEMICAL TREATMENT OPTIONS

CONVENTIONAL MEDICINE
Investigation may include a blood test for progesterone and prolactin levels, and a sperm count. Antibiotics may be prescribed to clear infections blocking the fallopian tubes. Other drugs include clomiphene, which helps trigger ovulation, and human chorionic gonadotrophin (HCG), which stimulates the ovaries (*see Drugs Glossary, page 179*).

Wild yam root and leaf

COMPLEMENTARY THERAPIES
Western Herbalism ❷ *(see page 127)*
A practitioner will suggest herbs that regulate hormones and aid conception. These include agnus castus, false unicorn root, black cohosh, sarsaparilla and wild yam.
Nutritional Therapies ❷
(see pages 128–29)
Vitamin and mineral deficiencies and exposure to chemical toxins are claimed to promote miscarriage. A therapist may suggest an organic diet and supplements

such as essential fatty acids, folic acid and vitamins B6 and B12. A diet rich in vitamin E and alkaline foods is said to regulate acidity of cervical and vaginal secretions. Food intolerance tests and a detoxification regime may be advised.

SELF-HELP TECHNIQUES
• Have sex at the time of ovulation (urine dipsticks and daily waking temperature charts detect ovulation)
• Stop smoking • Try to maintain a healthy weight.

STRUCTURAL TREATMENT OPTIONS

CONVENTIONAL MEDICINE
Investigations include an ultrasound scan of the ovaries, special X-rays of the uterus and an examination of the uterus, ovaries and fallopian tubes with a laparoscope (an illuminated viewing tube). Blocked fallopian tubes may be cleared by surgery. Various kinds of "test-tube" or in-vitro fertilization techniques (IVF) are available, but will only be suggested as a last resort.

COMPLEMENTARY THERAPIES
Acupuncture ❷ *(see page 125)*
Chinese studies have suggested that acupuncture is helpful for PID or endometriosis.
Massage ❸ *(see page 116)*
Massage or other bodywork therapies may be used, with a detoxification programme, to improve circulation and reduce mucus. This might be suggested for tubal blockage or endometriosis.

SELF-HELP TECHNIQUES
• Use the "missionary position" during sex with the man on top and a folded pillow under your hips. Remain on your back with your knees raised for the 20–30 minutes the cervix needs to take up the semen • Do not use artificial lubricants that can inhibit sperm movement • Do not douche after sex
• Take regular, moderate exercise.

PSYCHO-SOCIAL TREATMENT OPTIONS

CONVENTIONAL MEDICINE
If aged over 35, consult your doctor after trying to conceive for 6–9 months, or after two years if under 32. Sometimes seeking advice and feeling more in control may be sufficient to promote conception.

COMPLEMENTARY THERAPIES
Psychotherapy & Counselling ❷
(see pages 132–33)
The prospect of starting a family sometimes provokes unconscious fears. Discussing these issues may help put them in perspective. A programme of

cognitive therapy, relaxation techniques and group support may aid conception.
Hypnotherapy ❸ *(see page 134)*
Hypnotherapy can reduce stress levels and help some women to conceive. It may uncover fears about labour, motherhood or the baby's potential threat to the relationship.

Meditation, Visualization, Autogenic Training ❷ *(see pages 134–36)*
Techniques that help you achieve deep relaxation may relieve tension.

SELF-HELP TECHNIQUES
• Practise relaxation and breathing techniques (*see pages 170–71*)
• Talk openly about your feelings with your partner
• Focus on other goals apart from conception.

Discuss your feelings with your partner

PREGNANCY

Pregnancy is a natural process, although modern medicine has, until quite recently, tended to treat it as a medical problem. Today there is a movement towards a less clinical approach and greater acceptance of the mother's involvement in monitoring her health and that of her unborn baby. As well as relieving ailments and enhancing well-being, complementary therapies can be useful in pregnancy if they encourage a woman's sense of control of her body. Therapies work well in tandem with conventional medical approaches and some midwives, especially in the UK, integrate aromatherapy and acupuncture into their care.

CASE STUDY

George, a doctor trained in homeopathy, saw Trisha early in her second pregnancy. Her first had ended in a difficult forceps delivery and this time she wanted to do everything possible to maintain well-being and avoid medical intervention. George recommended the homeopathic remedy *Sepia 6c* and elasticated acupressure wrist bands to relieve morning sickness. He encouraged her to follow a healthy diet and to join a natural childbirth class to learn relaxation, breathing techniques and gentle antenatal yoga postures. To relieve lower-back pain in the last three months, George suggested McTimoney chiropractic, and a month before delivery he recommended the homeopathic remedy *Caullophylum*, which is derived from a Native American plant and is said to promote the normal onset of labour. The delivery of Trisha's son was easier and happier than the birth of her first baby and she breastfed him straightaway.

BIOCHEMICAL FACTORS

Women planning to conceive should take the opportunity to aim for optimum health. They should attempt to improve their diet and lifestyle, consult a doctor about any medical disorders and avoid unnecessary medication. Adequate nutrition is vital at all stages of pregnancy as, increasingly, studies show that a mother's diet has long-term effects on her child's health. There is, for instance, a strong link between low birthweight and diabetes and heart disease in adult life.

PSYCHO-SOCIAL FACTORS

Emotional highs and lows can result from hormonal changes and also from the expectation of a major life change. Our ancestors were group-living creatures and during pregnancy women may feel in particular need of companionship.

STRUCTURAL FACTORS

Many women feel easily exhausted and tired during pregnancy, especially if they are working and/or have other small children. All body systems are under strain, especially during mid to late pregnancy, although they usually adapt. Strain on circulation is reflected in fluid retention; on the back in lower-back pain; and on the digestion in acid reflux and indigestion.

PRECAUTIONS

Avoid people with German measles, or get vaccinated at least three months before trying to conceive. Do not take herbs in medicinal doses in the first three months of pregnancy and consult a trained medical herbalist thereafter. Do not take any essential oils internally and do not use thyme or chamomile essential oils externally. See a doctor immediately for: prolonged nausea and inability to eat properly; frequent urination for more than two days, especially if accompanied by pain; prolonged flu-like illness; fluid retention that has not decreased after three days; unusual headaches or unexplained pain; vaginal bleeding.

Realms of the Body (see page 20)

● **BIOCHEMICAL**
Body systems,
such as digestion.

● **STRUCTURAL**
Muscles, bones,
joints and nerves.

● **PSYCHO-SOCIAL**
Thoughts, feelings
and relationships.

Key: Evidence of Efficacy (see page 182)

❶ ❷ ❸ ❹ ❺

least evidence ◄—————————————► most evidence

BIOCHEMICAL TREATMENT OPTIONS

CONVENTIONAL MEDICINE
Consult a doctor or midwife as
soon as you suspect you are
pregnant. You will be told to take
folic acid (400mcg daily) to prevent
defects in the baby's spinal cord and
nervous system. Iron, zinc and
calcium supplements are sometimes
recommended. Small, regular meals are
advised for morning sickness.

COMPLEMENTARY THERAPIES
Western Herbalism ❸ (see page 127)
A practitioner may suggest chamomile

Chamomile tea
is soothing

tea to induce sleep,
ginger capsules for
morning sickness
and a compress
with witch hazel for
haemorrhoids.

Nutritional Therapies ❸
(see pages 128–29)
Suggested supplements may include
zinc for the baby's growth; vitamin B6
and B12 for energy and to enhance the
working of folic acid in the body;
vitamin C; and essential fatty acids for
brain growth. A therapist may suggest

bromelain (an enzyme in pineapple) to
reduce swelling after an episiotomy (see
Glossary, pages 177–78).

SELF-HELP TECHNIQUES
• Avoid large doses of multivitamins,
as too much vitamin A possibly causes
birth defects • Avoid foods that may
contain listeria: unpasteurized cheese,
raw or undercooked meats, and food
with uncooked egg such as homemade
mayonnaise • Limit fatty foods, sugar
and salt • Avoid alcohol in the first 12
weeks and give up smoking throughout.

STRUCTURAL TREATMENT OPTIONS

CONVENTIONAL MEDICINE
Regular checks are made to ensure you
are not suffering from problems such
as anaemia, fluid retention, high blood
pressure or poor placental growth.

COMPLEMENTARY THERAPIES
Chiropractic ❸ (see page 118) and
Osteopathy ❸ (see page 119)
Back pain is common in mid to late

pregnancy. A practitioner will gently
stretch and manipulate the lower back
to ease symptoms.
Acupuncture ❹ (see page 125) and
Acupressure ❹ (see page 125)
A practitioner may show you how to
stimulate Pericardium 6, which is an
acupoint just below the wrist (see page
124), as clinical trials have shown it
can relieve nausea in early pregnancy.

Acupuncture is useful for pain relief in
labour and moxibustion has been used
to avoid breech births.

SELF-HELP TECHNIQUES
• Get plenty of rest • Continue your
normal exercise programme but replace
high-impact activities with walking, yoga
or swimming • Practise pelvic floor
exercises before and after the birth.

PSYCHO-SOCIAL TREATMENT OPTIONS

CONVENTIONAL MEDICINE
Antenatal classes help you to prepare
for all aspects of birth and parenthood.
Postnatal support groups are
increasingly available.

COMPLEMENTARY THERAPIES
Visualization ❸ (see page 134)
You will be encouraged to focus on
positive feelings about your baby
during and after pregnancy. In one
study, mothers of premature babies
who listened to a guided imagery and
relaxation tape produced 63 per cent
more breast milk than the control group.

Hypnotherapy ❸ (see page 134)
A practitioner will teach you
techniques that can provide effective
pain relief in labour.

SELF-HELP TECHNIQUES
• Get support from family, friends,
other mothers and community
groups • Talk about your
feelings with your partner
and family and share
practical advice and
experiences other parents
may have to offer
• Use relaxation

techniques (see pages 170–71) to relieve
tension • Your baby can hear in the
uterus as early as 20 weeks: talk
reassuringly to your unborn
baby and play soothing
music • Take
opportunities to enjoy
art and the beauty of
nature to enhance
your own well-being
as well as that of
your baby.

A hug is comforting
and reassuring

MENOPAUSE

The cessation of menstrual periods, which signals the end of child-bearing years, is known as the menopause. It occurs around age 45–55, although it may take place as early as 35. The surgical removal of the uterus (hysterectomy) and ovaries results in an immediate menopause. Hormonal changes before and after periods stop take place over several years. Known as the perimenopause, this period may be accompanied by symptoms such as hot flushes, aches and pains, skin changes and emotional upset. The severity of symptoms varies and it is thought that women with positive attitudes to ageing suffer less than others.

CASE STUDY

Li, an acupuncturist, treated Clare, aged 51, for hot flushes, night sweats, insomnia, vaginal dryness and anxiety. Clare's doctor had suggested HRT but recommended she try acupuncture first.

Li used methods of diagnosis from Traditional Chinese Medicine (TCM): "Clare's pulse was thin and rapid, and her tongue red – classic signs of *yin* deficiency. In TCM, Kidney *yin* energy is the body's cooling process and deficiency causes a slow, rumbling internal heat." She stimulated points on the Heart and Kidney meridians, chiefly Kidney 6 on the inside of the ankle.

"My night sweats disappeared after one treatment," reported Clare. "The other symptoms improved within six sessions."

BIOCHEMICAL FACTORS

A woman's oestrogen levels decrease in her 40s, so eggs mature less regularly in the ovaries, producing less progesterone. This makes the uterus lining build up less, so periods become erratic and then cease. Many menopausal symptoms may be due to the effect of less oestrogen reaching the hypothalamus, an area of the brain which acts as a link between the hormonal and nervous systems. Adrenal glands and fat cells in the hips and thighs still manufacture small amounts of oestrogen but are easily depleted by poor diet and stress. Falling oestrogen levels also result in the following problems: disturbed blood circulation, loss of bone-building calcium and tissue-building collagen, anaemia due to heavy periods in the perimenopause and increased likelihood of heart disease.

STRUCTURAL FACTORS

Although oestrogen's primary role is in reproduction, it also helps to preserve the health of the bones, heart and arteries, gut, skin and even the brain. Common menopausal complaints include night sweats, hot flushes, headaches, palpitations, dizziness, weight gain, fatigue, itching and vaginal dryness, thrush, cystitis, loss of skin-elasticity and moisture, hair loss caused by thinning tissues, muscular aches and pains, increased urinary tract infections, osteoporosis and increased risk of bone fractures. Menopausal problems are caused by declining oestrogen levels, and most disappear when the menopause is over; the exceptions are osteoporosis and complaints related to thinning tissues.

PSYCHO-SOCIAL FACTORS

Common psychological menopause complaints include forgetfulness and difficulty in concentrating, loss of libido, depression, mood swings and insomnia. Hormonal changes may disturb levels of endorphins, the body's natural painkillers and mood-enhancing chemicals. The menopause often coincides with life changes, and some women may lose their sense of identity as children grow up and leave home. Women with a positive attitude to ageing and those who work, seem to suffer less than others. Studies show women with premenstrual syndrome or dysmenorrhoea (painful periods) are more likely to have menopausal complaints.

Realms of the Body (*see page 20*)

● BIOCHEMICAL
Body systems,
such as digestion.

● STRUCTURAL
Muscles, bones,
joints and nerves.

PSYCHO-SOCIAL
Thoughts, feelings
and relationships.

Key: Evidence of Efficacy (*see page 182*)

❶ ❷ ❸ ❹ ❺
least evidence ◄————————► most evidence

BIOCHEMICAL TREATMENT OPTIONS

CONVENTIONAL MEDICINE
Hormone replacement therapy (HRT), in the form of pills, skin implants, patches and creams, is prescribed to replace oestrogen. Treatment prevents many menopausal changes but may increase the risk of breast cancer if used long-term. Biphosphonates (*see Drugs Glossary, page 179*) and SERMs (Selective Oestrogen Receptor Modulators) prevent bone loss.

HRT patches and cream

COMPLEMENTARY THERAPIES
Western Herbalism ❸ (*see page 127*)
A practitioner may prescribe agnus castus, liquorice and hops for hot flushes and night sweats; St. John's wort for mild depression; and valerian for insomnia.
Caution: Do not take liquorice if you have high blood pressure, valerian if you are taking sleeping pills, or St John's wort with antidepressants.
Nutritional Therapies ❸ (*see page 128–29*) Suggested supplements may

include vitamin E for hot flushes, night sweats and vaginal dryness, evening primrose oil for dry skin; calcium, magnesium, vitamin D and boron for bone health; and vitamin B^6, B^{12} and folic acid for heart and brain health.

SELF-HELP TECHNIQUES
• Follow a low-fat, high-fibre diet • Eat phytoestrogen-rich fruit and vegetables (*see Glossary, page 177–78*) • Limit salt, red meat and alcohol • Take 1500mg calcium daily (1000mg if on HRT).

STRUCTURAL TREATMENT OPTIONS

CONVENTIONAL MEDICINE
Symptoms are treated individually (*see Headaches, pages 24–25, Persistent Muscle Pain, pages 60–61, Thrush, pages 74–75, and Cystitis, pages 76–77*).

COMPLEMENTARY THERAPIES
Massage ❷ (*see page 116*)
Visiting a practitioner for a regular massage can relieve tension and enhance feelings of well being.
Aromatherapy ❷ (*see page 117*)
German chamomile, sandalwood or

rose are among the essential oils recommended for hot flushes and mood swings.
Yoga ❷ (*see page 123*)
A teacher will demonstrate helpful poses. By focusing the mind on breathing, physical movement and postures, yoga may relieve tension and improve body image.
Acupuncture ❹ (*see page 125*)
A practitioner will stimulate acupoints to regulate the hormonal system and relieve hot flushes.

SELF-HELP TECHNIQUES
• Exercise to reduce the severity of hot flushes
• From your 20s do weight-bearing activities such as walking to maintain bone density
• Use lubricants such as KY jelly to counteract vaginal dryness.

Jogging maintains bone density

PSYCHO-SOCIAL TREATMENT OPTIONS

CONVENTIONAL MEDICINE
A doctor may prescribe antidepressants if depression is severe. Stress-management techniques may be advised (*see pages 168–69*).

COMPLEMENTARY THERAPIES
Psychotherapy & Counselling ❷
(*see page 132–33*)
Talking through feelings can help to resolve issues around the loss of fertility and self-esteem. Cognitive behavioural therapy may promote a

more positive approach to ageing. The period of psychological transition from fertility to post-fertility can be an anxious time.

Focusing on a serene image can relieve anxiety

SELF-HELP TECHNIQUES
• Stress can make symptoms worse: practise relaxation, visualization and breathing techniques (*see pages 170–71*) to relieve tension, promote relaxation and improve coping skills
• Keeping a stress diary (*see page 175*) helps to pinpoint triggers • Share experiences with friends and make time for yourself and activities you enjoy • Stay as positive as possible: an optimistic outlook helps people cope successfully with life changes.

VAGINAL THRUSH

This infection, which is also known as candidiasis, causes soreness and itching of the vulva, the skin around the opening of the vagina. A curdy, white discharge is a tell-tale sign. Vaginal thrush is common, particularly during pregnancy or after a course of antibiotics, and in some cases it can prove difficult to keep at bay. Conventional treatment usually helps, but recurrences are frequent. Close attention to all the contributing factors is important, especially if the condition is recurring. Since thrush is not the only infection to cause vaginal soreness, it is important to get the diagnosis confirmed with medical tests.

CASE STUDY

Cathy, a nurse in her 30s, had recurrent vaginal infections. A swab test had confirmed a diagnosis of thrush, and although antifungal medication had reduced her symptoms, it failed to prevent the infection recurring. Maria, a medical herbalist, was asked to help. She gave Cathy vaginal pessaries, containing tea tree, marigold and thyme extracts, to use each night for a week. A cream with the same constituents was given for daytime use, and Cathy's partner was advised to use it too. Cathy found that the itching and discharge quickly cleared up. She also followed Maria's advice to eat a very low-sugar, high-fibre diet and increase her fresh fruit and vegetable intake to raise her levels of infection-fighting antioxidants.

BIOCHEMICAL FACTORS

"Friendly" bacteria in the vagina, mouth and gut convert glucose into lactic acid, which helps to keep the areas free of harmful micro-organisms. Certain conditions, however, encourage the bacterium *Candida albicans* to overwhelm the friendly bacteria, resulting in thrush. Broad-spectrum antibiotics (*see Glossary, pages 177–78*) kill friendly bacteria, so vaginal thrush is common after antibiotics.

BIOCHEMICAL TRIGGERS
• Lowered immunity • Nutritional deficiencies
• Medication such as antibiotics, steroids and immunosuppressants • Hormonal changes due to pregnancy or oral contraceptives
• Raised blood sugar levels, as in diabetes
• Allergies

STRUCTURAL FACTORS

Uncontrolled growth of *Candida albicans*, a common micro-organism in the mouth, gut and vagina, causes thrush. Many practitioners believe "candida overgrowth" in the gut contributes to problems ranging from chronic fatigue syndrome and irritability to irregular periods and irritable bowel syndrome. They suspect that the micro-organism damages the intestinal lining, allowing toxins to be absorbed into the bloodstream (*see page 159*). If the vagina is dry, its lining may be damaged during sex, increasing the likelihood of thrush.

STRUCTURAL TRIGGERS
• Sexual intercourse with an infected partner
• Overuse of douches, spermicides and bath products which can disturb the acid/alkali balance in the vagina

PSYCHO-SOCIAL FACTORS

Recurrent attacks of thrush may suggest the immune system is impaired. Stress is known to increase susceptibility to infection in general.

PSYCHO-SOCIAL TRIGGERS
• Overwork and lack of adequate sleep
• Anxiety • Depression • Traumatic life events

Realms of the Body (see page 20)

 BIOCHEMICAL
Body systems,
such as digestion.

STRUCTURAL
Muscles, bones,
joints and nerves.

PSYCHO-SOCIAL
Thoughts, feelings
and relationships.

Key: Evidence of Efficacy (see page 182)

❶ ❷ ❸ ❹ ❺

least evidence ◀——————————▶ most evidence

BIOCHEMICAL TREATMENT OPTIONS

CONVENTIONAL MEDICINE

If thrush is recurrent, a doctor
will advise women taking oral
contraceptives to consider barrier
methods for contraception.

COMPLEMENTARY THERAPIES

Naturopathy ❸ (see page 126)
A therapist sees thrush as possibly also
indicating an overgrowth of candida in
the gut. Apple-cider vinegar douches
and *lactobacillus* yoghurt may restore
"friendly" bacteria and pH balance.

Nutritional Therapies ❸
(see pages 128–29)
A practitioner may advise you to
exclude all dietary yeast, mould and
fungi, such as yeast-based bread, blue
cheese or mushrooms, as well as
starches and refined sugar on
which yeast feeds. "Live"
yoghurt may be suggested
to restore friendly bacteria in
the gut, as well as natural
antifungals, which include
garlic, onions, aloe vera juice

Coconut extract has
antifungal properties

and caprylic acid, an extract of
coconut. Supplements may be advised
to revive the immune system, including
vitamin B complex, betacarotene,
vitamin C and vitamin E as well as zinc,
selenium, magnesium, essential
fatty acids and folic acid.

SELF-HELP TECHNIQUES

• Eat a healthy diet (see
pages 158–59) • Avoid junk
food and refined sugar.

STRUCTURAL TREATMENT OPTIONS

CONVENTIONAL MEDICINE

Examination of the vaginal discharge
will confirm diagnosis. A doctor will
prescribe vaginal tablets of
antifungal drugs, or nystatin or
clotrimazole (see Drugs Glossary,
page 179), or oral medication such
as fluconazole. A vaginal swab
tests for other infections such as
gardnerella or trichomoniasis,
which cause soreness or
discharge. A partner should
be treated at the same time.

Tea tree plant and oil

Doctors believe candidiasis in the
gut only affects people with
impaired immune systems,
such as those with AIDS.

COMPLEMENTARY THERAPIES

Aromatherapy ❸ (see page 117)
A practitioner may advise
you to add antifungal or
antiseptic essential oils,
such as tea tree, to the
bathwater.

Acupuncture ❷ (see page 125)
In cases when infection is recurrent,
acupuncture may help to boost an
impaired immune system.

SELF-HELP TECHNIQUES

• Wear cotton underpants and avoid
nylon tights and close-fitting clothes
that create a warm, moist environment
• Avoid vaginal deodorants and do not
use scented soaps, bubblebaths and
other products • Exercise regularly to
enhance immunity.

PSYCHO-SOCIAL TREATMENT OPTIONS

CONVENTIONAL MEDICINE

If thrush is recurrent, doctors will
advise you to learn stress-management
techniques (see pages 168–69).

COMPLEMENTARY THERAPIES

Psychotherapy & Counselling ❷
(see page 132–33)
Recurrent thrush may be part of an
underlying sexual difficulty. It can
also cause sexual problems and
relationships may suffer. Talking
such problems through may help.

Visualizing pleasant images can help to calm the
mind and induce relaxation

Visualization ❷ (see pages 136)
You are encouraged to focus on
calming scenes or use guided imagery
to help you relax at will.

SELF-HELP TECHNIQUES

• Keep a stress-trigger and symptom
diary (see pages 147 and 175) • Try to
get plenty of sleep • Practise stress-
management skills (see pages 168–69)
• Learn relaxation and breathing
techniques (see pages 170–71) to
help you cope with stressful events.

CYSTITIS

Over 20 per cent of women have a cystitis attack once a year, and many cases result in a kidney infection. Cystitis is usually caused by a bacterial infection inflaming the lining of the bladder and urethra. Symptoms include burning or stinging when urinating, wanting to pass urine more often, abdominal pain and unpleasant-smelling urine. Blood in the urine, chills or fever may also be experienced. Recurrent cystitis indicates a low resistance to infection, which can be caused by a number of factors ranging from stress to oral contraceptives or a poor diet. If attacks persist, a doctor may advise seeing a gynaecologist.

CASE STUDY

Gillian, a homeopath, saw Jill, a 24-year-old with recurrent cystitis. Jill was keen to come off the permanent low-dose antibiotics prescribed by her doctor because they seemed to give her indigestion. She said she felt depressed, and had no interest in sex. She was better when busy but felt cold and craved sour tastes: characteristics that are typical of the *Sepia* constitution. "Jill was well informed about self-help measures recommended for cystitis," said Gillian. "All I had to do was prescribe a remedy." With her doctor's agreement, Jill finished her course of antibiotics two weeks later and took a one-off dose of *Sepia 200c*.

A month on, she was much happier and had had no further attacks. In the next six months she had two minor bouts, which were managed with the homeopathic remedies *Nux vomica 6c* and *Cantharis 6c*.

BIOCHEMICAL FACTORS

Recurrent attacks of cystitis suggest that the immune system is depleted and resistance to infection lowered. Poor diet can reduce resistance to infection, as can hormone deficiency during and after the menopause. Chemicals in bubble baths, condoms and spermicides can sometimes irritate the urethra.

BIOCHEMICAL TRIGGERS

• Spermicidal gels and contraceptive diaphragms • Oral contraceptives
• Sugar in the urine (caused by diabetes) which may encourage infection • Hormone deficiency during and after menopause
• Inadequate diet and food intolerances

STRUCTURAL FACTORS

Women are more susceptible to cystitis than men because their urethra is shorter and the opening is closer to the anus. Anything that prevents the bladder from emptying completely, for example the expanding uterus during pregnancy, allows bacteria to multiply in stagnant urine. Diaphragms can cause cystitis by putting pressure on the urethra and bladder.

STRUCTURAL TRIGGERS

• Prolapsed uterus, fibroids • Blockage in the bladder due to a stone or tumour • Diaphragms
• Bruising during intercourse ("honeymoon cystitis") • Enlarged prostate gland (in men)

PSYCHO-SOCIAL FACTORS

Stress can put a strain on the immune system so that resistance to infection is low.

PSYCHO-SOCIAL TRIGGERS

• Stress in the work place • Problems with relationships • Anxiety and depression
• Emotionally traumatic events

Realms of the Body *(see page 20)*

● **BIOCHEMICAL**
Body systems,
such as digestion.

● **STRUCTURAL**
Muscles, bones,
joints and nerves.

PSYCHO-SOCIAL
Thoughts, feelings
and relationships.

Key: Evidence of Efficacy *(see page 182)*

❶ ❷ ❸ ❹ ❺

least evidence ◄──────────► most evidence

BIOCHEMICAL TREATMENT OPTIONS

CONVENTIONAL MEDICINE

If tests show a bacterial infection, antibiotics are prescribed. Though effective, they may lead to thrush *(see pages 74–75)*. You will be told to drink plenty of fluids to flush out the bladder.

COMPLEMENTARY THERAPIES

Western Herbalism ❸ *(see page 127)*
A practitioner will suggest you drink unsweetened cranberry juice, which helps to stop bacteria sticking to the lining of the urinary tract. Dandelion

and German chamomile are soothing, and echinacea helps to boost the immune system.
Nutritional Therapies ❷
(see pages 128–29)
If attacks recur, you may be tested for food intolerances, allergies or *Candida albicans*. Supplements of vitamin C, zinc, bioflavonoids and betacarotene can boost the immune system.
Homeopathy ❷ *(see page 130)*

Echinacea can improve immunity

Remedies include: *Cantharis 6c* if urination is painful; *Sarsaparilla 6c* for burning after urination; *Staphysagria 6c* for "honeymoon cystitis" *(see opposite)*.

SELF-HELP TECHNIQUES

• Drink 1 tsp of bicarbonate of soda dissolved in 300ml (10fl oz) of water once an hour for the first three hours of an attack • Eat a wholefood diet with garlic and onions • Avoid tea, coffee, alcohol, sugar, spices and acidic foods (e.g. tomatoes, citrus fruits and spinach).

STRUCTURAL TREATMENT OPTIONS

CONVENTIONAL MEDICINE

In cases when a urine sample test finds no trace of bacterial infection, symptoms may be due to an inflammation of the vagina or the urethra, the outlet from the bladder (urethritis). Bruising of the urethra during sex may also be a cause of cystitis. In some cases a gynaecological examination, an X-ray of the kidneys or a cystoscopy (examination of the bladder with a viewing instrument) may be necessary to obtain an accurate diagnosis.

COMPLEMENTARY THERAPIES

Acupuncture ❸ *(see page 125)*
A practitioner may stimulate the Bladder, Kidney, Spleen, Liver and Conception Vessel acupoints. In a Norwegian study, when these points were stimulated twice a week for four weeks, 85 per cent of women in the study were clear of cystitis.

SELF-HELP TECHNIQUES

• To prevent cystitis, drink lots of water and urinate frequently

• Use lubrication during sex to avoid bruising, and pass urine afterwards
• Avoid bubble baths, scented soaps and vaginal deodorants
• Keep the genital area clean • Avoid tight-fitting or synthetic-fibre underwear • Hold a hot water bottle to your lower back or between your legs to ease cystitis pain.

Water helps flush away cystitis bacteria

PSYCHO-SOCIAL TREATMENT OPTIONS

CONVENTIONAL MEDICINE

Doctors may suggest stress-management techniques *(see page 168–69)*.

COMPLEMENTARY THERAPIES

Psychotherapy & Counselling ❷
(see pages 132–33)
Recurring cystitis may reflect or prompt sexual difficulties, so talking through relationship problems can help.
Relaxation & Breathing ❶
(see pages 170–71)
Learning relaxation and breathing

techniques can help you to recognize tension in your body, and teach you to calm your mind and relax your deep pelvic muscles.

Alternate nostril breathing is part of a yogic technique that reduces stress *(see page 123)*

SELF-HELP TECHNIQUES

• Keep a diary of cystitis attacks *(see page 147)*, noting any triggers and take steps to avoid them • Keep a stress-trigger diary *(see page 175)* • Examine your lifestyle for persistent sources of stress and deal with them if possible
• Practise meditation *(see page 135)* or stress-management skills *(see pages 168–69)* • Try mind-body techniques such as yoga *(see page 123)* which are useful for relaxing the muscles and calming the mind.

ENLARGED PROSTATE

The prostate is a small, walnut-shaped gland, surrounding the urethra below the bladder, which secretes a fluid that contributes to semen. Enlargement of the prostate, known as *benign prostatic hyperplasia* (BPH), is increasingly common with age: more than 90 per cent of men over 70 are affected. There may be no symptoms until the gland begins to press on the urethra and interfere with urine flow. Troublesome symptoms include frequent urination, incontinence, difficulty in urinating, urine and kidney infections, back pain and pain between the legs. Symptoms of prostate cancer, the third most common cancer in men, are similar to those of BPH.

CASE STUDY

Carl, aged 66, consulted Jean, a medical herbalist, for help with his prostate problem. He complained of frequency and urgency in urination, and disturbed sleep because he had to get up in the night to urinate. A urologist had recently diagnosed BPH and suggested surgery. Carl hoped to find another approach, and his doctor was keen to support his efforts while he was waiting for the operation. Jean gave Carl saw palmetto and nettle root to protect the prostate from further enlargement, and couchgrass and horsetail to heal irritated urinary membranes. She also suggested a daily 15mg zinc supplement. Carl's symptoms reduced steadily and within six months he had no discomfort or urgency when urinating and was getting up less in the night. His doctors were happy with his progress and no longer saw any immediate need to operate.

BIOCHEMICAL FACTORS

The cause of prostate enlargement is unclear, but hormonal changes related to ageing may play a role. Falling levels of the male hormone testosterone, combined with relatively higher levels of the hormone prolactin, encourage the conversion of testosterone to the powerful androgen dihydrotestosterone (DHT), which stimulates the growth of prostate tissue.

BIOCHEMICAL TRIGGERS

• Zinc and essential fatty acids deficiencies, which encourage the conversion of testosterone to DHT • High alcohol intake (more than 4 units a day) • High intake of saturated fat • Environmental pollution, which increases oestrogen production in males

PSYCHO-SOCIAL FACTORS

Embarrassment can prevent men from being examined soon enough for effective treatment. The symptoms of prostate enlargement can be humiliating and worrying, and may affect work and personal and sexual relationships. Stress increases levels of the hormone prolactin, possibly leading to a build-up of DHT (*see above*).

PSYCHO-SOCIAL TRIGGERS

• Overwork and anxiety • Fatigue due to the need to urinate during the night • Shame and loss of self-esteem • Sexual difficulties • Stress

STRUCTURAL FACTORS

The bladder muscle may become over-developed from forcing urine through the compressed urethra. If the bladder is unable to expel all the urine, the tubes connecting it to the kidneys can become distended. Urine stagnating in the tubes may lead to a kidney infection and can leak around the obstruction causing incontinence. The bladder may also become overactive, leading to a more frequent need to urinate.

STRUCTURAL TRIGGERS

• Ageing • Lack of exercise • Poor posture or constipation, restricting circulation in the pelvis

PRECAUTIONS

Report any prostate problems to your doctor. Symptoms of BPH and prostate cancer are similar, so men over 50, and especially those with a close relative with prostate cancer, should consider an annual examination and a prostate-specific antigen (PSA) test.

Realms of the Body *(see page 20)*

● BIOCHEMICAL
Body systems,
such as digestion.

● STRUCTURAL
Muscles, bones,
joints and nerves.

● PSYCHO-SOCIAL
Thoughts, feelings
and relationships.

Key: Evidence of Efficacy *(see page 182)*

❶ ❷ ❸ ❹ ❺
least evidence ◄————————► most evidence

BIOCHEMICAL TREATMENT OPTIONS

CONVENTIONAL MEDICINE
Doctors screen for PSA (prostate-specific antigen). High levels indicate prostate cancer, but slightly raised levels may not be significant. Alpha-adrenergic blockers (*see Drugs Glossary, page 179*), which help improve urine flow, may be prescribed, as may the drug finasteride, which can shrink the prostate gland (although it occasionally causes impotence or loss of libido).

COMPLEMENTARY THERAPIES
Western Herbalism ❺ *(see page 127)*
Conventional doctors in Europe often prescribe herbal remedies. Several

Saw palmetto berries shrink the prostate gland

studies have shown that saw palmetto extract can improve symptoms as effectively as finasteride and with fewer side-effects, but it may take 6–8 weeks for benefits to show. Other herbal remedies that may also be suggested include rye-grass pollen, extracts of flower pollen, pygeum bark extract and stinging nettles.
Nutritional Therapies ❸
(see pages 128–29)
Zinc supplements seem to shrink the prostate, but more studies are needed.

(The increase in oestrogen levels in older men may inhibit zinc absorption.) Supplements of essential fatty acids, selenium and vitamin A may be given.

SELF-HELP TECHNIQUES
• Eat foods rich in zinc, essential fatty acids and soya – natural sources of phytoestrogens which reduce BPH
• Avoid saturated fats and cholesterol
• Limit alcohol intake, especially beer.

Eat foods rich in zinc

STRUCTURAL TREATMENT OPTIONS

CONVENTIONAL MEDICINE
A rectal examination will indicate whether the prostate is enlarged, a urine test will reveal any infection and a blood test will assess kidney function. A physician may use ultrasound, a bladder X-ray and urine-flow test to help diagnosis. If symptoms are mild, medical treatment may not be necessary. A procedure called transurethral resection (TURP) uses heat to destroy the enlarged prostate, and in more severe cases, the prostate gland may be removed

surgically (prostatectomy). Both procedures may cause sexual difficulties. Microwave treatment, laser surgery and a new, high-frequency radiowave procedure are alternative methods used to shrink the prostate.

COMPLEMENTARY THERAPIES
Alexander Technique ❷
(see page 121) Learning to improve posture can help

The Shoulderstand posture

circulation of blood in the pelvis.
Yoga ❷ *(see page 123)*
The Triangle and Shoulderstand postures are recommended to reduce prostatic swelling, and the Half Shoulderstand and Supine Butterfly are suggested to improve pelvic circulation.

SELF-HELP TECHNIQUES
• Do not simply tolerate symptoms in the hope they will improve: get advice and help • Take steps to improve general fitness.

PSYCHO-SOCIAL TREATMENT OPTIONS

CONVENTIONAL MEDICINE
Doctors recognize the embarrassment and sexual difficulties associated with BPH and may advise counselling.

COMPLEMENTARY THERAPIES
Psychotherapy & Counselling ❷
(see pages 132–33)

Talking through feelings may help you to deal with symptom-related problems.

SELF-HELP TECHNIQUES
• Practise relaxation and breathing techniques *(see pages 170–71)* and stress-management methods *(see pages 168–69)* • See a doctor when

symptoms first appear. Diagnosis is reassuring and natural treatments should begin early • Take practical steps to minimize embarrassment, for example establishing where lavatories are in public places • Be honest about the problem – people are more understanding than you think.

INFERTILITY IN MEN

Infertility of some kind affects about 15 per cent of couples, and male infertility may be the cause in 40 per cent of cases. In normal circumstances, each ejaculation releases three millilitres (less than a teaspoon) of semen, containing an average of 250 million sperm. A man's fertility is said to be impaired when

there are fewer than 20 million sperm in a millilitre of ejaculate. As well as a low sperm count, slow-moving, short-lived or misshapen sperm can also result in infertility. These conditions do not necessarily mean that a man will be unable to father a child, but they do indicate that he will need help and optimum conditions to do so.

CASE STUDY

Monica, an acupuncturist, was visited by Adam, aged 39. He and his wife wanted children but tests revealed a low sperm count and poor motility (slow-moving sperm). As well as offering advice about diet and stress-management, his doctor asked Monica to help. "My diagnosis showed that Adam's Kidney *jing*, his vital essence, was depleted," said Monica. "Adam was working 60 hours a week as a sales manager and had become exhausted." Monica stimulated points on the Kidney meridian and the Governor vessel (*see page 124*) to warm and tonify the Kidneys, and told Adam to rest, give up smoking and eat "warming" foods. Adam's sperm motility slowly improved and, two years after moving to a less stressful job, his son was conceived.

BIOCHEMICAL FACTORS

Falling sperm counts are reported in many countries, while the number of boys born with genital abnormalities is increasing. Both conditions may be due to a range of factors, possibly related to lifestyle and environment in developed countries, which can disrupt production of the male hormone testosterone.

BIOCHEMICAL TRIGGERS

• Smoking • X-rays • Various drugs, especially steroids • Alcohol • Caffeine • Drinking water contaminated with traces of pesticides, detergents and other products containing forms of the female hormone oestrogen, which may reduce sperm counts

STRUCTURAL FACTORS

The complex, partly external arrangement of the male genitals makes them vulnerable to a range of problems that can reduce fertility. Disorders of the testes, obstruction of the urethra or problems that prevent erection or ejaculation can each be a factor. Ill health may affect sperm production.

STRUCTURAL TRIGGERS

• Abnormal or undescended testes
• Varicocele (varicose vein in the scrotum)
• Mumps or other infections that cause inflammation of the reproductive tract
• High fevers • Being over- or underweight
• Too much or too little semen • Blockage of the sperm ducts, due to injury or a sexually transmitted disease • Ejaculation problems, such as retrograde ejaculation, in which semen is forced back into the bladder • Erectile dysfunction (*see pages 82–83*) • Vasectomy

PSYCHO-SOCIAL FACTORS

Constant production of stress hormones can interfere with the hormones regulating sperm production. In addition, anxiety and depression can contribute to problems in achieving and maintaining an erection (which are actually not affected by a low sperm count). Anxiety about infertility can also reduce libido and undermine the ability to enjoy lovemaking.

PSYCHO-SOCIAL TRIGGERS

• Stress at work or in personal relationships
• Loss of confidence and self-esteem
• Depression

Realms of the Body *(see page 20)*

● BIOCHEMICAL
Body systems,
such as digestion.

● STRUCTURAL
Muscles, bones,
joints and nerves.

● PSYCHO-SOCIAL
Thoughts, feelings
and relationships.

Key: Evidence of Efficacy *(see page 182)*

❶ ❷ ❸ ❹ ❺

least evidence ◄————————► most evidence

BIOCHEMICAL TREATMENT OPTIONS

CONVENTIONAL MEDICINE
A doctor will investigate underlying hormonal problems, which can occasionally cause male infertility. If low sperm counts are due to hormonal imbalance, testosterone injections or drugs such as clomiphene or gonadotrophin may be prescribed *(see Drugs Glossary, page 179)*.

COMPLEMENTARY THERAPIES
Traditional Chinese Medicine ❶
(see pages 124–25)
Practitioners treat infertility, with acupuncture and herbal remedies, but there is little supporting research.

Western Herbalism ❷
(see page 127)
A practitioner may suggest ginseng and and saw palmetto, which are traditionally used to improve male reproductive function.
Caution: do not take ginseng if you have high blood pressure.

Dried ginseng

Ginseng capsules

Nutritional Therapies ❸
(see pages 128–29)
A nutritionist might recommend foods or supplements with the following nutrients that are potentially beneficial

for healthy sperm function: zinc, folate, selenium, vitamins C and E, arginine and essential fatty acids. In one study in 1993, folinic acid, a type of folate, successfully treated a type of male infertility called round cell idiopathic syndrome, and a 1995 study at Sheffield University in the UK showed that a three-month course of vitamin E may help sperm bind to the egg.

SELF-HELP TECHNIQUES
• Eat a balanced, wholemeal diet of organic produce, free of pesticides
• Avoid smoking, caffeine and alcohol
• Maintain a healthy weight.

STRUCTURAL TREATMENT OPTIONS

CONVENTIONAL MEDICINE
A sperm analysis is usually carried out early in the investigation of a couple's fertility. If the sperm count is found to be low and the woman is fertile, artificial insemination may be an option to consider. Surgery can correct a varicocele (varicose vein in the scrotum) and occasionally reverse a vasectomy.

COMPLEMENTARY THERAPIES
Massage ❷ *(see page 116)*
Massage by your partner can be introduced as a useful aid for stress-management and may act as a welcome boost to libido and lovemaking.

Sensual massage can aid relaxation and improve lovemaking

SELF-HELP TECHNIQUES
• Avoid tight clothing, hot baths and saunas, as overheating the testicles can slow sperm production • If necessary, use a non-artificial lubricant (such as cocoa butter) that will not interfere with sperm quality • Do not over-exercise • Immersing the testicles in cold water for ten minutes three times daily is said to improve the circulation and raise sperm count.

PSYCHO-SOCIAL TREATMENT OPTIONS

CONVENTIONAL MEDICINE
As long as the sperm count is not very low, a small but effective increase may be achieved with an integrated approach that uses both conventional and complementary methods. If there is no structural or biochemical cause, a doctor may suggest making lifestyle changes to improve general health and practising relaxation and stress-management techniques *(see pages 168–69)*.

COMPLEMENTARY THERAPIES
Psychotherapy & Counselling ❷
(see pages 132–33)
If sperm production problems are not treatable, talking through feelings about fatherhood with a counsellor may help you come to terms with the situation.
Autogenic Training and
Biofeedback ❸ *(see page 136)*
It is possible that cognitive behavioural approaches, including autogenic training

and biofeedback, may make a difference if sperm production is borderline.

SELF-HELP TECHNIQUES
• Practise relaxation and breathing techniques *(see pages 170–71)* and stress-management skills to relieve tension and reduce the effects of stress
• Consider changing your job if you work with lead, radiation, pesticides, solvents or in a hot environment.

MALE SEXUAL DYSFUNCTION

Most men, particularly as they grow older, have problems in achieving or maintaining an erection at some time. When this problem is short-term or occasional, it is usually psychological. However, one in ten men experience *persistent erectile failure* – often, though incorrectly, known as impotence – which is likely to have a structural or biochemical cause, although there is often an accompanying psychological element. Ninety per cent of all such sufferers could be successfully treated, but many men are reluctant to seek help. Any persistent problem may be the first symptom of a disease and should always be referred to a doctor.

BIOCHEMICAL FACTORS

The taking of prescribed and other drugs is a frequent cause of difficulties in achieving and maintaining an erection. Hormonal imbalances are a less common cause.

BIOCHEMICAL TRIGGERS

• Alcohol and medication, especially antidepressants, antihypertensives and diuretics *(see Drugs Glossary, page 179)*
• Low levels of the male hormone testosterone
• High levels of the female hormone prolactin (all men produce small amounts of female hormones) • High blood cholesterol levels, resulting in atherosclerosis *(see pages 48–51)*

STRUCTURAL FACTORS

When there is a physical cause, erectile dysfunction usually begins gradually and occurs in all sexual situations. Structural causes of persistent erectile failure include disorders of the nervous system and circulation problems that affect the flow of blood into the penis.

STRUCTURAL TRIGGERS

• Deficient blood flow into the penis due to atherosclerosis *(see pages 48–51)* • Excessive drainage of blood from the penis ("leaking veins") • Damage of the nerves going to and from the penis due to injury, surgery or disease • Diabetes, alcohol, smoking and drug abuse, which can cause nerve or circulatory problems • Conditions that damage the central nervous system, such as stroke and spinal cord injury • Pelvic surgery, for example removal of the prostate gland

CASE STUDY

Asha, a psychologist, was visited by Mick, 32, who had enjoyed a good sex life before falling in love with his current partner. Lately, however, he was unable to maintain an erection. "I can't understand it," he said. "I love her more than I've ever loved anyone." Asha wondered why Mick was having problems with emotional intimacy. When Mick relaxed after a few sessions, he told Asha of a failed love affair when he was 20, which had hurt him a great deal. Asha encouraged Mick to acknowledge that, subconsciously, he believed being close to somebody meant getting hurt. She suggested that the couple try being physically intimate without intercourse for a month. Six months later, Mick was enjoying lovemaking once again.

PSYCHO-SOCIAL FACTORS

If erectile dysfunction begins suddenly and occurs in some circumstances and not in others, then there is usually a psychological cause. In competitive macho societies, size of penis and sexual prowess are given disproportionate importance. Erectile dysfunction and other genito-urinary conditions may influence a man's attitude towards sex and affect relationships. In one study, 21 per cent of patients' relationships broke up as a result of sexual dysfunction.

PSYCHO-SOCIAL TRIGGERS

• Fear of failure and worry about poor sexual performance • Stress and anxiety • Marital conflict and dissatisfaction • Sexual boredom • Unresolved sexual orientation • Loss of libido due to prostate problems, depression or chronic illness

Realms of the Body (*see page 20*)

● **BIOCHEMICAL**
Body systems,
such as digestion.

● **STRUCTURAL**
Muscles, bones,
joints and nerves.

● **PSYCHO-SOCIAL**
Thoughts, feelings
and relationships.

Key: Evidence of Efficacy (*see page 182*)

❶ ❷ ❸ ❹ ❺

least evidence ◄————————► most evidence

BIOCHEMICAL TREATMENT OPTIONS

CONVENTIONAL MEDICINE
A doctor may prescribe sildenafil (Viagra – see *Drugs Glossary, page 179*), which helps to relax blood vessels in the penis, allowing blood to flow in and cause an erection. It should be taken an hour before sexual activity and requires sexual desire and stimulation to be effective. However, there are side-effects and it is not suitable if you have heart or liver problems. Testosterone replacement may be prescribed, if laboratory tests indicate a deficiency.

COMPLEMENTARY THERAPIES
Traditional Chinese Medicine ❶
(*see pages 124–25*)
Erectile failure is associated with Kidney weakness and Liver *qi* stagnation. Ginseng may be given to enhance potency. Acupuncture points on the Conception meridian and certain Spleen and Bladder points may be stimulated to increase the flow of *qi* to sexual organs. **Caution:** avoid ginseng if you have high blood pressure.
Needles are used to stimulate acupoints

Western Herbalism ❸ (*see page 127*)
A practitioner may recommend saw palmetto, a traditional tonic for the male reproductive system, and ginkgo. In one study ginkgo helped 50 per cent of men with erectile problems due to poor blood flow in the arteries.

Ginkgo leaves

SELF-HELP TECHNIQUES
• Follow a healthy, organic wholefood diet to optimize well-being.

STRUCTURAL TREATMENT OPTIONS

CONVENTIONAL MEDICINE
If there is a mild vascular problem, a doctor may offer a constriction device. This uses a pump to create a vacuum around the penis to draw blood into it. Penile implants can be inserted to stiffen the penis. Several drugs, including sildenafil, can be injected into the penis to produce an erection; alprostadil (*see Drugs Glossary page 179*) is inserted into the urethra.

COMPLEMENTARY THERAPIES
Massage ❷ (*see page 116*)
Partners may help arouse each other by massaging areas of one another's bodies in ways they find mutually relaxing and erotic.

SELF-HELP TECHNIQUES
• If erectile dysfunction is due to leaking veins, try Kegel exercises, which can be as effective as surgery.

Stop mid-flow when urinating and note which muscle is used. Hold for four seconds then continue. Contract this muscle for four seconds then relax and repeat four times, at least twice a day. After a week try holding the contraction for eight seconds, then ten. You should see some improvement in 4–12 weeks • Exercise regularly to improve cardiovascular fitness • Reduce alcohol intake.

PSYCHO-SOCIAL TREATMENT OPTIONS

CONVENTIONAL MEDICINE
Depression is a major cause of sexual difficulty. Erectile problems often respond well to placebo medication. A doctor may also suggest stress-management (*see pages 168–69*), psychotherapy, hypnotherapy, marital counselling and sex therapy.

COMPLEMENTARY THERAPIES
Psychotherapy & Counselling ❸
(*see page 132–33*)
A therapist might explore underlying subconscious reasons for the condition,

especially as sexual difficulties are often a result of unacknowledged relationship problems. Sexual counselling encourages activities that do not depend on an erection, such as affectionate cuddling and caressing. Men are asked to concentrate on communication and the enjoyment of sensual touch rather than on penetration, and are told to avoid intercourse for an agreed period of time. Erection often follows spontaneously once the expectation to "perform" is removed.

SELF-HELP TECHNIQUES
• Practise relaxation and breathing (*see pages 170–71*) and other stress-management techniques to relieve anxiety and tension.

Meditation relieves underlying anxieties

STRESS

We experience psychological and physical stress in situations that tax our resources or endanger our well-being. Too little stimulation leaves us bored and inert, so a certain amount of stress has a positive effect, prompting us into action. Stress becomes a problem if body and mind remain in "emergency" mode because of continuing external stresses or internal conflicts. Persistent stress can lead to lifestyles that harm individuals and their relationships. People vary in their response to stress, depending on their ability to cope psychologically, structurally and biologically, and this capability can be boosted in all three areas.

CASE STUDY

Claudia, a nutritional therapist, helped Steve, a middle manager in his 30s, to deal with stress more effectively. Steve's energy levels had recently plummeted, he had mood swings and could not sleep for worrying about deadlines. He was using coffee as an "upper" and drank 10–12 cups a day, but still could not manage to pick himself up. "The caffeine in coffee is a stimulant," explained Claudia. "Combined with other repetitive stressors, over time, it can exhaust the adrenal glands and cause extreme fatigue." Steve gave up coffee and suffered caffeine-withdrawal headaches for four days. He switched to natural coffee substitutes and herbal teas, started a regular exercise routine and used a relaxation tape. "After seeing you I had to take stock of my lifestyle and the way I was working," he told Claudia a few months later. "My energy levels are better and I'm less moody now."

BIOCHEMICAL FACTORS

The body's reaction to an emergency is called the "fight or flight" response (see pages 168–69). It causes the stress hormones adrenaline, noradrenaline and cortisol to enter the system. In response, the digestion slows down as blood is diverted to the muscles, the liver releases sugar and fats for immediate energy, saliva dries up and perspiration increases. Persistent stress reactions can weaken the immune system and lead to recurring infections.

BIOCHEMICAL TRIGGERS
- Poor nutrition • Alcohol • Caffeine
- Nicotine • Additives • Recreational drugs
- Environmental chemicals and pollution

PSYCHO-SOCIAL FACTORS

In modern life, the causes of stress are more often emotional rather than physical. People most vulnerable to stress are obsessive, silent worriers and impatient, "hostile", "type A" personalities (see page 49). Psychological symptoms of persistent stress include lack of concentration, irritability, tearfulness, anxiety and panic attacks, sexual difficulties, insomnia, compulsive eating, obsessive behaviour, addictions and depression.

PSYCHO-SOCIAL TRIGGERS
- Stress-prone personality • Repressed strong emotions, such as fear, anger or grief
- Unresolved conflicts • Loneliness, bereavement or major loss of any kind
- Traumatic events or shock • Inability to relax and feel calm • A challenge, exam or competition • Time pressure or long or irregular working hours • Monotony and boredom
- Feelings of hopelessness and helplessness

STRUCTURAL FACTORS

The "fight or flight" response (see pages 168–69) anticipates physical action: the heart pumps faster, blood pressure rises and muscles tense. If the body does not discharge this tension, the effects accumulate. Persistent stress can cause muscle tension in the back, neck and shoulders. Tension in the gut, heart and diaphragm can lead to poor digestion, irritable bowel syndrome, constipation or diarrhoea, nausea, hyperventilation and palpitations. Skin irritation and nervous system problems, like fatigue or dizziness, may also occur.

STRUCTURAL TRIGGERS
- Injury • Poor posture • Noise • Lack of exercise and physical relaxation

Realms of the Body (*see page 20*)

- **BIOCHEMICAL**
Body systems,
such as digestion.
- **STRUCTURAL**
Muscles, bones,
joints and nerves.
- **PSYCHO-SOCIAL**
Thoughts, feelings
and relationships.

Key: Evidence of Efficacy (*see page 182*)

1 **2** **3** **4** **5**

least evidence ◄──────► most evidence

BIOCHEMICAL TREATMENT OPTIONS

CONVENTIONAL MEDICINE
Tranquillizers and sedatives (*see Drugs Glossary, page 179*) are now seldom prescribed, except if circumstances are causing severe problems

COMPLEMENTARY THERAPIES
Western Herbalism 3
(*see page 127*)
Traditional remedies include Siberian ginseng, to help

Valerian can induce calm

the body withstand stress, valerian to calm the mind and induce sleep, and kava kava to relieve anxiety and muscle tension. A practitioner will suggest a combination of herbs based on individual symptoms.
Caution: do not take ginseng if you have high blood pressure or are pregnant. Do not take valerian if you already take sleep-inducing drugs.
Nutritional Therapies 2
(*see pages 128–29*)
Certain nutrients are used up more

rapidly during stressful periods. To support the nervous system, a practitioner may recommend B-complex supplements, as well as a diet rich in this vitamin, and vitamin C and zinc, which increase resistance to infection.

SELF-HELP TECHNIQUES
• Eat a wholemeal diet with plenty of antioxidant-rich vegetables and fruit (*see pages 158–59*) • Limit caffeine, alcohol and smoking, and avoid other non-prescription stimulants.

STRUCTURAL TREATMENT OPTIONS

CONVENTIONAL MEDICINE
A doctor may advise regular exercise, as it discharges tension and releases endorphins (mood-enhancing chemicals) into the bloodstream.

COMPLEMENTARY THERAPIES
Massage 3 (*see page 116*)
All forms of touch can release endorphins (*see above*). Massage can relieve muscle tension and induce the relaxation response (*see page 170*).
Aromatherapy 3 (*see page 117*)
Lavender, rose, ylang ylang, neroli or

geranium essential oils may reduce tension and induce relaxation.
Yoga 3 (*see page 123*)
A teacher will recommend stretching and breathing exercises to promote the relaxation response, relieve tension and calm the mind. The Corpse posture and Alternate Nostril Breathing can be particularly useful.
Traditional Chinese Medicine 3
(*see pages 124–25*)
Acupuncture can promote deep calm and the mental focus induced during t'ai chi and qigong encourages the

relaxation response. Research shows t'ai chi can lower stress-hormone levels.

SELF-HELP TECHNIQUES
• Exercise regularly to release endorphins, break down accumulated stress chemicals and discharge tension.

The flowing movements of t'ai chi relieve stress

PSYCHO-SOCIAL TREATMENT OPTIONS

CONVENTIONAL MEDICINE
As many as 80 per cent of visits to a family doctor are for stress-related complaints. Your doctor will suggest you try to identify causes of persistent stress and will help you to find ways of dealing with them.

COMPLEMENTARY THERAPIES
Psychotherapy & Counselling 4
(*see pages 132–33*)
Cognitive behavioural therapy can help

you to change the way you perceive and respond to pressure.
Visualization 3 (*see page 134*)
This is one of the many established techniques that induce the relaxation response.
Meditation 4 (*see page 135*)
Studies in the US show that regular meditation can reverse the "fight and flight" response to stress. Meditation can also induce a state of deep physical relaxation and mental alertness.

Autogenic Training 3 (*see page 136*)
A practitioner will teach you a series of exercises that involves elements of relaxation, self-hypnosis and meditation. Once taught you will be able to treat yourself.

SELF-HELP TECHNIQUES
• Practise relaxation and breathing techniques (*see pages 170–71*) • Keep a stress diary (*see page 175*) • Discover your own healthy coping strategies.

ANXIETY & PANIC ATTACKS

nxiety is a normal reaction to threatening situations. It is part of the "fight or flight" response to stress (*see pages* 168–69), when the mind and body go on alert. Prolonged stress can lead to a variety of physical ailments, including headaches, raised blood pressure and palpitations. Panic attacks – sudden surges of intense anxiety – may occur at random. They are usually accompanied by disturbing physical sensations and can be so intense they interfere with daily life. About one in ten people suffer from intense anxiety, irrational fears, phobias and obsessive compulsive behaviour at some time in their lives.

CASE STUDY

Andrew, a psychologist, treated Jenny, a 21-year-old student who had started to get panic attacks. She told Andrew, "I feel frightened; my heart pounds, I get breathless, then my hands sweat and my lips and fingers tingle. I was sure I must have a bad heart, but doctor's tests showed I had nothing to worry about." Apparently her grandmother had suffered a stroke just before Jenny's exams, when she was unable to visit, and had died soon after. "At the time she had to put it out of her mind," explained Andrew. "Her tingling and numbness were due to hyperventilation, but made her feel as if she was going to have a stroke." Andrew taught Jenny diaphragmatic breathing, and arranged bereavement counselling. Once she began to accept the link between her panic attacks and her grief, she began to feel in control.

BIOCHEMICAL FACTORS

Stress triggers the "fight or flight" response, when stress hormone levels rise, the heart pumps faster and muscles tense. Breathing becomes rapid, shallow and irregular, coming from the upper chest instead of the diaphragm. This causes hyperventilation because too much carbon dioxide leaves the body, affecting blood chemistry, circulation and nerves. The hyperventilating person can feel breathless or faint, with tingling or numbness, muscle pain or spasms; they may even feel as if they are dying, which accentuates panic.

BIOCHEMICAL TRIGGERS
• Low blood sugar (hypoglycaemia)
• Stimulants, such as caffeine or alcohol
• Inadequate nutrients in diet • Food intolerance • Body chemistry changes due to overbreathing • Persistent high levels of adrenaline

STRUCTURAL FACTORS

Physical effects from the strain of being on a constant state of alert can be mistaken for symptoms of serious illness, which further increases anxiety. In the long term, anxiety may undermine the immune response and contribute to disorders such as high blood pressure or irritable bowel syndrome. Structural symptoms include sweating, chest pains and palpitations, digestive disturbances, headaches and back and neck pain.

STRUCTURAL TRIGGERS
• Muscle tension • Lack of exercise
• Overbreathing

PSYCHO-SOCIAL FACTORS

The causes of anxiety are not always clear. Anxious tendencies may partly be genetic, or may be rooted in past events. Pessimistic, perfectionist, impatient or neurotic people are more likely to suffer from stress. Many anxious people "overbreathe". Hyperventilation increases anxiety and causes physical symptoms.

PSYCHO-SOCIAL TRIGGERS
• Over-awareness of small changes in the body, for example, minor pain, heart rhythm and gut movements • A conviction that symptoms are dangerous • Family behaviour patterns
• Overload from a combination of generalized stresses • Bad experiences in the past

Realms of the Body (*see page 20*)

 BIOCHEMICAL
Body systems,
such as digestion.

STRUCTURAL
Muscles, bones,
joints and nerves.

PSYCHO-SOCIAL
Thoughts, feelings
and relationships.

Key: Evidence of Efficacy (*see page 182*)

❶ ❷ ❸ ❹ ❺

least evidence ◀─────────▶ most evidence

BIOCHEMICAL TREATMENT OPTIONS

CONVENTIONAL MEDICINE
Short-term minor tranquillizers or beta-blockers (*see Drugs Glossary, page 179*) reduce symptoms of acute anxiety. Antidepressants may be prescribed to help panic.

COMPLEMENTARY THERAPIES
Western Herbalism ❸
(*see page 127*)
At least one study has shown that the traditional Polynesian

Passion flower

herb kava kava can reduce anxiety. A practitioner may prescribe valerian to stop the mind racing; passionflower for long-term anxiety and St. John's wort for associated depression.
Caution: Do not take St. John's wort with antidepressants or valerian with sleeping pills.
Nutritional Therapies ❸
(*see pages 128–29*)
A practitioner might suggest an exclusion diet to reveal a mood-affecting food intolerance. Some

nutritionists link magnesium and calcium deficiencies to anxiety and prescribe supplements; others suggest taking vitamin B-complex supplements for the nervous system.

SELF-HELP TECHNIQUES
• Eat regular meals high in protein and complex carbohydrates • Avoid caffeine and alcohol • In an acute panic attack, rebreathe into a bag to increase blood carbon dioxide levels

STRUCTURAL TREATMENT OPTIONS

CONVENTIONAL MEDICINE
Your doctor may suggest one of the complementary therapies below.

COMPLEMENTARY THERAPIES
Massage ❸ (*see page 116*)
Regular massage can relieve muscle tension and reduce stress and anxiety.
Aromatherapy ❸ (*see page 117*)
Many people find massage with calming essential oils such as lavender, neroli and clary sage helpful. In hospital studies, patient anxiety decreased after

massage with Roman chamomile oil and neroli oil.
Caution: do not use chamomile essential oil during the first 16 weeks of pregnancy.
Therapeutic Touch ❸
(*see page 122*)
A practitioner will use touch to balance your "energy flow". Therapeutic touch has reduced anxiety in hospital patients more

Therapeutic touch reduces anxiety

efficiently than casual touch or conversation.
Acupressure ❷ (*see page 125*)
Acupressure points Liver 3, Lung 14, Heart 7, Pericardium 6 and yintang may be stimulated to relieve anxiety.

SELF-HELP TECHNIQUES
• Yoga and t'ai chi (*see pages 123 and 125*) can ease physical tension
• Regular aerobic exercise, boosts mood-enhancing brain chemicals and encourages relaxation.

PSYCHO-SOCIAL TREATMENT OPTIONS

CONVENTIONAL MEDICINE
If symptoms are severe, a doctor will refer you to a psychiatrist. Counselling can be especially important if anxiety attacks follow a traumatic event (Post-traumatic Stress Disorder). Obsessive-compulsive disorders and phobias that interfere with daily life need expert help.

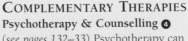
Counselling can restore perspective

COMPLEMENTARY THERAPIES
Psychotherapy & Counselling ❹
(*see pages 132–33*) Psychotherapy can help sufferers to recognize, understand and come to terms with the reasons for their anxiety. Cognitive behavioural therapy changes patterns of thinking and behaviour that reinforce anxiety.

Hypnotherapy ❸ (*see page 134*)
During treatment you will be taught techniques that may be helpful in undoing conditioned responses, such as exam fear.
Meditation ❹ (*see page 135*)
Studies show that "mindfulness" techniques can relieve panic disorders.

SELF-HELP TECHNIQUES
• Relaxation and breathing techniques (*see pages 170–71*) help • Remember symptoms are harmless and will pass.

DEPRESSION

The term "depression" is used to describe a range of negative feelings, from feeling unhappy or low on occasion to being so crippled by despair that life does not seem worth living. The incidence of clinical depression is rising, affecting one-third of all people during their lives and five per cent of people at any one time. Two-thirds of diagnosed depression sufferers are women, with an equal number of men likely to develop manic depression, a genetically based disorder in which moods swing between extremes. Complementary therapies can help mild cases, but clinical and manic depression require conventional medical help.

RED FLAG SYMPTOMS

See your GP if at least four of the following symptoms have applied to you for more than two weeks with no obvious cause:

- Loss of interest and enjoyment in life
- Lack of drive and motivation that makes even simple tasks seem impossible
- Overwhelming fatigue and loss of energy
- Unexplained aches and pains
- Agitation, irritability and restlessness
- Loss or gain in appetite and weight
- Sleeplessness, early morning waking or excessive sleeping
- Loss of affection for those close to you
- Loss of interest in sex
- Loss of self-confidence
- Feelings of uselessness, guilt, inadequacy, shame, helplessness and hopelessness
- Mood swings
- Thoughts of suicide – a certain sign that help is needed

BIOCHEMICAL FACTORS

A reduction in neurotransmitters (brain chemicals), is thought to be a factor in depression. Many drugs and supplements seek to treat depression by raising levels of serotonin and other neurotransmitters, which affect mood by stimulating certain brain cells. Physical illness or hormonal changes can affect mental state and cause depression, and the condition tends to run in families which suggests it could be partly genetic.

BIOCHEMICAL TRIGGERS

- Genetic predisposition • Hormonal changes caused by pregnancy (postnatal depression), premenstrual syndrome, oral contraceptives, and the menopause • Alcohol • Certain drugs • Depression after viral illnesses, such as flu, hepatitis or Epstein-Barr disease (glandular fever) • Some types of disease, including cancer and endocrinal, neurological and auto-immune conditions • Food intolerances

STRUCTURAL FACTORS

Most depressed people first see a doctor with symptoms such as extreme fatigue or pain. Depression manifests itself in other physical ways: depressed people are more prone to heart disease and osteoporosis. Research shows that recurrent depression disrupts nerve cell connections that generate positive feelings. Environmental triggers may be important: seasonal affective disorder is a type of depression related to low levels of daylight during the winter months.

STRUCTURAL TRIGGERS

- Physical illness • Chronic pain • Infections • Inadequate sleep • Lack of sunlight

PSYCHO-SOCIAL FACTORS

Stress-related events are thought to trigger 50 per cent of all cases of depression, and stress encountered in early life could predispose people to depression at a later stage. Those with certain personality types, for example people who are pessimistic, introverted and anxious, are more vulnerable to depression.

PSYCHO-SOCIAL TRIGGERS

- Stressful events in childhood and adolescence • Family traits • Personality type, such as anxious, pessimistic, perfectionist or introverted • Loss or bereavement • Anxiety • Unemployment • Overwork • Loneliness • Relationship problems

Realms of the Body (*see page 20*)

● **BIOCHEMICAL**
Body systems,
such as digestion.

● **STRUCTURAL**
Muscles, bones,
joints and nerves.

● **PSYCHO-SOCIAL**
Thoughts, feelings
and relationships.

Key: Evidence of Efficacy (*see page 182*)

❶ ❷ ❸ ❹ ❺

least evidence ◄————————► most evidence

BIOCHEMICAL TREATMENT OPTIONS

CONVENTIONAL MEDICINE
A course of antidepressants (*see Drugs Glossary, page 179*) can be life-saving for a depressed person. Three main types of antidepressant are commonly prescribed: selective serotonin re-uptake inhibitors (SSRIS), such as Prozac; tricyclics; and monamine oxidase inhibitors (MAOIS). Noradrenaline re-uptake inhibitors, which are relatively new, may also be given. Lithium is useful for recurrent depression and manic-depressive illness.

COMPLEMENTARY THERAPIES
Western Herbalism ❹
(*see page 127*)
St John's wort may be suggested since it has been shown to be as effective as antidepressants in treating cases of mild depression, but with far fewer side-effects.
Caution: Do not take St. John's wort if you have been prescribed conventional antidepressants.

St. John's wort

Nutritional Therapies ❸
(*see pages 128–29*)
Vitamin B⁶ and magnesium may help premenstrual depression. A therapist may suspect deficiencies affecting brain chemistry, including lack of folic acid and B vitamins, or test for food intolerances. Supplements 5-HTP and SAM-e need more research.

SELF-HELP TECHNIQUES
• Eat a healthy, balanced diet • Avoid alcohol and recreational drugs.

STRUCTURAL TREATMENT OPTIONS

CONVENTIONAL MEDICINE
Regular exercise can help relieve moderate depression by triggering natural mood-enhancing chemicals. Aerobic exercise has proved as effective as psychotherapy and relaxation techniques with mild depression. Studies show that it can help prevent depression, and that working on physical inertia and negative body image can be highly therapeutic. In the future, people with depression may be offered treatment in which high-powered magnetic pulses are directed at specific brain areas, as in experiments it temporarily relieved severe depression.

COMPLEMENTARY THERAPIES
Massage ❷ (*see page 116*)
Massage aids relaxation, enhances mood and relieves depression.
Aromatherapy ❷ (*see page 117*)
Aromatherapists use various essential oils to promote relaxation and lift mood including bergamot, rose, neroli, ylang ylang and lavender.

Acupuncture ❸
(*see page 125*)
Acupuncture, especially electro-acupuncture, can help.

SELF-HELP TECHNIQUES
• Yoga (*see page 123*) may improve posture and provide a supportive environment.

Regular aerobic exercise is
an excellent way to lift mood

PSYCHO-SOCIAL TREATMENT OPTIONS

CONVENTIONAL MEDICINE
Depression may be associated with bottled-up feelings, particularly those of rage and loss. Mild depression might not require any medication, as counselling and help with practical difficulties may be sufficient. A doctor may recommend cognitive behavioural therapy as studies show it can be as effective as antidepressants in relieving mild to moderate depression. Medication and psycho-social approaches work well together.

COMPLEMENTARY THERAPIES
Psychotherapy & Counselling ❹
(*see pages 132–33*)
A cognitive behavioural therapist may suggest the following: more involvement in pleasant activities; identifying negative behaviour and pessimistic thought patterns; and improving social skills to relate to other people more easily.

SELF-HELP TECHNIQUES
• Practise any stress-reduction method that appeals to you (*see pages 168–69*)

• Learn relaxation and breathing techniques (*see pages 170–71*) to reduce tension and relieve anxiety
• Listen to favourite pieces of music
• Do not bottle things up: learn to talk through problems with others • Break larger problems down into smaller, achievable tasks that can be tackled one day at a time • Try not to brood over problems • Take care of your appearance to boost your self-esteem
• Remind yourself that negative feelings will eventually pass.

INSOMNIA

Adequate sleep can help the body repair and regenerate tissue, build bone and muscle and strengthen the immune system. The inability to get enough of the right kind of sleep can lead to fatigue and irritability. Insomnia is common when people are over-stressed or depressed, particularly as they get older. Sleeplessness falls into three categories: being unable to go to sleep, which is linked to anxiety; falling asleep but waking frequently; and waking early in the morning then being unable to go back to sleep. Difficulty in remaining asleep may be linked to depression, illness, persistent pain or changes in daily body-clock rhythms.

CASE STUDY

Jane, a medical herbalist, treated Joe for long-term insomnia. After many years of shiftwork he found it difficult to drift off and his sleep was often disturbed by dreams. Sometimes he was getting no more than five hours' sleep a night. Jane prescribed a herbal mix to take as a tea in the evening. It included valerian and passionflower to promote relaxation and peaceful sleep, and kava kava to relax the body and relieve the anxiety that may have been causing his restless dreaming. Jane told him where he could get a good relaxation tape and suggested he exercise for half an hour a day. Joe gradually found he went to sleep more quickly and woke refreshed, without the "hangover" sleeping pills had produced.

BIOCHEMICAL FACTORS

During deep, non-dreaming (NREM) sleep, human growth hormone (HGH) is secreted, which stimulates tissue and liver regeneration, maintains the immune system and helps convert fat to muscle. The pineal gland responds to darkness by producing melatonin, a chemical that helps make us feel sleepy. Other chemicals promote wakefulness and the overall balance of brain chemicals influences when we feel tired or wakeful. For as yet unexplained reasons, deep sleep decreases with age and at least half of those aged between 40 and 55 have occasional problems in sleeping.

BIOCHEMICAL TRIGGERS

• Changes in daily body-clock rhythms due to jet-lag or shift work • Caffeine • Alcohol • Nicotine • Drugs such as beta-blockers or thyroid preparations

STRUCTURAL FACTORS

Sleep entails alternating periods of rapid eye movement (REM) sleep, when most dreaming occurs, and deep slow-wave sleep (SWS), also known as non-REM (NREM) sleep. The body needs to be comfortable enough to relax during sleep. Opinions vary, but 7–8 hours' sleep is generally considered the optimum amount of sleep for adults, and most people seem to need six hours to function without feeling tired.

STRUCTURAL TRIGGERS

• Lack of exercise • Illness or chronic pain • A poor sleeping environment – too hot, too cold, too noisy or uncomfortable

PSYCHO-SOCIAL FACTORS

Dreaming (REM) sleep is thought to be important in helping people to process the day's events and emotional issues. Stress and anxiety, work deadlines, concern over family, health and personal crises, probably account for at least 50 per cent of sleep-disturbances; these factors are most commonly the cause if the insomnia began suddenly. In the absence of such factors, depression or an anxiety disorder should be considered. Psychological strategies can be most effective in helping people to sleep.

PSYCHO-SOCIAL TRIGGERS

• Worry (associated with trouble falling asleep) • Depression (linked to difficulty in remaining asleep)

Realms of the Body (*see page 20*)

 BIOCHEMICAL
Body systems,
such as digestion.

STRUCTURAL
Muscles, bones,
joints and nerves.

PSYCHO-SOCIAL
Thoughts, feelings
and relationships.

Key: Evidence of Efficacy (*see page 182*)

❶ ❷ ❸ ❹ ❺

least evidence ◄————————► most evidence

BIOCHEMICAL TREATMENT OPTIONS

CONVENTIONAL MEDICINE
Your doctor will advise sleeping pills
or tranquillizers (*see Drugs Glossary,
page 179*) only as a short-term solution
or last resort. Waking early due to
depression usually responds well to a
course of antidepressants.

COMPLEMENTARY THERAPIES
Western Herbalism ❹ (*see page 127*)
St. John's wort can help especially
if moderate depression is the
cause. Valerian, passionflower
and hops are traditional remedies and
studies support the use of valerian.
Caution: Do not take valerian with
other sleep-inducing drugs. Do not
take St. John's wort if you have been
prescribed conventional antidepressants.
Nutritional Therapies ❸
(*see pages 128–29*)
You may be prescribed
supplements of the
hormone melatonin,

Passionflower
infusion

which can help revive a body clock
disturbed by jet-lag or shift work.

SELF-HELP TECHNIQUES
• Avoid stimulants such as caffeine,
alcohol and nicotine before bedtime
• Do not eat a meal within two hours
of bedtime, as digestion interferes with
sleep • Snack on bananas, milk or
wholemeal biscuits – carbohydrate foods
high in natural tryptophan, which makes
melatonin • Go to bed at a regular
time: late nights disrupt the body clock.

STRUCTURAL TREATMENT OPTIONS

CONVENTIONAL MEDICINE
Light therapy can help synchronize
the body clock: bright light in the
morning helps those who go to bed
progressively later and cannot wake
up; light in the evening helps those
who go to bed progressively earlier.

COMPLEMENTARY THERAPIES
Massage ❷ (*see page 116*)
Massage can relieve muscle tension,
reduce anxiety and promote sleep-
enhancing brain chemicals.
Aromatherapy ❸ (*see page 117*)
Lavender essential oil, either inhaled,
added to a bath or used in massage,
may enhance sleep. In one study, the
constant odour of essential oil of bitter
orange was sedative and improved
sleep even for those under mental stress.
Hydrotherapy ❷ (*see page 126*)
A warm bath before bed can improve
circulation, relax muscles and encourage
deep sleep just as well as exercise.

SELF-HELP TECHNIQUES
• Exercise regularly to reduce stress
hormones and increase secretion of
HGH (*see opposite*) • Avoid strenuous
activity (excluding sex) within three
hours of bedtime • Ensure your
bedroom is well-ventilated: 24°C (75°F)
is the optimum room temperature
• Choose a firm mattress • Avoid
drinking before bedtime • If early
daylight wakes you, use an eyemask
or invest in heavy curtains.

PSYCHO-SOCIAL TREATMENT OPTIONS

CONVENTIONAL MEDICINE
A doctor may suggest "sleep hygiene"
(learning habits to help you sleep) and
sleep-restriction therapy, which allows
only six hours in bed. Stimulus control
therapy restricts bed for sleep or sex
only, breaking the association between
bed and sleeplessness.

COMPLEMENTARY THERAPIES
Hypnotherapy ❹ (*see page 134*)
Self-hypnosis can induce and enhance
sleep. Intrusive thoughts are calmed by
focusing on relaxation and breathing.

Meditation ❸ (*see page 135*)
By releasing tension and helping
relaxation, meditation, either on
its own or combined with another
relaxing therapy, can aid sleep.
Biofeedback ❸ (*see page 136*)
This technique can allow you to calm
the body by monitoring your stress
levels on sensitive instruments.

SELF-HELP TECHNIQUES
• Stop any work an hour before
bedtime to calm mental activity, and
keep work materials out of the bedroom

• Practise relaxation and breathing
techniques (*see pages 170–71*) in bed.

Getting up and
reading a book is
a useful distraction
technique for those
who are unable to sleep

FOOD SENSITIVITY

Any kind of abnormal reaction to a food or food additive is known as a *food sensitivity*. An acute *food allergy* is relatively rare but can be very dangerous. The body's immune system reacts immediately to a particular food protein or carbohydrate as if it were harmful, forming immunoglobulin E (IgE) antibodies that cause acute inflammation of the skin and mucous membranes, a sudden fall in blood pressure and shock (known as anaphylaxis). In severe cases, this type of acute allergic reaction can be fatal.

The far more common type of food sensitivity is *food intolerance*. Symptoms occur after eating certain foods, but reactions are not acute or severe. They generally either appear one or two days after eating the trigger food, or build up gradually with regular intake. The immune system does not react in the same way as in food allergy. Tests show no trace of IgE antibodies, although other types may be detected. The sensitivity may go unrecognized for years because continued intake appears to be tolerated. However, problems eventually develop and only improve if treatment for food sensitivity begins. Then the trigger food should be avoided for at least six months, after which it can usually be eaten in moderation.

Although some conventional doctors are sceptical, sometimes food intolerance can be a factor in certain long-term illnesses. These include: chronic fatigue syndrome; hypoglycaemia (low blood sugar); arrhythmia (abnormal heartbeat); persistently swollen glands; skin disorders; digestive conditions such as irritable bowel syndrome; urinary problems; frequent infections; musculo-skeletal disorders such as muscle pain, migraine, arthritis and back pain; and psychological problems, for example, depression, hyperactivity and anxiety disorders.

BIOCHEMICAL FACTORS

IN CASES OF FOOD ALLERGY, it is the production of immunoglobulin E antibodies (*see above*) that triggers the acute allergic response. A substance called histamine is released, which in turn causes inflammation in various body tissues. Food allergies often occur in people who also suffer from other allergic conditions, such as eczema or hay fever. In cases of food intolerance, there is recent scientific evidence suggesting that faulty non-IgE antibodies (known as IgA and IgG) may allow incompletely digested food molecules to cross the lining of the intestinal tract and enter the bloodstream.

BIOCHEMICAL TRIGGERS
Food allergies: • Early exposure to inappropriate food proteins, e.g.cow's milk • Family tendency to allergy • Peanuts and other nuts • Shellfish, eggs • Strawberries
Food intolerances: • Lack of specific digestive enzymes (e.g. lactase, responsible for the digestion of cow's milk) • Dairy products • Gluten – a protein in wheat (coeliac disease) • Preservatives (especially benzoic acid) • Colourings (especially tartrazine) and other food additives • Pesticides • Antibiotics and other drugs

See over for Biochemical Treatment Options

Realms of the Body (*see page 20*)

○ **BIOCHEMICAL**
Body systems,
such as digestion.

○ **STRUCTURAL**
Muscles, bones,
joints and nerves.

○ **PSYCHO-SOCIAL**
Thoughts, feelings
and relationships.

STRUCTURAL FACTORS

IN AN ACUTE ALLERGIC REACTION to a food (*see left*), the release of histamine and other chemicals causes blood vessels to widen and blood pressure to fall dramatically. Other reactions may include an itchy raised rash, constriction of the airways in the lungs so that breathing is difficult, swelling of the tongue and throat, pain in the abdomen, and diarrhoea. Practitioners of nutritional therapies believe many cases of long-term food intolerance are due to "dysbiosis" (the overgrowth of "unfriendly" gut bacteria) and a "leaky gut" that lets partly digested substances be absorbed into the bloodstream,

affecting all body systems (*see page 159*). Over-consumption of certain foods, particularly wheat, dairy products and refined sugar (for which the gut is poorly adapted), may also be responsible.

STRUCTURAL TRIGGERS

Food intolerance: • Poor blood circulation in the intestines • Irritated gut lining • "Leaky gut lining", allowing absorption of partly digested food proteins into the bloodstream (*see below*)

See over for Structural Treatment Options

PSYCHO-SOCIAL FACTORS

STRESS AFFECTS DIGESTION and is a common factor in food intolerances (*see below*). People with food intolerances may also have difficulties in coping with stress because they feel under par. Those with allergies of all kinds tend to find their condition is worse when they are stressed.

PSYCHO-SOCIAL TRIGGERS

• Stress • Poor health • Lack of coping skills • Anxiety Depression • Overwork, lack of sleep • Traumatic events

See over for Psycho-social Treatment Options

Stress leads to biochemical imbalances

Toxin-induced ailments lead to pain and general poor health, which is stressful

Effect on gut:
• Fewer digestive enzymes
• Poor intestinal circulation
• Irregular peristalsis (*see Glossary, pages 177–78*)

Various biochemical waste products can act as irritating "toxins"

Toxins overload the liver and kidneys and irritate other organs

Food is not properly broken down or absorbed

May lead to:
Dysbiosis: poorly digested food in the gut encourages overgrowth of "unfriendly" bacteria, resulting in candidiasis, for example
Leaky gut: toxins from poorly digested food "leak" from the gut into the blood

FOOD SENSITIVITY

Key: Evidence of Efficacy (see page 182)

① ② ③ ④ ⑤

least evidence ◄————► most evidence

BIOCHEMICAL TREATMENT OPTIONS

CONVENTIONAL MEDICINE

If you have an acute allergic reaction, a doctor will suggest a RAST (Radio Allergo Sorbent Test), which is a very reliable method of detecting food allergies. Antibodies are extracted from a blood sample and added to the suspect allergen. Radioactive or coloured markers indicate an allergic reaction. A food allergy is lifelong, so you will be advised to avoid the food responsible permanently. Acute food allergies are treated with adrenaline injections and antihistamine and corticosteroid drugs (see Drugs Glossary, page 179) which can be lifesaving.

COMPLEMENTARY THERAPIES
Nutritional Therapies ④
(see page 128–29)

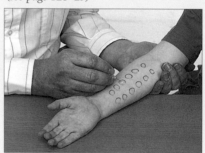
The skin reacts to foods causing sensitivity

A practitioner is likely to recommend diagnostic tests such a skin-prick test (see page 131) or a RAST (see above), but only if they suspect a true food allergy. For food intolerance they will suggest an elimination or exclusion diet (see page 128) to identify the culprit food. Compared with the plant-rich, raw and unrefined diet for

which our bodies evolved, the modern Western diet is unsuitable for many people, containing too much protein, refined sugar and wheat, as well as excess fat and additives. Short fasts and "detox" diets give the body a rest from irritant foods and allow the digestion and elimination to recover. A practitioner will suggest supplements to suit your needs, as people with food sensitivities are sometimes deficient in various vitamins and minerals. If dysbiosis (see page 159) is suspected, live yogurt and *lactobacillus* supplements will be given to promote healthy gut bacteria.

Environmental Medicine ③
(see page 131)
Clinical ecologists believe that the Western diet, combined with exposure to synthetic chemicals, encourages food intolerances. These intolerances are, they claim, the cause of chronic illnesses. Controversial diagnostic methods include cytotoxic tests, pulse-testing, hair analysis, Vega-testing and applied kinesiology (see Glossary, pages 177–78), but most conventional doctors doubt their accuracy. Some doctors and nutritionalists test for immunoglobulin G (IgG) abnormalities, but this is a relatively new procedure. You may be recommended Enzyme Potentiated Desensitization (EPD), in which an enzyme is used to make the skin absorb a safe dilution of common allergens.

Desensitization drops are placed under the tongue

Some complementary practitioners prepare highly diluted "desensitization drops", taken by mouth and believed to work by "turning off" the intolerance. This is a controversial form of treatment.

SELF-HELP TECHNIQUES
• Keep a food-trigger diary (see page 147) to help identify those foods that may be the cause of sensitivities
• Consider a "Stone Age" diet (see page 129) if you have any chronic illness
• Remember that excluding food triggers from your diet may initially make your symptoms worse, as will the reintroduction of any food to which you have a sensitivity.

A detox diet includes raw fruit and vegetables, as well as wholegrain cereals and plenty of filtered or mineral water

PRECAUTIONS

Call an ambulance immediately if you suspect an acute allergic reaction. Those at risk of an acute allergic reaction should avoid the food responsible, carry a syringe that has been preloaded with adrenaline and wear a medical alert tag. The following symptoms are all associated with acute allergic reactions to food. Consult a doctor if any of them develop within an hour or two of eating: itching or swelling in the mouth or on the skin on any part of the body, breathlessness, severe diarrhoea and abdominal cramps.

Practising yoga postures and breathing exercises can reduce the severity of symptoms

STRUCTURAL TREATMENT OPTIONS

CONVENTIONAL MEDICINE
Doctors see allergies as biochemical problems with no structural component. However, some doctors believe that food intolerance can be a significant underlying factor in certain long-term diseases.

COMPLEMENTARY THERAPIES
Yoga ❷ (*see page 123*)
In common with other movement therapies, yoga may be of help in alleviating mild food intolerance. Any exercise that improves circulation to the gut, lungs and kidneys can be beneficial, helping body systems to function efficiently. Yoga practitioners are likely to recommend postures that support digestion, and elimination including the Half Shoulderstand and Relaxation pose, as well as breathing exercises (*pranayama*).

SELF-HELP TECHNIQUES
• Exercise regularly to improve the circulation, aid digestion and to relieve tension (*see page 152*).

Aerobic exercise such as jogging can help body systems function efficiently

PSYCHO-SOCIAL TREATMENT OPTIONS

CONVENTIONAL MEDICINE
Doctors believe that no practitioner should attempt to offer psychological treatment for a condition as dangerous as an acute food allergy. However, in the case of long-term intolerances, the severity of the reaction will often vary according to the patient's stress levels. Psychotherapy may be of use in helping patients to cope with stress and to identify the times when they are most likely to suffer a reaction.

COMPLEMENTARY THERAPIES
Psychotherapy & Counselling ❷
(*see pages 132–33*)
Sometimes food intolerances are blamed inappropriately for ill health and psychological problems. In addition, some people become over-concerned about food sensitivity and condition themselves to expect symptoms. Talking through problems with a trained counsellor can help to identify unacknowledged areas of psychological difficulty.
Relaxation & Breathing ❷
(*see page 170–71*)
Hyperventilation (rapid breathing) stimulates the release of histamine, involved in the allergic response. A practitioner will demonstrate techniques to regulate breathing in order to reduce the severity of the stress response. Relaxation techniques also help to relieve muscle tension and stress.

SELF-HELP TECHNIQUES
• Keep a stress diary (*see page 175*) and choose a stress-management technique (*see page 168–69*). Food sensitivity is often a matter of poor resilience to the trigger food, and personal unhappiness can drastically undermine normal immune responses.

HAY FEVER & RHINITIS

Harmless airborne substances trigger allergic reactions in some people. Membranes lining the nose, throat, sinuses and eyes become inflamed, increasing mucus production. Symptoms can include itchy, watery eyes, a blocked or runny nose, sneezing, drowsiness, fatigue and a sore throat. Some allergens, notably pollen, cause *seasonal rhinitis*, or hay fever. This affects one in five people, with half also suffering from asthma, while many have eczema too. Non-seasonal allergens, such as dust, can cause year-round *perennial rhinitis*, although food intolerances (*see pages 92–95*) can contribute. Allergies often ease with age.

CASE STUDY

Guy, 36, dreaded the summer, when his hay fever led to a stuffy nose and very itchy, sore and swollen eyes. Antihistamines helped, but made him rather drowsy. Jill, a medical herbalist, prescribed a herbal remedy containing ephedra to reduce allergic reaction, and eyebright, elderflower, goldenseal and plantain to reduce mucus production and soothe the membranes of his eyes and nasal passages.

Within a few hours of taking his first dose, Guy found that his symptoms were much relieved, and he was able to go outside and enjoy the summer weather. He continues to take his herbal remedy when the pollen count is high. Several seasons later, he feels he is becoming less susceptible to pollen.

Caution: only take ephedra with professional supervision.

BIOCHEMICAL FACTORS

Hay fever and rhinitis are more likely to occur in "atopic" individuals (those with a family history of asthma, eczema and hay fever). For unknown reasons, their immune system over-reacts to proteins in airborne pollens and dust, and produces immunoglobulin E (IgE) antibodies which stimulate an excessive release of histamine. (This normally helps protect the body from infection by dilating blood vessels so they are more permeable to white blood cells which fight invading organisms.) The result is inflammation with pain and swelling.

BIOCHEMICAL TRIGGERS

• Genetic disposition to allergies • Grass and tree pollen • Fungal spores • House-dust mites • Animal dander (particles of skin, fur and feathers) • Food intolerances

STRUCTURAL FACTORS

Once inflamed, the mucous lining of the nose, throat and sinuses becomes increasingly sensitive. It then takes fewer allergens to trigger an attack and non-seasonal irritants, such as perfume, environmental chemicals, dust or cigarette smoke can exacerbate symptoms. Swollen mucous membranes may lead to blocked sinuses, sinusitis and headaches.

STRUCTURAL TRIGGERS

• Cigarette smoke • Environmental chemicals, such as pesticides • Perfumes • Airborne particles, such as traffic fumes

PSYCHO-SOCIAL FACTORS

Allergy symptoms are stressful in themselves but, according to complementary practitioners, stress from other sources can exacerbate the immune system's reaction. Other allergies, such as eczema and asthma, are known to be made worse by psychological stress. A study of 128 patients with perennial rhinitis or hay fever concluded that psychological factors are of more significance in perennial rhinitis than in hay fever.

PSYCHO-SOCIAL TRIGGERS

• Anxiety • Overwork • Lack of adequate sleep • Traumatic life events

Realms of the Body *(see page 20)*

● **BIOCHEMICAL**
Body systems,
such as digestion.

● **STRUCTURAL**
Muscles, bones,
joints and nerves.

● **PSYCHO-SOCIAL**
Thoughts, feelings
and relationships.

Key: Evidence of Efficacy *(see page 182)*

❶ ❷ ❸ ❹ ❺

least evidence ◄————————► most evidence

BIOCHEMICAL TREATMENT OPTIONS

CONVENTIONAL MEDICINE
Antihistamine tablets, eye drops, nasal inhalers and sprays (*see Drugs Glossary, page 179*) may be prescribed to reduce inflammation. Decongestant sprays and drops are effective but may damage nasal membranes if overused. Sodium cromoglycate eye drops, ointments, inhalers and nasal sprays inhibit allergies and anti-inflammatory corticosteroids can ease severe cases. Immunotherapy is a specialist treatment that involves injecting increasing

Eyedrops can be soothing

amounts of an allergen under the skin monthly for two years.
Caution: Some remedies react with one another; consult a pharmacist first.

COMPLEMENTARY THERAPIES
Western Herbalism ❸ *(see page 127)*
Herbalists may suggest a course of echinacea or liquorice to help boost the immune system before the pollen season.
Caution: avoid liquorice if pregnant.
Nutritional Therapies ❷
(see pages 128–29)
Practitioners may recommend a 48-hour detoxifying fast, followed by a raw-food, cleansing diet to help the body rid

itself of toxins. Vitamin C is said to support the mucous membranes. You might be advised to avoid wheat, dairy products and food additives.
Homeopathy ❹ *(see page 130)*
Taking homeopathically potentized pollens (*see page 130*) before the pollen season begins may help prevent symptoms. Several studies have found *Galphimia glauca* effective. Proprietary hay fever remedies are available in pharmacies and health shops.

SELF-HELP TECHNIQUES
• Eating garlic and onions may help to boost the immune system.

STRUCTURAL TREATMENT OPTIONS

CONVENTIONAL MEDICINE
Masks or caps that cover the mouth or nose help sufferers by filtering air.

COMPLEMENTARY THERAPIES
Aromatherapy ❷ *(see page 117)*
A steam inhalation can ease congestion. Adding 3–4 drops of menthol or eucalyptus essential oils may help. **Caution:** If you have asthma, use steam inhalations with care.
Acupuncture ❸ *(see page 125)*
Traditional Chinese Medicine regards hay fever as "Wind invasion", occurring

Eucalyptus

because the body's defences (*wei chi*) are weak. Medical acupuncturists in the West claim that acupuncture can affect nerves controlling mucus production and swelling of nasal blood vessels.

SELF-HELP TECHNIQUES
• Try to stay inside and keep windows closed, especially mid-morning and early evening when the pollen count is highest • Smear petroleum jelly inside your nostrils • Vacuum regularly and

dust surfaces with a damp cloth
• Keep pets out of bedrooms • Splash your face with cold water to flush away pollen and dust • Shower and wash your hair to remove pollen each evening
• Cover your bed during the day
• Wash bedding and pillows at over 60°C (140°F) to kill dust mites.

Wash your hair to remove allergens

PSYCHO-SOCIAL TREATMENT OPTIONS

CONVENTIONAL MEDICINE
Your doctor may recommend you reduce stress levels with one of the therapies listed below.

COMPLEMENTARY THERAPIES
Hypnotherapy ❷ *(see page 134)*
A practitioner may demonstrate breathing techniques that can help

to alleviate symptoms.
Visualization ❷ *(see page 134)*
You will be shown techniques to relieve physical and mental tension which may reduce stress.
Biofeedback ❷ *(see page 136)*
This technique allows you to monitor your reactions to stress. Used with methods of relaxation and meditation,

it may help to relieve the swelling of perennial rhinitis.

SELF-HELP TECHNIQUES
• Keep a symptom diary (*see page 147*) to identify possible allergic triggers including foods • Practise stress-management techniques (*see pages 168–169*).

ASTHMA

The episodes of breathlessness and wheezing that are characteristic of asthma result when the membranes lining the small airways of the lungs (the bronchioles) become constricted and inflamed, and airflow is restricted. Production of phlegm then increases and worsens the obstruction.

Asthma is becoming very common, especially in industrialized countries, and affects over 200 million people worldwide, including one child in seven. About a quarter of sufferers have severe attacks with sweating and a racing pulse, which can be frightening and dangerous and must be treated with conventional medicine.

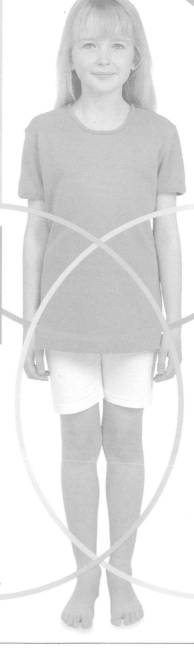

CASE STUDY

Louise, a homeopathic doctor, treated Rebecca, aged 10, for worsening asthma attacks. She advised continuing with the steroid inhalers and carried out skin tests for common allergens. Louise decided that Rebecca had the typical characteristics of a *Phosphorus* constitution and prescribed *Phosphorus 30c* daily for a week. Ten days later she added a daily homeopathic dilution of house-dust mite, the allergen to which Rebecca had reacted most strongly. Louise continues to see Rebecca: "The steroid dose she was on has been slowly reduced and she has had no further severe attacks."

PRECAUTIONS

Always keep emergency medicines to hand. If an attack does not respond quickly to self-administered bronchodilator drugs, call a doctor or go to hospital immediately.

STRUCTURAL FACTORS

A combination of tense bronchial tube muscles and inflamed, swollen membranes narrows the airways so that air flow is restricted. Production of white sticky phlegm increases, making the blockage worse, and breathing becomes a struggle. The chest feels tight and attempts to clear the airways may produce a dry cough, especially at night.

STRUCTURAL TRIGGERS

• Vigorous physical exertion, especially in cold, dry air • Cold, damp, dry or stormy weather
• Body-rhythm fluctuations make attacks more likely between midnight and 3 a.m.

BIOCHEMICAL FACTORS

When an asthmatic person inhales airborne allergens or irritants, the immune system overreacts, producing immunoglobulin E antibodies. These stimulate histamine release in the lining of the bronchial tubes, causing inflammation. Dietary factors or even viral infections can also trigger the immune response in susceptible individuals.

BIOCHEMICAL TRIGGERS

• House-dust mites, cockroaches, mould or pollen from grasses, trees and other plants
• Animal dander (particles of fur, skin and feathers) • Environmental pollutants such as tobacco smoke, exhaust fumes and industrial fumes • Allergy to foods such as dairy products, seafood, yeast, nuts and wheat, and to food additives and alcohol *(see page 92)*
• Food intolerances may increase susceptibility to inhaled allergens • Monosodium glutamate; preservatives • Deficiency of nutrients such as vitamin C, magnesium or essential fatty acids • Viral infections

PSYCHO-SOCIAL FACTORS

An asthma attack can be triggered by any kind of psychological stress, be it anxiety, overwork, relationship and family problems, depression, or even apprehension about the next attack. Anxiety constricts the bronchial tubes and the severity of an attack is often related to the degree of anxiety felt.

PSYCHO-SOCIAL TRIGGERS

• Stress and anxiety • Strong emotions
• Fear of the next asthma attack
• Repressed feelings

Realms of the Body *(see page 20)*

● **BIOCHEMICAL**
Body systems,
such as digestion

● **STRUCTURAL**
Muscles, bones,
joints and nerves

● **PSYCHO-SOCIAL**
Thoughts, feelings
and relationships

Evidence of Efficacy *(see page 176)*

  ❶ ❷ ❸ ❹ ❺

least evidence ◄————————► most evidence

BIOCHEMICAL TREATMENT OPTIONS

CONVENTIONAL MEDICINE
Your doctor will discuss a treatment plan with you and might perform skin or blood tests to identify allergens. Sodium cromoglycate or inhaled corticosteroid sprays, which reduce inflammation and mucus, are prescribed for daily use to prevent attacks (*see Drugs Glossary, page 179*).

COMPLEMENTARY THERAPIES
Western Herbalism ❸ (*see page 127*)
A practitioner may prescribe coleus,

Ginkgo leaves

which German studies found dilated bronchial tubes almost as powerfully as conventional drugs, and ginkgo to prevent bronchial constriction.
Nutritional Therapies ❹
(*see page 128–29*)
Exclusion or rotation diets help identify food intolerance. Supplements of vitamin C and B⁶ may be suggested.
Homeopathy ❹ (*see page 130*)
In a study published in *The Lancet* in

1994, asthmatics taking homeopathic remedies showed an improvement.

SELF-HELP TECHNIQUES
• Eat oily fish and wholegrain cereals, rich in omega-3 fatty acids and magnesium (*see page 158*), and avoid salt • Protect against house-dust mites with synthetic bedding and carpets, and an anti-allergy vacuum cleaner • Avoid animals, tobacco smoke and polluted air • Consider a new job if you are exposed to allergens at work.

STRUCTURAL TREATMENT OPTIONS

CONVENTIONAL MEDICINE
You may be prescribed bronchodilators such as salbutamol (*see Drugs Glossary, page 179*). During an attack, these are taken via nebulizers or inhalers to open the airways.

Asthma inhaler

COMPLEMENTARY THERAPIES
Osteopathy ❸ (*see page 118*) and
Chiropractic ❸ (*see page 119*)
Practitioners use manipulation to relax

and stretch the chest muscles and diaphragm so breathing is easier.
Yoga ❹ (*see page 123*)
Breathing and stretching postures help chest muscles to work better, expand the lungs, and calm mind and body.
Acupuncture ❸ (*see page 125*)
Studies suggest that stimulating acupoints may relieve symptoms.

SELF-HELP TECHNIQUES
• Regular exercise increases lung capacity and strengthens the heart

(*see pages 152–53*) • If asthma attacks are brought on by exercise, use a bronchodilator inhaler beforehand • Diaphragmatic breathing and progressive muscle relaxation (*see pages 170–71*) can help • In the controversial Buteyko breathing method, asthma is attributed to hyperventilation (rapid breathing). Patients are taught how to shallow breathe and hold their breath, but there is still very little evidence for this method's effectiveness.

PSYCHO-SOCIAL TREATMENT OPTIONS

CONVENTIONAL MEDICINE
Discuss any family, social or psychological problems with your doctor, who may suggest counselling (*see below*). There is evidence that repressed feelings make people more susceptible to asthma attacks.

COMPLEMENTARY THERAPIES
Psychotherapy & Counselling ❹
(*see pages 132–33*)
Cognitive behavioural therapy can reduce the frequency of attacks by

reducing the expectation of panic and giving a greater sense of control.
Hypnotherapy ❸ (*see page 134*)
By teaching you to relax and cope with unpleasant sensations, hypnosis can relieve symptoms and reduce the need for medication.

SELF-HELP TECHNIQUES
• The unpredictability of an attack is wearing; keep a diary (*see page 147*) to identify stresses, environmental factors, dietary factors, and even

emotions that trigger attacks • Join a support group • Learn coping skills (*see pages 172–73*).

A diary helps pinpoint factors involved in attacks

CANCER

The second biggest killer after heart disease, cancer affects about a third of people who live in developed countries. It occurs when cells in certain tissues multiply uncontrollably and most commonly affects the breasts, lungs, bowel, skin, stomach, ovaries, pancreas, prostate, bladder and lymph glands. Cancer is not a single disease and its severity depends, among other things, on the kind of tissue affected. Some forms are relatively mild and, if caught in time, have a 100 per cent cure rate. The incidence of certain cancers varies considerably from country to country and differences in diet and lifestyle are significant. It seems as many as 70 per cent of cancer cases could be prevented if people avoided known triggers such as tobacco, environmental toxins, ultraviolet light and certain foods.

In the past, complementary medicine sometimes claimed "miracle" cures for cancer which were proved later to be ineffectual or even fraudulent. Now a combination of conventional and complementary therapies offers a promising way forward, and many leading cancer treatment centres, hospices and self-help groups have adopted the integrated approach, using gentle therapies such as massage, relaxation and healing to help relieve symptoms. Complementary therapists aim to ease pain and anxiety, alleviate the side effects of conventional medicine, help patients come to terms with their situation and, where outlook is poor, to enjoy whatever time is left. There is some evidence that the resulting enhancement of emotional and spiritual well-being prolongs life.

BIOCHEMICAL FACTORS

THERE ARE MORE THAN 200 FORMS OF CANCER, but all have one thing in common: abnormal cells whose growth is out of control. Cells multiply by splitting in two, a process stimulated by genes called oncogenes and slowed by others known as tumour suppressors. Genetic mutations can throw this process out of balance, so that cells divide at breakneck speed, faster than the tumour suppressors can restrain them. As the tumour grows, it invades neighbouring tissues and tumour cells metastasize (spread) through the bloodstream and lymph system to distant parts of the body where they form "secondary" tumours. A tendency for cells to mutate can be inherited. Certain types of cancer – like colon and breast cancer – run in some families. Other types might be triggered by viral infections and lifestyle factors. Diet is estimated to account for up to 80 per cent of cancers of the bowel, breast and prostate.

BIOCHEMICAL TRIGGERS
• Genetic disposition • Infection with hepatitis B and C, or HIV viruses and *Helicobacter pylori* • Smoking (lung, mouth, throat, oesophagus, pancreas, bladder and cervix) • Heavy drinking (mouth, oesophagus, pharynx, larynx and liver) • Obesity (breast, uterus and gallbladder) • Chemicals and food additives • Processed and smoked foods, charred food • Diet high in red meat and other foods containing saturated animal fats • Diet low in selenium and other antioxidants

See over for Biochemical Treatment Options

Realms of the Body (*see page 20*)

● **BIOCHEMICAL**
Body systems,
such as digestion.

● **STRUCTURAL**
Muscles, bones,
joints and nerves.

● **PSYCHO-SOCIAL**
Thoughts, feelings
and relationships.

STRUCTURAL FACTORS

EXTERNAL FACTORS SUCH AS POLLUTION, industrial chemicals and radiation may trigger cell mutation and abnormal cell growth. Cultural differences seem to make certain cancers more prevalent in some countries. Breast cancer rates, for example, are higher in the affluent US (where early onset of menstruation and the postponement of childbearing are common) than in poorer countries like Poland, where slower growth rates delay menstruation. There are more cases of stomach cancer in Japan than in other countries, possibly due to the high salt intake and greater rates of infection with

the stomach bacteria *Helicobacter pylori*, which some experts believe might trigger cancer of the stomach.

STRUCTURAL TRIGGERS
● Ultraviolet radiation (skin cancer) ● Environmental and chemical irritants ● Pesticides, traffic fumes ● Ionizing radiation (for example excessive X-rays) ● Inactivity (in studies inactive men were twice as likely to develop cancer as active men) ● Unprotected sex (cervical and anal cancer are linked to a sexually transmitted virus)

See over for Structural Treatment Options

PSYCHO-SOCIAL FACTORS

A PERSON'S SUSCEPTIBILITY TO CANCER has been attributed to stress, personality and emotional events. Some books have even implied that cancer is caused by repressed emotions or a lack of "spiritual development". These theories and the related idea that recovery depends on the amount of mental effort put into it should be treated with scepticism. There is no firm evidence that stress, personality, emotional states, thoughts or feelings in themselves can *cause* cancer, nor that negative feelings will make tumours grow faster.

On the other hand, most experts now believe that the onset of the disease is complex. It requires a number of predisposing factors, from genes to lifestyle, which all need to be involved before one acts as a trigger. A stressful situation, such as

bereavement or loneliness, may undermine normal immune processes, but this might only trigger tumour formation if the person is already suffering from poor nutrition, adverse environmental factors or has a genetic tendency to develop cancer.

POSITIVE ATTITUDE
How we cope with cancer may be important. One study of women with early breast cancer found that those who had a positive "fighting spirit", fared better than those who felt negative or helpless. There is also evidence that supportive social environments and psychological factors may increase chances of recovery or lengthen the survival time of patients.

See over for Psycho-social Treatment Options

RED FLAG SYMPTOMS

Cancer can cause a variety of symptoms. Consult a doctor as soon as possible if you have any of the following:
● Unexplained, persistent weight loss
● A mole that changes shape, gets bigger, itches or bleeds
● Sores, scabs or ulcers on the skin that do not heal
● A lump in the breast; discharge or bleeding from the nipple or flattening of the nipple; change in the shape or size of the breast; dimpling or puckering of the skin
● Change in the shape or size of the testicles

● Unexplained severe headaches
● Constant hoarseness; persistent sore throat; nagging cough; difficulty in swallowing; repeatedly coughing up blood
● Persistent abdominal pain or indigestion
● Blood – either red or black – in the stools or urine
● Change in bowel habits, e.g. constipation for no obvious reason (especially in those over 40)
● Vaginal bleeding between menstrual periods, after sex or after the menopause

CANCER

BIOCHEMICAL TREATMENT OPTIONS

CONVENTIONAL MEDICINE

You may be offered radiotherapy *(see Glossary, page 177–78)* to mop up cancer cells left after surgery, or chemotherapy to destroy cells that have travelled to other parts of the body. The success of these methods varies, depending on the type of cancer. Retinoids, carotenoids, aspirin and hormones such as tamoxifen are being investigated as treatments, and new approaches include biological therapies and gene therapy. Vaccine therapy may eventually help the immune system to fight specific cancers, notably skin and prostate cancer.

COMPLEMENTARY THERAPIES
Traditional Chinese Medicine ❸
(see page 124–25)

You may be given remedies to alleviate the side-effects of chemotherapy and radiotherapy. *Fu zheng* therapy, which relies on a herbal formula with ginseng and astragalus, is claimed to improve patients' life expectancy. A number of studies have shown that ginseng has protective qualities.

Western Herbalism ❷ *(see page 127)*
Practitioners aim to boost the body's defences. A cleansing programme with herbs such as burdock may be followed by restorative remedies for the liver,

Lycopene in tomatoes and peppers helps protect against cancer

digestion, circulation and nervous system. Canadian herbalists have developed a remedy known as Essiac, based on a Native American formula, but their claims of its effectiveness require more research.
Caution: Take herbal remedies only under professional supervision and with the consent of your doctor.
Nutritional Therapies ❸ *(see pages 128–29)* Some foods seem to have protective qualities and the natural combination of nutrients, especially in fruit and vegetables, may be more powerful than taking supplements. Many doctors as well as nutritional therapists recommend fibre to improve elimination and mop up potentially carcinogenic substances, and foods rich in antioxidants *(see page 162)*, which protect against "free radicals" that can stimulate cancer-cell growth. Key antioxidants include: vitamins A and E to improve immune function; vitamin C to prevent carcinogenic nitrosamines *(see Glossary, page 177–78)* forming; selenium to protect cell membranes; and bioflavonoids to strengthen the capillaries. B-complex vitamins help to neutralize certain carcinogens.
Healing foods A nutritionist might recommend you eat garlic and onions, which contain allicin, said to help prevent gastrointestinal and bladder cancer; tomatoes and red peppers,

which are rich in lycopene, shown to lower the risk of prostate and cervical cancer; oily fish, which seems to have an anti-tumour effect; cabbage, broccoli and

Shiitake mushrooms may be protective

soya, which protect against prostate, ovarian and breast cancer; and shiitake and maitake mushrooms, which may inhibit cancer cell development.
Cancer-fighting diets There are a number of dietary therapies, such as the Gerson raw-foods diet, the Hippocrates wheat-grass diet, the Kelley-Gonzalez and Livington-Wheeler programmes that claim to *treat* cancer. However, no single programme has been scientifically proven to cure cancer or stop its spread, and these extreme regimes can cause weight loss and psychological strain in people who may already be stressed and underweight. The Bristol Diet, devised in the late 1980s at the Bristol Cancer Help Centre in the UK, is a less rigorous regime with an emphasis on natural, unprocessed foods.
Homeopathy ❸ *(see page 130)*
Iscador, an extract of mistletoe, may be suggested. Tests show it can increase white blood cell activity, but there is no conclusive evidence for its effectiveness.

SELF-HELP TECHNIQUES
• Eat more organic vegetables, fruit and wholegrains • Cut down on fat, red meat, salt-cured, salt-pickled and smoked foods • Only drink alcohol in moderation • Throw away mouldy food.

Protect against cancer with oily fish, vegetables and grains

PRECAUTIONS

If you have cancer, consult a doctor before undertaking any complementary therapy and do not stop taking conventional medication.

STRUCTURAL TREATMENT OPTIONS

CONVENTIONAL MEDICINE

Diagnosing cancer may require a biopsy (*see Glossary, page 177–78*) to determine if a tumour is malignant. A CT or MRI scan may be arranged, or nuclear medicine imaging, which allows three-dimensional views of tumours. Surgery aims to remove the cancer, possibly along with the local lymph nodes.

COMPLEMENTARY THERAPIES

Massage ❹ (*see page 116*)
Therapeutic massage, now available in many cancer centres and hospices, can relieve muscle pain and tension, reduce anxiety and encourage relaxation. After a mastectomy you may be offered a very gentle form of massage called lymphatic drainage to help reduce the swelling. Massaging someone with cancer demands knowledge and skill, but family and friends can also learn techniques that bring comfort and reassurance through touch.

Reflexology is relaxing and may help to relieve cancer symptoms

Reflexology ❷
(*see page 120*)
Reflexology is increasingly available in British cancer centres and hospices, where it is often given by nurses. It is relaxing and practitioners claim it can help relieve symptoms, including pain, constipation and nausea.
Healing ❸ (*see page 122*)
Healers are available in some cancer centres, and many patients and their families report that healing, or "laying on of hands", provides support, strength, symptom-relief and spiritual solace.
Therapeutic Touch ❸ (*see page 122*)
A growing number of nurses, particularly in the US, use therapeutic touch, and studies report that it can help pain management.

Acupuncture ❺ (*see page 125*)
A practitioner will show you how to stimulate acupoints, especially Pericardium 6, to relieve nausea caused by chemotherapy. Acupuncture can encourage the release of endorphins, natural painkillers which increase feelings of well-being.

SELF-HELP TECHNIQUES

- Exercise regularly to improve digestion and circulation
- Examine your skin, breasts or testicles regularly • If living with cancer, get as fit as your age and condition allows.·

Gentle qi gong is excellent exercise (*see page 125*)

PSYCHO-SOCIAL TREATMENT OPTIONS

CONVENTIONAL MEDICINE

A doctor may suggest one of the therapies below. Once considered "non-conventional", they are now widely recommended to cancer patients and their families.

COMPLEMENTARY THERAPIES

Psychotherapy & Counselling ❹
(*see pages 132–33*)
Therapy aims to promote a relaxed, optimistic outlook, which studies show seems to increase the activity of natural killer cells that destroy cancerous cells. One US study found that weekly support groups, coupled with relaxation and self-hypnosis, doubled the length of survival of women with advanced breast cancer.
Visualization ❷ (*see page 134*)
Visual imagery can be used to alleviate symptoms and promote healing, although there is no definite evidence that it affects the outcome. While in a state of relaxation, you will be asked to

focus on feeling stronger or better, or to picture the destruction of tumour cells. One technique, in which patients visualize remaining calm and relaxed at each step during various treatment procedures before chemotherapy can help to control nausea.
Hypnotherapy ❸ (*see page 134*)
Hypnosis can help people cope with pain and other symptoms of cancer, and with nausea and vomiting, which are side-effects of chemotherapy.
Art Therapy ❷ (*see page 137*)
Drawing, painting and sculpture, available in many cancer centres, can enable people to find a non-verbal way of expressing strong feelings, and encourage pleasure in creativity.

Art therapy can help people with cancer to express emotions

SELF-HELP TECHNIQUES

- Practise relaxation and breathing and stress-management techniques regularly (*see pages 170–71 and 168–69*)
- Encourage a sense of connectedness by developing a supportive network of friends and becoming involved in community life • Enjoy pleasurable and creative activities as much as possible (*see page 173*).

CHRONIC FATIGUE SYNDROME

Characterized by extreme physical and mental exhaustion, chronic fatigue syndrome (CFS) can last for years. Symptoms may begin suddenly, sometimes after a viral infection, and can be wide-ranging. They include: muscle aches, joint pains, headaches, depression, swollen glands, memory loss, inability to concentrate, recurring minor infections, digestive disorders and food intolerances. CFS is now accepted by doctors as a diagnosable disease, and experts believe it may be caused by a complex interaction between factors such as stress, viral infections, brain chemistry, psychological problems and social factors.

CASE STUDY

Georgia, 31, had suffered from CFS for three years following a flu-like viral infection. Medical tests had found nothing wrong so her doctor suggested she try complementary therapies. Adam, a naturopath, advised a calcium and magnesium bedtime drink to ensure a good night's sleep, and breathing techniques, massage and autogenic training to help her relax. Georgia cut back on milk and cheese after an exclusion diet suggested a mild dairy intolerance, and took *lactobacillus acidophilus* and b*ifidobacteria* supplements to normalize gut bacteria, as well as echinacea, goldenseal and barberry. Adam suggested Georgia visit a counsellor and, rather to her surprise, she found herself expressing intense grief over her mother's death three years previously. Georgia slowly improved and 12 months later was able to return to full-time work.

BIOCHEMICAL FACTORS

It is uncertain how viral infections are involved in CFS although they can clearly trigger it. However, high levels of antibodies to certain viruses, for example to the Epstein-Barr virus, which causes glandular fever, are sometimes found in CFS patients. These viruses can possibly interfere with the body's normal homeostatic processes (*see Glossary, pages 177–78*). Hormone imbalances, genetic susceptibility, vaccinations, environmental chemicals and other toxins have all been implicated, but not conclusively.

BIOCHEMICAL TRIGGERS

• Epstein-Barr virus (glandular fever) • Viral hepatitis, viral meningitis • Any viral infections if already run down

PSYCHO-SOCIAL FACTORS

CFS was thought to be more prevalent among educated, professional people, but research suggests it affects all social classes and cultures. A particular personality profile appears most susceptible: perfectionist, conscientious people who feel obliged to take on too much, come under a lot of stress, find it hard to relax and are inclined to become depressed and introverted. Many people with CFS rightly resist the idea that it is "all in the mind". Nevertheless, psychological elements seem to be involved, whether as causes or effects.

PSYCHO-SOCIAL TRIGGERS

• Stress and overwork • Anxiety • Depression • Perfectionism, inability to delegate and excessive conscientiousness • Pessimistic expectations about illness

STRUCTURAL FACTORS

Inactivity can lead to muscle cell abnormalities. There is little evidence that CFS is caused by a muscle disorder, but persistent muscle pain (*see page 60*) is often associated with it. Some sufferers have a form of low blood pressure in which the nervous system mistakenly tells the body to lower blood pressure when standing. Since CFS often makes people feel anxious, sufferers may overbreathe (hyperventilate). If persistent, this can intensify CFS symptoms.

STRUCTURAL TRIGGERS

• A form of low blood pressure (neurally mediated hypotension) • Excessive bed rest, lack of exercise and loss of fitness

BIOCHEMICAL TREATMENT OPTIONS

CONVENTIONAL MEDICINE
Prolonged fatigue is a symptom of other diseases, including anaemia, chronic infection, diabetes, cancer and autoimmune or thyroid disorders. Only when these have been ruled out should CFS be diagnosed, then a healthy diet and vitamin and mineral supplements might be suggested.

COMPLEMENTARY THERAPIES
Western Herbalism ❷ (*see page 127*)
A herbalist may advise echinacea and astragalus to improve immunity,

Siberian ginseng to increase resistance to stress, St John's wort to improve mood, and ginkgo to boost circulation.
Caution: Avoid ginseng in pregnancy or if you have high blood pressure. Do not take St. John's wort with conventional antidepressants.
Nutritional Therapies ❸
(*see pages 128–29*) A practitioner will consider dysbiosis (*see page 93*) and

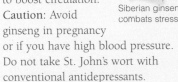
Siberian ginseng combats stress

food sensitivities. Exclusion diets, detoxification programmes and high-energy diets may be recommended. Suggested supplements might include evening primrose oil, coenzyme Q10, vitamins A (as betacarotene), C, E and B-complex, and probiotics (*see Glossary, page 177–78*). Injections of magnesium or vitamin B12 help some people.

SELF-HELP TECHNIQUES
• Eat a healthy balanced diet with fruit, vegetables and wholegrains
• Limit caffeine and alcohol.

STRUCTURAL TREATMENT OPTIONS

CONVENTIONAL MEDICINE
Doctors will advise gentle but gradually increasing levels of exercise. Avoiding all activity may be tempting but it can make CFS worse, as underused muscles lose power and bulk or tense up, causing even more aches and pains.

Gentle exercise can relieve debility and pain

COMPLEMENTARY THERAPIES
Massage ❷ (*see page 116*)
Massage can help to combat CFS by relieving muscular discomfort and tension and encouraging relaxation.
Acupuncture ❷ (*see page 125*)
Practitioners associate CFS with deficiencies of Kidney and Liver energy, defined by exhaustion and a low ability to cope with stress. Combining acupuncture with Chinese herbal remedies and *tuina* (Chinese massage therapy) may be even more effective than acupuncture alone.

Yoga, T'ai chi and Qigong ❷
(*see pages 123 and 125*)
All three therapies make use of gentle stretching movements and breathing techniques that focus the mind and may increase energy levels.

SELF-HELP TECHNIQUES
• Take daily exercise • Pace yourself, avoiding sudden exertion that might set you back • Allow time to relax, particularly after an infection: remember any improvement could take several months.

PSYCHO-SOCIAL TREATMENT OPTIONS

CONVENTIONAL MEDICINE
Antidepressants might not relieve CFS as such, but they can be highly effective at alleviating associated symptoms, such as anxiety, depression or disturbed sleep.

COMPLEMENTARY THERAPIES
Psychotherapy & Counselling ❹
(*see pages 132–33*)
Counselling can help those with CFS.

Patients need someone to acknowledge how frustrated and anxious the illness makes them feel. It can also help them re-evaluate lifestyle and career goals and manage stress more effectively. Several studies have found that cognitive behavioural therapy helps people with CFS. People who learn to view their illness in a more positive light improve more quickly than those who do not.

Relaxation & Breathing ❸
(*see pages 170–71*)
Diaphragmatic breathing improves circulation and helps counter a tight chest due to hyperventilation, which some people with CFS suffer from.

SELF-HELP TECHNIQUES
• Learn to pace yourself and allow time to relax • Practise stress-management techniques (*see pages 168–69*).

PERSISTENT PAIN

Short-term acute pain, which ranges from nagging discomfort to excruciating agony, is the body's warning signal that something specific is wrong, whether a cut finger or an acute appendicitis. Chronic, or persistent pain, is defined as pain lasting for six months or longer. It may have a clear source, such as chronic inflammation (a symptom of some types of arthritis), nerve damage from shingles infection, or tumour growth. However, very often there is no clear explanation, even after extensive examination and testing. This kind of persistent, incapacitating pain, which can affect work and relationships, is viewed by doctors not so much as a symptom, but as a disorder in its own right.

About 75 per cent of people who visit complementary practitioners do so because of various sorts of painful condition, and usually because they have found conventional treatments inadequate. Often the cause of pain is clear and, as in migraine, it comes and goes. However, persistent pain usually involves physical *and* psychological factors and so holistic approaches that take account of a person's lifestyle and attitudes may ultimately increase the chances of relief.

Certain manipulative therapies and acupuncture can stimulate the production of endorphins, the body's natural painkillers. Other techniques, such as hypnosis and relaxation, aim to help people improve their tolerance of pain. Increasingly these approaches are employed alongside conventional treatments in hospital pain clinics. Practitioners have found that a combination of methods within an overall pain-management regime often achieves good results.

BIOCHEMICAL FACTORS

SENSORY NERVE ENDINGS, or receptors, are highly concentrated in the skin. When stimulated by pressure, extreme temperature or prostaglandins (chemicals released by injured cells), they relay biochemical and electrical messages to the spinal cord and on to the brain, where they are interpreted as pain. According to the "gate control" theory, information carried on the limited number of pain nerve pathways to the brain passes through "gates". Various factors close the gates or hold them open. For example, endorphins (opiate chemicals that are the body's natural painkillers)

slot into receptors located in the brain, spinal cord and nerve endings, blocking pain impulses. How wide pain gates open and how much information reaches pain receptors, partly depends on the levels of endorphins in circulation at any one time.

BIOCHEMICAL TRIGGERS
• Substances produced in tissues that are inflamed (for example arthritic joints) or congested (for example chronically tense muscles) may open pain gates

See over for Biochemical Treatment Options

Realms of the Body (*see page 20*)

● BIOCHEMICAL
Body systems,
such as digestion.

● STRUCTURAL
Muscles, bones,
joints and nerves.

● PSYCHO-SOCIAL
Thoughts, feelings
and relationships.

STRUCTURAL FACTORS

ANY KIND OF STIMULATION along the path of a pain nerve will register at its tip. For example, if a finger pain nerve is pinched at the elbow, pain is felt shooting down to that finger. The pain in the finger is called "referred" pain. Continual pain can affect a pain pathway so that it becomes "facilitated", or more easily set off, long after the original problem has healed. This is thought to be due to "pain gates" remaining open somewhere in the brain and spinal cord, as a result of changes in the way the nervous system structures itself. Such changes may mean that people with chronic pain can be trapped in a vicious circle. They tend not to exercise, which would release painkilling endorphins, thus closing the "pain gates", and decreasing their sense of fear and depression. Lack of activity weakens, shortens and tenses muscles, creating further spasms and more pain.

STRUCTURAL TRIGGERS
• Injury or surgery • Disease, inflammation or damage to sensory nerves (neuropathy) • Lack of movement • Postural changes • Muscle tension anticipating pain

See over for Structural Treatment Options

PSYCHO-SOCIAL FACTORS

TOLERANCE OF PAIN varies between individuals and also changes according to mood. Pain seems worse and is more noticeable when people are depressed than when they feel well or happy or when they are distracted by something enjoyable. Emotional states can influence the levels of painkilling endorphins in the body, which explains why soldiers have been known to carry on in the heat of battle, unaware of devastating injury.

The way in which someone interprets pain, their ideas about its causes and consequences, as well as past experiences and associations with pain will all affect the person's ability to tolerate it. Psychological states can also directly affect areas of the body that have become accustomed to sensing pain. In one experiment, just thinking about painful experiences caused the back muscles of people who complained of chronic back pain to become tense. By anticipating the worst when an attack begins, migraine sufferers were found to stiffen their muscles and restrict blood flow, thereby making the attack longer and more severe. The tendency to breathe rapidly when made anxious by pain can lead to hyperventilation (abnormally rapid breathing). This in turn can engender a state of panic, making muscles more prone to spasm, and opening "pain gates" by altering the way nerve impulses are transmitted in the brain.

PSYCHO-SOCIAL TRIGGERS
• Stress • Fear • Depression • Previous experiences of pain • Attitudes towards pain • Anticipation of pain

See over for Psycho-social Treatment Options

CASE STUDY

Tania, an aromatherapist, treated Joan, 42, who suffered with persistent pain. Instead of gradually getting better in the normal way, a frozen shoulder had become weaker, with muscle wasting and skin changes. Eventually Joan felt pain from her head to finger tips on one side of her body. Her doctor prescribed a tiny dose of the antidepressant amitriptyline, which dulled the pain a little, and referred her to the hospital pain clinic. Here a doctor gave her some acupuncture, which helped, and suggested she saw an aromatherapist. Tania used various essential oils according to Joan's condition at the time of her appointment, but lavender and rosemary in particular. Joan found that aromatherapy really made a difference and continues to have aromatherapy every three or four weeks. Tania also gave her a relaxation tape which she found very helpful. She says can now live with the pain, even though she knows she may never be entirely free of it.

PERSISTENT PAIN

Key: Evidence of Efficacy (see page 182)

❶ ❷ ❸ ❹ ❺

least evidence ◄─────────────► most evidence

BIOCHEMICAL TREATMENT OPTIONS

CONVENTIONAL MEDICINE

Painkillers

Painkillers are very helpful for acute pain but can make persistent pain worse. Five out of six people with persistent pain take painkillers, but an estimated 70 per cent continue to feel severe pain. Painkillers include over-the-counter analgesics like paracetamol, non-steroidal anti-inflammatory agents (NSAIDS) such as aspirin and ibuprofen, muscle relaxants and opioids (see Drugs Glossary, page 179). The latter range from mild codeine to morphine and mimic endorphins by acting directly on the brain and spinal cord to alter perception of pain. Very severe pain arising from surgery or serious injury may be treated with injections of opioids, and morphine and diamorphine are prescribed to cancer patients. Small doses of amitriptyline, an antidepressant, seem to alter the pain experienced, and the anti-epileptic drug carbamazepine is useful for neuralgic pain. Research shows that cannabis may relieve muscle pain in multiple sclerosis but its prescription is a controversial issue in most countries.

COMPLEMENTARY THERAPIES

Western Herbalism ❸ (see page 127)
In clinical studies a cream containing capsaicin has proven useful in alleviating some persistent pain, and is now being used in some pain clinics. Relaxant herbs valerian and skullcap are often prescribed. St. John's wort is both antidepressant and anti-inflammatory and may be useful for persistent pain. **Caution**: do not take St. John's wort with antidepressants.

Nutritional Therapies ❸ (see page 128–29) Practitioners find that pain tolerance is decreased if levels of magnesium are low. Supplements might be suggested.

Skullcap

SELF-HELP TECHNIQUES
• Eat a well-balanced diet rich in fruit, vegetables and wholegrains.

STRUCTURAL TREATMENT OPTIONS

CONVENTIONAL MEDICINE
In many cases, no cause for the pain can be detected by medical diagnostic tests. Sometimes persistent pain may be helped by physiotherapy, massage, vibration and the application of heat and cold. Transcutaneous electrical nerve stimulation (TENS) in which impulses are applied to nerve endings, may be given to block pain signals. Local anaesthetics, or nerve blocks, can relieve pain for a time, and, in extreme cases, neurosurgery can sever nerve pathways, but it is irreversible and can cause loss of sensation and movement.

COMPLEMENTARY THERAPIES
Caution: consider structural therapies as a back-up to conventional pain-management, but not as a substitute.
Massage ❸ (see page 116)
Therapists will aim to alleviate pain by reducing the local muscle tension that can intensify pain sensations.

Aromatherapy ❷ (see page 117)
When used with massage, essential oils aid relaxation and may even help to stimulate the release of endorphins.
Osteopathy ❷ (see page 118) and
Chiropractic ❷ (see page 119)
Although manipulation alone is unlikely to cure persistent back pain, practitioners aim to relieve tension and improve posture (see also page 55).
Alexander Technique ❷ (see page 121)
Posture and chronic pain are closely linked. A practitioner will aim to improve posture to help relieve pain, especially neck and back pain.
Therapeutic Touch ❷ (see page 122)
A practitioner will pass her hands around the body to "balance energy fields".

Healing energy is directed to the patient

In a study, therapeutic touch reduced the pain of chronic tension headaches in 90 per cent of patients.
Hydrotherapy ❷ (see page 126)
Exercise in heated pools can ease chronic joint and muscle pain.
Acupuncture ❹ (see page 125)
Practitioners aim to restore the flow of qi by stimulating acupoints. Pain control is the one aspect of acupuncture that most conventional doctors accept; they believe it works by stimulating the release of endorphins and prostaglandin-suppressing corticosteroid hormones (see Glossary, page 177–78). It also appears to relieve pain from trigger points (see Glossary, page 177–78), a common cause of persistent pain.

SELF-HELP TECHNIQUES
• Exercise to prevent muscles from stiffening.

PSYCHO-SOCIAL TREATMENT OPTIONS

CONVENTIONAL MEDICINE

Pain is not measurable. Pain specialists ask about the level of pain the patient feels, what it is like and how it restricts activities. Their aim is to improve pain tolerance. Psychologists are important members of pain-management teams, as it is now recognized that the experience of pain affects the entire person, because of its impact on how he or she thinks, feels and behaves.

COMPLEMENTARY THERAPIES

Psychotherapy & Counselling ❹
(*see pages 132–33*)
Our thoughts, beliefs, moods and emotions can act as a kind of "volume control", capable of turning the pain experience up or down. Preoccupation with pain and anticipation and worry distorts thinking and raises the volume. Cognitive behavioural therapy can help replace these feelings with positive attitudes that encourage control.

Hypnotherapy ❸ (*see page 134*)
A hypnotherapist makes suggestions to help you alter pain perception and show that control of pain is possible. In studies, hypnotherapy has been effective in relieving pain from fibromyalgia (muscle pain) and cancer. Self-hypnosis can be very effective for pain, although its effects tend to wear off.

Visualizing a peaceful scene can help to distract the mind and reduce perception of pain

Visualization ❸ (*see page 134*)
Guided imagery is best used alongside other techniques and helps to distract from pain. You may be asked to picture yourself in peaceful, pain-free environments or to imagine your pain has a colour or shape and then visualize another colour or shape that will soothe or control it: a red-hot bar, for example, turning into ice-cream and melting away.

Biofeedback ❸ (*see page 136*)
Research shows that biofeedback may help 40–60 per cent of people with

headaches or pain in the jaw from temperomandibular joint disorder (TMJ), and can ease back pain and fibromyalgia.

Meditation ❹ (*see page 135*)
Learning to relax the body and calm and focus the mind may distract from pain. After four years of mindfulness meditation, 60 per cent of patients in a study reported in 1986 said their persistent pain had improved.

Relaxation & Breathing ❸
(*see pages 170–71*)
Muscle relaxation involving diaphragmatic breathing is probably one of the most effective ways to ease and control pain. It reduces muscle spasms and helps regulate brain chemicals, blood flow and other body processes involved in pain tolerance, and can relieve anxiety, distract from pain and encourage sleep.

Diaphragmatic breathing reduces tension

SELF-HELP TECHNIQUES

• To identify triggers, keep a diary to record episodes of pain and your emotional responses (*see page 147*)
• Practise relaxation and breathing (*see pages 170–71*): imagine a warm glow entering the painful area of your body as you slowly inhale, and pain and tension carried away as you exhale • Plan any outings ahead and pace yourself to avoid fatigue • Listen to music to keep your mind occupied.

While in a trance, the patient is told by the practitioner that he can control his pain

HIV & AIDS

Acquired immune-deficiency syndrome (AIDS) covers a range of diseases that usually follow infection with the human immunodeficiency virus (HIV). This destroys infection-fighting T-lymphocytes, leaving the body open to a range of potentially fatal diseases. HIV infection is symptomless at first and may take ten years or more to develop into AIDS. Although conventional treatment for HIV is effective, it is complicated, expensive and often causes unpleasant side-effects. Because complementary therapies emphasize health promotion and touch, they can integrate well into "packages" of care alongside high-tech treatments.

CASE STUDY

Stephen, a naturopath, treated Ian, 50, who was HIV-positive and had frequent infections and mouth ulcers despite conventional drug treatment. Stephen recommended a wholefood diet high in fresh vegetables and fruit, with supplements of vitamin B-complex and the antioxidants vitamin C, zinc and selenium. "I also suggested the amino acid lysine to balance out the arginine that was provoking his mouth ulcers, plus short courses of echinacea to boost his immune system." Ian was told to have a long daily soak in a hot bath to increase his internal temperature. Stephen felt this could "burn off the viral load" and stimulate the elimination of toxins. He also suggested Ian find an autogenics class to learn a deep-relaxation technique. After some months, Ian reported fewer infections and tests showed his disease-fighting white-cell count had improved.

BIOCHEMICAL FACTORS

HIV spreads through exchanges of body fluids and is usually transmitted sexually or by contaminated hyperdermic needles and transfusion of infected blood products. It takes between three weeks and three months from the time of infection to show in blood tests, and many people are unaware they are HIV-positive until AIDS develops. When HIV invades the T-lymphocyte cells, it changes their genetic codes so that they make more HIV genes instead of fighting the virus. As the level of healthy T-cells falls, HIV spreads and the immune system is weakened. Infections tend to become more frequent and recovery from them more difficult.

BIOCHEMICAL TRIGGERS
• Recurrent infections • Poor nutrition
• Drug abuse

PSYCHO-SOCIAL FACTORS

Some researchers believe that other factors, besides HIV, may contribute to the development of AIDS. Studies show that stress, isolation, pessimism and depression adversely affect the immune system. In HIV-positive people, this could *theoretically* promote a faster progression to AIDS. Coming to terms with being HIV-positive is unlikely to be easy and people are led to expect a bad prognosis. The ways in which HIV is contracted, and the stigma and alienation associated with it, add an extra socially isolating dimension. As attitudes towards HIV and AIDS change with increasing survival times, the notion that being HIV-positive is a literal and social death sentence should change.

STRUCTURAL FACTORS

Typical early symptoms of full-blown AIDS include swollen glands, fatigue, fever, weight loss, night sweats, shortness of breath, a dry cough and thrush. *Kaposi's sarcoma* (skin tumours that appear as purple blotches), diarrhoea and pneumonia are characteristic as the disease progresses. Finally, the brain may be affected by a form of encephalitis that causes dementia.

STRUCTURAL TRIGGERS
• Unprotected sexual intercourse • Sharing contaminated needles or syringes when injecting drugs • Contaminated blood products and blood transfusion • Mother-to-child infection in the uterus or during breast-feeding

Realms of the Body (see page 20)

● **BIOCHEMICAL**
Body systems,
such as digestion.

● **STRUCTURAL**
Muscles, bones,
joints and nerves.

● **PSYCHO-SOCIAL**
Thoughts, feelings
and relationships.

Key: Evidence of Efficacy (see page 182)

❶ ❷ ❸ ❹ ❺

least evidence ◄─────────► most evidence

BIOCHEMICAL TREATMENT OPTIONS

CONVENTIONAL MEDICINE
Antiviral, antibacterial and antifungal drugs are used to prevent or combat infection. Chemotherapy involves powerful drug combinations, including a protease inhibitor and AZT (see Drugs Glossary, page 179). These often have unpleasant side-effects, but may eliminate 99 per cent of detectable HIV.

COMPLEMENTARY THERAPIES
Herbalism ❸ (see pages 125 and 127)
Practitioners of Western and Chinese herbal medicine use a range of plant-based remedies to improve immunity

and inhibit HIV. These include artemisia, astragalus, bitter melon, echinacea, germanium-132 (a mineral found in ginseng, garlic and watercress) and prunellin, a compound isolated from Prunella vulgaris (self-heal). **Caution: only take remedies with professional supervision.**
Nutritional Therapies ❸
(see pages 128–29)
A diet high in immune-boosting nutrients and antioxidants will be recommended. Practitioners may

suggest selenium, zinc, bioflavonoids and vitamins A, C, E and B-complex to improve immunity.

SELF-HELP TECHNIQUES
• Take a good quality antioxidant supplement • Follow a balanced, ideally organic, diet with plenty of fruit, vegetables and wholegrains • Avoid caffeine, junk foods, alcohol, smoking and illegal drugs.

An antioxidant diet boosts the immune system

STRUCTURAL TREATMENT OPTIONS

CONVENTIONAL MEDICINE
A doctor will offer advice about preventing HIV transmission.

COMPLEMENTARY THERAPIES
Massage ❸ (see page 116)
An empathetic practitioner can provide the kind of caring touch that the stigma of AIDS denies many patients. Gentle

Regular massage can help support AIDS patients

massage can relieve emotional distress, and enhance body image and self-esteem as well as improve circulation, lymph drainage and muscle relaxation.
Acupuncture ❷ (see page 125)
A practitioner will aim to alleviate symptoms and boost immune functions by reducing stress.

SELF-HELP TECHNIQUES
• Practise safer sex by using a condom • Intravenous drug users should use only new, disposable

syringes; never share a needle or syringe or use an old one • Ensure that dentists, dental hygienists, acupuncturists, tattooists and body-piercers have adequate sterilization procedures and use disposable needles • If HIV-positive and pregnant, discuss delivery and breast-feeding with your doctor or midwife • Cover any cuts if you are HIV-positive • In developing countries, avoid blood transfusions and carry a sterile hypodermic needle and syringe in case an injection or infusion is necessary.

PSYCHO-SOCIAL TREATMENT OPTIONS

CONVENTIONAL MEDICINE
Counselling should be offered before HIV testing, and afterwards to support a person whose result is positive.

COMPLEMENTARY THERAPIES
Psychotherapy & Counselling ❸
(see pages 132–33)
Therapists can play an important role both before and after diagnosis, not

only for basic information and advice, but also because anger, fear, denial, grief and depression may have to be dealt with. Sharing experiences in a support group can help in a similar way. Research has shown that appropriate support combined with a positive attitude towards the disease can raise T-cell counts, reduce symptoms and possibly extend lifespan.

SELF-HELP TECHNIQUES
• Be aware of your physical, psychological and spiritual needs
• Find a stress-management technique (see pages 168–69) that works for you
• Supportive relationships with those who accept and understand the situation are important. Many people living with HIV say they find a new sense of meaning and purpose in life.

THE NATURAL MEDICINE CHEST

Medical emergencies require expert help and conventional treatment as soon as possible. Complementary remedies have no place in urgent life-threatening situations, but may be used to treat minor injuries. They have a role in relieving pain, calming the mind and helping the body heal itself. Keep emergency numbers by the telephone and a first aid kit (*see below*) in an easily accessible place, along with information on resuscitation and the recovery position, and on how to deal with choking, drowning, head and back injuries, heart attacks and stroke, bleeding, electric shock, burns, poisoning, shock, fractures and dislocations. Organizations such as the Red Cross and St. John Ambulance (*see pages 186–87*) provide information and first-aid courses to help you manage situations promptly and appropriately.

FIRST AID KIT

Conventional Items
• Painkillers: paracetamol, aspirin (also for heart attack) • Antiseptic wipes and cream • Plasters • Sterile dressings (various sizes) • Bandages: roller, triangular, tubular • Sterile eye pad
• Disposable gloves • Safety pins
• Scissors • Tweezers • Thermometer

Suggested Complementary Items
• Herbal remedies: aloe vera gel, arnica cream, echinacea tincture or capsules, pot marigold (calendula) cream, St. John's wort (hypericum) tincture or cream (with calendula), witch hazel, slippery elm powder, ginger and rosemary teas
• Essential oils: camphor, lavender, tea tree, rosemary, peppermint, eucalyptus
• Homeopathic remedies (store away from essential oils): *Arnica, Aconite, Calendula, Hypericum* and *Urtica urens*
• Bach Flower Rescue Remedy
• Nutritional: vitamin E capsules, garlic capsules

Slippery elm powder for indigestion

Vitamin E capsules to break for burns and stings

Paracetamol capsules ease pain

Tea tree oil disinfects minor cuts

Lavender oil to calm and relax

Valerian tablets for stress and insomnia

Garlic capsules help fight infection

Witch hazel soothes stings and abrasions

Plasters

Bandages

Thermometer

Arnica cream to relieve bruising and strains

Pot marigold cream speeds healing of minor wounds

Urtica urens cream heals minor burns

Bach Flower Rescue Remedy may aid recovery from shock

Eucalyptus oil for steam inhalation

FAINTING

First aid: If you feel faint, sit with your head between your knees or lie down. Put a person who has fainted on his side, loosen his collar and elevate his legs to 30cm (12in). Ensure the airways are clear, pull the jaw forward and upwards. When he recovers, give sips of water. Call emergency help if the patient does not regain consciousness within two minutes. See a doctor if fainting is frequent or accompanied by unusual symptoms such as chest pain.

Aromatherapy (*see page 117*)
A few drops of essential oils of rosemary, camphor or peppermint on a handkerchief held under the nose may stimulate the senses. (Pregnant women should not inhale essential oils.)

Western Herbalism (*see page 127*)
After regaining consciousness, sip ginger or rosemary tea.

Bach Flower Rescue Remedy (*see page 177*) For emotional shock, place four drops on the tongue.

MINOR CUTS & BRUISES

First aid Elevate the area and apply pressure for ten minutes to stop any bleeding. Clean the wound, apply antiseptic cream and cover with a dry dressing. Ice packs or cold compresses reduce bruising. Call a doctor if bleeding cannot be controlled, if the wound is deep and may need suturing, if it becomes infected, if debris cannot be removed, or if bruising persists. Check your tetanus status: a booster injection is recommended every 5–10 years.

Aromatherapy (*see page 117*) Essential oil of tea tree is antiseptic and antibacterial. It helps to relieve pain and aid healing. Add a few drops to the water when cleaning the wound.
Western Herbalism (*see page 127*) Pot marigold (calendula) is an antiseptic and astringent that helps

Tea tree helps to prevent infection

blood to clot. St. John's wort (hypericum) has astringent, sedative, anti-inflammatory and antimicrobial properties. Add tinctures of both to warm water to wash the wound, or apply as a cream. The two are often combined in commercial preparations.
Homeopathy (*see page 130*) *Arnica 6c* (granules and cream) is recommended for bruising; *Calendula 6c* to prevent infection and aid healing; *Hypericum 6c* if a graze is sensitive.

BITES & STINGS

First aid Remove an insect sting by scraping it out with a thumbnail or blunt blade rather than tweezers. Wash with soap and water and apply an ice pack. Elevate the area to reduce swelling. Some people are allergic to insect bites so call emergency medical help if the lips, tongue or throat swell, or if

breathing is difficult. Allergic reactions may lead to collapse or even to death.
Naturopathy (*see page 126*) Apply alkaline sodium bicarbonate to neutralize acidic bee and ant stings; and acidic vinegar to neutralize alkaline wasp and hornet stings. Vitamin E oil or 3–4 tablets of vitamin C crushed

with water applied to the sting may relieve pain and reduce swelling.
Western Herbalism (*see page 127*) Onions contain enzymes said to deactivate insect poisons; place half a raw onion on the sting for ten minutes. An application of distilled witch hazel is particularly good for mosquito bites.

SHOCK

Physiological shock may follow an injury. Blood supply to the brain and gut is depleted, causing nausea, rapid pulse, clammy skin and, in some cases, even loss of consciousness and death. Emotional shock may follow bad news.
First aid For physiological shock, call emergency medical help. Lie the patient

in the recovery position (*see Fainting*). Ensure the mouth and airways are clear and turn her head to one side. Keep the patient covered and warm. Do not give her food or drink.
Western Herbalism (*see pages 127*) For emotional shock only, teas and tinctures of chamomile, lemon balm

and skullcap are calming and restorative.
Homeopathy (*see page 130*) For emotional shock, take *Arnica 30c* or *Aconite 30c*.
Bach Flower Rescue Remedy (*see page 177*) Place four drops on the tongue, as required, for emotional shock.

BURNS

First-degree burns damage the skin's surface, causing redness, pain and swelling, and second-degree burns raise blisters. Third-degree burns destroy all the layers of the skin.

Hold the burned area under cold running water for 10 minutes

First aid Immerse first- and second-degree burns in cold water for ten minutes. Keep the area clean and cover blistered skin with a sterile, non-stick dressing. Drink plenty of fluids. Call emergency medical help at once for third-degree burns. Do not put water on these or try to remove clothing sticking to the skin, instead cover the

area with a clean dry cloth. Get medical advice if a burn is larger than the patient's hand, if it is still painful after 24 hours or if the patient is in shock or collapses.
Naturopathy (*see page 126*) Practitioners recommend frequent applications of vitamin E oil or cream, or pure aloe vera gel to speed healing.
Homeopathy (*see page 130*) *Urtica urens 6c* taken every 10 minutes is advised for first-degree burns.

chapter 3

Not all complementary therapies combine well with conventional medicine. Here we feature those that doctors who are interested in an integrated approach are likely to accept. Some, such as acupuncture, are

GLOSSARY OF THERAPIES

supported by clinically controlled trials, while others are backed by a body of anecdotal evidence. We explain each one's principles and treatments and indicate its effects on biochemical, structural and psycho-social health. Our aim is to help you decide whether a therapy would improve your health, either on its own or as an adjunct to conventional treatment.

STRUCTURAL THERAPIES

MASSAGE

BIOCHEMICAL EFFECTS

Changes brain and tissue chemistry by encouraging the relaxation response.

STRUCTURAL EFFECTS

Pressure and stretching movements encourage muscle relaxation and improve circulation. Relieves pain by reducing the congestion of inflamed tissue.

PSYCHO-SOCIAL EFFECTS

A range of feelings may be evoked, from sedation to arousal. The effect depends on the individual – one person may be reassured, another alarmed.

INTRODUCTION

Massage may be the oldest and simplest form of medical care. It has been used for thousands of years around the world to promote well-being, ease pain of all kinds and relieve anxiety. A number of studies support its healing role in lowering blood pressure, improving circulation, muscle tone and digestion and promoting relaxation. Massage is an integral part of most traditional health systems around the world, and different techniques have been developed and incorporated into various complementary therapies.

HISTORY OF MASSAGE

The ancient Egyptians, Greeks and Romans used massage for therapeutic purposes and it has long been an important part of Traditional Chinese Medicine and Ayurveda, the traditional Indian system of medicine. For many centuries in the West, massage had a dubious connection with sin and sensuality, but at the end of the 19th century, the Swedish gymnast, Per Henrik Ling, made therapeutic massage respectable again. Awareness of the healing value of massage is growing rapidly. In both the UK and the US, some physiotherapists and nurses are bringing

Massage can be used to promote relaxation and combat stress

massage therapy into conventional healthcare. Increasingly, massage is used in intensive-care units, for children, babies in incubators, the elderly, and patients with cancer, AIDS, heart attacks or stroke. It is available in some family practices, hospices, drug rehabilitation units and pain clinics.

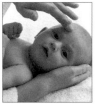
Babies can be soothed and calmed by gentle massage

A head massage can relieve headaches and aid relaxation

MAIN PRINCIPLES

Touch is our first sensual experience and remains, along with smell, the most immediate and evocative link between mind and body. The skin is the body's largest sensory organ, with millions of specialized receptors that react to heat, cold and pressure. Massage can stimulate the release of endorphins, the natural painkillers produced by the body. It also induces a feeling of comfort and well-being that can aid relaxation and reduce levels of stress hormones, such as cortisol and noradrenaline, that may otherwise eventually weaken the immune system.

Vigorous massage can directly affect body systems that govern heart-rate, blood pressure, respiration, digestion and pain. As local circulation improves, so does the supply of oxygen and nutrients to the skin and body tissues, and excess tissue fluids are flushed away. The lymphatic system can then work more effectively to eliminate waste products,

which cause pain and stiffness in joints and muscles. Massage also relieves tension in the muscles, improving mobility and flexibility.

Psychologically, massage can calm the mind and reduce anxiety so that people are better equipped to cope with stress. A heightened awareness of the way the mind and body affect one another may help some people take more control of their own well-being.

TREATMENT

Techniques vary according to which massage method is used, but usually include stroking, where the hands glide rhythmically; kneading, in which the hands alternately squeeze and release flesh; friction, when thumb pressure is steadily applied to a point for deep penetration; and hacking, when the sides of the hands deliver alternate short, sharp taps to the body. Massage techniques are used in other therapies, notably aromatherapy, reflexology, Rolfing, hellerwork and osteopathy.

MAIN USES

• Stress-related conditions, such as insomnia, irritable bowel syndrome and headaches • Muscle and joint disorders like arthritis, sports injuries and back pain • Pain relief • Anxiety • Depression • Digestive disorders.

PRECAUTIONS

Massage of the abdomen should be avoided in the first three months of pregnancy. Consult a doctor before having a massage if you have phlebitis, thrombosis, varicose veins, acute back pain, cancer, a personality disorder or psychotic illness. Do not massage bruises, fractures or skin infections. (See also page 21.)

AROMATHERAPY

BIOCHEMICAL EFFECTS

Some essential oils may have direct and specific effects on brain and tissue chemistry. The relaxation response is also encouraged.

STRUCTURAL EFFECTS

Massage with essential oils encourages muscle relaxation and improved circulation, aiding pain relief and tissue regeneration.

PSYCHO-SOCIAL EFFECTS

The smells of certain oils can evoke and become strongly associated with feelings and emotions such as relaxation and well-being.

INTRODUCTION

Essential oils have been used in many cultures throughout history for healing and relaxation. Aromatherapists believe that different oils have distinct therapeutic properties: certain oils are calming, others stimulating and uplifting. Molecules in the oils are absorbed into the bloodstream either through the skin during massage, or by inhalation of the scent through the nose and lungs. The biochemical effects on the body are not fully established, but smell is known to have psychological effects.

HISTORY OF AROMATHERAPY

Essential oils, for example myrrh, are mentioned in the Bible, and the ancient Egyptians used them to embalm the dead. In around AD 1000, the Persian physician Ali ibn-Sina developed the method of distillation used today. Oils such as sandalwood, cedar and rose have always been at the heart of perfumery, and highly aromatic oils like eucalyptus, mint and camphor have long been used medicinally.

Medical interest in essential oils was rekindled in the early 20th century by Réné-Maurice Gattefossé, a French chemist, who was impressed by the healing powers of lavender oil, which he had applied to a burn. Some French doctors now prescribe essential oils for oral use or in a vaporizer as substitutes for certain conventional medicines, for example to control infections.

MAIN PRINCIPLES

Plant roots, flowers, leaves and stalks (and trees, in some cases) are processed to extract the essential oils that form the basis of aromatherapy. Extraction is usually by means of distillation, in which the plant is heated by boiling or steaming until it vaporizes. Chemicals in the scents released by the oils are thought to act on the hypothalamus, the part of the brain influencing mood and the hormonal system. Studies on hospital patients show that massage with certain oils can relieve anxiety, for example. Some oils also have obvious chemical effects when applied to the skin: tea tree, for instance, is a proven antiseptic.

TREATMENT

Massage: essential oils are diluted in a vegetable-based carrier oil for massage. An aromatherapy massage is usually based on Swedish massage techniques that relieve tension and improve circulation.

An inhalation is an excellent way to treat respiratory problems

Inhalation: add 4 drops of essential oil to a bowl of steaming hot water. Cover your head with a towel, lean over the bowl with eyes closed and inhale for 10 minutes. Alternatively, moisten a tissue with 4–5 drops of oil, hold to your nose and inhale.
Bath: run a warm bath and add 6 drops of essential oil. Relax in the bath for at least 10 minutes.
Vaporizers: Place 2–3 drops of essential oil in the vaporizer bowl with a small amount of water, and light a candle beneath.

Essential oils can be burned in vaporizers to fill a room with scent

Essential oils are diluted in vegetable-based carrier oils for use in massage

OILS AND EFFECTS

Calming: bergamot, chamomile, clary sage, geranium, jasmine, lavender
Uplifting: clary sage, grapefruit, jasmine, lavender, neroli, rose, rosemary, ylang ylang
Stimulating: black pepper, cinnamon, eucalyptus, ginger, peppermint, pine
Antiseptic, antibacterial and antifungal: tea tree, lavender
Decongestant: eucalyptus, lavender, peppermint, pine.

MAIN USES

• Stress-related conditions, such as insomnia and headaches • Digestive disorders • Colds • During pregnancy and labour • Menstrual problems • Relaxation and well-being.

PRECAUTIONS

Take care when using inhalations if you have asthma or are prone to nosebleeds. Do not swallow oils, unless supervised by a medically qualified practitioner. Never apply neat essential oils to the skin (except lavender and tea tree). Keep essential oils away from naked flames and out of reach of children. Consult a qualified practitioner if you are pregnant, epileptic or have high blood pressure. *(See also page 21.)*

CHIROPRACTIC

BIOCHEMICAL EFFECTS

Improves tissue chemistry as pain and inflammatory substances and waste products disperse following local and general relaxation.

STRUCTURAL EFFECTS

Increases range of movement. Reduces muscle tension, which leads to better local circulation and reduction of swelling.

PSYCHO-SOCIAL EFFECTS

By diminishing pain, increases confidence to stretch and exercise; provides knowledge and skills to help prevent future problems.

INTRODUCTION

Chiropractors use manual techniques to diagnose and treat disorders of the spine, joints and muscles. They treat the body as a mechanism, with the spine as its key support, linking the brain to the body. When body systems work in harmony, self-healing processes can function efficiently, and chiropractors believe that any distortion of the spine affects other parts of the body and disturbs these processes. Chiropractic is practised in all developed countries, and a number of studies have demonstrated its effectiveness in relieving back pain.

HISTORY OF CHIROPRACTIC

Chiropractic – from the ancient Greek *cheiro*, or "hand", and *praktikos*, or "doing" – was developed in 1895 by Daniel D. Palmer, a Canadian. Palmer claimed to have restored the hearing of his office janitor, who had been deaf for 17 years following a back and neck injury. The therapy became popular throughout the West during the early part of the 20th century. Condemned as an "unscientific cult" by the American Medical Association (AMA) in the

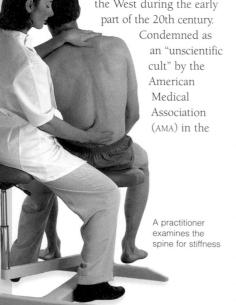

A practitioner examines the spine for stiffness

1960s (the AMA lost the ensuing legal battle in 1987), chiropractic has now gained widespread recognition and is available in the American, British and Australian healthcare systems.

Offshoots of chiropractic include Network Spinal Analysis, which concentrates on the interaction of the vertebrae and uses a sequence, or "network", of 12 adjustment techniques, and also McTimoney chiropractic, which focuses on the patient's whole body at each session and uses low impact, relatively uncomplicated forms of adjustment.

MAIN PRINCIPLES

The spinal cord carries nerves to the whole body. Chiropractors think that any distortion of the spinal column will have an effect on other parts of the body. Accordingly, the spine should be properly aligned in order for the body systems to work in harmony and to enable the body's self-healing processes to function efficiently. Any strain, damage or distortion of the spine is said to promote problems in the internal organs, glands and blood vessels, and can undermine the body's self-regulating and healing processes.

TREATMENT

A chiropractor takes a detailed medical history, asks questions about lifestyle and may carry out standard diagnostic tests, especially X-rays. She will manoeuvre you into various positions, using her hands to examine the functioning of your spinal column, joints and muscles. Treatment of stiff or "locked" joints usually takes place on a specially adjustable chiropractic couch, and consists of precise, controlled techniques known as "adjustments".

The practitioner begins by moving the joint as far as it will go (mobilization), then gives a rapid, measured thrust to move it slightly further. With any adjustment, there may be an audible but painless "click" in the joint, which

Patients often lie on a special couch for manipulation of the spine

is caused by the collapse of a tiny gas bubble created by the change in pressure when the joint is suddenly stretched. Initial chiropractic sessions last 30–60 minutes; subsequent ones may be less. The total number of sessions depends on how quickly the condition responds to treatment.

MAIN USES
- Spine and neck disorders
- Muscle, joint and postural problems
- Sports and repetitive strain injury
- Sciatica • Headaches and migraine
- Digestive disorders • Tinnitus
- Vertigo • Menstrual pain • Asthma.

PRECAUTIONS

If you have osteoporosis or inflammation, infections, tumours, circulatory problems or a recent fracture, practitioners may decide not to treat you using manipulation. However, chiropractors are skilled in other pain-relief methods. Avoid vigorous manipulation if you have badly prolapsed (slipped) discs. *(See also page 21.)*

OSTEOPATHY

BIOCHEMICAL EFFECTS

Improves tissue chemistry as pain and inflammatory substances and waste products disperse following local and general relaxation.

STRUCTURAL EFFECTS

Increases range of movement. Reduces muscle tension, which leads to better local circulation and reduction of swelling.

PSYCHO-SOCIAL EFFECTS

By diminishing pain, increases confidence to stretch and exercise; provides knowledge and skills to help prevent future problems.

INTRODUCTION

The relaxed, harmonious working order of muscles, bones and joints is held to be essential to well-being because it supports the optimum functioning of all body systems. Osteopaths use touch and manipulation to diagnose problems and to restore or improve mobility and balance. They employ a variety of therapeutic techniques, from soothing massage to high velocity mobilization of joints. Although more clinical research needs to be done, osteopathy is well established, and its role in treating acute back pain is generally accepted by conventional medicine.

HISTORY OF OSTEOPATHY

Osteopathy – from the Greek *osteon*, meaning "bone", and *pathos*, meaning "suffering" – was developed in the late 19th century by an American army doctor, Dr. Andrew Taylor Still, after his wife and three children died from meningitis. He sought ways to stimulate the body's self-healing powers and founded the American School of Osteopathy in 1892. In 1917, his pupil, Dr. John Martin Littlejohn, founded the British School of Osteopathy. Despite early opposition from conventional medicine, osteopaths were licensed in the US in 1972 and the first British state register of osteopaths opened in 1999.

MAIN PRINCIPLES

Posture and the way we move express how we feel. Physical and emotional stress, injury and poor posture can all adversely affect the musculo-skeletal system, which supports and protects the body organs. Pain creates muscle tension, which in turn creates more pain. Osteopaths ease muscle tension and improve joint mobility in order to restore the body's ability to heal itself. While chiropractors have tended to

concentrate on joint manipulation, osteopaths traditionally focus more on "soft tissue" treatment, but today this distinction is often blurred. Practitioners are as concerned about what has triggered and is maintaining the musculo-skeletal dysfunction as with the problem itself, and will look for any psychological, occupational or lifestyle factors.

Cranial osteopathy, developed by an American osteopath, Dr. William Garner Sutherland, in the 1930s, uses delicate touch around the skull and lower spine to ease the tension believed to disturb the flow of cerebrospinal fluid. Cranial osteopathy is claimed to be particularly successful for babies and young children and in treating problems following trauma and injury.

Practitioners believe manipulation of the cranial bones improves the flow of cerebrospinal fluid

TREATMENT

After taking a thorough medical history, an osteopath asks about lifestyle and emotional health, carries out standard medical tests and examines posture and movements for stresses and strains.

Treatment is tailored to individual needs. It may consist simply of massage

The osteopath carefully feels each vertebra to detect problems

and stretching techniques, or it may involve manipulation of the joints. The practitioner may also position you in such a way that tension from areas of strain or injury is released spontaneously. Another type of treatment, known as "muscle energy techniques", involves working against resistance provided by the practitioner in order to release tension in the muscles. One visit may be enough, but three to six sessions are average, depending on your problem and state of health.

MAIN USES

- Spine and neck disorders
- Muscle, joint and postural problems
- Sports and repetitive strain injury
- Sciatica • Headaches and migraine
- Digestive disorders • Tinnitus
- Vertigo • Menstrual pain • Asthma.

PRECAUTIONS

If you have osteoporosis or inflammation, infections, tumours, circulatory problems or a recent fracture, practitioners may decide not to treat you using manipulation. Avoid vigorous manipulation if you have badly prolapsed (slipped) discs.
(See also page 21.)

REFLEXOLOGY

BIOCHEMICAL EFFECTS

Changes brain and tissue chemistry by encouraging the relaxation response.

STRUCTURAL EFFECTS

Encourages muscle relaxation and improves circulation; some evidence that it can relieve pain.

PSYCHO-SOCIAL EFFECTS

Practitioners aim to address underlying stress-related factors that trigger or prolong health problems.

INTRODUCTION

Reflexologists believe that the feet and hands mirror the body, and stimulation of specific reflex points on them can affect associated organs and systems. The big toe, for example, reflects the head and brain. A combination of massage, pressure and pinching over all parts of the feet (or in some cases, the hands) can produce deep relaxation. Consequently, despite lack of evidence, reflexology is one of the most popular complementary therapies and is even offered in hospital cancer centres, pain clinics and special-care baby units.

HISTORY OF REFLEXOLOGY

Foot massage dates back to ancient Egypt and China, but reflexology as practised today was introduced in 1915 by Dr. William H. Fitzgerald, a US ear, nose and throat specialist. Known at the time as "zone therapy", it was based on the theory that energy flows in vertical zones through the body, from the feet to the head, so that pressure

applied to a reflex point on the foot can affect all the organs, glands, bones and muscles in that zone. In the 1930s, Eunice Ingham, a US physiotherapist, mapped the reflex points on the feet and developed techniques for stimulation. Her map is still widely used today. One of Ingham's students, Doreen Bayley, introduced reflexology to the UK in the 1960s and its popularity spread rapidly.

Practitioners stimulate reflex points on the feet

MAIN PRINCIPLES

Zones on the left side of the body are said to correspond to reflex points on the left foot and hand, and those on the right to the right foot and hand. Practitioners believe that granular or crystalline accumulations of waste products, possibly uric acid and calcium, collect around reflex points. The more tender the points to the touch, the greater the "imbalance" in the body. The practitioner tries to break down

these deposits to free "energy flow" along the zones and stimulate circulation to flush away "toxins". Mental health is also said to be reflected in the feet, so reflexology is used to treat emotional as well as physical problems.

Although similar in theory to Traditional Chinese Medicine's concept of meridians (*see page 124*), reflexology claims to be a separate approach. Doctors concede that pressure on the 7,200 nerve endings in each foot seems to promote feelings of deep relaxation, which may induce useful, non-specific healing effects.

TREATMENT

Most practitioners prefer to work on the foot, so expect to take off your footwear and relax in a reclining chair with your feet raised. The practitioner stimulates the reflex points by massaging each foot with her knuckles and thumbs, observing areas of pain or tenderness. When worked on intensely, even extremely sensitive areas usually become less so. Most people find the treatment relaxing, but occasionally it is followed by a worsening of symptoms, believed to indicate that the body's natural healing processes are removing "toxins".

MAIN USES
- Stress-related conditions
- Insomnia • Back pain.

PRECAUTIONS

Avoid in the first three months of pregnancy and check with your doctor before treatment if you have a long-term health problem. Tell the practitioner if you are taking medication. (*See also page 21.*)

REFLEX POINTS ON THE SOLES OF THE FEET

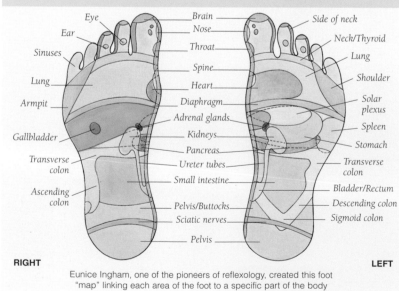

Eye, Ear, Sinuses, Lung, Armpit, Gallbladder, Transverse colon, Ascending colon — Brain, Nose, Throat, Spine, Heart, Diaphragm, Adrenal glands, Kidneys, Pancreas, Ureter tubes, Small intestine, Pelvis/Buttocks, Sciatic nerves, Pelvis — Side of neck, Neck/Thyroid, Lung, Shoulder, Solar plexus, Spleen, Stomach, Transverse colon, Bladder/Rectum, Descending colon, Sigmoid colon

RIGHT   **LEFT**

Eunice Ingham, one of the pioneers of reflexology, created this foot "map" linking each area of the foot to a specific part of the body

THE ALEXANDER TECHNIQUE

BIOCHEMICAL EFFECTS

Changes brain and tissue chemistry by encouraging the relaxation response.

STRUCTURAL EFFECTS

Improves posture and co-ordination; promotes efficient body movement; encourages the relaxation response; may improve circulation to internal organs.

PSYCHO-SOCIAL EFFECTS

Promotes an attitude of active self-care; also improves self-image and esteem.

INTRODUCTION

Years of poor posture, hunching and slumping, have a detrimental effect on the working of the joints and muscles. The Alexander technique helps people to stand and move more effectively, so that stresses on the body can be eased and each body system is able to function more efficiently. As the body works in a more relaxed way, the ability to cope with stress improves. Conventional medicine generally supports the use of the Alexander technique to treat persistent back pain and stress, and it has a wide international following. Many actors, dancers, opera singers and musicians say that practising the Alexander technique improves their performance.

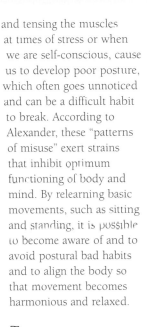

The practitioner corrects posture and shows how to stand in a way that exerts minimum strain on the body

HISTORY OF THE ALEXANDER TECHNIQUE

In the late 19th century, Frederick Matthias Alexander, an Australian actor, discovered that he could prevent his voice becoming strained by improving his posture and relaxing his muscles, especially those of the throat. He moved to London in 1904 and developed his techniques, establishing strong links with educationalists and the performing arts. In 1931 he set up a training school for teachers in London. Recent studies at Columbia University, New York, and Kingston Hospital, London, indicate that the technique can help relieve chronic back pain and improve breathing.

MAIN PRINCIPLES

Young children possess a natural grace, but years of sitting and standing in awkward positions, lifting incorrectly and tensing the muscles at times of stress or when we are self-conscious, cause us to develop poor posture, which often goes unnoticed and can be a difficult habit to break. According to Alexander, these "patterns of misuse" exert strains that inhibit optimum functioning of body and mind. By relearning basic movements, such as sitting and standing, it is possible to become aware of and to avoid postural bad habits and to align the body so that movement becomes harmonious and relaxed.

TREATMENT

The principles of the Alexander technique are best learned on a one-to-one basis from a teacher in a series of between 15 and 30 lessons. The teacher usually begins the course by making gentle adjustments as you lie flat on a couch; she will then help you to your feet. The object of this exercise is to give you personal experience of "optimum body use". Subsequent classes focus on all kinds of everyday movements – sitting, standing, walking, lifting, even ironing – while the teacher adjusts your

movements and teaches you how to get the fullest use from your muscles with minimum effort. She will aim to make you aware of your posture, both at rest and in activity. These so-called "thought in activity" exercises concentrate on the sensation of sitting or standing without strain, following Frederick Alexander's directions: "Free the neck; let the neck go forward and upward; let the back lengthen and widen." Postural changes can be difficult to make at first, but with practice at home, relaxed and effective body use can become second nature.

MAIN USES

- Back pain and other musculo-skeletal problems • Stress and anxiety
- Headaches • Stress-related gastro-intestinal disorders • Muscle strain caused by repetitive movement
- Postural pain during pregnancy.

To help this musician, the practitioner works on the head-neck-spine alignment, and the position of the wrists and elbows

PRECAUTIONS

Always check with a doctor before consulting a therapist if you have any medical condition or symptom of illness. (See also page 21.)

HEALING

BIOCHEMICAL EFFECTS

Changes brain and tissue chemistry by encouraging the relaxation response.

STRUCTURAL EFFECTS

Can encourage muscle relaxation and improve circulation; there is some evidence that it relieves pain and helps tissue regenerate.

PSYCHO-SOCIAL EFFECTS

A therapeutic relationship has potentially powerful effects and may change self-perception and improve tolerance of pain and the ability to cope.

INTRODUCTION

Healers claim to use an indefinable benign healing energy that can activate a patient's natural self-healing processes. They do this by laying on hands or by offering healing at a distance through the medium of thought or prayer. Explanations for the source of healing powers vary, but most healers are ordinary people who see themselves as "channels" for some kind of healing energy. Although medical science can find no explanation, many doctors concede that healing can help people, and some healers practise in hospitals and medical centres.

HISTORY OF HEALING

Most cultures have a tradition of laying on of hands and prayers or ceremonies for recovery from illness. Usually they are linked to religion or to ritual magic. Christian healing shrines such as Lourdes draw thousands of pilgrims, and some churches have revived healing services. Healing organizations exist in the UK and Canada, and there is active interest in the US, Australia and New Zealand. Dr. Daniel Benor, a US psychiatrist and healer, published an extensive review of healing in 1993 claiming there were enough positive results to warrant serious consideration and further research.

MAIN PRINCIPLES

The nature of the "healing energy" thought to be at work varies according to the healer's beliefs, though many believe in a divine or "higher" source. Some claim to work with the human aura, perceived as layers

of colour or radiance that surround each person. *Spiritualist* healers say that a spirit of the dead assists them, whereas *spiritual* healers regard themselves as conductors of supernatural healing power.

TREATMENT

After asking questions about your lifestyle and complaint, a typical healer will take time to "centre" himself, relaxing and focusing his mind before mentally "attuning" to you. Most healers regard their hands as conduits of healing power and place them on or slightly above the surface of the body. By touching you lightly or making sweeping movements, healers are able to assess any "imbalances" in your "energy field" and can then concentrate on allowing healing energy to flow into your body.

THERAPEUTIC TOUCH

Practitioners of this type of healing believe people are a unique part of a universal energy field. They use their hands in a series of sweeping movements to re-balance disruptions in the flow of "energy" with the intention of stimulating natural processes of self-healing. Therapeutic Touch (TT) was developed in the 1960s by Dr. Dolores Krieger, Professor of Nursing at New York University, as a way of introducing healing techniques into the patient-nurse relationship. It is now widely practised by nurses in US hospitals and is also becoming increasingly popular in the UK and Australia. Research

The TT practitioner passes her hands over the body without making contact

suggests it can relieve anxiety, speed wound healing, decrease post-operative pain and reduce the effects of stress on the immune system.

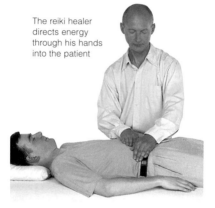

The reiki healer directs energy through his hands into the patient

REIKI

Founded in the late 19th century by Dr. Mikao Usui, a Japanese theologian, and allegedly based on ancient Buddhist healing rituals, reiki is one of the fastest-growing healing therapies. The name is derived from the Japanese *rei* (universal) and *ki* (life energy). Practitioners claim to channel "reiki energy" to areas of need, not only in their patients but also in themselves. Reiki is said to work at an atomic level, making the body's molecules vibrate so intensely that "energy blockages" are dissolved.

MAIN USES

• As an adjunct to conventional medicine in serious, chronic and painful conditions of all kinds • Stress-related problems • Wound-healing.

PRECAUTIONS

Do not consult a healer who demands your unquestioning faith in order for treatment to succeed. Healers should never offer a diagnosis or promise a cure. *(See also page 21.)*

YOGA

BIOCHEMICAL EFFECTS

Changes brain and tissue chemistry by encouraging the relaxation response.

STRUCTURAL EFFECTS

Reduces tension in involuntary muscles (e.g. in gut and blood vessels) and in voluntary muscles (e.g. in back and neck); improves circulation to internal organs.

PSYCHO-SOCIAL EFFECTS

Changes mood, attitude, self-image; increases the level of active self-care; improves pain tolerance and coping skills; aids mental relaxation.

INTRODUCTION

Yoga, a regime of mental and physical training, is part of Ayurveda, the traditional Indian health system, and was originally a preparation for mental and spiritual development. Various forms are now popular in developed countries, and are often initially valued for their ability to increase suppleness and relieve stress. Most doctors accept the benefits of yoga, and studies have shown that it may improve asthma, arthritis and heart conditions. Interest is now growing in yoga therapy, which uses specific postures to treat particular conditions.

HISTORY OF YOGA

Yoga (the word is derived from the Sanskrit for "union") was traditionally practised by Hindu ascetics, or yogis. Originating 5,000 years ago, the system was introduced to the West in the 19th century and became very popular in

the 1960s, along with other Eastern disciplines. It is also used as part of some US healthcare programmes, notably Dr. Dean Ornish's regime to treat heart disease (*see page 50*).

MAIN PRINCIPLES

Yoga is a philosophy concerned with life and how it should be lived. Yogic principles can be applied to all aspects of life. At its simplest, it is a system for healthy eating habits and personal hygiene, but it progresses through physical postures and breathing techniques to meditation, whose goal is the experience of clear consciousness. There are many types of yoga, the most popular in developed countries being hatha yoga. *Hatha* means balance of mind and body: a calm mind is achieved through regular breathing and a relaxed body. It uses *asanas*, which are postures designed to stretch and

strengthen muscles and stimulate nerve centres and organs, and *pranayama*, which involves breathing techniques to influence the flow of *prana*, or life energy, in the body in preparation for meditation. Popular variants of hatha yoga are Iyengar yoga and the fast-moving ashtanga, or "power yoga".

TREATMENT

People of all ages can benefit from yoga, which is probably best learned in a class. Most classes last 1–1½ hours. After gentle warm-up exercises, the yoga teacher shows the correct way to perform *asanas*, which the class then practises. You should never be tempted to push yourself too far or be competitive. If practising yoga for medical reasons, always consult a teacher trained in yoga therapy.

MAIN USES

- Stress, anxiety, fatigue, moderate depression • Headaches, migraine
- Circulatory disorders • Asthma, bronchitis • Irritable bowel syndrome
- Persistent back problems
- Menstrual problems • To improve mobility • General well-being.

PHYSICAL BENEFITS OF YOGA

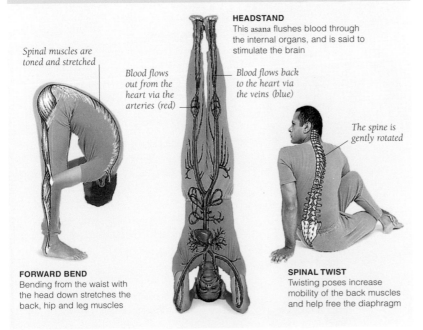

Spinal muscles are toned and stretched

FORWARD BEND
Bending from the waist with the head down stretches the back, hip and leg muscles

HEADSTAND
This asana flushes blood through the internal organs, and is said to stimulate the brain

Blood flows out from the heart via the arteries (red)

Blood flows back to the heart via the veins (blue)

The spine is gently rotated

SPINAL TWIST
Twisting poses increase mobility of the back muscles and help free the diaphragm

---

PRECAUTIONS

Take care if you are practising yoga during pregnancy or menstruation. The Headstand, and some other asanas, should be avoided during pregnancy; some experts also advise against this asana during your monthly period.

Consult a yoga therapist if you have neck or back problems, high blood pressure, circulatory problems, heart disease or disorders of the brain, ears or eyes, as some asanas are not advised. *(See also page 21.)*

TRADITIONAL CHINESE MEDICINE

BIOCHEMICAL EFFECTS

Plant substances, nutritional approaches and insertion of needles into acupoints alter biochemical processes and improve organ function.

STRUCTURAL EFFECTS

Acupuncture, tuina and exercise regimes like t'ai chi and qigong can improve range of movement and lessen muscle tension.

PSYCHO-SOCIAL EFFECTS

Practitioners take into account and treat stress-related factors that trigger or maintain health problems; improved well-being brings psychological benefits.

INTRODUCTION

This ancient system of healing views symptoms as signs of "disharmony" (rather than a named disease) and attributes illness to a disruption in the flow of *qi*, or "life energy". Acupressure, acupuncture, herbalism, diet, qigong, t'ai chi, tuina and shiatsu are different aspects of Traditional Chinese Medicine (TCM), whose aim is to harmonize the flow of *qi*. Although Western doctors are sceptical about the concept of *qi*, the proven effectiveness of acupuncture in treating some conditions makes it one of the most widely accepted complementary therapies.

HISTORY OF TCM

There is evidence that acupuncture was practised in China some 3,500 years ago. The *Nei Jing* (*The Yellow Emperor's Classic of Internal Medicine*), which dates from between 200BC and AD100, is one of the earliest documents to explain the principles of balance, harmony and moderation underpinning TCM.

After its introduction to China in the 16th century, Western medicine threatened to supersede TCM. However, the establishment of the People's Republic in 1949 led to a revival of ancient medicine. In China, TCM is now taught at universities and practised in hospitals alongside Western medicine.

New York Times journalist James Reston had an emergency appendectomy while visiting China in 1972. His account of how acupuncture relieved his post-operative pain re-awakened Western medical interest. Since then, acupuncture has been widely studied, and "medical acupuncture" is now often used to help relieve pain and nausea in hospitals and pain clinics.

MAIN PRINCIPLES

TCM is about the body's processes rather than its physical anatomy. Practitioners view the body as an integrated whole, linked by energy and information transfer known as the flow of *qi*. According to TCM, *qi* moves along a network of channels, called meridians, that run through the body. Twelve meridians are named after the main internal organs through which they pass. Two further meridians, the Conception and Governing channels,

MERIDIANS AND ACUPOINTS

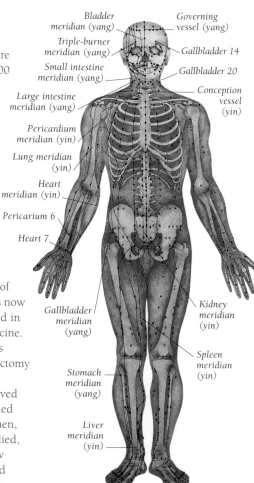

Bladder meridian (yang)
Triple-burner meridian (yang)
Small intestine meridian (yang)
Large intestine meridian (yang)
Pericardium meridian (yin)
Lung meridian (yin)
Heart meridian (yin)
Pericarium 6
Heart 7
Gallbladder meridian (yang)
Stomach meridian (yang)
Liver meridian (yin)
Governing vessel (yang)
Gallbladder 14
Gallbladder 20
Conception vessel (yin)
Kidney meridian (yin)
Spleen meridian (yin)

control the 12. Disruption of *qi* on a meridian can cause a problem at any point along it, thus a disorder in the Stomach meridian, which passes through the upper gums, could cause toothache. *Qi* moves between *yin* and *yang* – opposite but complementary tendencies in the body – either to the centre (*yin*), or outwards to the surface (*yang*). Various factors, including diet, the strength of the organs, environment, temperament and stress levels, will determine the balance between *yin* and *yang*. If the balance is disturbed, *yin* conditions ("hardenings", such as osteoarthritis) or *yang* conditions (inflammations) will ensue.

Yin and yang, opposites in harmony

Fire, earth, metal, water and wood are the five elements (or "processes") considered in TCM to be inherent in all things in the universe, including the body's organs. Each element has a *yin* organ and a *yang* organ, as well as associated tastes and emotions. Qualities common to one particular element are said to support one another. So, to treat a disorder of the Spleen, which is a *yin* organ of the element earth, a Chinese doctor might prescribe sweet-tasting herbs, which are associated with earth. The 12 organs in TCM might be better translated as 12 "functions", the Chinese concept of an organ being broader and less literal than its Western equivalent. The organs are nourished by "vital substances", namely *qi*, blood, body fluids, and *jing*, or "Kidney essence", which is a hereditary factor governing growth, sexuality and constitutional strength.

TREATMENT

A TCM practitioner uses four methods of diagnosis to assess a patient's condition: asking, observing (this involves looking at the tongue, noting the tone of the skin and the way a patient moves), listening and smelling, and touching. The latter includes pulse-taking: checking the rhythm and strength of all 12 meridian pulses (six on each wrist). The practitioner looks for "'patterns of disharmony", for example, *yin* or *yang* excess or deficiency in particular organs, and will then suggest a programme of herbal remedies, acupuncture and other treatments.

Acupuncture

Main uses: pain relief, anaesthesia; arthritis and other musculo-skeletal problems; addictions; asthma, hay

The practitioner inserts a fine needle at an acupoint on the Kidney meridian to stimulate the flow of *qi*. The procedure is usually painless

fever; depression, anxiety; migraine, nausea and other digestive disorders; high blood pressure; women's health.
Treatment: there are about 365 acupoints along the meridians at which *qi* is concentrated and enters and leaves the body. The acupuncturist inserts fine stainless steel needles to a depth of about 4–25mm at these sites to stimulate or suppress the flow of *qi*. Needles may be left in place for a few minutes or as long as an hour. Sometimes a practitioner will burn moxa, a herb, over the acupoint to create a stimulating heat.

Acupressure and Tuina

Acupressure is acupuncture without needles. It involves the use of finger and thumb pressure to stimulate acupoints. Tuina, a vigorous form of body massage, is popular in China. Both acupressure and tuina provide useful self-help techniques for many common ailments.

Shiatsu

Main uses: musculo-skeletal problems such as arthritis; stress, insomnia and fatigue; headaches and migraine; asthma; digestive disorders; menstrual problems; circulatory disorders; health promotion.
Treatment: developed early in the 20th

century from *anma*, the Japanese form of tuina, the modern therapy of shiatsu (the word means "finger pressure"), has its roots in TCM. Practitioners use fingers, thumbs, elbows, knees and even feet in a combination of massage techniques that apply pressure to acupoints (*tsubos* in Japanese) in order to stimulate and influence the flow of *qi*.

Qigong and T'ai Chi

Main uses: fatigue; stress-related conditions; high blood pressure, heart disease; problems of ageing; musculo-skeletal pain and stiffness; to promote well-being.
Treatment: translating as "energy work", qigong is an ancient system of movement, breathing techniques and meditation, designed to develop and improve the circulation of *qi* around the body. T'ai chi is a dynamic form of qigong and is sometimes described as "meditation in motion" because of its sequences of slow, graceful movements.

Chinese Herbalism

Main uses: eczema and other skin conditions; migraine; menstrual disorders; fatigue, chronic fatigue syndrome; digestive disorders including irritable bowel syndrome (IBS).
Treatment: remedies are used to rebalance organ functions. Each herb is classified as sweet, sour, bitter, pungent or salty, as well as "hot" or "cold". Herbs are usually prescribed in a mixture, which is adapted to suit the individual. They are generally taken as

Bai Xian Pi (dittany)

Bamboo leaf

Huang Bai (phellodendron)

Yin Yin Hua (honeysuckle)

Di Huang (rehemannia)

Mu Dan Pi (peony)

A herbal remedy to treat eczema might include a combination of the above herbs

boiled-up herbal teas, but may also be prescribed as pills, powders, pastes, ointments, creams and lotions. Western studies show that Chinese herbs can successfully treat eczema and IBS, but many doctors in the West are concerned about the possible side-effects of certain remedies.

MAIN USES

• As a complete medical system, TCM claims that it can contribute to the treatment of every medical problem. Chinese hospitals use it most for conditions not easily treated with Western drugs, for example migraine, skin problems and irritable bowel syndrome.

Qigong exercises are designed to develop and improve the circulation of *qi*

PRECAUTIONS

Always consult a qualified practitioner (*see page 180*).

Ensure that your practitioner uses disposable needles. Sterilization is not foolproof, and contaminated needles can spread hepatitis and HIV.

Tell your practitioner if you are pregnant, and do not take Chinese herbs without expert advice.

TCM herbs have been known to cause liver damage. If you have had hepatitis or other liver diseases you may be at greater risk than other people.

Avoid alcohol, large meals, hot baths or showers and strenuous exercise immediately before or after any type of TCM treatment.

Take care if driving or working immediately after acupuncture, as you may feel tired and lack concentration. (*See also page 21.*)

NATUROPATHY

BIOCHEMICAL EFFECTS

Plant substances and nutritional therapies alter biochemical processes and improve organ function.

STRUCTURAL EFFECTS

Makes use of exercise regimes, relaxation techniques and bodywork therapies to improve overall movement and support circulatory function.

PSYCHO-SOCIAL EFFECTS

Practitioners take into account and treat stress-related factors that trigger or maintain health problems.

INTRODUCTION

Naturopaths believe that the body's "vital force" strives to achieve a state of equilibrium in which all systems, especially digestion and excretion, function in harmony. An unhealthy lifestyle can disturb organ function and weaken this vital force. Practitioners use natural methods, such as wholefoods, medicinal herbs and exercise, to stimulate the body's self-healing processes. Naturopathy is practised widely in developed countries, and many of its basic ideas have been adopted – often unknowingly – by conventional medicine.

HISTORY OF NATUROPATHY

Naturopathy grew out of the "nature cure" practised in 19th-century Austrian and German health spas, and was introduced to the US by a German, Benedict Lust, who founded the American School of Naturopathy in 1896. John Kellogg famously used natural therapies at his sanatorium in Battle Creek, Michigan. Advances in surgery and pharmaceuticals eventually overshadowed natural methods, however, and it was not until the 1960s that interest in naturopathy revived. In some US states, naturopaths are now recognized as family practitioners and Germany has several thousand state-licensed naturopaths (*Heilpraktiker*).

MAIN PRINCIPLES

An unhealthy lifestyle – inadequate diet, lack of sleep, exercise or fresh air, emotional or physical stress, and environmental pollution – can allow waste products and toxins to build up in the body and upset natural self-regulation. This overloads the immune system and weakens organ function so that the body becomes susceptible to illness. Naturopaths believe that symptoms are signs that the body's self-healing processes are at work, and that chronic and serious diseases are the result of accumulated toxins. Rather than treating symptoms as such, they aim to build up resilience and improve elimination processes.

Herbs support the body's healing powers

TREATMENT

At the initial visit, the naturopath builds a detailed picture of the patient. As well as routine medical tests (for example testing blood pressure and taking blood and urine samples), he may carry out less conventional tests, such as analysing samples of blood, sweat or hair for evidence of nutritional deficiencies. If the condition is caused by an accumulation of waste products, treatment may include fasting and other detoxifying measures. Nutritional supplements and dietary changes may be suggested if digestion is poor. Treatments vary according to the practitioner, who is often multi-skilled, but generally include nutritional therapy, acupuncture, hydrotherapy, manipulation, massage or physiotherapy, herbal medicine, homeopathy, reflexology and yoga. Between four and 30 weekly sessions may be needed depending on the condition.

Plenty of fruit and vegetables help the body fight disease

HYDROTHERAPY

All forms of water therapy can help cleanse, revitalize and restore health. Hydrotherapy improves the circulation, which in turn feeds and decongests tissues, helps flush waste products from the body and can even boost the immune system. Traditionally, treatment involves baths, steam rooms and compresses, but whirlpools and water jets are now included. Cold water constricts surface blood vessels, sending blood to nourish internal organs, and relieves external inflammation. Hot water dilates surface blood vessels, reducing blood pressure and increasing blood flow to the skin.

Warm baths help relieve arthritic conditions

MAIN USES

• Arthritis • Allergic conditions, such as asthma • Fatigue • High blood pressure, hardening of the arteries • PMS • Gastrointestinal problems • Skin conditions.

PRECAUTIONS

Do not fast or follow a restricted diet without supervision of a qualified naturopath. *(See also page 21.)*

WESTERN HERBALISM

BIOCHEMICAL EFFECTS

Plant substances alter biochemical processes and improve organ function.

STRUCTURAL EFFECTS

Some herbs applied as ointments or packs have a local effect on joints and muscles.

PSYCHO-SOCIAL EFFECTS

Some herbs can stimulate or calm the mind; practitioners also take into account and treat stress-related factors that trigger or maintain health problems.

INTRODUCTION

Herbal remedies have long been the most important element of folk medicine. While many conventional drugs are derived from single active chemical ingredients in plants, herbalists make use of the whole plant. They believe its components have greater therapeutic power when they work together in synergy than when used separately. Conventional medicine is showing cautious interest as evidence mounts for some herbal treatments, but their integration with conventional drug treatments requires care.

HISTORY OF WESTERN HERBALISM

The world's ancient civilizations relied on medicinal herbs. The writings of Roman, Greek and Arab physicians provided the basis of Western herbalism, culminating in 16th-century texts by Paracelsus, John Gerard and Nicholas Culpeper. Herbal medicine began to decline with the growth of science in the

Berries may be dried in an oven before being used to make herbal remedies

18th century, but the 19th century saw a revival in Europe, where it is now well established and can even be studied as a university course. In Europe and Australia, herbal products require minimal scientific backing for medicinal claims to be made, but in the US it is illegal to state therapeutic uses for herbal products, so they are marketed as "food supplements".

MAIN PRINCIPLES

Herbalism matches specific treatments to certain diseases. However, like all traditional systems, herbalism seeks to restore the body's self-healing processes, so remedies can be tailored to suit the patient's health as a whole rather than to combat individual symptoms. Practitioners look for the cause of illness, such as poor diet, an unhealthy lifestyle or excessive stress, which may have disrupted the body's natural state of harmony, or homeostasis (see pages 12–13). Much of the herbalist's skill lies in knowing the action of specific plants on different body systems; for example, a plant may stimulate the circulation or or may calm the digestive system.

TREATMENT

A medical herbalist will take a detailed history and may give you a physical examination or carry out simple tests. From her conclusions she may prescribe one or more herbal remedies tailored to your individual condition, which are normally made up on the spot. Over-the-counter

Aloe vera gel is scraped away from the inside of the leaf to apply to burns and chapped skin

herbal products are useful for common ailments. Modern production methods aim to ensure they have consistent levels of known active constituents. Choose products from reputable suppliers and follow the instructions on the label. Remember that herbal remedies may take longer to work than conventional medicines.

MAIN USES

• Most illnesses, including persistent conditions, such as migraine and arthritis • Respiratory, digestive and circulatory problems • Skin conditions • Mild depression and insomnia • Benign prostatic disease • Cystitis, PMS and menopausal problems.

PRECAUTIONS

Tell your practitioner what drugs and supplements your are taking and if you are pregnant, have heart disease, high blood pressure or glaucoma.
Remember herbal remedies can have side-effects or may interfere with some conventional drugs, so always consult a qualified medical herbalist.
Do not discontinue a prescribed medicine without telling your doctor.
(See also page 21.)

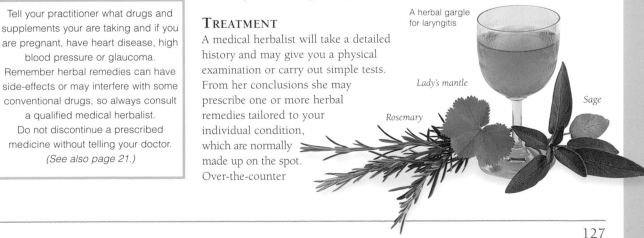

A herbal gargle for laryngitis

Lady's mantle

Rosemary

Sage

NUTRITIONAL THERAPIES

BIOCHEMICAL EFFECTS

Uses nutritional approaches to alter biochemical processes and improve the function of different organs.

STRUCTURAL EFFECTS

Treats food intolerances, believed by practitioners to irritate body organs and so cause or contribute to a wide range of disease. Practitioners may suggest ways of improving fitness, strength and flexibility.

PSYCHO-SOCIAL EFFECTS

Treats physical conditions believed to affect mental states (i.e. some mental illnesses are thought to be related to allergies and intolerances). Takes into account and treats stress-related factors.

INTRODUCTION

The role of diet in causing and preventing conditions such as heart disease and cancer is well established, as is the importance of vitamins and minerals in maintaining health. Nutritional therapists and specialists go a step further than most conventional doctors by using diet and food supplements to *treat* as well as to prevent illness. They look for nutritional deficiencies, allergies or intolerances to food and for lifestyle and environmental factors that disturb digestion and the absorption of nutrients into the bloodstream.

HISTORY OF NUTRITIONAL THERAPIES

Foods such as garlic have long been valued for their therapeutic properties, but it was 19th-century naturopaths (*see page 126*) who believed in the idea of "diet as medicine". Most modern nutritional therapists continue in this tradition. In 1912 a Polish biochemist, Casimir Funk, coined the term "vital amines" or "vitamines" for minute substances found in food. Further discoveries in biochemistry led to a greater understanding of the need for a balanced diet and the role of different nutrients. Recognition of the importance of antioxidants (*see page 162*) in maintaining health, preventing and treating disease and delaying ageing processes is a recent development. Other landmark advances of the 1980s and 1990s have tended to support naturopathic theories about diet. They include the importance of

Vitamins are often prescribed

Pesticides sprayed on crops can cause a build-up of toxins in the body

fibre, the discovery of plant oestrogens and the effects of saturated fats, food additives and pesticides on the body.

MAIN PRINCIPLES

Practitioners believe that good health is directly related to the quality of food eaten, and that an inadequate diet affects mood, fitness and well-being and even hastens ageing. These are important ideas as crops grown in poor soil are low in essential micro-nutrients, and toxic chemicals in pesticides and antibiotics fed to livestock have found their way into the food-chain. Highly processed "junk" foods are deficient in essential vitamins and minerals and high in refined sugar, salt, fats and chemical additives. Many practitioners believe that even if you eat a balanced diet and have an otherwise healthy metabolism, you can be adversely affected by toxins. Industrialization and traffic pollution mean the environment contains excessive levels of heavy metals, namely lead,

The practitioner may examine the central nervous system for signs of nutritional deficiencies

cadmium, mercury and aluminium. Coping with these puts a strain on the body, which practitioners are convinced causes problems that range from frequent infections, vague aches and pains and fatigue to serious conditions, including severe depression, high blood pressure and even cancer. According to practitioners, the "toxic overload" helps to upset the body's homeostatic processes (*see pages 12–13*) by over-taxing the liver and kidneys – organs responsible for detoxification and elimination – and causing problems of toxic accumulation and irritation elsewhere in the body, such as the skin and joints. A number of practitioners believe environmental factors and nutritional deficiencies are so serious that dietary adjustments alone may be insufficient. They advise high doses of vitamins and minerals, well above the accepted recommended daily levels. This practice is known as megavitamin therapy or orthomolecular therapy. Conventional doctors tend to be uneasy about the lack of research into possible side-effects of such high doses.

TREATMENT

People tend to consult nutritional therapists when suffering from long-term health problems that have not responded to conventional treatment and for which no cause can be found; for example, fatigue, headaches, bloating, and skin or digestive problems. Practitioners take a medical history and ask detailed questions about diet and lifestyle. Some use less conventional methods of diagnosis to determine nutritional deficiencies and food sensitivities. These may include tests on samples of blood, hair, urine or sweat, and also a procedure known as kinesiology, which tests the strength of muscles to confirm a suspected food sensitivity. Some practitioners also employ the Vega test, in which patients are connected to an electrical device designed to detect the presence of deficiencies and sensitivities.

Exclusion diets are, however, the most reliable way of detecting a food sensitivity. If the practitioner believes you have a nutritional problem, he will probably recommend and monitor one of various diets. Herbal remedies, enzymes, "live" bacteria to normalize levels of gut bacteria, and vitamin and mineral supplements may be suggested, as well as lifestyle changes or even other complementary therapies. You will probably be advised to eat fibre-rich foods and organic fruit and vegetables in order to reduce your intake of toxins.

MAIN USES

- Headaches, migraine • Fatigue, CFS
- Irritable bowel syndrome, digestive disorders • Arthritis • High blood pressure • Circulatory disorders
- Menstrual problems • Asthma, eczema • Allergies and food sensitivities.

PRECAUTIONS

If you are taking medication, check with your doctor before beginning a course of nutrient supplements, as these may react with or counteract the effects of prescribed drugs.

Do not take high doses of vitamins or minerals without consulting a properly trained nutritionist. Excessive supplementation can have adverse side-effects.

Do not follow a strict diet for long periods without the supervision of a qualified nutritionist.

COMMON DIET THERAPIES (see also page 165)

Stone Age Diet
This diet is sometimes recommended for irritable bowel syndrome or for people with a wheat sensitivity. The theory behind the Stone Age diet is that our digestive system has not evolved beyond the diet of Stone Age hunter-gatherers. Plain fish, lamb, vegetables, and moderate amounts of fruit are allowed, but cultivated wheat and unrefined grains as well as dairy products are restricted.

Raw Food Diet
This diet, which is based on the work of Swiss doctor Max Bircher-Benner in the late 19th century, includes 70 per cent raw fruit and vegetables and 30 per cent grains, nuts, dairy products and meat. The "enzyme activity" of uncooked food is said to benefit the digestive system and promote well-being.

Macrobiotic Diet
Macrobiotic diets aim to balance foods according to yin (light) and yang (dense) properties (see page 124). The most extreme forms, intended as short-term detoxification, consist almost entirely of brown rice and vegetables, and in the long term could lead to malnutrition.

Vegan Diet
A vegan diet is entirely free of animal products – no meat, poultry, fish, eggs, milk or honey. Adequate protein depends on a careful balance of pulses, nuts, grains and seeds. Vegans need to ensure they get enough vitamin B12 and folate, especially during pregnancy. Non-animal sources of calcium are available.

The Hay Diet ("Food Combining")
American Dr. William Hay developed his diet in the early 1900s. He believed that protein and carbohydrate could, in the long term, cause disease if eaten together. He based this notion on the theory that proteins need an acidic environment for digestion, and carbohydrates an alkaline one. Protein and carbohydrate foods are eaten separately and "neutral" foods can be combined with either group. Although the Hay diet has no proven scientific basis – plant foods contain both protein and carbohydrate and the human digestive system is designed

to cope with both – it is enormously popular and many followers say they feel better for it. If your resilience and energy levels are low and your digestion seems poor, the Hay diet may be worth considering.

HOMEOPATHY

BIOCHEMICAL EFFECTS

Research confirms homeopathic doses affect tissue chemistry.

STRUCTURAL EFFECTS

Practitioners may suggest ways of improving fitness, strength and flexibility.

PSYCHO-SOCIAL EFFECTS

Strong therapeutic-relationship effects. Brings about beneficial changes in mood and self-perception. Improves ability to cope with a health problem.

INTRODUCTION

Based on the theory that "like cures like", homeopathy is a system of medicine that aims to encourage the body's self-healing ability, or "vital force". This force is believed to maintain the body's health, and symptoms of illness are regarded as a sign that the body is using its self-healing powers to fight infection. Homeopathic medicines do not work in the same way as conventional drugs. Instead, they are given to boost the vital force, so that the body fights back. Remedies are repeatedly diluted to reduce side-effects but are still believed to be potent enough to trigger self-healing processes.

HISTORY OF HOMEOPATHY

Hippocrates, the "father of medicine", outlined the principle of "like curing like" in the 5th century BC. In Germany in the 1790s, Dr. Samuel Hahnemann rediscovered this principle and called it homeopathy, from the Greek *homoios* (same) and *pathos* (suffering). Using himself as a guinea pig, Hahnemann took the malaria cure quinine and developed malaria-like symptoms. He concluded that a substance that caused symptoms in a healthy person could cure the same symptoms in an ill person. He went on to test or "prove" other substances such as arsenic, and began to use them as cures. Homeopathy quickly spread across the world to Europe, Asia and the Americas, and is currently undergoing a revival in the US.

MAIN PRINCIPLES

Homeopathic remedies are derived from substances that induce symptoms similar to those of an illness. The symptoms of poisoning by deadly nightshade for

Deadly nightshade

example, resemble those of scarlet fever, so *Belladonna*, a remedy derived from deadly nightshade, was given to treat scarlet fever. Hahnemann noticed that his patients got worse before improving. To reduce the side-effects, he developed the law of "potentization", according to which doses are repeatedly diluted in the belief that the weaker the remedy, the more potent it becomes. The diluted liquid is believed to keep a "footprint-like" image of the original substance so that, even when there is no trace of the original ingredient, the liquid retains a "memory" of it. Remedies are diluted on the decimal scale (x) with a dilution factor of 1:10, or on the centesimal scale (c) with a dilution factor of 1:100.

TREATMENT

Hahnemann discovered that when he found out more about his patients, he was more likely to prescribe the correct remedy. So-called "classical" homeopaths still offer treatment based on their assessment of a patient's "constitution", taking stock of appearance, personality, likes and dislikes, among other factors.

At the initial consultation, homeopaths question their patients closely about medical health, lifestyle, moods, likes

and dislikes. They then prescribe one of the 2,000 remedies available, which come in many different forms, including lactose pills, tablets and powders, as well as ointments and tinctures. Homeopaths advise taking remedies between meals so that flavours do not interfere with the remedy.

Homeopathic treatment is said to work according to the "laws of cure" – that is, symptoms getting better starting from the top of the body, improving inside before the outside and in reverse order of appearance. The longer a condition has taken to develop, the longer it takes to treat, and remedies may be changed according to how symptoms progress.

MAIN USES

• Long-term disorders, such as asthma and other allergies • Anxiety, nervous tension • Menstrual or menopausal problems • Ailments in pregnancy, including morning sickness.

PRECAUTIONS

Tell your practitioner if you are using essential oils; in certain cases they are thought to be incompatible with homeopathic remedies.

If you are allergic to milk-based products, ask for lactose-free tablets. *(See also page 21.)*

The liquid, which homeopaths call the "mother tincture", is strained into a dark glass bottle

The tincture is diluted (one drop to 99 drops of alcohol), then shaken (known as "succussion")

After repeated dilution to the required potency, a few drops are added to lactose tablets

ENVIRONMENTAL MEDICINE

BIOCHEMICAL EFFECTS

Nutritional and environmental approaches alter biochemical processes helping improve the function of different organs.

STRUCTURAL EFFECTS

Treats a wide range of diseases and food and environmental allergies and intolerances, which practitioners believe chronically irritate the organs of the body. Practitioners may suggest ways of improving fitness, strength and flexibility.

PSYCHO-SOCIAL EFFECTS

Practitioners believe that some mental illness is not "all in the mind" (e.g. that allergies and intolerances can affect how we think, feel and behave); they take into account and treat stress-related factors that trigger health problems.

INTRODUCTION

Environmental medicine, also known as clinical ecology, attributes many disorders to environmental factors. These include some types of food and the pesticides and preservatives used in food production, as well as pollen, dust and exhaust fumes. Most people are able to withstand the effects of these toxins, but in susceptible individuals they may trigger allergy-related disorders, such as eczema or hay fever, or less severe reactions, known as "intolerances" or "sensitivities". Different tests are used to identify these irritants and patients are encouraged to avoid them if possible.

HISTORY OF ENVIRONMENTAL MEDICINE

Viennese paediatrician Baron Clemens von Pirquet, working early in the 20th century, was the first person to use the word "allergy" to describe unusual responses to the environment. Allergies are now defined as immune system reactions, identified by a positive skin-prick test. More controversially, some doctors in the US went on to claim that common foods and environmental chemicals caused "delayed" or "hidden" reactions (*see pages 94–95*), ranging from headaches and fatigue to asthma and arthritis.

MAIN PRINCIPLES

Practitioners believe that we ingest a whole range of synthetic chemicals every day, in the form of unfiltered tap water and the foods that make up a typical Western diet. These chemicals are derived from pesticides, herbicides, the residues of drugs fed to the animals we eat, and also from preservatives contained in processed foods. People who are susceptible to allergies, or who have a poor diet, may find it difficult to cope with high levels of toxins and have a tendency to develop adverse reactions.

TREATMENT

A practitioner asks questions about the patient's medical history, typical diet and lifestyle. He will then check for swollen glands and other signs of sensitivity. The patient may be given a skin-prick test, hair and blood tests to determine mineral and nutritional deficiencies. Research suggests that these methods are far from reliable for detecting food sensitivities. A radioallergosorbent blood test (RAST) reveals any immunoglobulin E, the sign of an allergic reaction. Unproven tests for sensitivities include muscle-strength testing, a Vega test (*see page 129*) and cytotoxic testing, in which a blood sample is mixed with the irritant and then checked

Plant pollens can trigger allergic reactions when they are inhaled

In an elimination diet the patient eats "neutral" foods such as cabbage, lamb, sunflower oil, pears and water

for cell damage. The practitioner may suggest an exclusion or elimination diet (*see page 129*) to identify irritant foods.

When contact is unavoidable some practitioners use desensitization treatments. These can involve placing irritants with an enzyme on the skin, or giving decreasing amounts by injection or as drops under the tongue.

MAIN USES

• Asthma, hay fever, eczema, psoriasis
• Headaches, migraines • Digestive disorders, fluid retention, weight loss
• Depression, fatigue, CFS • Arthritis.

PRECAUTIONS

Never follow an elimination diet without the supervision of a qualified practitioner. (*See also page 21*.)

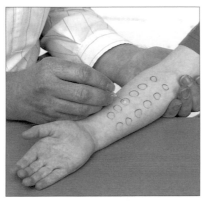
In a skin-prick test, a dilution of the suspect irritant is placed on an area of scratched skin

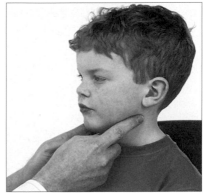
The practitioner checks for swollen glands, which may indicate sensitivity to certain substances

PSYCHOTHERAPY & COUNSELLING

BIOCHEMICAL EFFECTS

Probably helps induce helpful changes in mood-related brain chemistry.

STRUCTURAL EFFECTS

Relieves distress that can disturb body function (some therapists attribute a wide range of diseases to psychosomatic problems); some forms of psychotherapy involve bodywork and movement.

PSYCHO-SOCIAL EFFECTS

Influences thoughts, feelings, attitudes and behaviour; allows memories to emerge and new ideas to form; changes in self-perception improve pain tolerance and ability to cope with health problems.

INTRODUCTION

In general, psychotherapy and counselling involve a "talking cure". Psychologists assess and treat problems, often working with cognitive and behavioural approaches, to change ways of thinking and behaving. Although techniques vary greatly, psychotherapy and counselling usually entail discussing with a skilled listener thoughts, feelings, memories and situations that contribute to a personal difficulty. Whether following loss or trauma, or triggered by unknown events, it offers an opportunity for insight and resolution. Hospitals and medical practices increasingly employ psychotherapists and counsellors, and treatment is widely available through state and private insurance schemes.

HISTORY OF PSYCHOTHERAPY & COUNSELLING

Dr. Sigmund Freud developed the foundations of psychoanalysis in the 1880s. He introduced the notion of the "unconscious mind" and tried to relate disturbed thoughts, feelings and actions to buried memories. By letting patients talk freely he hoped to help them heal lost parts of themselves.

Other therapists took up Freud's theories in various ways. Dr. Carl Jung believed in a deep human need to unify one's "essential self" and in the existence of a "collective unconscious" shared by all human beings. In the 1920s, Wilhelm Reich explored body-centred psychotherapy, working with feelings directly through the body. "Behavioural" psychologists claimed that human behaviour and feelings were "conditioned" and, once learned, could be corrected. In the 1960s, "humanistic" psychologists, led by Abraham Maslow, Carl Rogers and Fritz

Psychotherapists and counsellors help clients to articulate their feelings

Perls, evolved techniques to encourage "personal growth". A growing understanding of how the mind uses language and relationships has led to modern "brief" psychotherapy methods, which are problem-focused and solution-oriented.

PRINCIPLES & TRAINING

Analytic and psychodynamic therapies are based on the idea that thoughts and behaviour are shaped by earlier experience. Traumatic memories and feelings can be repressed and return unrecognized to disturb the mind and body. Clients are encouraged to talk about their experiences and express feelings freely. *Cognitive and behavioural therapies,* on the other hand, tend not to deal with the unconscious at all, but aim to forge new ways of thinking and behaving. *Humanistic therapies* lie between these two extremes.

The distinctions between practitioners may be blurred, particularly in the case of psychotherapists and counsellors, but all should undertake rigorous training and have regular professional supervision. Psychoanalysts follow the teachings of Freud, Jung or Melanie Klein, whose theories on childhood thought processes are influential. Training lasts for five to seven years,

including personal analysis, and some may also be medically qualified. Psychologists take a science-based university degree, studying the mind and behaviour. Clinical psychologists undergo further training. Psychotherapists should train for at least four years with a recognized institution and experience personal therapy. They tend to specialize in a particular technique, either psychodynamic or humanistic.

Counsellors should also be highly trained. The better qualified undergo several years' training and use similar approaches to psychotherapists.

TREATMENT

It is important that you understand the therapist's approach. A session usually lasts 50–60 minutes and generally takes place once a week, but analysis may be more often. Treatment can span a few sessions or go on for several years, depending on the method. Therapists encourage you to speak freely, interrupting only to help you focus on your problem, and some will employ techniques from different approaches where appropriate. Sometimes disturbing emotions emerge, so the therapist must be trained to help you work through them.

TYPES OF THERAPY

Psychoanalysis

Treatment is usually a lengthy process as an intense relationship has to build up with the analyst, mirroring earlier relationships in a process known as transference. Gradually the unconscious, in the form of unacknowledged and repressed ideas, feelings, memories, thoughts and attitudes, is "re-owned".

Group Therapy

Clients meet in small groups (ideally the same people) over several months to share experiences and feelings with the help of a practitioner, or "group facilitator". Group work can be analytical or may use humanistic approaches, such as the 12-step programmes for addiction. The shared situation often intensifies the experience of the therapy.

Family Therapy

Some people become unwell as a way of coping with family tensions. When a family sits down with a therapist, communication difficulties and hidden conflicts between family members can become obvious. It may be possible to resolve them and even change patterns of behaviour.

Counselling

Practitioners usually focus on specific problems, such as bereavement or redundancy, rather than on deep-seated personal issues. Specialist counsellors deal with marital, relationship and sexual problems, working with couples or on a one-to-one basis.

Cognitive Behavioural Therapy

This term takes in everything from basic desensitization for phobias to stress-management programmes and mind-body techniques like relaxation, biofeedback, visualization and meditation. They all aim to identify and change unhelpful thoughts, expectations and behaviour, but do not

Neuro-linguistic programming helps people connect with the world on six levels: environment, behaviour, capability, belief, identity and spirituality

Group therapy enables clients to learn more about themselves by sharing feelings with others

seek to understand the deeper psychological origins of a problem. Such methods have proved most effective in treating stress-related conditions, phobias, obsessions and eating disorders, as well as the less severe forms of depression.

Humanistic Psychotherapy

Clients are encouraged to explore their feelings and to take responsibility for their thoughts and actions. Emphasis is on self-development and achieving one's human potential. How this is defined depends on the therapist. Social or financial success, spiritual development or emotional openness are typical goals. Techniques include experimenting with unfamiliar ways of behaving and relating to others; for instance, trying out different body language or disclosing feelings, as in Gestalt therapy (*see Glossary, pages 177–78*) and psychodrama.

Neuro-linguistic Programming

This approach combines cognitive behavioural techniques and ideas from hypnotherapy. The practitioner helps you to understand how you organize your thoughts, feelings and perceptions, and how to re-organize them in ways that work better.

Transactional Analysis

Not a psychoanalytic method, transactional analysis is a way of looking at the individual that encourages the recognition of potentially conflicting roles: the creative but needy child; the realistic adult and the nurturing but judgmental parent.

Transpersonal Approaches

The therapeutic value of enhanced feelings of love, altruism and connectedness to the universe is taken up by transpersonal approaches, such as psychosynthesis, which explore dreams, inner heroes, creativity and aspirations.

MAIN USES

• Stress, anxiety, depression • Phobias, obsessions, compulsions • Eating disorders • Bereavement, grief • Relationship and sexual problems • Emotional instability • Psycho-somatic illness • Personal development.

PRECAUTIONS

Research shows people gain most benefit when they trust and relate to their practitioner, regardless of technique; but check his or her training and qualifications, and whether he or she belongs to a professional body (*see page 180*). Shop around and remember that you are entitled to stop therapy whenever you wish.

If you have a psychotic condition, such as schizophrenia, or are manic depressive, only seek psychotherapy with the backing of your psychiatrist.

(*See also page 21.*)

HYPNOTHERAPY

BIOCHEMICAL EFFECTS

Triggers healing processes. Causes changes in brain and tissue chemistry by inducing the relaxation response.

STRUCTURAL EFFECTS

Profoundly reduces tension of voluntary (e.g. in back and neck) and involuntary muscles (e.g. in gut or blood vessels).

PSYCHO-SOCIAL EFFECTS

Brings about valuable changes in perceptions, attitudes and mood, and promotes active self-care.

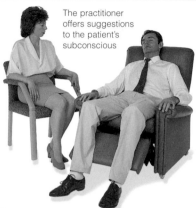

The practitioner offers suggestions to the patient's subconscious

INTRODUCTION

When profoundly relaxed, as if in a daydream, most people become open to suggestion. Modern hypnotherapy makes use of this state of heightened susceptibility to alleviate pain, to foster self-confidence, to overcome phobias or even to treat conditions like asthma.

HISTORY OF HYPNOTHERAPY

Hypnotherapy evolved from the work of the controversial 18th-century Austrian, Franz Anton Mesmer. Freud used some hypnosis in early psychoanalysis, but the modern form of hypnotherapy was developed in the 1950s and 1960s by US psychotherapist Milton H. Erickson. It is supported by clinical research and has considerable credibility – if not total acceptance – among doctors.

MAIN PRINCIPLES

After inducing a state of hypnosis in the patient, the practitioner seeks to plant positive suggestions in the subconscious mind, which is more open to influence than during normal waking life. Practitioners claim that patients are aware of their surroundings and are unlikely to do anything against their will.

TREATMENT

You will be asked about your medical history and why you are seeking help. Depending on your problem and on the practitioner's training, you may be asked to recall past experiences to help shed light on your condition, or be taken progressively deeper into a relaxed state of mind and encouraged to overcome your problem.

MAIN USES

• Pain relief • Phobias • Stress, anxiety
• Depression • Addictions • Asthma
• Skin conditions • Digestive disorders.

PRECAUTIONS

Hypnotherapy may not be suitable for those with severe depression, psychosis or epilepsy. (See also page 21.)

VISUALIZATION

BIOCHEMICAL EFFECTS

Triggers healing processes. Causes changes in brain and tissue chemistry by inducing the relaxation response.

STRUCTURAL EFFECTS

Reduces tension of voluntary (e.g. in back and neck) and involuntary muscles (e.g. in gut or blood vessels).

PSYCHO-SOCIAL EFFECTS

Brings about valuable changes in perceptions, attitudes and mood, and promotes active self-care.

HISTORY & MAIN PRINCIPLES

Also known as "guided imagery", this technique, which can be practised either alone or with the help of a practitioner, harnesses the imagination to help people cope with stress, achieve their potential and stimulate the body's self-healing ability. The aim is to visualize positive images and desired outcomes. Following research by US psychologist Dr. Carl Simonton in the 1960s, many cancer patients have been taught to picture the destruction of their cancer cells. Psychologists, athletes and performers use visualization to improve motivation and change negative attitudes.

SELF-HELP

To do this exercise, you first need to learn a relaxation technique (see pages 170–71). Lie down or sit comfortably with eyes closed. Breathe slowly, relax and mentally "let go" before focusing on your chosen image. To leave the imagery behind, simply wriggle your toes.
Fighting Illness: create a picture of your ailment in your mind, and picture the treatment you are receiving aiding your self-healing powers. Some people like to "turn down" pain on an imaginary dial.
Achieving Success: think about your goal. Tell yourself you are in control, and picture yourself performing well.

Combating Stress: picture yourself in a tranquil scene, making it as real as possible. Repeat phrases such as "I am relaxed and content".

MAIN USES

• Pain relief • Phobias • Stress and anxiety • Heart conditions • Cancer.

Visualizing a peaceful scene aids relaxation

MEDITATION

BIOCHEMICAL EFFECTS

Triggers healing processes. Causes changes in brain and tissue chemistry by inducing the relaxation response.

STRUCTURAL EFFECTS

Induces immediate and long-term reduction in tension of voluntary (e.g. in back and neck) and involuntary muscles (e.g. in gut or blood vessels).

PSYCHO-SOCIAL EFFECTS

Brings about valuable changes in perceptions, attitudes and mood, and promotes active self-care. Improves tolerance of pain and ability to cope with a health problem.

INTRODUCTION

Various techniques can be used to induce "relaxed awareness", the basic meditative state of mind. All involve focusing the mind and ignoring distractions. The practice is widely recommended for stress-related conditions. People who meditate claim they have greater clarity of thought, calmness and energy, and research suggests that it can help improve conditions including anxiety, migraine, irritable bowel syndrome and PMS.

HISTORY OF MEDITATION

Meditation is a part of all major religions, practised as prayer and contemplation in Christianity, Judaism and Islam, and as a way of exploring consciousness and attaining bliss in Buddhism and Hinduism. The Indian yogi Maharishi Mahesh introduced transcendental meditation (TM) to the West in the 1960s, prompting scientific research in the US. From this, Dr. Herbert Benson of Harvard University developed the concept of the "relaxation response", encouraging the practice of a non-religious style of meditation.

MAIN PRINCIPLES

By triggering the relaxation response, meditation reverses the physiological effects of stress (*see page 84*), reducing heart-rate and slowing metabolism. Brainwaves change to a distinctive alpha pattern that indicates the mind and body are resting deeply, although still mentally alert. Regular meditators deal more effectively with stress and appear to have better health.

MEDITATION TECHNIQUES

Be prepared to try several methods until you find one that is right for you.
Mantra Meditation: a word or phrase is continually chanted or repeated in your head. The word may be an expression of your personal beliefs, or simply one that holds some positive meaning for you.
Breath Awareness: you focus on your breathing and count "one", or think of a word that induces a sense of peace, each time you exhale.
Vipassana (Mindfulness): you enter a state of "diffuse openness", in which you are fully conscious of, but detached from, your immediate experience and thoughts.
Object Meditation: you focus with eyes open on an object, dwelling on its shape, weight and texture.

A rosary can aid meditation

A flame may be a focus of meditation

MAIN USES

• Stress and anxiety • High blood pressure • Headaches • Fatigue, depression, insomnia • Pain • Addictions • Boosting the immune system • Personal development.

MEDITATION SEQUENCE

IT IS POSSIBLE to learn to meditate from books, tapes or videos, but consulting a teacher or joining a group is advisable.

1 Begin with 5–10 minutes and build up to 15–20 minutes once or preferably twice a day. To keep track of time, place a clock nearby. Eventually you will not need it.

Regular meditation relieves stress-related ailments

2 Sit with your back straight. You may fall asleep if slumped or lying down. A cross-legged pose can be adopted, or you could sit in an upright chair. Keep your feet firmly on the ground or on a support, and place your hands on your lap or knees. Close your eyes and relax.

3 Inhale through your nose and feel the air descending to your abdomen. Note any areas of tension in your body and, as you exhale, imagine your muscles relaxing. Notice the slow, rhythmic movement as you breathe in and out.

4 Concentrate on the focus of your meditation. This may be the rhythm of your breathing, an image, or a word or phrase repeated silently each time you breathe out (*see above*).

5 Your attention should be relaxed but focused. If you find yourself thinking of other things, simply allow your mind to drift back to the focus of meditation.

6 Try to remain still and relaxed. You might feel restless or get the urge to move. These feelings will usually disappear.

7 When you are ready, wait a full minute before opening your eyes and for another minute before letting yourself return to full activity. Stretch and stand up slowly. If your meditation is interrupted, try to return to it later, re-emerging slowly this time.

BIOFEEDBACK

BIOCHEMICAL EFFECTS
Changes in brain and tissue chemistry by encouraging the relaxation response.

STRUCTURAL EFFECTS
Regulates unwanted tension in involuntary muscle (e.g. in gut or blood vessels) or voluntary muscles (e.g. back and neck).

PSYCHO-SOCIAL EFFECTS
Decreases anxiety and promotes an attitude of active self-care. Also improves ability to cope with stress.

INTRODUCTION
People can learn to control involuntary body functions such as heart rate or skin temperature using "biofeedback" machines that electronically monitor pulse rate, brainwaves, skin sweat and other physical responses. Scientific research supports biofeedback's role in teaching people to relax muscles and so relieve headaches or persistent back pain, for example, or to control pelvic floor muscles in order to prevent incontinence. Many doctors believe biofeedback is set to become widely available in the future.

HISTORY OF BIOFEEDBACK
In the 1960s, American scientists found that, if linked to a monitoring device, people could learn to influence their brainwaves and heart rate. Further studies showed that other biological functions could be controlled in this way. Advances in computer technology have led to increasing use of biofeedback.

TREATMENT
Different types of biofeedback device measure changes in body functions. With the sensors in place you are taught to recognize which signals indicate relaxation or tension. Techniques such as breathing and muscle relaxation can help achieve the desired response, which might include lowered heart rate or reduced blood pressure. Mastering these takes practice, and at least six half-hour sessions may be necessary, with further follow-up sessions at home.

MAIN USES
- Stress, tension, anxiety, insomnia
- Headaches, migraine • High blood pressure • Irritable bowel syndrome • Asthma
- Raynaud's disease
- Incontinence.

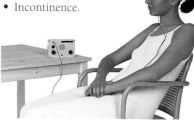
Electrodes measure brainwave activity

AUTOGENIC TRAINING

BIOCHEMICAL EFFECTS
Changes brain and tissue chemistry by encouraging the relaxation response.

STRUCTURAL EFFECTS
Regulates unwanted tension in involuntary muscle (e.g. in gut or blood vessels) or in voluntary muscles (e.g. back and neck).

PSYCHO-SOCIAL EFFECTS
Decreases anxiety and promotes an attitude of active self-care. Also improves ability to cope with stress.

INTRODUCTION
A series of six mental exercises trains the mind to switch off the "fight-or-flight" stress response. Once learned, autogenic training (AT) offers a no-nonsense way to relax at will and stimulate the body's self-healing processes. As such, it is a useful self-help treatment for stress-related conditions. It is also claimed to have a beneficial effect on personal relationships and on performance at work, and to enhance creative skills. AT is widely available and most doctors are comfortable with its highly structured approach to relaxation.

HISTORY OF AUTOGENIC TRAINING
In the 1920s Dr. Johannes Schultz, a German neurologist and psychiatrist, devised six silent verbal exercises to calm the mind and relax the body. Known as "autogenic" (from the Greek, "generated from within"), the exercises were further developed in Canada by Dr. Wolfgang Luthe, a colleague of Dr. Schultz.

TREATMENT
Students are carefully questioned about their medical history and psychological suitability, before learning the exercises in small groups or one-to-one over eight 90-minute weekly sessions. Each exercise aims to induce relaxation in different areas of the body: heaviness in the neck, shoulders and limbs; warmth in the limbs; a calm heartbeat; relaxed breathing; warmth in the stomach, and coolness in the forehead. Students can enter a state similar to that of meditation.

MAIN USES
- Stress, migraine, insomnia, depression, nervous tension, ulcers • High blood pressure • Irritable bowel syndrome
- PMS • Eczema • Addictions • HIV.

Autogenic training induces deep relaxation

ART THERAPY

BIOCHEMICAL EFFECTS
Probably induces helpful changes in brain and body chemistry.

STRUCTURAL EFFECTS
Engages the body in expressing thoughts and feelings.

PSYCHO-SOCIAL EFFECTS
Allows memories to emerge, ideas to form, feelings to be connected with.

INTRODUCTION
Art has the ability to promote the expression of feelings that seem too difficult or threatening to articulate verbally. Through painting, drawing and sculpting, people may come to terms with traumatic experiences and find therapeutic relief from emotional distress. Art therapy is often available to cancer, AIDS and Alzheimer's patients, particularly those who find it hard to talk about their concerns. The technique is also used by some psychiatrists and psychologists to treat mental and emotional disorders and addictions.

HISTORY OF ART THERAPY
Art has a long history as a vehicle of emotional expression. Sigmund Freud and Carl Jung recognized its therapeutic potential as a reflection of a patient's subconscious state. After World War II, art therapy was used in the rehabilitation of war veterans and it is now widely practised in the US and the UK.

TREATMENT
Sessions may be one-to-one or in small groups, led by a therapist. Patients are encouraged to express their feelings by making images. As emotions can surface visually before they are verbalized, art therapy may help patients to face issues they have repressed. The act of releasing emotions through creative art is thought to be healing in itself, and the work may contain personal symbols that the patient is encouraged to interpret.

MAIN USES
• Mental and emotional problems
• Learning and communication difficulties • Eating disorders • Stress, including stress-relief in serious disease
• Addictions • Bereavement
• Alzheimer's • Personal development.

Images and colours often have symbolic meaning

MUSIC THERAPY

BIOCHEMICAL EFFECTS
Probably induces helpful changes in brain and body chemistry.

STRUCTURAL EFFECTS
Engages the body in expressing thoughts and feelings.

PSYCHO-SOCIAL EFFECTS
Allows feelings to be connected with; encourages communication.

INTRODUCTION
The power of music to stir and soothe the emotions and enable the expression of feelings that are too profound for words is unquestioned. Its association with healing is ancient, but music has only recently come to be employed as a therapy for those with serious disabilities, mental illness or psychological distress. Research indicates that listening to music may stimulate neurochemicals that promote relaxation and even enhance immunity. Certainly many dentists' surgeries, intensive care units and obstetric suites use music to reduce patients' anxiety.

Children respond to the stimulus of music

HISTORY OF MUSIC THERAPY
Music therapy developed in the US at the end of World War II, when it was used in the psychological rehabitation of war veterans. In the UK, the concert pianist Paul Nordoff and teacher Clive Robbins began training therapists in 1974 to work with autistic and emotionally disturbed children.

TREATMENT
Sessions are in groups or one-to-one, and treatment varies according to the condition. Musical knowledge is unnecessary. Singing or improvizing with percussion and other instruments, led by the practitioner, may help patients release tension and express emotions in a non-verbal way, enabling them to deal with problems more effectively. Listening to certain types of music can be soothing and so provide relief for those with stress-related conditions. Music can also relieve physical pain or stimulate memories, making it of particular use in work for the elderly.

MAIN USES
• Learning and communication difficulties, especially autism • Mental, emotional and behavioural problems
• Depression • Stress, anxiety • Care for the elderly • Pain relief, especially in labour or in terminal illness.

chapter

Assuming control of your health is empowering, and

active self-care is a cornerstone of integrated medicine.

The questionnaire on the following page is designed

to help you evaluate different aspects of your life,

YOUR HEALTHCARE PLAN

from diet to relationships, and to pinpoint areas for

improvement. We introduce you to a range of health

skills that improve well-being and resistance to disease,

from eating well and learning how to relax to finding

the best type of exercise for your lifestyle and

personality. Following the advice here sets you on the

road to zestful well-being and an active old age.

HOW HEALTHY ARE YOU?

Well-being depends on body and mind working in harmony, allowing you to enjoy optimum health. If you are healthy with plenty of zest for life, and if you have a partner, friends or relatives to whom you can turn for support, you should find that you can meet most of life's challenges successfully. Good health relies on biochemical, structural and psycho-social factors. Relationships, lifestyle, environment, and the way you cope with problems can all both undermine health or support it. Psychological strain (for example from an unhappy relationship) or a bad work environment, perhaps due to poor air quality or the presence of toxic chemicals, can increase susceptibility to illness, as can a diet of junk food or an aversion to exercise. If you want to strengthen your resilience, cope with disease or just improve general well-being, start by identifying how different factors affect you and try to change your lifestyle if necessary. Bear in mind that even if it is difficult to adjust one aspect, strengthening others can compensate. This questionnaire can help you to learn about the areas of your life that influence your well-being, and to identify those that may be undermining your health. The colour wheel (*see page 143*) gives an at-a-glance picture of your overall well-being.

BIOCHEMICAL HEALTH

A DIET LOW IN FAT and high in fruit, vegetables and fibre can protect against disease. Many of us have a tendency to eat too much junk and processed food, which is low in fibre and high in fat, sugar and chemical additives. Our genetic make-up can sometimes help us to resist disease, but an unhealthy lifestyle can cancel out inherited advantages.

GENETIC MAKE-UP

Have you or has a close relative (i.e. parent, sibling or child) suffered from any of the following complaints? If you answer yes to any question, you may need to pay particular attention to your diet. In the case of questions 1–4, a doctor might recommend that you follow a low-fat diet; for questions 5–8 a low-sugar, high-fibre diet is likely to be advised; for questions 7 and 8 you should drink plenty of water.

A NO
C YES

1 High blood pressure   A   C

2 Heart attack before age 40   A   C

3 Very raised cholesterol   A   C

4 Breast cancer   A   C

5 Diabetes   A   C

6 Bowel cancer   A   C

7 Gout   A   C

8 Kidney stones   A   C

DIET/LIFESTYLE

A YES/USUALLY
B SOMETIMES
C NO/NEVER/RARELY

1 Is your diet well balanced, low in fat and high in fibre, with plenty of fresh fruit and vegetables?   A   B   C

2 Is your daily fat intake less than 30 per cent of your total calorie intake?   A   B   C

3 Do you limit your salt and sugar intake?   A   B   C

4 Do you eat pulses, poultry and fish in preference to red meat?   A   B   C

5 Do you drink sufficient water to keep your urine pale in colour?   A   B   C

6 Do you avoid eating junk and processed food?   A   B   C

7 Do you resist the temptation to eat when you're not hungry?   A   B   C

8 Do you skip meals only on rare occasions?   A   B   C

9 Do you avoid strict diets, except under medical advice?   A   B   C

10 Do you restrict your caffeine intake (coffee, tea, cola)?   A   B   C

11 Do you limit your alcohol intake (three drinks a day or less if a man, two if a woman)?   A   B   C

12 Are you a non-smoker?   A   B   C

13 Do you avoid recreational drugs?   A   B   C

YOUR SCORE

A If you scored mostly As, your healthy diet is helping you to maintain optimum well-being.

B A score of mostly Bs indicates that you should rethink your diet (*see pages 158–65*) and pay greater attention to your health.

C A score of mostly Cs strongly suggests that you are eating unhealthily. See your doctor for checkups and advice on diet.

STRUCTURAL HEALTH

KEEPING PHYSICALLY FIT is essential if you are to stay in good health. Regular exercise also helps to prevent many serious diseases, both physical and mental. Health checks, particularly as you get older, can identify problems before it becomes difficult to treat them. Good living and working conditions are another important factor in maintaining well-being.

A YES/USUALLY
B SOMETIMES
C NO/NEVER/RARELY

1 Do you have plenty of energy? A B C

2 Do you get enough sleep? A B C

3 Do you take aerobic exercise for at least 20–30 minutes three times a week? A B C

4 Can you climb three flights of stairs non-stop without becoming breathless? A B C

5 Do you regularly take part in sport or exercise, either before or after work or at weekends? A B C

6 If necessary, could you run to catch a bus or train? A B C

7 Are you free of unexplained physical symptoms? A B C

8 Do you feel happy with your physical health, weight and body shape? A B C

9 Do you use dental floss every day? A B C

10 Do you have a dental checkup at least once a year? A B C

11 Do you limit your exposure to the sun and use a sunscreen where necessary? A B C

12 Do you have a good sex life, or if celibate, are you happy to be so? A B C

13 If you use contraception and/or practise safe sex, are you satisfied with the form you use/practise? A B C

14 Do you work in a pollution-free environment (e.g. without exposure to harmful chemicals or to excessive noise)? A B C

15 Are you able to work without physical discomfort and without placing strain on your back, joints, muscles or eyes? A B C

16 Are you able to work under stressful conditions without experiencing any of the following symptoms: palpitations, breathlessness, insomnia, indigestion or fatigue? A B C

WOMEN

17 Do you have a cervical smear test at least once every three years? A C

18 Do you make regular checks (at least once a month) for lumps and other changes in your breasts? A C

MEN

19 Do you make regular checks (at least once every three months) for lumps and other changes in your testicles? A C

OVER 40

20 Do you have an eye test for glaucoma at least every four years? A C

21 Do you have a checkup for abnormal blood pressure at least once a year? A C

OVER 50

22 Have you asked your doctor whether you need to be tested for bowel cancer? A C

23 Do you have a regular mammogram? A C

YOUR SCORE

A If you scored mostly As, you are maintaining a healthy lifestyle and should feel physically fit enough to lead the life you want.

B A score of mostly Bs indicates you should see a doctor for checkups and advice on exercise (see pages 154–55). Your work may be affecting your health (see page 151).

C A score of mostly Cs strongly suggests that you need to take better care of yourself and improve your work environment.

Genetic make-up can sometimes make us prone to disease, but a healthy lifestyle may offset these disadvantages.

PSYCHO-SOCIAL HEALTH

STRESS IS AN EVERYDAY PART OF LIFE, but constant or excessive levels of stress undermine physical and mental health. Remember that the degree to which pressure affects you depends on how you perceive it and how much you feel in control of it. Your reaction to stress may be influenced by your personality: those who react with aggression (so-called "hot" reactors) can expose themselves to heart disease, while "cold" reactors, who often suffer from low self-esteem, may deplete their immune system and so be prone to infection. People who can discuss their problems with partners or close friends are less vulnerable to stress. A life of creative and spiritual fulfilment can also help you cope with challenges.

SOURCES OF STRESS
Have you experienced any of the following life events in the past year?

A NO
C YES

1 The death of someone close to you. A C

2 Major changes in close relationships (e.g. marriage or the birth of a baby). A C

3 A new job or home, or a change in your finances. A C

4 A major illness (either your own health problem or that of a close friend or relative). A C

5 Marital or other family problems. A C

6 Long-term day-to-day stress that has left you feeling exhausted. A C

ATTITUDES TO STRESS

A NO/NEVER/RARELY
B SOMETIMES
C YES/USUALLY

1 Do you ever feel a compulsion to work, eat, smoke or drink? A B C

2 Do you feel that you are no longer in control of your life? A B C

3 Do you experience any of the following problems or emotions when under stress: insomnia, fear of serious illness, lack of concentration, indecisiveness, lack of a sense of purpose, inability to enjoy life? A B C

4 Do you have problems relaxing and enjoying yourself? A B C

5 Do you find it difficult to maintain close and supportive relationships with other people, even (or especially) partners, parents or children? A B C

"HOT" AND "COLD" REACTIONS
Questions 1 and 2 describe characteristics typical of those whose reactions when under stress are said to be "hot"; questions 3, 4 and 5 describe typical "cold" reactions.

A NO/NEVER/RARELY
B SOMETIMES
C YES/USUALLY

1 When under pressure, do you become angry and blame other people? A B C

2 When under pressure, do you fume inwardly? A B C

3 When under pressure, do you deny the existence of a problem? A B C

4 Do you panic easily under pressure? A B C

5 Do you blame yourself when things go wrong? A B C

COPING SKILLS

A YES/USUALLY
B SOMETIMES
C NO/NEVER/RARELY

1 Do you laugh easily? A B C

2 Do you find it easy to express emotions? A B C

3 Do you have someone you can talk to about personal problems? A B C

4 Can you tolerate differences of opinion in your relations with others? A B C

5 Do you take time out to relax every day? A B C

6 When you're busy at work or at home, do you prioritize your tasks and plan ahead to avoid potential problems? A B C

7 Are you good at making decisions? A B C

8 Do you make your wishes and feelings known to others? A B C

9 Do you find it easy to delegate or share tasks? A B C

10 Do you feel your life has a sense of purpose? A B C

11 Is your work consistent with your values? A B C

12 Do you feel there is enough creativity and stimulation in your life? A B C

13 Does your spiritual life sustain you? A B C

YOUR SCORE

A If you scored mostly As, your self-confidence, self-esteem, commitment, sense of priorities and assertiveness enable you to cope well with pressure. No one can afford to be complacent, however. You might wish to consider how you would react in the face of unexpected life events.

B A score of mostly Bs indicates that you can deal with some situations but not others, and would be well advised to learn strategies for coping with stress (see pages 168–71). Look at areas of conflict and self-doubt and consider making changes in your behaviour and attitude.

C A score of mostly Cs strongly suggests that you could be vulnerable to illness when under stress. Are there ways you could learn to manage stress better, perhaps by avoiding over- or under-stimulation? What might improve your self-esteem? If you are prone to depression, consider talking to a doctor about this. Relationships and communication with others (see page 175) may not always be easy. Is there anything that would help to change that?

ASSESSING YOUR LEVEL OF WELL-BEING

THIS COLOUR WHEEL is designed to help you identify those factors in your life that could be undermining your physical and mental well-being. The three sections of the wheel are colour-coded to match the three sections of the questionnaire, and the inner, middle and outer zones of each section have been subdivided to represent your scores for A, B and C respectively. Mark your combined score (As, Bs and Cs) in the form of dots on the corresponding segments of the wheel.

INTERPRETING YOUR RESULTS

Together the three segments of the wheel – Biochemical, Structural, Psycho-social – make up an overall picture of your potential for well-being. By looking at the pattern of dots in each circle you can quickly assess your level of susceptibility. Is there an imbalance between the sectors? Remember that even if you can't improve in every area, steps taken in one sector probably pay dividends in the others.

INNER CIRCLE A

The inner circle (A) represents the highest level of well-being that you can achieve. The higher your score here, the greater your ability to handle stressful situations and to maintain good health.

MIDDLE CIRCLE B

A high score in the middle zone (B) indicates that you're doing some things right, but that there is room for improvement. Ask yourself what you can do to make your lifestyle a healthier one than at present.

OUTER CIRCLE C

Any dot recorded in the outer zone (C) is a red-light signal. A high score in any one section of this zone is a strong indication that you need to give particular attention to making changes in this area of your life.

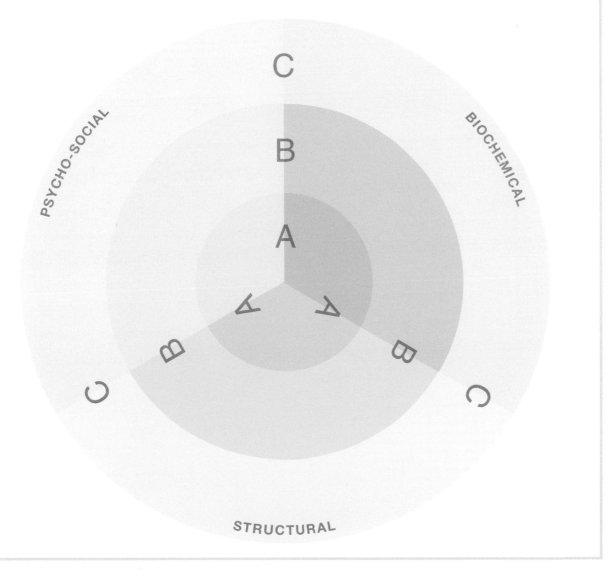

FINDING THE RIGHT THERAPY

I t is important to find a therapy with which you feel comfortable, since you are more likely to respond well to it if its approach suits your personality and views on health. Some people enjoy touch or movement therapies, for example, while others prefer those that are more mind- or emotion-orientated.

Filling in the health questionnaire (*see pages 140–43*) will help you to understand the factors that are influencing your health, while this questionnaire guides you towards a therapy that is most appropriate for you. There are no "right" or "wrong" answers, however, and you may prefer to use a combination of different therapies.

QUESTIONNAIRE

CIRCLE THE BOXES according to whether you agree with the statements. You should not have to spend a long time thinking about your answers. Then check whether most of your answers fall in the A, B or C columns. Once you have read the conclusions, the flow chart opposite can help you find an appropriate therapy. For therapies, see pages 114–37.

1 Which five of the following do you think are most essential to your health?

	A	B
A diet high in fruit and vegetables.	yes	no
A body that functions efficiently.	yes	no
The ability to relax and deal with stress.	no	yes
Family and friends.	no	yes
Job satisfaction.	no	yes
The flow of healing energy through me.	no	yes
Removal of toxins and waste products.	yes	no
A high standard of living.	yes	no

CONCLUSION

A Mostly As: you see your health primarily in physical terms; your diet, physical condition and environment are extremely important to you.

B Mostly Bs: you are emotionally and spiritually oriented: factors such as relationships, emotions and spiritual harmony are central to your health and well-being.

2 How responsible do you feel about your own health?

	A	B
If I am ill, I can probably make myself well again.	yes	no
My health is largely a matter of luck: it is influenced by events and factors beyond my control.	no	yes
I am directly responsible for my own health.	yes	no
I can only stay in good health if I consult a health professional.	no	yes
My physical health depends on how well I eat, exercise and take care of myself.	yes	no
When I am ill, I have to let nature and time heal my body.	no	yes

CONCLUSION

A Mostly As: you aim to be as healthy as possible. You take care of your health and if you are ill, you like to be actively involved in treatments.

B Mostly Bs: you see good health mostly as a matter of luck. If you are ill and need treatment, you are happy to let doctors and other health professionals take charge.

3 How do your individual preferences affect the type of therapy you choose? (For "no", circle both boxes.)

	A	B	C
I am content to be touched or massaged.	yes	no	no
I would like to use therapies that harness mental powers.	no	no	yes
I am happy "popping" pills and can remember to take them.	no	yes	no
I am comfortable with the idea of needles being used.	yes	no	no
I would change my eating habits completely if required.	no	yes	no
I am content to explore my feelings with other people	no	no	yes
I don't mind being undressed in front of a practitioner.	yes	no	no
I find it easy to picture scenes and events in my mind.	no	no	yes

CONCLUSION

A Mostly As: you are likely to be comfortable with structural therapies that involve manipulation.

B Mostly Bs: you might think about biochemical therapies, using diet, medicines or remedies.

C Mostly Cs: as you are happy exploring emotional factors, try a psycho-social therapy.

INTERPRETING YOUR ANSWERS

USE YOUR ANSWERS to the three questions opposite to work through the flow chart and find a therapy that may suit you. For therapies, see pages 114–37.

Mostly As: consider a structural therapy that you can practise on your own, once you have learnt the techniques, e.g. aromatherapy, Alexander technique or yoga.

Mostly Bs: think about a biochemical therapy for which you can eventually take responsibility, e.g. nutritional therapies or Western herbalism.

Mostly Cs: you may benefit from a psycho-social therapy that you can practise in your own time, such as relaxation and breathing or autogenic training.

Mostly As: you may prefer a patient-led therapy

QUESTION 3

QUESTION 2

Mostly As: consider a structural therapy with practitioner involvement, e.g. massage, chiropractic or osteopathy.

Mostly Bs: a biochemical therapy with practitioner guidance may suit you, e.g. Western herbalism or megavitamin therapy (*see nutritional therapies*).

Mostly Cs: you may prefer a psycho-social therapy with practitioner support, e.g. hypnotherapy or biofeedback.

Mostly As: you may be comfortable with a body-oriented therapy

Mostly Bs: you may prefer a practitioner-led therapy

QUESTION 3

QUESTION 1

Mostly As: consider a structural therapy which, once learnt, you can follow on your own, e.g. acupressure, qigong, t'ai chi or yoga.

Mostly Bs: think about a biochemical therapy in which you can take some responsibility for treatments, e.g. over-the-counter homeopathic remedies.

Mostly Cs: you may respond well to a psycho-social therapy that you can follow in your own time, e.g. meditation, visualization or self-hypnosis.

Mostly Bs: you may be comfortable with a mind- or spirit-oriented therapy

Mostly As: you may prefer a patient-led therapy

QUESTION 3

QUESTION 2

Mostly As: consider a structural therapy with practitioner involvement and control, e.g. reflexology or acupuncture.

Mostly Bs: you may prefer a biochemical therapy with practitioner guidance, e.g. homeopathy or Traditional Chinese Medicine.

Mostly Cs: a psycho-social therapy with practitioner support may suit you, e.g. psychotherapy and counselling or hypnotherapy.

Mostly Bs: you may prefer a practitioner-led therapy

QUESTION 3

WORKING WITH YOUR DOCTOR

We no longer have the blind faith in the medical profession that our parents had. We expect to be involved in our own healthcare and are readier to provide doctors with relevant information about lifestyle, eating and drinking habits and sexuality than generations who feared medical disapproval. We know that cures are not always possible and are aware that a symptom could be due to a variety of illnesses, for each of which there might be a range of treatments. Taking an active part in our own healthcare is an important step on the road to recovery: studies at the Health Institute of the New England Medical Center in Boston and at Guy's Hospital in London, for example, show that if patients become involved with their care and understand what to expect, they are likely to recover faster and feel less anxious. Many people want to negotiate the kind of relationship with their doctors that will enable them to feel comfortable about asking questions and expressing worries and reservations about treatment, including discussing options connected with non-conventional therapies.

THE DOCTOR-PATIENT RELATIONSHIP

PROBABLY ONE IN TEN people in the UK uses complementary therapies regularly, and three-quarters of the population would definitely consider doing so. Yet how many tell their doctor about herbal or nutritional supplements they are taking or discuss their visits to a reflexologist or homeopath?

Not all doctors are happy with a "patient-centred" approach and not all are good communicators. If it is awkward to discuss conventional treatment with such practitioners, bringing up the subject of complementary therapies may be even more daunting. However, at least a third of family doctors surveyed in 15 countries have practised therapies or referred their patients to complementary practitioners, so it is likely that if patients were more forthcoming, their doctors' reactions might surprise them, since clearly more physicians are taking an active interest in what complementary medicine has to offer.

If you enjoy a good working relationship with your doctor, the integration of conventional and non-conventional treatments could be relatively easy. But even if the physician is not enthusiastic, he or she will usually be tolerant, provided you do not abandon necessary conventional treatment. If the combination of therapies proves effective, and you find your need for drugs or other procedures diminished, then it is important to let your doctor learn from the experience.

GETTING THE BEST FROM YOUR DOCTOR

• Make a list of symptoms and questions so you will be sure to discuss them.
• If you do not understand what the doctor is saying, say so, and take notes if a consultation is likely to be complicated.
• Discuss the pros and cons of a procedure with the doctor. Ask about possible side effects and risk factors. Say if you are not entirely happy.
• Never use a minor complaint as an excuse to see the doctor when really you are worried about depression, stress or an unexplained lump.
• Tell the doctor of any side effects of treatment before abandoning it. A switch may be possible.
• Tell the doctor about any over-the-counter medication or complementary remedies or treatments you are taking.
• Tell your doctor if a treatment worked, either conventional or non-conventional. Feedback is much appreciated.
• Make separate appointments for each family member.

• Only ask for an emergency appointment if you really cannot wait.
• When making an appointment, say if you think you will need extra time.
• Try to be punctual, but if unavoidably late call the surgery.
• Always keep surgery appointments. Cancel them beforehand if you cannot make them.

QUESTIONS TO ASK YOUR DOCTOR

• What caused my illness?
• How is it normally treated?
• How do you intend to treat it and what are the alternatives?
• What can I do to help myself?
• Is there any danger in my trying a complementary therapy before, or as well as, the treatment you recommend?
• Are there any long-term consequences of my illness?
• Why are you sending me to that surgeon, specialist centre or hospital?
• What evidence is there that the treatment would work? What would happen if I did nothing? Are there any alternatives?

KEEPING A SYMPTOM DIARY

KEEPING A RECORD OF SYMPTOMS for any long-term health problem will enable you to track signs of improvement or decline. This will help you keep your doctor or practitioner fully informed. Note any changes in severity as well as what you ate and drank every day, and your activities and feelings. Watch out for any emerging patterns. For example, did you develop a migraine after eating cheese? Did a stressful event precede an asthma attack? Once you start a treatment, evaluate any changes in symptoms, mood or energy levels. Progress can be slow and it may take weeks or even months before you can really be sure an improvement has taken place. In that case, use the medical outcome profile below to monitor your main problem symptoms at the end of each week.

Sample Weekly Symptom Diary

	MON	TUE	WED	THUR	FRI	SAT	SUN
Headache	3	0	4	4	0	0	0
Skin rash	2	2	2	4	1	1	1
Stressors	slept badly last night		too much cheese for supper?	grape fast today			

Medical Outcome Profile

1. Choose one or two problems that bother you the most. Write them on the dotted lines below. Now consider how bad each problem was over the previous week, and score it by circling the appropriate number.

PROBLEM 1

.................................0   1   2   3   4   5   6

PROBLEM 2

.................................0   1   2   3   4   5   6

Key: 0 = As good as it could be

2. Now choose one activity of daily living, such as walking briskly, that your problem prevents you from doing. Score how badly the problem has affected you in the last week

ACTIVITY

.................................0   1   2   3   4   5   6

3. Finally, rate your general feeling of well-being during the week.

.................................0   1   2   3   4   5   6

6 = As bad as it could be

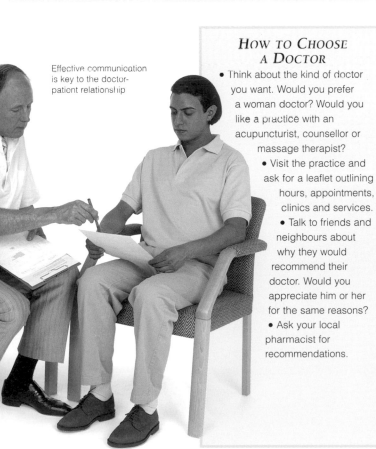

Effective communication is key to the doctor-patient relationship

HOW TO CHOOSE A DOCTOR

- Think about the kind of doctor you want. Would you prefer a woman doctor? Would you like a practice with an acupuncturist, counsellor or massage therapist?
  - Visit the practice and ask for a leaflet outlining hours, appointments, clinics and services.
  - Talk to friends and neighbours about why they would recommend their doctor. Would you appreciate him or her for the same reasons?
- Ask your local pharmacist for recommendations.

RED FLAG SYMPTOMS

Consult a doctor for:
- Chest pain or breathlessness; call an ambulance for acute pain in the chest radiating into the arms, jaw or throat
- Unexplained dizziness
- Persistent hoarseness, cough, sore throat
- Difficulty in swallowing
- Persistent abdominal pain or indigestion
- Persistent weight loss or fatigue
- A mole changing shape, size or colour, or itching or bleeding
- Change in bowel or bladder habits
- Passing blood in the stools
- Unusual vaginal discharge; bleeding between periods, after sex or after the menopause
- Lump in a breast or change in shape or size; discharge or bleeding from a nipple
- Swelling or lump in a testicle, or change in shape or size; persistent failure to get an erection
- Severe headaches; persistent one-sided headaches; vision disturbance
- A sore that does not heal; swellings; lumps
- Frequent and persistent back pain
- Unexplained leg pain and swelling.

YOUR STRUCTURAL HEALTH

The body's flexible framework of muscles, bones and joints protects the internal organs and allows us to move. The flow of blood, which transports nutrients, warmth and waste products round the body, depends on the heart and its network of arteries and veins. All the body's processes are co-ordinated by the neuroendocrine system, which centres on the brain and spinal cord. Together, these structural systems support the health of other organs and the mind, so their optimum functioning is essential for well-being. Muscle tension, for example, can influence psychological states, and narrowed arteries can reduce the supply of blood to the tissues, adversely affecting cell biochemistry.

HEALTH OF THE MUSCULO-SKELETAL SYSTEM

The spinal column consists of a stack of 33 vertebrae, which protect the spinal cord and support the entire skeleton. Many bodywork therapists believe that tension in the muscles attached to the spine or misalignment of the vertebrae produce pain elsewhere and can even interfere with internal organ function.

The musculo-skeletal system is vulnerable: accumulated postural strain, habitually tense muscles or joints stiff from neglect can make injury and pain likely. Disorders of the musculo-skeletal system are a major cause of health problems today, accounting for over a quarter of all visits to the doctor and they are the commonest cause of long-term disability.

MUSCLES, BONES & JOINTS

Bone is composed of a mixture of fibrous and connective tissue in which calcium is deposited. Where two bones meet is known as a joint. Some joints, such as those in the skull, are fixed, while others such as those of the knuckles are mobile and move within sheaths of fibrous tissue whose linings produce a lubricating fluid. Tendons attach the muscles to the skeleton, and the contraction and relaxation of the muscles enable the body to move. Voluntary muscles, such as those of the leg, are under our control, while involuntary muscles, like those of the heart or gut are not.

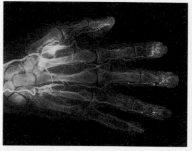

An angiogram reveals the hand's structure – its bones and blood vessels

STRUCTURAL EFFECTS OF EXERCISE

- Hand-eye co-ordination controls actions

- Sweat is produced and evaporates to cool the body

- Nervous and musculo-skeletal systems work closely to control balance and co-ordination

- Bloodflow to the gut decreases as more blood is directed to the muscles and lungs

- Endorphins ("feel-good" chemicals) and adrenaline affect body systems, boosting performance

- Blood comes to the surface of the skin to radiate away excess heat

- Heart pumps faster, blood pressure rises, breathing rate quickens, and air flow and lung capacity increase

- Spine twists and bends and back muscles contract to increase force in the hand and arm

- Weight-bearing joints experience high levels of "loading" and twisting

- Metabolic rate rises, burning up calories faster to provide more energy

THE HEART & CIRCULATION

In an 80-year lifespan, the heart beats more than 3000 million times. It pumps blood around the body through a network of arteries and veins, which are linked by tiny capillaries with walls thin enough to allow oxygen and nutrients to pass from the blood to the cells, and waste products to pass back into the blood. Deoxygenated blood flows to the heart from where it is pumped through the pulmonary artery to the lungs. Here, carbon dioxide diffuses into the alveoli – tiny sacs linked to the smallest air tubes (bronchioles) – and is exhaled. At the same time, oxygen passes into the capillaries, oxygenating the blood. The blood then returns to the left side of the heart to be pumped out around the body via the aorta, the body's largest artery.

The circulatory and respiratory systems face a number of hazards. In urban areas, the air may be so laden with industrial chemicals and traffic fumes that the respiratory system's mucous membrane defences are overwhelmed and environmental toxins can enter the bloodstream. In addition, damage to the artery walls – made worse by poor diet, chemicals, smoking, stress and high blood pressure – can lead to atherosclerosis (*see pages 48–51*). In this, toxins and calcium are deposited on the damaged lining of blood vessels, narrowing them, which is especially dangerous in the arteries supplying the heart muscle (coronary arteries) and in the brain because it reduces elasticity and impairs vital circulation. These fragile, narrowed arteries can also be blocked by a blood clot, or can leak. The result may be a heart attack, or a stroke, which can lead to brain damage.

THE BRAIN & NERVOUS SYSTEM

The human brain has been called the most complex object in the known universe. Together with the spinal cord, it comprises the central nervous system, which is composed of billions of interconnecting nerve cells, or neurons, which process information from sense organs and receptors throughout the body. Nerve fibres fan out from the central nervous system, networking to the muscles, internal organs and glands. The somatic nervous system controls muscles involved in voluntary movement, and the autonomic nervous system controls unconscious functions, such as the contraction of the gut. The autonomic system has two functions. Its sympathetic nerves stimulate glands and involuntary muscles, while its parasympathetic nerves reduce activity in the same tissues. The regulation of blood pressure, heart and breathing rate, muscle tension and the secretion of intestinal juices and enzymes depends largely on the balance between the two.

STRAIN & PAIN

When a muscle is strained or otherwise irritated, pain nerves fire off messages to the spinal cord, which sends back "reflex nerve impulses" that make the muscle tense up further (*see below*). At the same time, chemicals released by the inflammatory process and other waste products build up in the tense muscle, producing more pain. Just how susceptible a muscle is to such strain and how long it needs to recover depend on a number of factors, but especially on pre-existing bone and joint problems, postural and occupational "loading" and the general degree of psychological tension and stress.

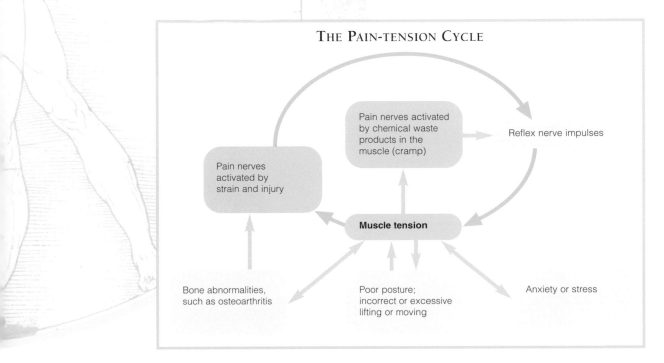

THE PAIN-TENSION CYCLE

Pain nerves activated by chemical waste products in the muscle (cramp)

Reflex nerve impulses

Pain nerves activated by strain and injury

Muscle tension

Bone abnormalities, such as osteoarthritis

Poor posture; incorrect or excessive lifting or moving

Anxiety or stress

BODYWORK

Daily activities like sitting and bending, subject joints and muscles to all sorts of mechanical strain. This may be harmful if movements are sudden, awkward, repetitive or unaccustomed, or if muscle weakness and tension have made the body susceptible to damage. Chronic back pain (*see page 52*) and repetitive strain injury (RSI) are just two of the conditions that can result from poor posture and inappropriate body use. Sitting exerts even more pressure on the back than standing; as the upper body shifts forward, the back muscles strain to keep the body upright. Fortunately, good posture, back fitness and well designed furniture can prevent problems by distributing pressure so that strain is taken off the back.

In evolutionary terms, standing upright is very recent. To avoid problems, the vulnerable back needs all the care it can get.

EVERYDAY GOOD POSTURE

THE BACK IS HELD TOGETHER by hundreds of muscles that not only move it but prevent it overstretching by protectively tensing. Twisting, swivelling and bending put the back muscles and joints under strain, especially if these are already sensitized by slouching. Learning how to stand, bend, lift and carry objects correctly will prevent problems in the future.

STANDING

Good posture distributes pressure so that the back does not take all the strain. Try standing against a wall so that your head, upper back and buttocks are touching it. Your hand should be able to slide easily into the space between your lower back and the wall, yet should almost touch both.

Neck is relaxed and shoulders are dropped

Lower back is slightly curved

Weight is evenly distributed

Good Posture

CARRYING

Distribute heavy loads, such as shopping, evenly between both hands. If carrying only one item, do not arch your back or twist your body. The bend-and-twist combination is the worst possible position for the lower back. Try to take the weight in your arms and abdominal muscles and alternate the load from one side to the other. Better still, carry the object in a rucksack, which distributes the weight more evenly, or pull it behind you on a set of wheels.

BENDING AND LIFTING

When lifting a heavy object, do not bend at the waist. Bend at the knees and let the leg muscles do the work. If the object is heavy, squat with a straight back and your legs apart; tighten your stomach muscles and lift, holding the object close to your body.

Box is carried close to the body

Spine stays in a straight line

1 Place your feet apart. Crouch down bending the hips and knees but avoid bending the back.

2 Stand up, taking the strain in the legs. Carry the load close to your body without twisting the back.

DESK SENSE

IF YOU WORK AT A DESK or a computer terminal, you can find yourself perched on the edge of your seat, leaning forward to read, with your neck bent and shoulders hunched. To maintain this position for the 25–45 hours a week expected of the average office worker requires a lot of what is known as "static" effort. Muscles in the back, arms, head and shoulders are forced to contract for long periods, causing tension and pain. Blood flow may be congested so muscles are fatigued, and breathing can be restricted because the stomach is compressed (*see Relaxation & Breathing, pages 170–71*). Adjustable chairs and desks should prevent much of this discomfort.

THE PERFECT CHAIR

If possible, try out a new chair for a day before buying. Choose one with a five-legged base and an adjustable back and seat, and check that all knobs and levers are easily reachable when sitting down. The chair should support the small of your back and you should be able to place both feet flat on the ground (if not, use a foot rest). The keyboard should be at, or just below, elbow height. A seat that tilts forwards is more comfortable for VDU users and desk work. The seat of the chair should be wide enough so that you can change position comfortably and have a curved "waterfall" edge. It should be deep enough to support the full length of the thighs, but not so deep that there is pressure behind the knees when leaning back.

THE PERFECT WORKSTATION

Many office workers complain of fatigue, but a well-designed chair and correct keyboard and screen positioning can prevent most of these problems. Fit your workstation to your body by adjusting the chair, screen, keyboard and phone, and place documents so that the most important task is directly in front of you. Try not to hunch over books, prop them up instead on an adjustable desk stand. Ideally, your worktop should slope upwards, like a Victorian desk.

SCREEN TIPS

• The top of the screen should be at or just below eye level
• Keep the screen at a comfortable distance
• Adjust contrast and brightness to avoid eye fatigue
• To reduce reflection, tilt the screen and use an anti-glare filter
• Avoid having an unshielded window either in front or behind you
• Check that overhead lighting does not reflect on the screen
• Keep the screen clean
• Arrange an eye test if you suffer from fatigue, headaches and eyestrain
• Take regular breaks. Get up and walk around every hour or so, and stand up and stretch every 20 minutes.

KEYBOARD TIPS

• Hold your wrists straight, with elbows at approximately 90 degrees
• Adjust seat and keyboard positions to be comfortable
• Do not hammer the keyboard
• Do not overstretch your fingers
• Do not rest your wrists on the keyboard or desk while typing (use a special wrist rest if necessary)
• Limit repetitive mouse movements by learning short-cut keystrokes.

DESK EXERCISES

• Alternately stretch out your fingers and clench your fists to combat stiffness and improve circulation in your hands
• Relax your neck by rolling your head across your shoulders from side to side
• Keeping your arms by your sides, roll your shoulders forwards and backwards to loosen a stiff neck and shoulders
• Relieve aching eyes by looking away from the screen and focusing on more distant objects. For relief from screen glare, occasionally cover your eyes.

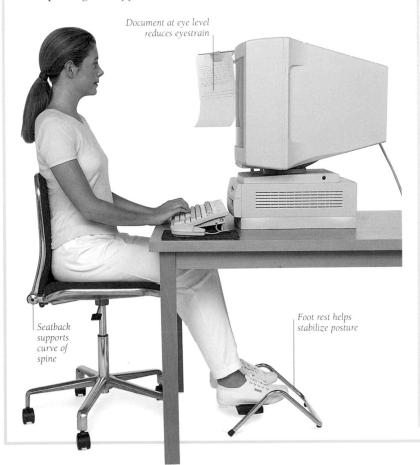

Document at eye level reduces eyestrain

Seatback supports curve of spine

Foot rest helps stabilize posture

BENEFITS OF EXERCISE

Regular exercise does more than keep you fit. It makes the heart and lungs work better, tones muscles and strengthens bones and joints. It stimulates circulation to the brain and internal organs, boosts the immune system and helps protect against insomnia, depression, heart disease, high blood pressure, cancer and osteoporosis (brittle bone disease). Exercise also triggers the release of endorphins, brain chemicals that lift mood and generate a sense of glowing well-being. What's more, it is not necessary to spend hours pounding machines in the gym to benefit from exercise. As little as 15 minutes of moderate physical activity twice a day five days a week can make a big difference to your health and will make you look better too, with glowing skin and a leaner body.

"My quality of life has been so much better since I started skating. I feel healthier, more energetic and no longer get tension headaches."

WHAT CAN EXERCISE DO FOR YOU?

THE SEDENTARY LIFE OF MOST PEOPLE in developed countries is bad for health. For example, those who exercise for less than 30 minutes a week have double the risk of dying from coronary heart disease. Activity is powered by energy from food and the oxygen we breathe. Overweight, sedentary people often lack energy because their circulation is sluggish and their muscles are deficient in oxygen. Exercise raises the heart rate so blood circulates more efficiently around the body and the number of capilliaries (tiny blood vessels) that feed the muscles increases. Muscle fibres – including those of the heart – flex and become stronger. The metabolic rate increases and bone density improves. Exercise can also:

LOWER THE RISK OF CANCER
According to a study at the University of California, women under 40 who exercise for at least four hours a week are half as likely to develop breast cancer as those who do not. Exercise also seems to protect against colon cancer, probably by stimulating the immune system and speeding up digestion.

WARD OFF HEART DISEASE & STROKE
Brisk walking for three hours a week can lower cholesterol and reduce the risk of stroke. Recent research suggests that strength training can lower blood-fat levels.

SHORTEN COLDS
Exercise tones up all body systems, including those that fight infection. In one study, brisk walking for 45 minutes five days a week halved the duration of colds.

EASE BACK PAIN
Weak back muscles are vulnerable to strain. Exercise, particularly yoga, swimming and Pilates, can treat and prevent backache by strengthening the muscles supporting the spine. Improving fitness is the single most helpful way to prevent and treat chronic back pain.

BUILD BONE
Weight-lifting and weight-bearing exercise, such as walking, aerobics and jogging, increase bone density among people of all ages.

BOOST BRAIN POWER
Improved circulation carries oxygen and glucose to the brain cells more efficiently. Exercise that requires co-ordination and mental agility, for example tennis, may generate nerve-cell connections in the brain.

IMPROVE SLEEP
Walking or low-impact aerobics for 40 minutes four times a week may help you fall asleep faster and for longer according to studies.

LIFT PMS AND MENSTRUAL PAIN
Moderate to vigorous exercise produces sweat, which offsets water retention, a symptom of PMS. It also promotes blood circulation and increases the production of mood-enhancing endorphins

ENHANCE MOOD
Exercise releases endorphins, the body's natural opiates, and mood-enhancing neurotransmitters such as serotonin. As body temperature rises, stress chemicals are burned off, making you feel relaxed.

HELP YOUR SEX LIFE
Exercise encourages the endocrine glands to produce more testosterone, the sex hormone in both men and women. In studies, people who exercised three times a week reported greater arousal, more frequent sex and more satisfaction.

EXTEND LONGEVITY
A Finnish study found six 30-minute brisk walks a month cut the risk of premature death by 44 per cent. Inactivity is even more life-threatening than smoking, according to the Cooper Institute for Aerobics Research in the US.

TYPES OF EXERCISE

THERE ARE THREE TYPES OF EXERCISE: aerobic, anaerobic and stretching. You should aim to include all three in a fitness programme, but it is important that you choose an appropriate activity, according to your age and ability, and build up levels of intensity gradually.

AEROBIC EXERCISE is any vigorous activity sustained for at least 12 minutes without a break. It should make you puff, but not so hard that you cannot carry on a conversation. During aerobic exercise, the heart pumps faster, forcing the lungs to work harder to bring in more oxygen. Blood is pumped faster around the body to nourish the cells, burn fat and carry away waste products. As muscles are developed, stamina and energy are increased so you can keep going longer without becoming exhausted. **Examples:** brisk walking, jogging, aerobics classes such as step, swimming, inline skating, dance, cycling, rowing.

Rowing is an excellent form of aerobic exercise

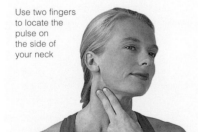

Press-ups develop arm, stomach and shoulder muscles

ANAEROBIC EXERCISE, or strength training, develops muscular strength and "resistance", which is the ability to carry, lift, push or pull a heavy load or to give extra power to a tennis serve or football kick. These are brief intense bursts of action, in which there is no time for the muscles to draw on oxygenated blood for energy. They rely instead on other chemical processes that produce lactic acid, a waste product, which can cause muscle fatigue and cramp unless muscles are strong and toned. **Examples:** weight-lifting, press-ups, resistance bands, abdominal crunches, leg raises.

STRETCHING improves the ability of the joints to move through their full range of motion. If muscle fibres are too tight, the ability to stretch, twist and turn with ease is hindered. Stretching exercises can prevent muscle tissue shortening and stiffening, avert pulled or torn muscles, relieve pain, improve muscle strength, length and tone, and enhance body awareness and appearance. Suppleness can reduce stiffness after exercise, improve your posture, keep you active as you age and even prevent falls. **Examples:** yoga, Pilates, tai chi.

Yoga is an effective way for people of all ages to improve their flexibility

Use two fingers to locate the pulse on the side of your neck

ASSESSING YOUR PULSE RATE

The number of times your heart beats per minute can be measured by taking your pulse. During aerobic exercise your heart rate should be 60–90 per cent of its maximum. To establish your maximum, subtract your age from 220. To measure your pulse rate, place two fingers on the pulse at the side of your neck or on your wrist. Count the number of beats over 15 seconds, then multiply the number by four to arrive at the number of beats per minute. As you become fitter, you will need to step up the intensity of exercise to maintain your optimum heart rate. Avoid obsessive pulse taking unless you have high blood pressure or heart disease or you are a competitive athlete.

YOUR EXERCISE PROGRAMME

Beginning an exercise programme is the best lifestyle change you can make for your health. However, embarking on an exercise programme will also be a challenge. It is easier to sustain enthusiasm if you choose an activity that you enjoy and which suits your personality, age and way of life. Set yourself realistic goals and begin gradually. There are many ways to incorporate exercise into your life:

use the stairs rather than the lift; walk to the shops instead of driving; join in a vigorous game with the children, or think of housework as a chance to be energetic. Remember anything that makes you feel out of breath counts as exercise.

"Now that I go to salsa classes, exercise is no longer a chore. I love dance and it's a great way to meet new people."

BECOMING MOTIVATED

It is never too late to start exercising. Even in your 70s, regular, moderate exercise can add a year to your life. However, the less active you have been the less energy you are likely to have, so starting an exercise programme can initially seem difficult. Remember you are bound to feel some muscle soreness and fatigue at first, and it may take up to six weeks to stop feeling lethargic. But once you are fit enough to enjoy exercise, you will begin to experience the feelings of well-being, calm and relaxation that follow a session. The key is to find an activity that you enjoy, which gives you an immediate payback in terms of having fun or learning new skills. Studies show that if you can keep exercising regularly for six months, you are likely to start thinking of yourself as an active person and to continue exercising.

EXERCISE GUIDELINES

• Make exercise part of your routine so that you spend less time thinking about it.
• Write fitness appointments in your diary as if they were business meetings.
• Choose a form of exercise that is convenient for your lifestyle and pocket. Travelling an hour each way to a swimming pool four times a week will soon become difficult and tedious.
• Set sensible goals, especially if you have not exercised for a while. Enrolling for an hour of aerobics every day could leave you tired and dispirited. Aim instead simply to complete a certain number of sessions a month.
• As you get fitter, notice how your heart and breathing rate take less time to settle down after exercise. After two months of exercising three times a week you will feel noticeably fitter.
• Plan fitness sessions with a friend, so that exercise becomes more of an enjoyable social occasion and is harder to cancel.
• Try different forms of exercise to prevent boredom. Change your schedule each week or try something innovative like inline skating, Pilates or salsa dancing.

Exercising at home to music is a good way to start a programme

AEROBIC EXERCISE TIPS

• Begin by aiming to do 15–30 minutes of moderate exercise every other day.
• Warm up for 5–10 minutes before exercise with gentle stretches and walking on the spot to stimulate heart rate and blood flow, and stretch muscles to reduce the risk of injury.
• Stop exercising if you feel any pain.
• Slow down if your muscles are sore after exercise.
• Wear appropriate clothing and footwear. The wrong kind of shoe can put strain on the knees, feet and ankles, hips and back. If exercising outdoors, dress in light layers to remove as you warm up.
• Drink plenty of fluids before, during and after exercise to prevent your becoming dehydrated.
• At the end of the workout, slow down gradually to let your heart rate return to normal.
• Stretch muscles after exercise to prevent cramps and stiffness. Hold each stretch for at least six seconds.
• Give your body a rest at least one day a week, as excessive exercising can depress the immune system.

PRECAUTIONS

Consult a doctor before starting an exercise programme if you are pregnant, over 45, obese or have a history of heart disease, high blood pressure, back pain or dizziness.

WHICH EXERCISE SUITS YOU BEST?

1. During exercise, do you like to:
    A *Push yourself to your limits?*
    B *Keep pace with a friend?*
    C *Work at your own pace?*

2. Do you see exercise as a chance to:
    A *Burn off energy?*
    B *Talk and socialize?*
    C *Think and mentally relax?*

3. Is the presence of other people when you are exercising:
    A *An inducement to perform as well as you can?*
    B *What you look forward to most?*
    C *Daunting, off-putting or distracting?*

4. Does most of the fun of exercising come from:
    A *Competing against others?*
    B *Improving on your last performance?*
    C *The joy of physical activity?*

5. Is your main reason to exercise:
    A *To improve zest and energy levels?*
    B *To feel better and look good?*
    C *To improve your sense of control?*

YOUR SCORE

MOSTLY As:
You like to test yourself and thrive on competition. Consider squash, tennis, marathon-running and triathlons.

MOSTLY Bs:
You are most likely to enjoy exercise that has a sociable element. Think about joining a gym, or a health, walking or cycling club, and try playing regular tennis or badminton for a taste of competition.

MOSTLY Cs:
You enjoy exercise because it is a chance to escape, to meditate and enjoy a peaceful period of physical activity. Consider a regular regime of repetitive exercise that you can practise at your own pace, such as swimming, walking or running.

Tennis is a good form of competitive exercise

WHICH ACTIVITY?

AEROBICS CLASSES include step, jazz, kick-boxing or even dynamic yoga. Take care if you are out of condition. Low-impact aerobics, where one foot stays on the floor, is easier on joints.
AQUAROBICS, workouts in water, is one of the safest forms of aerobic exercise. It works the heart, lungs and muscles without straining the joints.
CROSS-TRAINING, including biathlons and triathlons, combines two or three sports to overcome boredom and exercise more muscle groups.
CYCLING is excellent aerobic exercise and puts little stress on the joints.
DANCING – whether tango, salsa, jazz, Egyptian, flamenco or folk – is excellent aerobic exercise with socializing as an added bonus.
PILATES, which is fast becoming popular, claims to rebalance the body and develop strength, muscle tone, flexibility and mental concentration.
RACKET SPORTS including tennis, squash and badminton are good for improving agility and co-ordination. Playing singles is more aerobic than doubles.
ROWING can improve overall strength and endurance and provides the aerobic benefits of running with relatively little strain on the back, joints and muscles.
RUNNING AND JOGGING are excellent forms of aerobic exercise, but don't attempt either until you can walk two miles briskly without difficulty.
SKIING can be expensive but develops balance, agility and co-ordination. Cross-country skiing offers a more complete aerobic and muscle workout than almost any other sport.
SWIMMING works two-thirds of the body's muscles as well as the heart and lungs and improves muscle strength, endurance, posture and flexibility. The water takes 90 per cent of your weight so it is good for people with arthritis and asthma. Try to immerse your head if doing breaststroke to avoid neck and back damage.

WALKING is safe, simple, cheap and can be incorporated into any routine. It is both aerobic, provided your pace is at least four miles an hour, and weight-bearing (and so good for increasing bone density).
WEIGHT AND STRENGTH TRAINING is usually done with machines. It strengthens all major muscle groups and can increase bone density. It also increases the metabolic rate so more calories are burned.
YOGA is excellent for flexibility, breathing, muscle co-ordination, circulation and relaxation.

Weight-training strengthens muscle groups

EXERCISES

Key

△ **ACUTE**
For acute pain
and stiffness

□ **RECOVERY**
For when acute
pain has worn off

● **PREVENTIVE**
For long-term
prevention

Many muscle and joint problems can be prevented by developing strength and flexibility. Everyday activities, such as housework and gardening, as well as sports, can cause stresses and strains, but the more supple you are the more protected you will be from injury. Exercise routines can target specific muscle groups to hone your shape and improve posture. The back has to support the entire weight at all sorts of angles and cope with different loads, so strong, supple abdominal and lower-back muscles are vital. Avoid exercises that might strain the spine, such as straight-leg toe touches or backward bends, and always stop and rest if you feel any pain when exercising, as pushing on through the pain only risks injury.

Strong and supple abdominal and lower-back muscles will help prevent joint problems and back pain

BASIC EXERCISES

THESE EXERCISES are useful for strengthening and stretching the muscles that support and align the spine. Make them part of your regular routine if you are prone to back pain. If you do them each day they will strengthen the abdominals and prevent the back and leg muscles becoming tight and sore.

☐ ● SIDE STRETCH

1 With your feet at shoulder-width apart, stretch your right arm straight upwards with your left arm relaxed by your side.

2 Slide your left arm down your leg as far as you can and hold the position for 7 seconds.

3 Slowly return to the upright position. Repeat 3 times on each side.

● HAMSTRING STRETCH

1 Lie on your back with a leg raised and the knee bent at right angles.

Keep this leg flat on the ground

2 Slowly straighten your leg as much as you can, keeping the thigh vertical. Hold for 10 seconds. Repeat 3 times with each leg.

● CALF STRETCH

1 Stand facing a wall at an arm's length away with your right foot in front of the left. Place your hands on the wall at shoulder height.

2 Bend your elbows and lean towards the wall, keeping your back straight and your left heel on the ground. You should feel a stretch in your left calf.

3 Hold this position for 15 seconds. Repeat on each leg 3 times.

● ABDOMINAL STRENGTHENING

1 Lie on your back with your legs bent and your hands by your side.

Reach forward with your arms

2 Raise your head and shoulders off the ground. Hold for 7 seconds, then release carefully. Repeat up to 10 times.

BACK & NECK EXERCISES

THE FOLLOWING EXERCISES ease stiff joints slowly and gently. If you have acute back pain, use them as a first aid measure; rest in bed only if it is impossible to move, and then for no more than two days. Consult a doctor and start to mobilize the back and joints as soon as you can because prolonged inactivity results in stiffness, loss of strength and more pain.

A PELVIC TILT

1 Lie on your back with knees bent and feet flat on the floor.

2 Press the back of your waist against the floor, tighten your abdominal and buttock muscles and tilt your pelvis up and forwards. Hold for at least 6 seconds, then relax slowly. Repeat up to 10 times.

A R P GENTLE TWISTING

1 Lie on your back with knees bent and feet flat on the floor.

2 Keeping your knees together and your shoulders flat on the ground, let your legs gently fall over to one side as far as they will go. Hold this position for one minute. Repeat the exercise, twisting to each side, up to 5 times.

A R P CAT STRETCH

1 Position yourself on all fours. Look straight ahead, and arch your back downwards. Hold for 5 seconds.

If it is painful, raise the back a little

Keep hands and knees at shoulders' width apart

2 Curve your spine upwards until it forms an arc. Hold for 5 seconds. Repeat the whole exercise 10 times.

Slowly drop your head

A LOWER-BACK STRETCH

1 Lie on your back with knees bent and feet flat on the floor. Grasp your knees with both hands, and draw them up towards your chest.

2 When you feel a slight stretch in your lower back, inhale deeply and hold this position for 10 seconds. Slowly lower your legs ensuring that your back stays pressed against the ground. Repeat 3 times.

A PASSIVE EXTENSION

1 Lie on your front, looking straight ahead, with your hands flat on the ground either side of your head.

2 Slowly straighten your arms lifting your shoulders and chest off the ground. Repeat 5 times allowing your spine to arch more each time.

A NECK RETRACTION

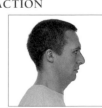

1 Sitting upright, look straight ahead. Pull your chin back to straighten your neck and elongate your spine.

2 Pull your chin further back and raise your shoulders. Keep your neck straight. Relax, then repeat 3 times.

YOUR BIOCHEMICAL HEALTH

The nutrients we absorb are crucial to biochemical health, and scientists are discovering that the foods we eat and how we prepare them can either help to prevent disease or directly contribute to ill health. The average Western diet is unhealthily high in refined and preserved foods. In developed countries, soaring rates of heart disease, gastrointestinal disorders and certain cancers are due to our appetite for foods high in fat and sugar. We should know better: one of the great nutritional discoveries of the last 15 years has been the role of antioxidants. These nutrients in fruit and vegetables actually seem to protect against disease and premature ageing. And continuing research reveals the unexpected importance of substances in such ordinary foods as broccoli and garlic. The adage "you are what you eat" is proving more true and more complex than anyone ever suspected.

THE DIGESTIVE PROCESS

Many practitioners pay close attention to diet and digestion. Clearing the gut of toxins and unfriendly bacteria so it can eliminate waste products, and a well-functioning liver are considered vital for good health. The inability to cope with stress can have an adverse effect on these processes. Digestion begins when the anticipation and smell of food trigger the secretion of saliva, which moistens food so that it is easier to chew. However, the fight or flight response to stress

dries the mouth and reduces the production of digestive enzymes and juices that break down food. Stress also slows down digestion so that energy can be diverted to the muscles for action. Less blood circulates to the stomach and to the intestines, and the rhythmic contractions of the gut becomes slower, faster or irregular (*see below*). Constant stress sustains these reactions, so that food remains inadequately digested and absorbed with damaging effects on health.

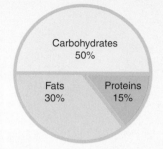

WHAT IS A BALANCED DIET?

Carbohydrates
50%

Fats
30%

Proteins
15%

In broad terms, a balanced diet consists of 50 per cent carbohydrates, 15 per cent protein, and no more than 30 per cent fats, with plenty of fibre, vitamins, minerals and water (*see pages 160–64*). Many people are hazy about nutrients such as different types of carbohydrate or essential fatty acids, let alone newly relevant nutrients such as lycopene (found in red vegetables and thought to prevent prostate cancer). Fortunately, most dieticians agree on easy-to-follow guidelines (*see right*) which concur with the so-called Mediterranean diet. (People in Greece and Italy have low rates of chronic diseases, which is thought to be linked to their diet rich in fruit and vegetables, olive oil and red wine.)

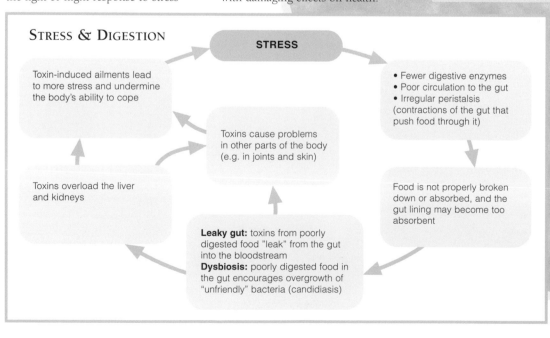

STRESS & DIGESTION

STRESS

Toxin-induced ailments lead to more stress and undermine the body's ability to cope

Toxins cause problems in other parts of the body (e.g. in joints and skin)

Toxins overload the liver and kidneys

Leaky gut: toxins from poorly digested food "leak" from the gut into the bloodstream
Dysbiosis: poorly digested food in the gut encourages overgrowth of "unfriendly" bacteria (candidiasis)

• Fewer digestive enzymes
• Poor circulation to the gut
• Irregular peristalsis (contractions of the gut that push food through it)

Food is not properly broken down or absorbed, and the gut lining may become too absorbent

A shared meal offers a chance to relax and communicate

Healthy Eating Habits

Many of us in developed countries have fallen into bad habits, grabbing meals on the run and wolfing junk food that lacks essential nutrients and is full of preservatives. With more people going out to work, there is an understandable trend towards relying on convenience foods. This is not intrinsically wrong, but it does mean that we must become aware of what we are eating and compensate for any dietary inadequacies.

Eating "little and often" is a worth-while axiom. Although short periods of fasting seem to sharpen mental alertness, persistent low blood sugar causes irritability, depression and mood swings. Several light meals a day with fruit and nut snacks maintain stable blood-sugar levels, and are easier to digest and less likely to make you sleepy than a hefty lunch and dinner laden with sugar and saturated fat. To avoid the post-lunch energy slump, eat a midday meal of protein and complex carbohydrates, such as lean chicken or fish with pasta or wholemeal bread.

Breakfast is worth making time for, no matter how busy your schedule, since it is necessary to stir the metabolism and restore energy after the overnight fast. Studies show that children who eat breakfast are more alert later in the morning than those who do not. But choose foods that are high in complex carbohydrates, like toast, cereals and fruit, rather than high-protein and fatty foods such as fried eggs and bacon or

cheese and ham. It is important to bear in mind that eating should be enjoyable. The whole performance of preparing and consuming a meal ideally should be a social event, shared with family and friends. Perhaps if we sat down to enjoy at least one meal together every day, without watching television at the same time or rushing off afterwards, not only would our digestive systems be under less strain, but we might also communicate better and feel less stressed.

Mood Foods

Certain foods are known to affect mood. Bananas and some high-protein foods including meat, milk and eggs contain the amino acid tryptophan, for example, which is metabolized to serotonin, a brain chemical that induces calm and sleep. Lowered levels of serotonin are linked to depression and hostility. A mid-morning cup of coffee whets concentration thanks to its caffeine, a stimulant also found in tea, chocolate and cola. However, six or more cups a day raises blood pressure and stress-hormone levels and can cause tremors, palpitations, insomnia and accelerated bone-calcium loss. More positively, cocoa and chocolate contain phenylethylamine, a chemical associated with mood enhancement.

12 Ways to Improve Your Diet

- Ensure half your daily calorie intake comes from starchy foods like bread, pasta, rice and potatoes.
- Eat at least five portions of fruit and vegetables every day.
- Limit your intake of saturated fat (found in meat and dairy products).
- Steam or stir-fry vegetables rather than frying or boiling them.
- Cook with pure, unrefined vegetable oils such as olive oil rather than with animal fats
- Use skimmed milk and low-fat dairy products instead of full-fat versions.
- Get more of your protein from poultry, fish, pulses, cereals and low-fat dairy products, rather than from red meat.
- Eat oily fish, such as salmon, twice a week for their essential fatty acids.
- Reduce your intake of coffee, tea and cola drinks. Drink herbal teas, fruit juices and water instead.
- Replace butter with a low-fat spread, high in polyunsaturated fats and low in trans-fats (look for "non-hydrogenated fat" on the label) and spread thinly.
- Avoid "junk" and processed foods loaded with preservatives, colourings and flavourings.
- Limit alcohol intake to no more than 14 units a week for women and 21 for men (a unit = 1 glass wine, ½ pint beer or 1 measure spirits). A daily glass of red wine may lower the risk of heart disease.

Probably the best single way to improve your diet is to increase your intake of fruit and vegetables

NECESSARY NUTRIENTS

Foods contain proteins, carbohydrates and fats in varying combinations. These molecular compounds are essential for good health, providing energy and playing a vital role in the growth and maintenance of cells. Food is also a source of vitamins and minerals, necessary only in tiny amounts, but each with a specific part to play in the body's metabolism. Fibre, from plants, is another essential nutrient, helping the digestive system to function efficiently. Our most precious nutrient, however, is water – nearly two-thirds of the human body is comprised of it. Without water, our body systems would stop working and we would die within days.

Most people in the Western world get more protein than they need. The excess is used for energy or converted into fat.

PROTEIN

THE PROTEIN WE EAT is broken down into its component amino acids, which are used by cells for growth, maintenance and repair. The body can make some amino acids itself, but there are nine, the so-called "essential" amino acids, that can be obtained only from food. In addition, amino acids are used in the body to produce enzymes, catalysts that allow complex chemical processes to take place, and DNA, which carries the genetic information controlling all metabolic activity. Ideally, around 10–15 per cent of calories should come from protein. If we do not get enough protein, the body will break down cells in order to provide it. In fact, most people in the Western world get more protein than they need. The excess is used for energy or converted into fat and stored.

Sources Meat, fish, poultry, eggs, cheese and soya beans are sources of the full range of amino acids, and one helping a day is sufficient. Incomplete sources of amino acids, such as pulses, bread, rice, pasta, potatoes and nuts, must be combined in meals to provide the whole range. Rice and lentils, baked beans on toast, and cereals with milk are all examples of protein-rich combinations.

CARBOHYDRATES

CARBOHYDRATES are the most readily available source of food energy and should account for 50 per cent of our diet. They are turned into glucose (the body's basic fuel) and glycogen, which is stored in the liver and muscles for conversion to glucose. Carbohydrates fall into two categories: *complex*, which are broken down slowly to provide energy over a long period (these should form two-thirds of carbohydrate intake) and *simple* (sugars) which provide instant energy. Some types of simple carbohydrates, such as cane sugar, are known as "empty" calories as they have no extra nutritional value.

Sources *Complex*: in starchy foods – bread, pasta, rice, potatoes, pulses, wholegrains and other cereals. *Simple*: in fruit, vegetables and honey (glucose and fructose), milk (lactose), sprouting grains (maltose) and cane or beet sugar (sucrose).

WATER

ALL THE BODY PROCESSES, including digestion and elimination, need water – ideally, about three litres a day. The best way to get enough water is to drink about two litres every day, or sufficient to keep your urine pale yellow. In hot weather, if exercising, or during a fever, you may need more water as your body loses fluid in the form of sweat. Filtered tap water may be preferable to some bottled waters, which can contain bacteria, nitrates and chemicals. When buying bottled water, read the label carefully.

Sources Fruit, vegetables, dairy products, bread, cereals and meat provide one-third of daily intake. The rest can be made up with plain water, juices, milk and other drinks. **Caution** Alcohol, tea, coffee and cola are diuretic, expelling more water from the system than they provide.

FATS

FATS, OR LIPIDS, ARE THE MOST CONCENTRATED source of food energy. High-fat foods are therefore high-calorie foods. A certain amount of fat is necessary for the body to function healthily, but too much can lead to health problems. In the West, the recommended maximum level is about 30 per cent of total calorie intake, although experts suggest it should be as low as 10 per cent for those who have a problem metabolizing fats. Fats are important for storing energy, for transporting fat-soluble vitamins (A, D, E and K) and for producing hormones. They also provide essential fatty acids (EFAs) which the body cannot produce by itself.

Fats make food palatable and delay its exit from the stomach. A balance of EFAs and the prostaglandins they produce (see Glossary, pages 177–78) is vital for good health. Deficiencies of EFAs have been linked to atherosclerosis or narrowing of the arteries, arthritis and allergies. Fats are classed as saturated or unsaturated (see below) – terms that refer to their chemical composition. Unsaturated vegetable oils are converted to saturated fats (e.g. margarines) by an industrial process known as hydrogenation. This creates trans-fatty acids, linked to heart disease. Vegetable oils are thus considered a healthy alternative to margarine.

SATURATED FATS

Mainly associated with meat and dairy produce, saturated fats are not an essential part of a healthy diet. A high intake raises blood cholesterol levels, and increases the risk of obesity, heart disease, atherosclerosis and cancer of the bowel, breast and pancreas.
Sources Butter, hard cheese, cream, palm oil, coconut and fatty meats, hard margarine, solid cooking fats, cakes and biscuits.

UNSATURATED FATS

Monounsaturated fatty acids are fats of plant origin and can replace saturated fats in the diet.
Sources Peanut oil, rapeseed oil, avocados, nuts, seeds and olive oil. The latter also contains poly-unsaturated fatty acids (see right), and features strongly in the diet of Mediterranean countries, which have low rates of heart disease. Where possible, use cold-pressed, unrefined olive oil from a single source.

Polyunsaturated fatty acids, or PUFAs, contain essential fatty acids, which cannot be produced by the body so must be obtained from the diet. They are important in maintaining cell membranes, transporting fats around the body and forming prostaglandins. These chemicals are produced as and when required for numerous body functions, including circulation, water balance and maintaining the immune system. Essential fatty acids are grouped in two families (see below).

Omega–6 polyunsaturated fatty acids are derived from linoleic acid.
Sources Seed oils such as sunflower oil, maize oil, peanut oil, olive oil and evening primrose oil.

Omega–3 polyunsaturated fatty acids are derived from alpha-linolenic acid. They are important in early brain development and protect against heart disease and cancer of the breast, bowel, colon and pancreas. They are advised to help relieve arthritis and psoriasis.
Sources Leafy vegetables, oily fish, fish oils and shellfish.

FIBRE

DIETARY FIBRE IS THE TERM used to describe a group of substances found in the cell walls of plants. Fibre is resistant to digestive enzymes, and so passes through the gut without being absorbed. It softens and increases the bulk of faeces, preventing constipation, and slows down the passage of food through the gut, giving digestive enzymes time to work. Fibre also absorbs the toxic by-products of digestion. Low-fibre diets are linked to bowel and gallbladder cancer and other intestinal diseases. The UK Department of Health advises eating at least 18g of fibre a day, while other experts suggest up to 35g. There are two main groups of fibre: soluble and insoluble. Insoluble fibre speeds the passage of food through the intestines and reduces the build-up of carcinogens which can cause colon cancer. Soluble fibre lowers blood-cholesterol levels and inhibits the absorption of glucose.
Sources
Insoluble fibre: brown rice, bran, nuts, wheat bran, wholegrains, dried fruit.
Soluble fibre: oat bran, pulses, fruit, vegetables.

VITAMINS & MINERALS

Vitamins and minerals are an essential part of our diet, since the body is unable to manufacture them for itself. Each vitamin has specific functions in the body, while at least 16 minerals are vital for life, growth or reproduction. Ideally, we should obtain all the vitamins and minerals we need from food, especially if we eat a well-balanced diet. However, scientific evidence increasingly suggests that mass-production of food may deplete some nutrients and that supplements may therefore be beneficial. They should not be taken as a substitute for a healthy diet, however, as research also suggests that the key to optimum nutrition lies in the way food components work together, rather than in the action of isolated vitamins or minerals.

SUPPLEMENTS

THE WORLD HEALTH ORGANIZATION and other agencies have established guidelines for daily levels of nutrients, known as RDAS (recommended daily allowances) or RNIS (reference nutrient intakes), but many nutritionists claim these are only minimum levels to prevent disease and not enough for optimum health. In any case, individual needs vary according to age, gender and state of health. Nutritional supplements can certainly be of benefit in some situations.

Some people need extra vitamins and minerals

For example, the occurrence of spina bifida and other birth defects is dramatically reduced when pregnant women take additional folic acid. In all adults, folic acid seems to protect against heart disease. Vitamin E supplements may reduce the risk of heart attack by up to 75 per cent. Vegans, those on a diet and heavy smokers may all be advised to take B complex vitamins. On the other hand, iron can cause health problems if taken in excess, as can vitamins A and D.

If you have cut corners nutritionally, a good antioxidant-rich multivitamin and mineral supplement may be useful until you improve your diet. Always consult your doctor before taking supplements if you are pregnant or on medication.

ANTIOXIDANTS

OVER 100 ANTIOXIDANTS have been discovered (*see below*). These nutrients are able to "scavenge" (seek out and destroy) potentially harmful molecules known as free radicals. The body produces free radicals as part of its normal metabolism and as a defence against infection but, in the few seconds they exist, they can damage DNA and cell membranes and affect cholesterol so that it "furs up" arteries. If unchecked, these reactions contribute to heart disease, cancer, premature ageing and other health problems. Eating an unhealthy diet (especially fried or burnt food), taking excessive exercise, and exposure to environmental chemicals, cigarette smoke, sunlight and radiation can all increase levels of free radicals.

VITAMINS	Vitamins A (beta-carotene, *see below*), C and E
MINERALS	Selenium, zinc, manganese and copper
BIOFLAVONOIDS	These are plant chemicals that boost vitamin C activity and appear to have anti-infective and anti-carcinogenic properties. They are found in prunes, citrus fruit, cherries, berries, plums, rosehips, grapes, papaya, melon, broccoli, tomatoes, tea and red wine.
CAROTENOIDS	These yellow and red pigments are present in many plants. The best known is beta-carotene, which the body converts to vitamin A. Others include lycopene (found in tomatoes), and lutein and zeaxanthin (found in spinach, kale, broccoli, turnips and mustard greens), which also prevent age-related macular degeneration.
GLUTATHIONE	This enzyme is produced by the body from foods rich in the amino acids L-cysteine and L-methionine (egg yolks, red peppers, garlic, onions, broccoli, sprouts, yogurt, wheatgerm and poultry).

Good sources of antioxidants include citrus fruits, tomatoes and spinach

VITAMINS

VITAMIN D, PRODUCED NATURALLY when the skin is exposed to sunlight, is the only vitamin the body can make efficiently on its own. All the others must be obtained from food. The fat-soluble vitamins A, D, E and K can be stored in the body, unlike the B complex vitamins (with the exception of B[12]) and vitamin C, which are water soluble (dissolvable in water). Stress, antibiotics and alcohol can all affect the body's absorption of water-soluble vitamins.

VITAMIN	MAIN USES	GOOD SOURCES	RDA
VITAMIN A	Antioxidant (*see left*); necessary for good vision; maintains skin and mucous membranes; in excess can cause birth defects, blurred vision and headaches	Present as retinol in animal foods (liver, butter, cheese, eggs, oily fish) and as beta-carotene in plant foods (carrots, tomatoes, spinach, broccoli)	Women, 600mcg; breastfeeding women, 950mcg; men, 700mcg
VITAMIN B[1]	Helps convert food into energy; prevents the build-up of toxic substances	Whole grains, brown rice, nuts, wholemeal pasta and bread, fortified white bread and breakfast cereals, dried beans, lean meats, fish	Women, 0.8mg; men, 1mg
VITAMIN B[2] (RIBOFLAVIN)	Helps convert food into energy	Nuts, dairy products, liver, yeast extract, eggs, lean meat, leafy vegetables, lentils, breakfast cereals	Women, 1.1mg; men, 1.3mg
NIACIN	Involved in the synthesis of DNA; helps convert food into energy; supports the nervous and digestive systems	Dairy products, liver, oily fish, chicken, turkey, wholemeal bread, brown rice, yeast extract, nuts	Women, 13mg; men, 17mg
VITAMIN B[6] (PYRIDOXINE)	Promotes brain activity; stimulates production of antibodies and formation of red blood cells; helps release energy from protein	Whole grains, dried beans, eggs, nuts, oats, fish, liver, brown rice, bananas, green leafy vegetables, yeast extract, wholemeal bread, soya beans	Women, 1.2mg; men, 1.4mg
VITAMIN B[12]	Protects the nerves; important for cell division, formation of red blood cells and enzyme function; involved in production of DNA and RNA	Foods of animal origin, e.g. meat, poultry, fish, eggs, dairy products; some fortified breakfast cereals	Men and women, 1.5mcg
BIOTIN	Stimulates body to produce energy; maintains enzyme function, healthy skin, hair and bone marrow; supports glands producing sex hormones	Almost all foods, especially liver, peanut butter, egg yolks, yeast extract	Men and women, 150mcg
FOLIC ACID (FOLATE)	Works with B[12] to form new cells, especially blood cells; important in making DNA and RNA; helps prevent birth defects such as spina bifida, therefore essential for pregnant women	Wheatgerm, liver, broccoli, green cabbage, pulses, nuts, yeast extract, fortified bread and breakfast cereals	Men and women, 200mcg; pregnant women, 300mcg (400mcg in first 12 weeks)
PANTOTHENIC ACID	Converts food into energy; promotes synthesis of cholesterol, fat and red blood cells, and formation of antibodies; supports nervous system and skin	All meat and vegetable foods, especially liver, yeast extract, nuts, kidney, wheatgerm, soya flour	Men and women, 3–7mg
VITAMIN C	Antioxidant (*see left*); makes collagen (important for healthy gums, teeth, bones and skin) and neurotransmitters (serotonin, noradrenaline, *see Glossary, pages 177–78*); aids absorption of iron and helps skin to heal; protects against infection	Oranges and other citrus fruits, blackcurrants, strawberries, kiwi fruit, tomatoes, spinach and other dark-green vegetables, potatoes, mango, papaya	Men and women, 40–60mg; smokers, at least 80mg
VITAMIN D	Important for absorption of calcium and phosphorus essential for healthy bones and teeth	Made by the skin in response to sunlight; also found in milk, oily fish, brown rice, eggs, butter, margarine	Produced by the body when skin is exposed to sun
VITAMIN E	Antioxidant; prevents formation of free radicals following ingestion of polyunsaturates; proven ability to protect against heart disease	Nuts, vegetable oils, whole grains, olives, asparagus, spinach, salmon, tuna, eggs, avocado, blackberries, wholemeal bread, brown rice	Women, at least 3mg; men, at least 4mg
VITAMIN K	Helps body digest certain proteins and prevents blood clots from forming	Green leafy vegetables (green cabbage, broccoli, Brussels sprouts)	Women, 65mcg; men, 70mcg

MINERALS

ALTHOUGH MINERALS ACCOUNT for only 3–4 per cent of body weight, some, such as calcium and iron, which are necessary for healthy bones and red blood cells respectively, are required in fairly large quantities. Others, such as iodine, zinc, molybdenum and chromium, are needed in such tiny amounts they are known as "trace elements", but are, nevertheless, essential constituents of particular enzymes or hormones. If you take supplements, consult a nutritionist or doctor as there is a delicate balance between different minerals and an excess of one can affect the efficacy of others. An excess of iron in the diet, for instance, inhibits the absorption of zinc.

MINERAL	MAIN USES	GOOD SOURCES	RDA
CALCIUM	Growth and maintenance of bones and teeth; blood clotting, muscle function and heartbeat regulation; especially important in women to prevent osteoporosis after menopause	Milk and dairy products (including low-fat), tinned sardines, eggs, spinach and other green leafy vegetables	Ages 11–18, 800–1000 mg; men and women over 18, 800mg; breastfeeding women, 1250mg
CHROMIUM	Regulation of blood sugar and cholesterol	Red meat, liver, egg yolks, seafood, wholegrain cereals, cheese	Men and women, 25mcg
COPPER	Building bones and connective tissue; aids absorption of iron	Offal, shellfish, nuts and seeds, mushrooms	Men and women, 1.2mg
FLUORIDE	Protection against tooth decay	Tap water, toothpaste, tea	No RDA
IODINE	Hormone production by thyroid gland	Iodized table salt, seafood, seaweed	Men and women 150mcg
IRON	Carrying oxygen to body cells	Liver, shellfish, dried fruits, dark-green leafy vegetables, wholemeal bread, pulses, red meat, fortified cereals	Women, 14.8mg; men, 8.7mg
MAGNESIUM	Bone growth and nerve and muscle function.	Wheat bran, whole grains, raw leafy vegetables, almonds, cashews, soya beans, bananas, apricots	Men and women, 300mg
MANGANESE	Bone growth and cell function	Nuts, whole grains, vegetables, fruits, tea, egg yolks, pulses	Men and women, 1.4mg
MOLYBDENUM	DNA production	Offal, yeast extract, pulses, whole grains, leafy vegetables	Men and women, 50–400mcg
PHOSPHORUS	Release of energy from food; nutrient absorption; maintenance of healthy bones and teeth	All protein foods (e.g. meat, poultry, fish, seafood, egg yolks, milk), dried peas, beans, nuts	Men and women, 550mg
POTASSIUM	Regulation of heartbeat; muscle contraction; transference of nutrients to cells; regulation of fluids and electrolyte balance (see Glossary, pages 177–78); nerve function	Citrus fruits, bananas, dried fruits, avocados, peanut butter, dried peas and beans, potatoes	Men and women, 3500mg
SELENIUM	Works with vitamin E as an antioxidant (see page 162); involved in sexual development and may help prevent cancer	Offal, white fish, tuna, shellfish, red meat, egg yolks, poultry, garlic, tomatoes, muesli, wholegrain cereals, wholemeal bread, dairy foods, lentils, avocados, Brazil nuts	Women, 60mcg; men, 75mcg
SODIUM	Regulation (with potassium) of fluid balance; nerve and muscle function	Table salt, anchovies, yeast extract, processed meats	Men and women, 1600mg
SULPHUR	Protein production	All protein foods – meat, poultry, fish, seafood, egg yolks, milk, dried peas, beans, nuts	No RDA
ZINC	Antioxidant (see page 162); growth and sexual development; immune function; enzyme action	Liver, red meat, oysters, peanuts, sunflower seeds, cheese, eggs	Women, 7mg; men, 9.5mg

SPECIAL DIETS

For various health or ethical reasons, some people need to modify their diet. Increasing numbers, for example, are giving up meat for health reasons or due to concern about the treatment of animals reared for consumption and about the levels of antibiotics, hormones and other drugs given them. Other people need to adapt their diet to lose weight, or to cure themselves of a food intolerance (*see pages 92–95*). Followers of rigorous regimes such as the "Stone Age" diet (*see page 129*) claim special benefits, and certain regimes such as the Pritikin diet or Gerson therapy aim to prevent or cure particular diseases, notably heart disease and cancer. Always consult a doctor before following a strict diet, since restricted diets risk malnourishment in the long-term. This is especially important for children.

Studies quite clearly show that people who eat a vegetarian diet run less risk of heart disease and colon cancer.

VEGETARIANISM

Studies show that vegetarians run less risk of contracting heart disease, gall bladder problems, diabetes, high blood pressure, osteoporosis, diverticular disease and colon cancer, while vegan diets have been prescribed for high blood pressure, arthritis, angina and asthma with some success. If you are vegetarian, it is essential to eat alternative sources of protein and, if vegan, to take enough vitamin B^{12} (*see page 129*).

WEIGHT LOSS

Obesity is common in industrialized countries and is clearly linked to diabetes, high blood pressure, heart disease, joint problems and, indirectly, to some forms of cancer, while an obsession with weight can lead to anorexia,

Regular exercise helps control weight

bulimia and faddy diets that risk malnourishment. To find out if your weight is healthy, assess your body mass index (*see below*). If under- or overweight, keep a food diary for a week. The average daily calorie intake should be 1800–2200, depending on gender, age and activity levels. The secret to increasing your weight healthily is to eat more complex carbohydrates (*see page 160*). To lose weight, reduce fat consumption (*see right*) to no more than 30 per cent of total calorie intake. In addition, take aerobic exercise for 30 minutes and anaerobic exercise for ten minutes three times a week (*see page 153*). There is no evidence that "wonder" pills cure obesity, although there are prescription drugs that inhibit nutrient absorption, reduce appetite and increase metabolic rate.

TIPS TO HELP REDUCE FAT INTAKE

- Remove fat from meat and skin from poultry before eating, or better still avoid red meat.
- Grill or roast meat on a rack.
- Avoid frying but if you do, drain food on absorbent kitchen paper before eating.
- Skim fat from casseroles while cooking and when cool.
- Remember that low-fat margarine still contains fat; spread thinly.
- Switch to skimmed or semi-skimmed milk and low-fat cheeses and yogurts.
- Use herbs and spices to add flavour to food.
- Avoid cakes, biscuits, pastry, confectionery and desserts made with fat or shortening.

BODY-MASS INDEX

THE EASIEST WAY TO ESTIMATE if you are the correct weight for your height is to work out your body mass index.

Note: if you exercise frequently, the calculation may be distorted by your increased muscle mass.

Divide your weight in kilograms by your height in metres squared (round up to the nearest decimal point).
For example, you are 1.6 m tall and weigh 63 kg:

1.6 x 1.6 = 2.6   63 divided by 2.6 = 24.2

(To convert pounds to kilos, multiply pounds by 0.45; to convert feet to metres multiply feet by 0.3.)

SCORE	
Under 20	underweight
20–25	healthy weight
25–30	overweight
Over 30	obese

Spicy stir-fries are excellent for those who wish to lose weight

HEALTH & THE ENVIRONMENT

The quality of food is a growing concern in industrialized countries and part of the fear that the natural world is under threat from pollution. Many people worry, for instance, about genetically modified crops and the effects of additives, pesticides and other environmental toxins on the body. The scare in the UK over beef infected with BSE (bovine spongiform encephalopathy) is just one example of an incident that has left consumers sceptical of official reassurances and anxious to find food that is as unprocessed and pure as possible. Environmental factors are thought to have wide-ranging effects: in some individuals they may be a factor in food sensitivities (*see pages 94–95*) and they can interfere with the way hormones work or affect how well the immune system responds to infection.

CHEMICALS IN FOOD

BOTH NATURAL and chemical substances are widely used in agriculture and food processing. While some are harmless, others can affect health.

ADDITIVES
Substances are added to food to preserve it and provide flavour and colour. In Europe, the E number or the actual name of all additives, except for flavourings, must be included in the list of ingredients. Not all of these additives are necessarily bad, and some are needed to prevent food from spoiling. Ascorbic acid (vitamin C), for example, is used to prevent fruit juices from turning brown and fatty foods from going rancid. The following additives, however, can cause problems:
Monosodium glutamate (MSG) can make some people unwell or trigger food intolerance symptoms.
Nitrites and nitrates, used to preserve processed meats and fish, may convert to potentially carcinogenic nitrosamines in the body.
Benzoic acid, added to soft drinks and beer, can cause adverse reactions.
Sulphur compounds in dried fruit and relishes may trigger asthma and other allergic reactions.
Colourings such as tartrazine, found in soft drinks and sweets, are said to contribute to allergic and behavioural problems in some children.

Crops are sprayed with a variety of insecticides

Guar gum and gum arabic, used to improve texture and smoothness, may cause flatulence in some people.

CHEMICALS IN FARMING
Pesticides are used in agriculture to kill insects, weeds and fungi, while antibiotics are routinely added to feed to prevent the infections prevelant when livestock are raised intensively.
Pesticides, such as organophosphates and dioxin, may affect the body, especially the central nervous system, in various ways.
Antibiotics and antifungals are linked with antibiotic-resistant bacteria.
Growth hormones may affect the body in ways we do not yet understand.
Heavy metals, such as cadmium, mercury and lead, are found in fish and shellfish from rivers and coastal waters polluted by industrial waste. These metals interfere with immune responses and affect the central nervous system.

ORGANIC PRODUCE
Where possible, it is wise to reduce the danger from chemicals by choosing organically produced foods. Although more expensive, demand for organic produce currently outstrips supply, and intensive farming methods for the time being may still be the only way to feed the world's population.

Those suspicious of of genetically modified food and the consequences of consuming crops laden with pesticides insist that long-term scientific testing is necessary.

Organic vegetables are better for health

THE IMMUNE SYSTEM

THE BODY'S DEFENCES PROTECT it from invading foreign substances – viruses, bacteria, pollen, dust and toxic chemicals – which could inflict damage, ranging from an infected cut to cancer. The frontline defences are the skin, mucous membranes (of the respiratory system, gut and genitals), small hairs in the nose and ears, and acid juices in the stomach.

If invaders breach these barriers and enter the bloodstream, they are met by defensive white blood cells called lymphocytes. These are formed in the bone marrow and circulate round the body in the lymphatic system, which is a network of vessels that filters debris and toxins out of body tissues. Lymphocytes engulf the invading microbes.

Antibodies are produced by a special kind of lymphocyte in response to a specific invader. A flu antibody, for example, is produced to attack a flu virus. Once programmed, the lymphocyte recognizes the invader if it appears again and rapidly produces more targeted antibodies. This is the main principle behind immunization. Although some immunity is passed on from mother to child in the womb and in breast milk, we acquire most of it by dealing with invading microbes as we grow up. It is widely accepted that exposure to infection develops a competent immune system.

IMMUNE DISORDERS

Special "suppressor" T-cells switch off antibodies when there are enough to fight invaders. Too many can block antibody production so the system is "immunodeficient". This may happen naturally, as in HIV (human immuno-deficiency virus), or with the use of drugs, after an organ transplant.

"Helper" T-cells prompt the production of antibodies. If they dominate, the body no longer recognizes the difference between invading substances and itself. It starts to attack its own cells in what are called autoimmune diseases, which include multiple sclerosis and rheumatoid arthritis.

Finally, the immune system can become hypersensitive and react against normally harmless substances, such as grass, dust, pollen and certain foods (*see pages 92–99*).

DAMAGE TO THE IMMUNE SYSTEM

Malnutrition and vitamin deficiency are linked to poor immune function. Environmental chemicals and toxic heavy metals such as cadmium, lead and mercury damage the immune system (*see left*), as do tobacco smoke and certain drugs. Stress (*see pages 84–85*), excessive exercise, ageing and certain infections (most notably HIV) reduce immune competence.

A lymphocyte engulfs an invading flu virus

HOW TO PROTECT THE IMMUNE SYSTEM

- Eat a balanced diet with plenty of fruit and vegetables, nuts, seeds and wholegrains, and cut down on saturated fats, sugars, processed products and chemical additives.
- Limit caffeine and drink alcohol in moderation. (One or two drinks a day are not harmful.)
- Stop smoking, as it increases susceptibility to infection.
- Top up your diet with a good quality antioxidant supplement on a "bad nutrition day".
- If you are elderly, pregnant or suspect your immune system is struggling because of an infection, environmental pollution or stress, consider taking a multivitamin and mineral supplement.
- Include in your diet herbs that stimulate the immune system: garlic, ginger, thyme, sage and rosemary
- Take aerobic exercise for 30 minutes three times a week.
- Practise stress-reducing techniques such as meditation (*see page 135*).
- Avoid environmental chemicals, such as petrol exhaust fumes, wherever possible.
- Enjoy social interaction with friends and family
- Ensure you have enough rest and sleep to repair your body.
- Develop positive beliefs and attitudes towards life and other people. Research shows that optimism and altruism actually promote health.
- If you get an infection, fight it with over-the-counter herbs such as echinacea, garlic or astragalus.

HORMONES

HOW WELL THE BODY can cope with stress, environmental change and fluctuating amounts of sleep and food depends on interweaving processes in the brain, nervous system and endocrine (hormone) glands.

The endocrine system and the brain secrete chemicals, known as hormones, that influence mood and vitality and regulate all body functions from digestion to the menstrual cycle,

blood circulation and the fight-or-flight response (*see page 84*).

The *pituitary gland* orchestrates all hormonal activity. It produces growth hormones as well as substances that control the output of other hormonal glands. These include the *thyroid gland* in the neck which regulates metabolism; the *adrenal glands* above the kidneys which co-ordinate the body's chemical balance and response to stress, physical

injury and infection; and the *pancreas* which secretes insulin to regulate blood-sugar levels. The pituitary gland also regulates the *ovaries'* production of oestrogen and progesterone and the *testes'* output of testosterone.

Endocrine disorders require conventional treatment. But if hormone levels are only mildly disturbed, complementary approaches might, with your doctor's support, be worth trying.

YOUR PSYCHO-SOCIAL HEALTH

Dealing with crises, life events and conflict is part of the constant adaptation to change that is essential to well-being. We tend to think about managing stress in purely psychological terms, but the process also requires energy, so it also puts a strain on the body. How well we cope will depend on how much energy, support and information are available. Certain challenges are inescapable, but difficulties arise when challenges are severe and sudden, such as injury or shock, or persistent and drawn out – the effects of poor nutrition perhaps, or of an impossible job or relationship. Stress- management techniques can help us adapt to and control stress.

WHAT IS STRESS?

We feel stressed in situations that tax our ability to cope and/or endanger well-being. These prompt the instinctive stress or "fight or flight" response, which was originally intended to be an immediate and short-term reaction to an external danger, such as a predatory wild animal. The physical act of running away or fighting would mop up the stress hormones, expend the energy

generated, and resolve the feelings of anger or fear aroused. After the crisis, a set of calming down reactions, known as the "relaxation response", reversed the arousal, preventing it from becoming harmful.

In the modern world, however, our challenges tend to be more mental and emotional, often involving successive episodes of psychological tension (for example a delayed train, being late for a

RECOGNIZING THE SYMPTOMS OF STRESS

Often people who suffer from stress are unaware of just how stressed they are, and even rely on a constant adrenaline surge to keep going. They have forgotten what it feels like to be relaxed and ignore the signs that their coping mechanisms are beginning to burn out. Key signs of too much stress include:

- Irritability
- Sleeping badly
- Constant tiredness
- Inability to wind down even at weekends or on holiday
- Finding it difficult to concentrate or to make decisions
- Tense muscles
- Skin irritations
- General aches and pains
- Frequent infections

If you suspect you are suffering from stress, *see pages 84–85*.

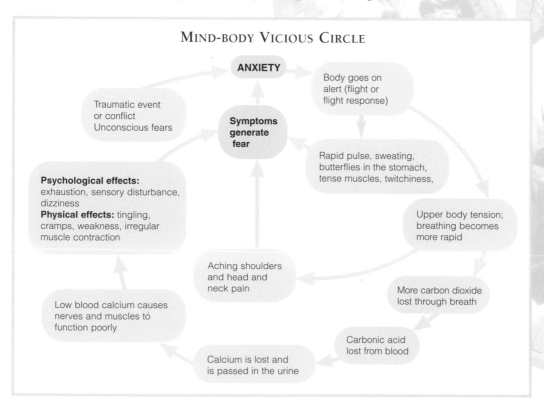

MIND-BODY VICIOUS CIRCLE

ANXIETY

Body goes on alert (flight or flight response)

Traumatic event or conflict Unconscious fears

Symptoms generate fear

Rapid pulse, sweating, butterflies in the stomach, tense muscles, twitchiness,

Psychological effects: exhaustion, sensory disturbance, dizziness
Physical effects: tingling, cramps, weakness, irregular muscle contraction

Upper body tension; breathing becomes more rapid

Aching shoulders and head and neck pain

More carbon dioxide lost through breath

Low blood calcium causes nerves and muscles to function poorly

Carbonic acid lost from blood

Calcium is lost and is passed in the urine

meeting, arguing with a partner). Stress chemicals have no chance to dissipate, and the body and mind may begin to act and feel as if in continual physical danger. Exhaustion and jitters from tense muscles, overactive circulation and senses, and finally damage to the immune system, are all likely outcomes.

Causes of stress, known as stressors, range from the life-threatening (mugging) to the trivial (a ringing phone). Between the two extremes is a spectrum of potential stressors, both external (life events like bereavement, or an environmental stimulant such as noise) and internal (memories, expectations, and feelings such as shame and rage). As stressors multiply in number and grow in magnitude, the ability to cope diminishes. Sometimes we are able to handle major issues but fall apart over interminable daily hassles, which are now understood to be as likely as major life dramas to provoke unhealthy coping strategies, such as turning to alcohol and "comfort" foods.

WHY LEARN TO RELAX?

The stress response should naturally be followed by the relaxation response, in which heart and breathing rates are lowered and stress-hormone levels are reduced. However, if you are constantly in a state of arousal, you can forget what deep relaxation and calm awareness feel like. Learning to switch on the relaxation response at will is an essential part of managing stress and it enables the vicious cycle of stress responses (*see left*) to be broken. See over for instructions on

deep breathing and muscle relaxation. It may also help to buy a relaxation tape that will talk you through the steps.

Breathing calmly and relaxing the mind and body are integral elements in many stress-management techniques, such as t'ai chi, yoga, meditation, autogenic training, visualization and self-hypnosis (*see Glossary of Therapies, pages 114–37*). Which one you follow is very much an individual choice and you may have to sample several. Some people also find that they relax deeply only after aerobic exercise; so take time to discover the strategy that works for you.

AN ANTI-STRESS PACKAGE

Relaxation techniques are not the whole answer. If your mind is buzzing with worries, conflicts, negative attitudes and prejudices, you may need to consider counselling or psychotherapy. Cognitive behavioural therapy (*see pages 174–75*) is a potent tool for changing the way you think and feel about stressors. Time-management techniques can clear the internal (and external) clutter and enable you to prioritize tasks, while assertiveness training and learning social skills may help you deal with people and gain control over situations in which you felt vulnerable. Self-confidence and self-esteem are important, but if a problem seems bigger than you are, it could be because it is. Seek help. Major crises always require support, help and energy to move forward. If you feel exhausted, do whatever you must to get some rest. You need respite and recuperation before you can begin to make sense of your situation.

Meditation is one of many techniques that induce the relaxation response

(see left)
(see Glossary of Therapies, pages 114–37)
(see pages 174–75)

12 WAYS TO CONTROL STRESS LEVELS

- Allow at least 20 minutes a day for the relaxation technique of your choice, even if you have to mark it in your diary
- Eat a healthy balanced diet (*see pages 158–61*).
- Exercise for at least 20 minutes four times a week.
- Be assertive: decide what it is you want or feel and say so specifically; say no to unnecessary requests.
- Delegate: hand over jobs that other people can do, so that you are not over-committed.
- Organize your day and prioritize tasks to make the most efficient use of your time.
- Make your workplace as comfortable as possible (*see page 151*).
- Try to avoid working late. Long working hours have been linked to mental and physical health problems.
- In the hour before bedtime detach yourself from the day's events with music, a book or some visualization. Aim for 6–8 hours sleep every night.
- Find time in the week for pleasure and creativity. Go to the theatre, cinema or an art gallery; have dinner with friends; paint, sing or garden.
- When you go away on holiday, leave work behind. Several short breaks can be more restful than one long holiday with stressful travelling.
- Seek help when you need it. Open up to friends, family and professionals who act as listeners. Being able to make use of social support in times of stress is good for mental and physical well-being.

Getting adequate sleep is a powerful way to cope with stress

RELAXATION & BREATHING

Simple breathing exercises and muscle-relaxing techniques can alleviate the physical and mental effects of stress by lowering the heart rate, reducing blood pressure and lowering levels of stress hormones. Such techniques have been used for thousands of years in Eastern health systems and fit in well with many complementary therapies. Western medicine is finding relaxation techniques increasingly valuable and they are often taught in health centres and hospitals.

THE MIND-BODY CONNECTION

Breathing is usually involuntary, but when consciously controlled, it forms a link between the mind and body. Yoga postures (*asanas*) and breathing techniques (*pranayama*) are used to calm body and mind (*see page 123*). Traditional Chinese Medicine uses breathing and movement exercises in t'ai chi and qigong to regulate the flow of *qi*, or "life energy", through the body (*see page 125*).

PROGRESSIVE MUSCLE RELAXATION

In the 1930s, American physiologist Dr. Edmund Jacobson developed one of the earliest relaxation techniques practised in the West. He called his systematic approach to relaxing "progressive muscle relaxation" (*see opposite*). In the 1960s, Dr. Herbert Benson of Harvard Medical School found that simply sitting in a quiet environment, breathing calmly and focusing the mind could reverse the physiological effects of stress. He called this state of relaxed awareness the "relaxation response" (*see right*).

FIGHT OR FLIGHT

When stress triggers the "fight or flight response" (*see pages 168–69*), breathing becomes quick and shallow, reinforcing the messages of alarm being sent to the brain. If this "over-breathing" continues, too much carbon dioxide is removed from the blood, which then loses its correct acidity. This directly affects the body's nerves and muscles, prompting symptoms such as faintness, palpitations and panic attacks. Calm abdominal breathing, particularly when practised with muscle relaxation and visualization (*see page 134*), may alleviate this condition by "turning off" the fight-or-flight response.

CALM ABDOMINAL BREATHING

ABDOMINAL, OR DIAPHRAGMATIC, breathing is a gentle, relaxing technique that allows the lungs to fill and empty with minimal effort. The diaphragm is a sheet of muscle between the chest cavity and the abdomen. When breathing in, it contracts and moves down, the abdomen rises and the chest expands slightly. On breathing out, the diaphragm relaxes and rises, making the chest cavity smaller and expelling air from the lungs.

1 Remove your shoes and loosen any tight clothing. Sit in a comfortable position with your back supported, either cross-legged or on a chair. Alternatively, you can lie on a mat or firm bed with a small pillow supporting your head.

2 Place one hand on your upper chest and the other on your abdomen, below your breastbone. Note which hand moves when you breathe. If the hand on your chest moves more than the one on your abdomen, you breathe mainly in the upper chest. Try to breathe so only your lower hand moves.

3 Place both hands on your abdomen below the ribs. Breathe in slowly through your nose, allowing your abdomen to rise as your diaphragm moves downwards.

4 Pause for a few seconds between breaths, then breathe out slowly through the nose, feeling your abdomen fall as your diaphragm relaxes. Let as much air out of your lungs as possible.

5 Repeat slowly several times. Try to relax your muscles and concentrate on your breathing, rather than on any thoughts that come to you.

Aim to let this hand stay motionless

TRY TO PRACTISE FOR
10–15 MINUTES A DAY

HOW TO RELAX YOUR MUSCLES

DURING STRESSFUL PERIODS, we tend to tense our muscles, resulting in aches, pains and fatigue. A practitioner trained in massage therapy (*see page 116*) or an osteopath (*see page 119*) can help you become aware of tension patterns in your body. Relaxation classes usually include the following progressive muscle-relaxation exercise. It involves tensing and relaxing all the major muscle groups in the body. As you release each muscle, repeat to yourself the words "relax and let go". Each time you tense and relax a muscle group, take time to feel the difference. If thoughts or worries drift into your mind, return to focusing on your breathing and how your body feels. Avoid holding your breath.

Making time to relax each day reverses the effects of stress, calms the mind and encourages peaceful sleep.

1 Remove your shoes and loosen any tight clothing. Lie on a mat placed on the floor, or on a firm bed, with your head supported by a small pillow. Your head, torso and legs should be in a straight line, with your feet apart and your hands by your sides.

2 Close your eyes and become aware of the weight of your body. Focus on the rhythm of your breathing and the rise and fall of your abdomen. Try to breathe more slowly than usual, emphasizing the out breath and pausing before you breathe in again.

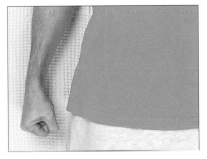

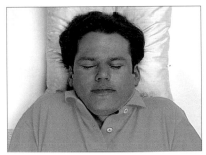

3 Tense the muscles in your right foot, hold for a few seconds then release. Tense and release the calf, followed by the thigh muscles. Repeat the process with the left foot and leg.

4 Tense and relax each buttock in turn, then your stomach muscles. Clench and release your right fist, then all the muscles in your right arm. Repeat with the left arm.

5 Lift your shoulders up to your ears, hold for a few seconds, then lower them again. Repeat two or three times. To free the neck, rock your head gently from side to side.

6 Yawn and then relax your face. Twist your mouth into a pout, and release. Frown, then scrunch up your nose and let go. Raise your eyebrows, then release and relax all the muscles in your face.

7 Focus on your breathing again, and tell yourself you feel peaceful and warm. When ready, wriggle your toes and fingers and ease your back muscles. Bend your knees, roll on one side for a while, then slowly get up.

> ▶ **TRY TO PRACTISE FOR 10–15 MINUTES A DAY**

YOUR EMOTIONS

Tears at losing someone dear, joy at a reunion, anger when hurt or frustrated: these powerful emotions are a normal part of life. They also show how intimately the mind and body are interconnected: pleasure triggers waves of endorphins that influence all the body's systems, while fear releases stress chemicals that speed up heart rate and contract the muscles of the gut. The ability to deal with feelings is essential for helping people manage challenging situations such as having a baby or losing a parent or a job. How individuals respond to life's demands depends partly on genetics, physical make-up and brain chemistry, but also on their personality and culture. Whereas northern Europeans might view crying as a sign of weakness, people from a Mediterranean culture are more likely to regard the same display of emotion as entirely normal. Childhood experiences are also a factor: children who are bullied, for example, often grow up to bully in turn.

Feelings of mistrust and aggression have been compared to a slow drip of poison.

COPING WITH DIFFICULT EMOTIONS

IT IS ENTIRELY NATURAL to be anxious or apprehensive, or to feel angry and guilty at times. Denying negative feelings can lead to problems, and one emotion may become the predominant reaction, distorting your way of coping with stress and emotions. You may adopt a self-blaming style whenever life becomes difficult for example, or always blame others.

Anger is potentially one of the most difficult emotions to handle, and those who are dominated by it tend to overreact to any form of stress. While the occasional explosion of righteous anger may be cathartic, violent outbursts of temper over everyday annoyances simply reinforce inappropriate behaviour and usually provoke unhelpful responses from other people.

Talking about disagreements can help to dissipate anger

Your way of coping with your emotions has a bearing on health: pessimists are more likely to suffer from ill health, for instance; whereas optimists, who interpret events in the best light, enjoy greater well-being. A personality profile known as "type A" – driven, tense, competitive, angry and aggressive – has been directly linked to heart disease (*see page 49*). The American research scientist Dr. Redford Williams has defined the relevant trait as "hostility": a combination of cynical mistrust, anger and aggression. He compares it to a slow drip of poison, especially when partnered with other negative emotions such as jealousy and resentment. In hostile people, angry reactions provoke strong physiological responses – extra stress hormones flood the system and blood pressure soars, straining the body and endangering long-term health.
If you think you are prone to anger, ask yourself the questions in "Are You Hostile?" (*page 49*) and follow the advice in "Tips to control anger" (*right*) and in "Steps to a trusting heart" (*page 51*). It is also important to learn stress-management techniques (*see pages 168–69*).

TIPS TO CONTROL ANGER
- Breathe slowly for several minutes to calm down (*see pages 170–71*).
- Walk away from a situation or mentally distance yourself. The old adage "count to ten" still holds good.
- Reframe the trigger event. For example, if annoyed by a rude shop assistant, tell yourself, "She must be under terrible pressure", and remind yourself, "I am not the target".
- Listen to the other person. Hold your tongue if necessary, but let them vent their feelings. Put your views calmly.
- Don't demonize your attacker. Remember that most arguments are about values, and the issues involved may not be black and white.
- Don't blame others for your anger. Apologize or compromise if appropriate.
- Don't endlessly replay events that have provoked you to anger.

There are various long-term measures you can take to help control anger:
- Practise stress-management techniques (*see pages 168–69*) to reduce tension and promote well-being.
- Practise a relaxation technique such as yoga or meditation (*see pages 123 and 135*) to help calm yourself at will.
- Take regular exercise (*see pages 152–53*) to relieve stress and alleviate feelings of frustration.

SELF-ASSERTIVENESS

LEARNING SKILLS that enable you to be more assertive is an effective way to overcome feelings of self-blame and melancholy. This type of psychological training will make you aware of your real needs and how to express them, and will encourage you to expect these needs to be met.

Long-term poor health can sometimes be traced to humiliating experiences never brought into the open, but continually replayed at an unconscious level and a perpetual source of distressing negative self-talk.

According to one study, finding a way to recount the shameful event can have real health benefits. Counselling might be a solution, but even just writing about the event can improve well-being. American students who practised creative writing were found to enjoy significantly better health than those who did not. Ideally, you should set down not only what happened but also how it made you feel, what you wish you had said or done, how you would have liked it all to have turned out, and how you feel it has affected you.

Creative writing can help you come to terms with emotions

POSITIVE EMOTIONS

HAPPINESS HELPS THE HEALING process along. Laughter and optimism, for example, have been linked with rises in antibody levels in the saliva and in hormones that boost the immune

Laughter has positive physical effects

system, increasing the activity of natural killer cells, which fight infection. Laughing, rather like exercise, also eases muscle tension, encourages diaphragmatic breathing (*see pages 170–71*), improves circulation and releases endorphins, the body's natural pain-relieving opiates. People with a good sense of humour tend to experience less fatigue, anxiety, anger and depression when under pressure.

Humour implies an exchange of feeling, and it is no surprise that "connectedness" – a network of friends and family, a readiness to find emotional support and to give and receive love – seems to encourage

good health. Lonely, isolated people are vulnerable to illness, and people who maintain caring relationships throughout their lives are likely to live longer than those who do not. Perhaps that is why some studies have found that those who go to church appear healthier than those with no religious belief. Other studies, however, suggest that health benefits derive from spiritual awareness and from active involvement in the community, rather than from organized religion. In a recent study, women with breast cancer who joined support groups were found to live twice as long after diagnosis as those who did not. This result can be attributed to the expression and sharing of emotions, encouraging feelings of optimism and a sense of control over the illness.

Sometimes it is difficult to express feelings in words. Music, art and dance can help touch the emotions directly and intuitively without having to pin them down verbally.

Sharing your emotions can help to promote a positive outlook

WAYS TO ENCOURAGE POSITIVE EMOTIONS

• Visualize yourself at a time when you were happy, relaxed and full of energy – try to recall your emotions and re-experience how you felt.
• Develop your sense of humour.
• Practise looking on the bright side.
• Work on closeness. If you are glad to see someone, or grateful for an act of kindness, say so without restraint.
• Let those who are dear to you know how much you love them.
• Learn yoga, qigong or meditation (*see pages 123, 125, and 135*) to help still the mind and focus thoughts.
• Altruism is healthy. Do something to help other people, whether voluntary work or visiting a sick neighbour.
• Link up your thoughts with feelings. Try writing an account of unpleasant or traumatic events, describing your emotions.

IMPROVING WAYS OF THINKING

Some people, by virtue of their psychological and physical make-up, seem to handle stress more effectively than others. In a study of American executives involved in a company reorganization, some succumbed to stress-related diseases, while others seemed to thrive. Researchers attributed the difference to characteristics that together constitute "hardiness": a sense of commitment to themselves, families and jobs; a feeling of being in control of their lives; and a belief that change is a challenge and an inevitable part of life.

The "hardy" executives had a flexibility and readiness to adapt, which seemed to give them better physical and mental health compared with the rigid, black-and-white thinkers, and they were also able to communicate more effectively. Fortunately, it is possible to change attitudes, beliefs and behaviour and to improve communication and reactions to events so that stress becomes easier to deal with.

Adapting to life's events and accepting change are key to stress-free living.

STRESS-MANAGEMENT PROGRAMME

MONITORING EVENTS IN A STRESS DIARY (*see opposite*) can help to define the kind of pressures that are stressful for you, and filling in the questionnaire on pages 142 identifies how you react to stress. Particularly if you are a silent, obsessive worrier or a hot-tempered blusterer, it is important to learn how to adapt your response to stress. Researchers at the Mind/Body Medical Institute of Harvard Medical School have devised the following approach to managing stress.

1 STOP!
When confronted by a stressful situation, think "STOP!" before your imagination runs amok in expectation of the worst possible scenario. Picture a big red STOP! sign, if you like. "Thought-stopping" helps to break the panic cycle.

2 BREATHE
Breathing diaphragmatically (*see page 170*) helps immediately to diffuse tension.

3 REFLECT
When panicking, people stop thinking logically. Ask yourself why you are so distressed. Is it really a crisis? What is the worst thing that can happen? Will worrying help? Reflecting calmly will help to identify irrational thinking and eliminate knee-jerk responses.

4 CHOOSE
Deciding what to do involves choosing an appropriate response.

5 TAKE ACTION
Depending on the situation, you could:
- Tackle the problem at once.
- Put it on hold until you are able to deal with it effectively.
- Make a full list of possible solutions to discover options and compromises.
- Relax and do something enjoyable to put yourself in a better, calmer mood.
- Look at the problem from a different perspective (sitting in a traffic jam, for example, might give you the opportunity to do some forward planning or breathing exercises).
- While you are considering what to do, repeat words or phrases with a particular positive meaning, for example "I am peaceful", or "I can organize my life".
- Talk to yourself constructively. For example, rather than fretting about a speech ("I hate talking in public", "I'll fluff my words and look silly"), try saying to yourself, "I'll take a deep breath and relax", and "They'll enjoy what I have to say".
- Talk about the problem. An amazing amount of stress can be eliminated simply with better communication.

COMMUNICATING WELL

VERBAL COMMUNICATION includes what you say, how you say it and how you listen and understand. Non-verbal communication encompasses your body language, eye contact and actions. If you communicate well, others will respond better to you, which in turn raises your self-esteem, improves your relationships and can actually prevent stressful situations. Simple rules to sum up the essence of good communication include:

• Maintain eye contact during a conversation (but avoid staring).

• State your message clearly and specifically: "I'm unhappy because the arrangements haven't allowed enough time for travelling," is more accurate than "I'm not happy about this".

• Support your words with appropriate non-verbal behaviour. Do not say, "It's OK, no problem", when you're frowning, biting your lips and drumming your fingers.

• Listen to what the other person actually says. Give them your full attention, don't interrupt, don't jump to conclusions or put your own interpretation on their words.

• Clarify any areas of doubt by reiterating what you think they said, for example, "You want me to double-check these figures with the marketing department."

• Accept other people's opinions and feelings as genuine, even when they are different from your own.

Plenty of eye contact aids communication

KEEPING A STRESS DIARY

Every week (or every day) describe in a diary a situation that caused you to feel stressed:

• How did you feel physically?

• What were your first thoughts?

• What emotions did you feel?

• What distorted beliefs may have lain behind your thoughts (for example, "Nobody loves me", "I'm always the one who gets dumped on", "I'm trapped in a situation that won't ever get better")?

• How did you behave during or immediately after the situation?

• What could you think or do differently to cope better next time?

• How might this make you feel and behave?

ACHIEVING HIGH SELF-ESTEEM

OVERCOMING POOR SELF-ESTEEM gives you the emotional "hardiness" to deal with stressful events. Even quite tiny shifts in how you perceive yourself can bring about profound changes. The Mind/Body Institute at Harvard University suggests you try to become aware of the origins of low self-esteem. Think of your life as a bus with every significant person from your past on board. When they make criticisms such as "Why are you so clumsy?", ask yourself: "Who is driving this bus? Who is in control?" Taking over the driver's seat yourself might entail putting some of the passengers off the bus – and out of your mind – permanently.

BUILDING CONFIDENCE

CONFIDENT, OPTIMISTIC PEOPLE take a positive approach to life and do not interpret events negatively. If an acquaintance suddenly crosses the road as they approach, for example, they attribute it to being unseen rather than deliberate avoidance. Sometimes behaving in a confident manner generates real confidence. If you hide your anxieties and act with self-assurance, people often respond by listening and assuming you know what you are talking about, which in turn reinforces your confident behaviour.

Behaving confidently builds self-esteem

TIPS FOR CONFIDENT BEHAVIOUR

• Visualize yourself behaving in a confident manner (*see page 134*) and practise deep breathing when you feel stressed (*see pages 170–71*).

• On meeting, look at people long enough to acknowledge them and then look away again.

• Watch your body language: confident people take up space and look relaxed. They don't twitch or fiddle, hunch their shoulders or cross their arms and legs defensively.

• When you speak, take time to pause and breathe evenly throughout.

• Lower your voice if you hear it rising.

• Be prepared: make notes and know your facts before going into a meeting or a difficult interview, for example.

• If you make a mistake, ask yourself "Will this matter in ten years' time?" Usually it won't.

• Remind yourself that other people have better things to do than analyse your shortcomings.

RESEARCH INTO THERAPIES

DESPITE THEIR POPULARITY, more research into complementary therapies is needed. Most conventional practitioners, quite rightly, want evidence that a complementary approach is safe and effective before using it or recommending it to their patients, and trials are under way in a number of areas.

Even in conventional medicine, "evidence-based" treatments are an increasingly important goal. With so many demands on funds, doctors and healthcare managers are reluctant to support treatments that are not proven to be effective. The development of new high-tech drugs and procedures is hugely expensive, so their cost-effectiveness and patient-acceptability have become big issues.

Complementary therapies will always be the alternative of choice for some people but, if they are to become truly integrated with conventional medicine, they will have to prove their worth. This may not be easy. Some practitioners argue that it is impossible to measure something as subtle as *qi*, "life energy" or "the healing process". In addition, how do you devise a trial to take account of treatment that has been tailored to a specific individual? And how do you judge the result of a treatment that might not cure someone, but makes them *feel* better? Many complementary practitioners maintain simply that there are enough reports from patients to support their claims.

Most research into complementary medicine has been done by doctors with an interest in the field, but few have the expertise to conduct a scientifically acceptable study. Colleges that train practitioners of complementary medicine have only just begun to include research as part of the curriculum, and few have linked up with university or hospital-based researchers.

Part of the problem is funding. Research organizations are often unwilling to make grants in unusual or controversial areas, and drug companies are unlikely to invest in research due to few financial incentives. A second difficulty is a lack of subjects. A trial with 30 people, no matter how promising the results, is not as impressive as one of 300 or 3000. Large numbers of patients are usually only available through big organizations like the UK National Health Service or a group of university hospitals, but the ailments complementary therapists tend to treat are seldom seen in hospitals.

Much of the necessary research into complementary medicine will therefore be done in collaboration with family doctors and with the participation of patients. Mobilizing the person's own efforts to become well is one of the most important aspects of integrated healthcare, so ways must be found of doing research *with* people, rather than *on* them.

Fortunately the situation is slowly beginning to change. European Community regulations now demand that products making medicinal claims must provide proof, and growing consumer awareness is encouraging investment in research. More complementary practitioners and their professional organizations are realizing the importance of submitting their therapies to scientific evaluation and exploring ways of doing

so. Other organizations, such as the UK's Research Council for Complementary Medicine and the Cochrane Collaboration, are establishing a database of randomized controlled trials involving non-conventional treatments. Several peer-reviewed journals such as the American *Alternative Therapies in Health and Medicine* publish research studies. On pages 182–85, we list some of the better studies that support complementary therapies.

In the US, the National Center for Complementary and Alternative Medicine (NCCAM), funded by the National Institutes of Health, currently supports 12 centres conducting complementary and alternative medicine research with an annual budget of more than $50 million. In 1998, the November issue of the *Journal of the American Medical Association* was devoted to complementary and alternative research studies and found, just as in the case of conventional medicine, that some treatments worked and some did not.

TYPES OF STUDY

The most rigorous engine for scientific proof is the clinical trial, which was originally devised to test pharmaceutical drugs. To be reliable it should contain all the following elements:

Controlled trial At least two groups are compared. The experimental group receives the treatment, the other group (the control) receives none.

Randomized trial Large numbers are used in the trial to cancel out individual differences. Bias is also overcome by assigning patients at random into experimental and control groups.

Randomized double-blind study If practitioners and researchers know which is the active treatment and which the placebo, their behaviour can be affected so that the patient may guess which is which. In this ultimate test, neither the patients nor the practitioners know who is receiving which treatment.

Placebo-controlled trial Any treatment, even a sugar pill, tends to make about a third of people feel better. This is known as the placebo effect and indicates the psychological power of belief over physical function. In fact, sceptics attribute much of the success of complementary therapies to this effect. In a clinical trial, the placebo is a treatment that appears indistinguishable from the experimental one but is inactive. The experimental treatment must perform significantly better than the placebo to be considered valid. Finding a placebo can be a challenge, especially with a therapy like acupuncture. Researchers either have to insert needles into sham, or non-acupuncture, points or use a plastic tube that feels like a needle insertion.

Meta-analysis, or systematic review These are ways of collecting together and analysing the results of a number of studies. Each study is assigned points according to its scientific reliability. The mathematical analysis of a whole group of trials gives a more accurate picture of the total evidence available.

GLOSSARY OF TERMS

Words in CAPITAL LETTERS are defined elsewhere in the glossary.

ACUPOINT Term used in Traditional Chinese Medicine for a point along a MERIDIAN at which the flow of QI is accessible. Acupoints are stimulated by acupressure or by acupuncture needles.

ACUTE Describes a disorder or symptom that comes on suddenly. See also CHRONIC.

AEROBIC Designed to increase oxygen uptake (when used in the context of vigorous exercise).

ALLERGEN An environmental or dietary irritant that triggers an allergic reaction in sensitive people.

ANAEROBIC Not designed to increase oxygen uptake (when used in the context of exercise such as lifting weights and performing stretches).

ANTIBODY Protein in the blood responsible for destroying invading substances that the body considers harmful.

ANTIFUNGAL Substances that destroy or inhibit fungal infections.

ANTIOXIDANTS Substances capable of neutralizing FREE RADICALS.

APPLIED KINESIOLOGY Detection of body system imbalances and food and environmental sensitivities by muscle-resistance testing.

ARACHIDONIC ACID Derivative of an essential fatty acid that produces substances causing inflammation.

ARGININE Amino acid essential for sperm formation. It appears to encourage the growth of the *herpes simplex* virus.

ASANA Physical posture adopted in yoga.

AUTO-IMMUNE DISEASE Disorder in which the immune system fails to distinguish between substances that are "self" and those that are "non-self", and produces ANTIBODIES to attack the body's own tissues.

AUTONOMIC NERVOUS SYSTEM Part of the nervous system that controls body functions such as breathing and heart-rate that are not under conscious control.

BACH FLOWER REMEDIES Infusions of plant materials in spring water, often taken to ease emotional problems.

BARIUM X-RAY Procedure to detect and monitor diseases of the gastrointestinal tract in which the element barium, opaque to X-rays, is either swallowed (barium meal) or introduced into the lower intestine through the rectum (barium enema).

BIOPSY Removal of a small piece of living tissue for examination in a laboratory.

BODY CLOCK The system that regulates eating, sleeping, metabolism and attention span. It is also known as the circadian rhythm because it is primarily set by sunlight and darkness.

BODYWORK Term used to describe manipulative therapies or techniques, such as massage.

CANDIDA Common but incorrect term for candidiasis, an over-growth of *Candida albicans*, a yeast-like micro-organism that occurs naturally in the mouth, gut and vagina and on the skin, and which is normally controlled by "friendly" bacteria.

CENTRAL NERVOUS SYSTEM Brain and spinal cord; receives and analyses information and initiates a response.

CHOLESTEROL Fat-like substance in the blood and most tissues. High levels in the blood can damage artery walls.

CHRONIC Term used for conditions of long duration and slow changes. It is the opposite of ACUTE.

CO-ENZYME Q10 ANTIOXIDANT nutrient, also known as ubiquinone, made by the body which helps release energy from food. It is also available as a supplement.

COGNITIVE BEHAVIOURAL THERAPY Form of psychotherapy pioneered in the 1960s and based on a belief in the ability of the mind to change negative patterns of thinking and behaviour.

COLONOSCOPY Examination of the inside of the colon, the major part of the large intestine, by means of a flexible, fibre-optic instrument called a colonoscope.

CT (COMPUTED TOMOGRAPHY) SCAN Diagnostic technique that uses X-rays and computers to produce a cross-section view of the tissue being examined.

CYTOTOXIC TEST Diagnostic technique in which damage to white blood cells when mixed with extracts of a possible ALLERGEN is said to suggest sensitivity.

DIURETIC Stimulates urine production.

DNA (DEOXYRIBONUCLEIC ACID) Principal molecule found in the cells of living organisms, carrying the genetic information that controls all metabolic functions.

DYSBIOSIS Condition in which poorly digested food in the gut encourages overgrowth of unfriendly gut bacteria.

ELECTROLYTE BALANCE Electrolytes, or body salts, are minerals present in body fluids and within cells that regulate water balance, blood acidity, nerve impulses and muscle contraction. Diarrhoea, vomiting and certain drugs can upset the balance between various salts and cause problems.

ENDOCRINE SYSTEM Collection of hormone-producing glands in the body.

ENDORPHINS Morphine-like substances produced naturally by the body to relieve pain; known as the body's natural opiates.

ENDOSCOPY Examination of a body cavity by means of an endoscope, a tube-like viewing instrument, used for diagnosis and treatment.

EPISIOTOMY Surgical procedure in which an incision is made in the perineum (tissue between the vagina and anus) to facilitate delivery of a baby.

FIGHT-OR-FLIGHT RESPONSE Physiological response to what the body sees as a threat. Chemicals are produced to make the body more efficient in either fighting or fleeing from the apparent danger.

FLAVONOIDS Chemicals with strong ANTIOXIDANT properties thought to help prevent certain forms of cancer. (Bio-)flavonoids are found in fruits such as lemons, plums and blackcurrants.

FREE RADICALS Potentially harmful molecules, produced naturally in the body, which can damage DNA and cause a range of physiological problems. They are linked to various health problems, including cancer and heart disease.

GESTALT THERAPY Method of psycho-therapy which helps clients to gain self-awareness through analysing their thoughts, feelings and behaviour in a variety of scenarios and situations.

HAIR ANALYSIS Diagnostic technique used by nutritional therapists and environmental medicine practitioners in which strands of hair are analysed in a laboratory to assess deficiencies or excesses of minerals in the body that might contribute to illness.

HOLISTIC Term used to describe an approach to treatment in which the "whole" person is taken into account rather than just their symptoms.

HOMEOSTASIS Processes by which the body maintains a constant internal environment (*see pages 12–13*).

HRT (HORMONE-REPLACEMENT THERAPY) Treatment of menopausal symptoms using hormones, often administered in the form of skin patches and/or pills, to counteract falling levels of oestrogen.

HYPERVENTILATION Very deep or rapid breathing, usually caused by anxiety. It can lead to abnormal loss of carbon dioxide from the blood, the symptoms of which include numbness of hands and feet, faintness, muscle spasms and twitches, and feeling unable to breathe properly.

ILEOSTOMY Operation in which the lower part of the small intestine (ileum) is severed and the end brought through the abdominal wall to allow the discharge of faeces into a bag attached to the skin.

IMMUNE SYSTEM Body organs responsible for resisting infection.

LYMPH Body fluid that contains lymphocytes (a type of white blood cell); has an important role in the IMMUNE SYSTEM, bathes all body tissues and is circulated into the bloodstream.

LYSINE One of the eight essential amino acids, obtainable only from food. It is thought instrumental in preventing and treating cold sores and herpes infections.

MERIDIANS Energy channels that are considered in Traditional Chinese Medicine to run up and down the body transporting QI (vital energy). Each meridian is related to a YIN or YANG organ.

METABOLISM General term for the chemical processes that take place in the body, governing all body functions.

MIND–BODY TECHNIQUES Approaches that harness thoughts, feelings, imagination and actions in order to influence biochemical and structural processes.

MOXIBUSTION An acupuncture procedure in which the herb moxa (mugwort) is burned over acupoints to create heat.

MRI (MAGNETIC RESONANCE IMAGING) Diagnostic technique that exposes body tissue to high-frequency radio waves; it is used particularly to examine the central nervous system.

NEBULIZER Device used to administer a drug in aerosol form through a mouthpiece or face mask.

NEEDLING Insertion and tweaking of acupuncture needles to stimulate the ACUPOINTS.

NEUROTRANSMITTER Chemical released from nerve endings that transmits impulses to another nerve cell or to a muscle cell.

NITROSAMINES Substances formed when nitrites (chemicals used as meat preservatives) react with amines (nitrogen compounds in food); they have been shown to cause cancer in laboratory animals.

NOSODE Homeopathic remedy originally made from bodily secretions and now made from many body tissues.

PELVIC FLOOR EXERCISES Precise exercises that strengthen the muscles surrounding part of the vagina, rectum and urethra.

PERISTALSIS Involuntary wave-like action of muscles in certain tubular structures of the body, for example in the intestines, that causes the contents to move forward.

PHYTOESTROGENS Chemicals of plant origin that have an action similar to that of the female hormone oestrogen; they are found in soya beans and other pulses.

PILATES A body-conditioning technique that increases flexibility and strength.

PLACEBO Chemically inert substance given in place of a drug; often used in scientific studies as a control.

PRANAYAMA Breathing techniques in yoga that aim to regulate *prana* ("vital life energy" in Ayurvedic medicine, akin to QI).

PRE-ECLAMPSIA Serious condition in which high blood pressure, accumulation of fluid in the tissues (oedema) and protein in the urine develops in the second half of pregnancy.

PROBIOTICS "Friendly", disease-destroying bacteria in the digestive tract that help in the manufacture of vitamins and enzymes, so improving digestion.

PROSTAGLANDIN Drug or naturally occurring substance within the body that has several actions, including causing muscle contractions and producing mucus in the stomach lining.

PULSE-TESTING Diagnostic technique that uses the pulse in the radial artery of the wrist. Western practitioners feel one pulse point to check the rate blood pumps from the heart. Traditional Chinese and Ayurvedic practitioners monitor nine pulse points, the strength of which are said to reflect the flow of "life energy".

QI "Life energy" force of Traditional Chinese Medicine that enters and can be accessed at ACUPOINTS on the body. It is said to be inherited at conception and is also derived from food and air.

RADIOTHERAPY The use of X-rays or other sources of radioactivity; used to treat cancer and occasionally other diseases.

REFERRED PAIN Sensation experienced as a result of spinal problems that can affect nerves and muscles linked to other parts of the body, causing pain in those areas.

SEROTONIN Substance found particularly in the blood, intestinal wall and central nervous system that acts as a NEUROTRANSMITTER, relaying information across nerve endings.

SICK-BUILDING SYNDROME Condition in which symptoms such as fatigue, lack of concentration and recurrent infections are attributed to poor ventilation and chemical fumes from furnishings and office machines.

SIGMOIDOSCOPY Examination of the rectum and lower parts of the large intestine (sigmoid colon) with a viewing instrument called a sigmoidoscope.

TENS (TRANSCUTANEOUS ELECTRICAL NERVE STIMULATION) Stimulation of body tissue with pulses of low-voltage electricity; used for pain relief.

TRANS-FATTY ACIDS Fats occurring naturally in meat and diary products and artificially in foods such as margarines, where edible oils are treated to become solid (hydrogenation). Research links artificial trans-fatty acids to heart disease.

TRIGGER POINTS Areas of muscle tension caused by pain from the spine and connected tissue; they feel like hard nodules when pressed.

ULTRASOUND Sound with a frequency higher than the range of the human ear, used to scan internal organs and the foetus in the womb, and to treat soft-tissue injuries.

UVA LIGHT Natural or artificial light containing ultraviolet wavelengths; its antiviral, antifungal and antibacterial properties make it effective in the treatment of psoriasis and other skin problems.

VEGAN Person who eats only foods of plant origin.

VEGA-TESTING Diagnostic technique which uses a machine that measures electrical resistance at various points on the body to homeopathic dilutions of suspect substances.

YIN and YANG Opposing but complementary energies in Traditional Chinese Medicine; all things are said to be a manifestation of *yin* or of *yang*.

DRUGS GLOSSARY

ACE INHBITORS Powerful VASODILATORS that block an enzyme involved in blood-vessel constriction; often prescribed for angina and high blood pressure.

ACYCLOVIR Antiviral for herpes infections.

ALPHA BLOCKERS Relieve urinary retention by relaxing the muscle of the sphincter.

ALPROSTADIL A PROSTAGLANDIN used to treat male impotence.

AMITRIPTYLINE A tricyclic ANTIDEPRESSANT used to improve mood, activity levels and encourage sleep in long-term depression.

ANALGESICS Drugs that relieve pain.

ANTACIDS Mildly alkaline compounds that neutralize excess stomach acid.

ANTIBIOTICS Bacteria-destroying drugs used to treat bacterial infections. Broad-spectrum antibiotics such as penicillins and tetracyclines can treat many common infections but increasing bacterial resistance is limiting their use.

ANTICONVULSANTS Inhibit excessive electrical activity in the brain. They are used to prevent and stop epileptic fits.

ANTIDEPRESSANTS Drugs used to treat moderate to severe depression.

ANTIFUNGALS Drugs used to treat fungal infections, particularly of the skin, mouth, throat and vagina, including thrush.

ANTIHISTAMINES Drugs that counter the effects of histamine, a chemical released in the body during an allergic reaction.

ANTIHYPERTENSIVES Drugs used to reduce high blood pressure.

ANTI-INFLAMMATORIES Drugs to relieve inflammation; the two major groups are NON-STEROIDAL ANTI-INFLAMMATORIES (NSAIDs) and CORTICOSTERIODS.

ANTIRHEUMATICS Drugs used to treat various rheumatic disorders, most commonly rheumatoid arthritis.

ASPIRIN As an ANALGESIC and NSAID, used to relieve pain, reduce fever and alleviate arthritis symptoms. In low doses, it helps prevent blood clots in people with coronary artery disease and reduces the chance of heart attacks and strokes.

AZT Also known as Zidovudine, an antiviral drug used to treat AIDS.

BARBITURATES Sleeping drugs. Rarely used due to risks of dependence and overdose.

BENZODIAZEPINES Anti-anxiety drugs that reduce excessive activity in the part of the brain that controls emotion.

BENZOYL PEROXIDE A topical preparation that treats acne and fungal skin infections by removing the top layer of skin and unblocking sebaceous glands.

BETA BLOCKERS Blocks noradrenaline, the main "fight-or-flight" hormone, reducing heart rate and preventing dilation of blood vessels. Used mainly for heart disorders, but sometimes for migraine, anxiety, overactive thyroid and glaucoma.

BIPHOSPHONATES A group of drugs (e.g. Etidronate) that treats bone disorders such as osteoporosis.

BROMOCRIPTINE Inhibits excessive secretion of the hormone prolactin. It can be used to treat female infertility and to relieve symptoms of Parkinson's disease.

CALCIUM CHANNEL BLOCKERS Help blood vessels dilate by preventing the movement of calcium in muscles that make the vessels contract. Treats angina, abnormal heart rhythm and high blood pressure.

CHLOROQUINE Antimalarial and antirheumatic drug.

CLOMIPHENE Drug used to treat infertility by increasing the output of pituitary gland hormones that stimulate ovulation.

CLOTRIMAZOLE An ANTIFUNGAL drug.

CORTICOSTEROIDS Often referred to simply as steroids, these are used to control inflammation (e.g. in eczema, inflammatory bowel disease, rheumatoid arthritis), and for conditions caused by deficiency of adrenal gland hormones.

CYCLOSPORIN Immuno-suppressant drug used to treat severe cases of psoriasis.

DITHRANOL Treats psoriasis by reducing excessive skin growth.

DOMPERIDONE An anti-emetic used for treating nausea caused by gastrointestinal disorders such as gastroenteritis.

ERGOTAMINE A vasoconstrictor used to treat headaches and migraines.

ERYTHROMYCIN Broad-spectrum ANTIBIOTIC.

FINASTERIDE An enzyme inhibitor used to treat benign prostatic enlargement.

FLUCONAZOLE An ANTIFUNGAL drug.

GONADOTROPHIN Human chorionic gonadotrophin (GCG), a hormone produced by the placenta and extracted from the urine of pregnant women; used to treat infertility by stimulating the ovaries to produce oestrogen and progesterone.

H2 BLOCKERS Anti-ulcer drugs (e.g. Cimetidine, Ranitidine) that help healing by preventing the release of histamine in the stomach, so reducing acid production.

HYDROCORTISONE A CORTICOSTEROID identical to the hormone cortisol produced by the adrenal glands.

IBUPROFEN An ANALGESIC and NSAID, similar to ASPIRIN but less likely to cause bleeding in the stomach.

IDOXURIDINE Antiviral drug commonly used to treat herpes infections.

INDOMETHACIN A NSAID used to treat arthritic conditions, including gout.

LITHIUM A metallic element used to treat manic and severe depression.

MEFENAMIC ACID A NON-STEROIDAL ANTI-INFLAMMATORY drug.

MESALAZINE Drug used to treat ulcerative colitis and sometimes Crohn's disease by relieving inflammation in the large intestine.

METHOTREXATE Cancer-therapy drug that inhibits the metabolic functioning of cells. It is also used to treat psoriasis.

MONOAMINE OXIDASE INHIBITORS (MAOIS) Antidepressant drugs that increase levels of serotonin and other mood-enhancing brain chemicals. They are especially effective for people with anxiety and phobias as well as depression.

MONTELUKAST Prevents and treats asthma by preventing contraction of the airways. Brandname: Singulair.

NON-STEROIDAL ANTI-INFLAMMATORIES (NSAIDS) A group of drugs used to relieve pain, stiffness and painful inflammation affecting the muscles, bones and joints.

NORADRENALINE RE-UPTAKE INHIBITORS An antidepressant that increases levels of noradrenaline, a chemical involved in mood.

NORATRIPTAN A serotonin-inhibiting drug used to treat headaches and migraines.

NYSTATIN An ANTIFUNGAL drug.

OPIOIDS A group of drugs (also known as narcotics) that relieve pain, treat diarrhoea and suppress coughs. Codeine (in over-the-counter preparations) is a mild opioid.

PARACETAMOL A non-opioid analgesic that does not cause stomach upset or bleeding, but can fatally damage the liver and kidneys if taken in slight overdose.

PROGESTOGEN Synthetic form of the female sex hormone, progesterone.

PROTEASE INHIBITOR Drugs that treat HIV by preventing formation of HIV proteins.

PROZAC Brand name for fluoxetine, one of the SSRIS (selective serotonin re-uptake inhibitors) group of antidepressants that boost levels of serotonin, the mood-enhancing brain chemical.

RANITIDINE An anti-ulcer drug. Brand name: Zantac.

RETINOIC ACID A form of vitamin A.

SALBUTAMOL A bronchodilator used to treat asthma, bronchitis and emphysema.

SALMETEROL One of a group of broncho-dilator drugs used to treat asthma and bronchitis by relaxing the muscles around the bronchioles (narrow lung airways).

SERMS (Selective Eostrogen Receptor Modulators) A form of HRT that mimics oestrogen's effects in some parts of the body but blocks it in others.

SILDENAFIL A drug to treat erectile dysfunction (impotence) by increasing blood flow to the penis to establish and maintain erection. Brand name: Viagra.

SODIUM CROMOGLYCATE An anti-allergy drug that prevents the release of histamine; inhaled to prevent asthma attacks.

STATINS Drugs that lower blood cholesterol, used to prevent stroke and heart atttack.

SUMATRIPTAN A serotonin-inhibiting drug used to treat headaches and migraines.

SULPHASALAZINE Treats symptoms of ulcerative colitis, Crohn's disease and rheumatoid arthritis.

TETRACYCLINE A broad-spectrum ANTIBIOTIC used to treat chlamydia and non-specific urethritis.

TRANQUILLIZERS Sedative drugs. Minor tranquillizers, such as benzodiazepines, are given in short courses to treat anxiety without risking dependence. Major tranquillizers control psychotic symptoms.

TRICYCLICS A group of antidepressant drugs (e.g. Amitriptyline) that raise levels of serotonin and noradrenaline, brain chemicals involved in mood.

VASODILATORS Widen blood vessels; used to treat angina and high blood pressure.

ZOLMITRIPTAN A serotonin-inhibiting drug used to treat headaches and migraines.

FINDING A PRACTITIONER

BEING ABLE TO TRUST YOUR PRACTITIONER and feeling a sense of rapport with him or her are vital factors in the healing process and should be considered when looking for a complementary practitioner. Competence is another key factor. Finding a good practitioner can be a matter of trial and error, so many people prefer word-of-mouth recommendations.

Establishing adequate standards of training, ethical practice and disciplinary procedures for complementary therapies has always proved a problem. Although some practitioners complete 3–4 years full or part-time degree studies, others operate on the basis of a weekend correspondence course.

This lack of regulation means you have little means of redress should anything go wrong or should you be dissatisfied with your treatment. At the very least, you need to feel confident that any undiagnosed serious condition would be recognized and that you would be advised to seek medical help if your practitioner suspected the problem lay beyond his or her expertise.

If you are considering chiropractic, osteopathy, acupuncture, psychotherapy, counselling or hypnotherapy, it is worth asking your doctor whether he or she can recommend a practitioner, as these therapies are becoming more accepted in mainstream medicine. Some conventional health professionals may also be qualified practitioners of acupuncture or homeopathy.

If you are choosing a complementary practitioner for yourself, you should consider the following issues, based on a checklist drawn up by the Royal College of Nursing which includes suggestions from the British Medical Association:

TRAINING AND CREDENTIALS

Always ensure that the practitioner is adequately trained and reputable, especially if the therapy involves the use of either physical manipulation or invasive techniques (e.g. if you swallow medication or have needles inserted into you) as they can be potentially harmful. Ask the following questions:
• What are the practitioner's qualifications?

• What sort of training was undertaken, and for how long?
• For how many years has the practitioner been in practice?
• Does the practitioner advise your doctor of any treatment?

PROFESSIONAL ORGANIZATIONS

Some disciplines have professional associations to regulate training, provide a code of conduct and maintain a register of members. For others, particularly non-invasive therapies, standards vary greatly and there may not be a single representative body. You should ask the following questions:
• Is the practitioner registered with a recognized organization, and does this organization have a public register of practitioners?
• Does the organization have a code of practice specifying the professional conduct required?
• Does the organization have a complaints system and an effective disciplinary procedure and sanctions?
• Can the practitioner give you the address and telephone number of the organization?

FINANCIAL CONSIDERATIONS

• Is treatment available at little or no personal cost on referral by your doctor? Some therapies, such as chiropractic, osteopathy, homeopathy, acupuncture and psychotherapy, may be available through a limited number of mainstream health practices.
• Can you claim for the treatment through your private health insurance scheme, if you have one?
• What is the cost (both short- and long-term) of treatment?
• How many treatments might you expect to require?
• Does the practitioner have professional indemnity insurance so that you receive compensation if he or she is negligent?

PRECAUTIONS

Avoid any practitioner you feel uncomfortable with. Trust and empathy are important, and treatment is unlikely to succeed without them. Treatment is often conducted on a one-to-one basis, and may involve removing clothes and being touched. Also avoid any practitioner who seems to be making excessive claims about the treatment or who guarantees a cure. No form of treatment – either conventional or complementary – is perfect, and miracles should be neither expected nor promised. After your initial consultation, ask yourself the following questions:

• Was the practitioner's conduct entirely professional?
• Did the practitioner answer any questions clearly and thoroughly?
• Were you given information to read in your own time?
• What was the practitioner's attitude towards any conventional medicine you may be receiving? Avoid any practitioner who suggests changing your conventional medicine without first consulting your doctor.

FINDING OUT MORE

KNOWING WHERE TO GO FOR INFORMATION and help enables you to become more actively involved in your own healthcare. When you understand the causes of illness, the meaning of symptoms and what treatment options are available, you may feel more in control of your well-being – and this is therapeutic in itself.

Good information is not always easy to find, but the following sources are good starting points:

WEBSITES

Although the web is brimming with advice on health matters, much of it can be ill-informed, biased or even downright wrong. This is especially true of interactive sites. If you put a health question to an "expert", make sure you check their credentials or know how much privacy you can expect. Be suspicious of "miracle cures" and note any sponsorship or advertising deals that could indicate a conflict of interest.

The following are reputable medical sites that provide reliable information and links to related sites, including complementary medicine. Although most are American, more localized information is becoming available:

www.bma.org.uk
British Medical Association's website offering general information on health.
www.healthfinder.gov/
Developed by the US Department of Health and Human Services, it directs visitors to selected online publications, databases, websites and support and self-help groups.
www.omni.ac.uk
Organizing Medical Networked Information, from Nottingham University, is the nearest UK equivalent to healthfinder, though mostly aimed at medical professionals.
www.intelihealth.com
Includes advice on self-care and diagnoses, as well as drug and research databases.
www.netdoctor.co.uk
News and advice on a wide range of health issues; offers links to other sources of information.

www.ncbi.nlm.nih.gov/pubmed
Medline is the world's largest database of medical papers at the US National Library of Medicine.
www.ama-assn.org
The American Medical Association site includes a consumer-health area.
cancernet.nci.nih.gov
Current information on cancer, sponsored by the US National Cancer Institute.
www.patient.co.uk
UK patient information and links to relevant organizations and support groups.
www.altmedicine.com
Alternative Health News Online covers major topics and offers links to other sources of information.
www.hon.ch
Internationally selected guidelines for responsible medical and health information on the internet.
www.nhsdirect.nhs.uk
Health information and advice from the UK National Health Service.

BOOKS

The following books provide basic information to enable an understanding of the structural, biochemical and psycho-social approach to integrated healthcare:

Benson, H. & Stuart, E. *The Wellness Book* (Fireside, Simon & Schuster, 1992)
Benson, H. *Timeless Healing: the Power and Biology of Belief* (Scribner, 1996)
Chevallier, A. *Encyclopedia of Medicinal Plants* (Dorling Kindersley, 1996)
Daniel, R. *Healing Foods: How to Nurture Yourself and Fight Illness* (Thorsons, 1996)
Gawain, S. *Creative Visualisation* (Bantam, 1982)
Goleman, D. *Emotional Intelligence* (Bantam, 1995)
Goleman, D. & Gurin, J. *Mind/Body Medicine* (Consumer Reports Books, 1993)
Kabat-Zinn, J. *Full Catastrophe Living* (Piatkus, 1996)
LeShan, L. *How to Meditate* (Thorsons, 1995)
Lockie, A. & Geddes, N. *Complete Guide to Homeopathy* (Dorling Kindersley, 1995)
Maxwell-Hudson, C. *The Complete Book of Massage* (Dorling Kindersley, 1988)
Moyers, B. *Healing and the Mind* (Doubleday, 1993)
Nagarathna, R., Nagendra H.R. & Monro, R. *Yoga for Common Ailments* (Gaia, 1990)
Ornish, D. *Dr Dean Ornish's Program for Reversing Heart Disease* (Ballantine Books, 1990)
Reader's Digest *Foods that Harm, Foods that Heal* (Reader's Digest Association, 1996)
Smith, T. (ed.), *The British Medical Association Complete Family Health Encyclopedia* (Dorling Kindersley, 1995)
Tanner, J. *Beating Back Pain* (Dorling Kindersley, 1987)
Williams, R. & Williams, V. *Anger Kills* (Times Books, 1993)
Woodham, A. & Peters, D. *Encyclopedia of Complementary Medicine* (Dorling Kindersley, 1997).

BIBLIOGRAPHY

Therapies: Evidence of Efficacy
In *Treating Ailments (see pages 22–111)*, the efficacy of each therapy for a particular ailment is rated 1–5 based on the available research.
Key to Ratings:
1 *Rumoured to be effective* (traditionally used but efficacy doubted; no research)
2 *Effective in practitioners' opinion* (practitioners are convinced, but no reliable research studies)
3 *Possibly effective* (some research, but results are inconclusive or conflicting)
4 *Probably effective* (positive evidence from randomized and/or controlled trials)
5 *Definitely effective* (good evidence available from several sound randomized controlled trials or a meta-analysis – *see page 176*)

HEADACHES
Chiropractic Boline P.D. *et al.* "Spinal manipulation vs. amitriptyline for the treatment of chronic tension-type headaches: a randomized clinical trial" *J. of Manipulative Physical Therapy* 1995, 18(3):148–54
Osteopathy Schoensee S.K. *et al.* "The effect of mobilization on cervical headaches" *J. of Orthopaedic & Sports Physical Therapy* 1995, 21(4):184–96
Visualization Blanchard E.B. *et al.* "The role of regular home practice in the relaxation treatment of tension headache" *J. of Consulting & Clinical Psychology* 1991, 59(3):467–70
Biofeedback Zitman F.G. "Hypnosis and autogenic training in the treatment of tension headaches: a two-phase constructive design study with follow-up" *J. of Psychosomatic Research* 1992, 36(3):219–28
Kuile M.M. *et al.* "Autogenic training and cognitive self-hypnosis for the treatment of recurrent headaches in three different subject groups" *Pain* 1994, 58(3):331–40
Therapeutic Touch Keller E., Bzdek V.M. "Effects of therapeutic touch on tension headache pain" *Nursing Research* 1986, 35(2):101–105
Hypnotherapy Melis P.M. *et al.* "Treatment of chronic tension-type headache with hypnotherapy" *Headache* 1991, (10):686–89

MIGRAINE
Nutritional Therapies Mansfield L.E. *et al.* "Food allergy and adult migraine: double-blind and mediator confirmation of an allergic etiology" *Annals of Allergy* 1985, 55:126–29
Western Herbalism Murphy J.J. "Randomised double-blind placebo-controlled trial of feverfew in migraine prevention" *Lancet* 1988, 2(8604):189–92
Chiropractic Parker G.B. *et al.* "A controlled trial of cervical manipulation for migraine" *Australian and New Zealand J. of Medicine* 1978, 8(6):589–93
Acupuncture Tavola T. *et al.* "Traditional Chinese acupuncture in tension-type headache: a controlled study" *Pain* 1992, 48(3):325–29
Vincent C.A. "A controlled trial of the treatment of migraine by acupuncture" *Clinical J. of Pain* 1989, 5(4):305–12

Hypnotherapy Olness K. "Comparison of self-hypnosis and propranolol in the treatment of juvenile classic migraine" *Pediatrics* 1987, 79(4):593–97
Biofeedback Blanchard E.B., Andrasik F. "Biofeedback treatment of vascular headache" *Biofeedback: Studies in Clinical Efficacy* ed. Hatch, J.P. *et al.* (1987, Plenum, New York) 1–79
Relaxation & Breathing Sorbi M. *et al.* "Long-term effects of training in relaxation and stress-coping in patients with migraine: a 3-year follow-up" *Headache* 1989, 29(2):111–21

ACNE
Aromatherapy Bassett I.B. *et al.* "A comparative study of tea-tree oil versus benzoylperoxide in the treatment of acne" *Medical J. of Australia* 1990, 153:455–58

PSORIASIS
Western Herbalism Gieler U. *et al.* *J. of Dermatological Treatment* 1995, 6:31–34
Wiesenauer M. *et al.* *Phytomedicine* 1996, (3) 231–35
Galle K. *et al.* *Phytomedicine* 1994 (1) 59–62
Syed T.A. *et al.* "Management of psoriasis with aloe vera extract in a hydrophilic cream: a placebo-controlled, double-blind study" *Tropical Medicine and International Health* 1996, 1:505–509
Biofeedback Winchell S.A. *et al.* "Relaxation therapies in the treatment of psoriasis and possible pathophysiologic mechanisms" *American J. of Academic Dermatology* 1988, 18:101–104

ECZEMA
Traditional Chinese Medicine Atherton D.J. *et al.* "Treatment of atopic eczema with traditional Chinese medicinal plants" *Pediatric Dermatology* 1992, 9:373–75
Sheehan M.P. *et al.* "Efficacy of traditional Chinese herbal therapy in adult atopic dermatitis" *Lancet* 1992, 340:13–17
Nutritional Therapies Soyland E. *et al.* "Dietary supplements with very long-chain-3 fatty acids in patients with atopic dermatitis: a double-blind, multicentre study" *British J. of Dermatology* 1994, 130:757–64
Sampson H.A. "Role of immediate food hypersensitivity in the pathogeneses of atopic dermatitis" *J. of Allergy & Clinical Immunology* 1983, 71:473–80
Hypnotherapy Ehlers A. *et al.* "Treatment of atopic dermatitis: comparison of psychological and dermatological approaches to relapse prevention" *J. of Consulting & Clinical Psychology* 1995, 63(4):624–35

HERPES
Western Herbalism Wolbling R.H., Leonhardt K. "Local therapy of herpes simplex with dried extract from *Melissa officinalis*" *Phytomed* 1994, 1:25–31
Visualization Kiecolt-Glaser J.K. *et al.* "Psychosocial enhancement of immunocompetence in a geriatric population" *Health Psychology* 1985, 4(1):25–41

COLDS & FLU
Traditional Chinese Medicine Kong X.T. *et al.* "Treatment of acute bronchiolitis with Chinese herbs" *Archives of Disease in Childhood* 1993, 68:468–71
Naturopathy Mossad S.B. *et al.* "Zinc gluconate lozenges for treating the common cold. A randomized double-blind placebo-controlled study" *Annals of Internal Medicine* 1996, 125:81–88
Ernst E. *et al.* "Regular sauna bathing and the incidence of common colds" *Annals of Medicine* 1990, 22:225–27
Western Herbalism Melchart D. *et al.* "Echinacea root extracts for the prevention of upper respiratory tract infections" *Archives of Family Medicine* 1998, 7:541–45
Zakay Rones Z. *et al.* "Inhibition of several strains of influenza virus *in vitro* and reduction of symptoms by an elderberry extract (*Sambucus nigra L.*) during an outbreak of influenza B in Panama" *J. of Alternative & Complementary Medicine* 1995, 1:361–69
Homeopathy Ferley J.P. *et al.* "A controlled evaluation of a homoeopathic preparation in the treatment of influenza-like syndromes" *British J. of Clinical Pharmacology* 1989, 27(3):329–35
Papp R. *et al.* "Oscillococcinum in patients with influenza-like syndromes: a placebo-controlled double-blind evaluation" *British Homeopathic J.* 1998, 87:69–76
Aromatherapy Saller R. *et al.* "Dose dependency of symptomatic relief of complaints by chamomile steam inhalation in patients with common cold" *European J. of Pharmacology* 1990, 183:728–29

IRRITABLE BOWEL SYNDROME
Naturopathy Nanda R. *et al.* "Food intolerance and the irritable bowel syndrome" *Gut* 1989, 30(8):1099–104
Western Herbalism Lech Y. *et al.* "Treatment of irritable bowel syndrome with peppermint oil: a double-blind study with a placebo" *Ugeskrift For Laeger* 1988, 150(40):2388–89
Psychotherapy & Counselling Read N. "The role of psychological and biological factors in post-infective gut dysfunction" *Gut* 1999, 44:400–406
Hypnotherapy Whorwell P.J. *et al.* "Hypnotherapy in severe irritable bowel syndrome: a further experience" *Gut* 1987, 28(4):423–25

INFLAMMATORY BOWEL DISEASE
Nutritional Therapies Riordan A.M. *et al.* "Treatment of active Crohn's disease by exclusion diet: East Anglian multicentre controlled trial" *Lancet* 1993, 342:1131–34
Beluzzi A. *et al.* "Effect of an enteric-coated fish-oil preparation on relapses in Crohn's disease" *New England J. of Medicine* 1996, 334:1557–60
Loescheke K. *et al.* "n-3 fatty acids only delay early relapse of ulcerative colitis in remission" *Digestive Diseases & Sciences* 1996, 41:2087–94
Massage Joachim G. "The effects of two forms of stress-management techniques on feelings of

well-being in patients with inflammatory bowel disease" *Nursing Papers* 1983, 15:(5)18
Biofeedback Marzyk P.M. "Biofeedback for gastrointestinal disorders: a review of the literature" *Annals of Internal Medicine* 1985, 103:240–44
Milne B. *et al.* "A stress-management programme for inflammatory bowel disease patients" *J. of Advanced Nursing* 1986, 11(5):561–67

HIGH BLOOD PRESSURE
Nutritional Therapies Witteman J.C.M. *et al* "Reduction of blood pressure with oral magnesium supplementation in women with mild to moderate hypertension" *American J. of Clinical Nutrition* 1994, 60:129–35
Margetts B.M. *et al.* "A randomized control trial of a vegetarian diet in the treatment of mild hypertension" *Clinical and Experimental Pharmacology and Physiology* 1985, 12(3):263–66
Auer W. *et al.* "Hypertension and hyperlipidaemia: garlic helps in mild cases" *British J. of Clinical Practice* 1990; (supplement 69):3–6
T'ai Chi Jin P. "Efficacy of T'ai Chi, brisk walking, meditation and reading in reducing mental and emotional stress" *J. of Psychosomatic Research* 1992, 36(4):361–70
Meditation Patel C. *et al.* "Controlled trial of biofeedback-aided behavioural methods in reducing mild hypertension" *British Medical J.* 1981, 282:2005–08; 2081–122
Biofeedback Glasgow M.S., Engel B.T. "Biofeedback and relaxation therapy" in *Biofeedback: Studies in Clinical Efficacy*, ed. Hatch J.P. *et al.* (Plenum 1987, New York)
Relaxation & Breathing Eisenberg D.M. *et al.* "Cognitive behavioral techniques for hypertension: are they effective?" *Annals of Internal Medicine* 1993, 118(12):964–72

HEART DISEASE
Naturopathy Ornish D. *et al.* "Can lifestyle changes reverse coronary heart disease? The Lifestyle Heart Trial" *Lancet* 1990, 336(8708):129–33
Nutritional Therapies Azen S.P. *et al.* "Effect of supplementary antioxidant vitamin intake on carotid arterial wall intima-media thickness in a controlled clinical trial of cholesterol lowering" *Circulation* 1996, 94(10):2369–72
Kushi L. *et al.* "Diet and 20 year mortality from coronary heart disease" *New England J. of Medicine* 1985, 312(13):811–18
T'ai Chi Lai J.S. *et al.* "Two-year trends in cardiorespiratory function among older T'ai Chi practitioners and sedentary subjects" *J. of the American Geriatrics Society* 1995, 43(11):1222–7
Osteopathy Morgan J.P. *et al.* "A controlled trial of spinal manipulation in the management of hypertension" *American Osteopathic Association* 1985, 85(5):308–13
Acupuncture Ballegaard S. "Acupuncture in severe, stable *angina pectoris*: a randomized trial" *Actor Medica Scandinavia* 1986; 220(4):307–13
Massage Bauer W.C. *et al.* "Effects of back massage in patients with acute myocardial infraction" *Focus on Critical Care* 1987, 14(6):42–46
Aromatherapy Stevenson C. "The psycho-physiological effects of aromatherapy massage

following cardiac surgery" *Complementary Therapies in Medicine* 1994, 2(1):27–35
Psychotherapy & Counselling Linden W. *et al.* "Psychosocial interventions for patients with coronary artery disease: a meta-analysis" *Archives of Internal Medicine* 1996, 156(7):745–52
Visualization Elliott D. "The effects of music and muscle relaxation on patient anxiety in a coronary care unit" *Heart & Lung* 1994, 23(7):27–35
Meditation (*see* **High Blood Pressure**)

BACK & NECK PAIN
Rolfing Cottingham J.T. *et al.* "Shifts in pelvic inclination angle and parasympathetic tone produced by Rolfing soft tissue manipulation" *Physical Therapy* 1988, 68(9):1364–70
Chiropractic Meade T.W. "Low back pain of mechanical origin: randomised comparison of chiropractic and hospital outpatient treatment" *British Medical J.* 1990, 2;300(6737):1431–37
Meade T.W. *et al.* "Randomised comparison of chiropractic and hospital outpatient management for low back pain: results from extended follow up" *British Medical J.* 1995, 311(7001):349–51
Osteopathy Shekelle P.G. *et al.* "Spinal manipulation for low-back pain" *Annals of International Medicine* 1992, 117(7):590–98
Koes B.W. *et al.* "Spinal manipulation and mobilisation for back and neck pain: a blinded review" *British Medical J.* 1991, 303:1298–303
Acupuncture White A.R., Ernst E. "A systematic review of randomized controlled trials of acupuncture for neck pain" *Rheumatology* 1999, 38:143–47
Ernst E, White A.R. "Acupuncture for back pain: a meta-analysis of randomized controlled trials" *Archives of International Medicine* 1998, 158:2235–41
(**Homeopathy, Massage** *see* **Persistent Muscle Pain**)

OSTEOARTHRITIS
Western Herbalism McCarthy G.M. *et al.* "Effect of topical capsaicin in the therapy of painful osteoarthritis of the hands" *J. of Rheumatology* 1992, 19:604–607
Nutritional Therapies Vaz A. "Double blind clinical evaluation of relative efficiency of ibuprofen and glucosamine sulfate in management of osteoarthrosis of the knee in outpatients" *Current Medical Research Opinion*, 1982, 8:145
Travers R. *et al.* "Boron and arthritis – a double-blind pilot study" *J. of Nutritional Medicine* 1990, 1:127–132
(**Osteopathy** *see* **Back Pain**)
Yoga Garfinkel M.S. *et al.* "Evaluation of a yoga-based regimen for treatment of osteoarthritis of the hands" *J. of Rheumatology* 1994, 21(12):2341–43
Acupuncture Ernst E. "Acupuncture as a treatment of osteoarthritis: a systematic view" *Scandinavian J. of Rheumatology* 1997, 26:444–47

RHEUMATOID ARTHRITIS
Nutritional Therapies
Kjeldsen-Kragh J. *et al.* "Vegetarian diet for patients with rheumatoid arthritis: two years after introduction of the diet" *Clinical Rheumatology* 1994, 13(3):475–82

Van de Laar M.A. *et al.* "Food intolerance in rheumatoid arthritis: a double-blind, controlled trial of the clinical effects of the elimination of milk allergens and azo dyes" *Annals of Rheumatic Disease* 1992, 51(3):298–302
Fortin P.R. *et al.* "Validation of a meta-analysis: the effects of fish oil in rheumatoid arthritis" *J. of Clinical Epidemiology* 1995, 48:1379–90
Gibson *et al. British Clinical J. of Pharmacology* 1978, 6:391–95
T'ai Chi Kirsteins A.E. *et al.* "Evaluating the safety and potential use of a weight bearing exercise, T'ai-Chi Chu'an, for rheumatoid arthritis patients" *American J. Physical Medicine and Rehabilitation* 1991, 70(3):136–41
Psychotherapy & Counselling Bradley L.A. *et al.* "Effects of psychological therapy on pain behaviour of rheumatoid arthritis patients: treatment outcome and six-month follow up" *Arthritis and Rheumatism* 1987, 30:1105–14
O'Leary A. *et al.* "A cognitive-behavioral treatment for rheumatoid arthritis" *Health Psychology* 1988, 7:527–44
(**Massage, Acupuncture** *see* **Persistent Muscle Pain**)

PERSISTENT MUSCLE PAIN
Homeopathy Fisher P. *et al.* "Effect of homeopathy on fibrositis (primary fibromyalgia)" *British Medical J.* 1989; 299:365–66
Massage Danneskiold-Samsoe B. *et al.* "Myofascial pain and the role of myoglobulin" *Scandinavian J. of Rheumatism* 1986, 15:175–78
Acupuncture Sprott H. *et al. Rheumatology International* 1998, 18:35–36
Hypnotherapy Haanen H.C.M. *et al.* "Controlled trial of hypnotherapy in the treatment of refractory fibromyalgia" *J. of Rheumatology* 1991, 18(1):72–75
Meditation Kaplan K.H. *et al.* "The impact of a meditation-based stress reduction program on fibromyalgia" *General Hospital Psychiatry* 1993, 15(5):284–89

SPORTS INJURIES
Western Herbalism Cichoke A. "The use of proteolytic enzymes with soft tissue athletic injuries" *American Chiropractor* October 1981, 32
Nutritional Therapies Moncada S. *et al.* "Leucocytes and tissue injury: The use of eicosapentenoic acid in the control of white cell activation" *Wien Klinische Wochenschrift* 1986, 98(4):104–106
Homeopathy Bohmer D. *et al.* "Treating sports injuries with Traumeel ointment: a controlled double-blind study" *Biological Medizin* 1992, 21(4):260–68
Chiropractic & Osteopathy (*see* **Back & Neck Pain**)
Massage Smith L.L. *et al.* "The effects of athletic massage on delayed-onset muscle soreness, creatine kinase, and neutrophil count: a preliminary report" *J. of Orthopaedic & Sports Physical Therapy* 1994, 19(2):93–99
Acupuncture Haker E. *et al.* "Acupuncture treatment in epicondylalgia: a comparative study of two acupuncture techniques" *Clinical J. of Pain* 1990, 6(3):221–26
Hypnotherapy Achterberg J. *et al.* "Behavioural strategies for the reduction of pain and anxiety associated with acute orthopoedic trauma" *Biofeedback and Self-regulation* 1989, 14(2):101–14

PREMENSTRUAL SYNDROME

Western Herbalism Dittmar "Premenstrual syndrome: treatment with a phytopharma-ceutical" *Therapiewoche Gynakol* 1994, 7:49–52

Nutritional Therapies Abraham G.E. "Nutritional factors in the etiology of the premenstrual tension syndromes" *J. of Reproductive Medicine* 1983, 28:446–64 Faccinetti F. *et al.* "Magnesium prophylaxis of menstrual migraine: effects on intracellular magnesium" *Headache* 1991, 321:298–301 London R. "Effect of nutritional supplement on PMS symptomatology in women with PMS – a double-blind longitudinal study" *J. American College of Nutrition* 1991, 10(5):494–99

Reflexology Oleson T., Flocco W. "Randomized controlled study of premenstrual symptoms treated with ear, hand, and foot reflexology" *Obstetrics and Gynecology* 1993, 82(6):906–11

MENSTRUAL PAIN

Chiropractic & Osteopathy Kokjohn K. *et al.* "The effect of spinal manipulation on pain and prostaglandin levels in women with primary dysmenorrhea" *J. of Manipulative and Physiological Therapeutics* 1992, 15(5):279–85 Boesler D. *et al.* "Efficacy of high-velocity low-amplitude manipulative technique in subjects with low-back pain during menstrual cramping" *J. of the American Osteopathic Association* 1993, 93(2):203–208, 213–14

Acupuncture Helms J.M. "Acupuncture for the management of primary dysmenorrhea" *Obstetrics and Gynaecology* 1987, 69(1):51–56

INFERTILITY IN WOMEN

Hypnotherapy Quinn P.D.R., Pawson M. "Conceptions of the mind; the role of hypno-therapy interventions in medically unexplained, functional and psychosomatic infertility" *European J. of Clinical Hypnosis* 1994, 1:(4)

PREGNANCY

Western Herbalism Fischer-Rasmussen W. *et al.* "Ginger treatment of hyperemesis gravidarum" *European J. of Obstetrics and Gynaecology and Reproductive Biology* 1990, 38:19–24

Nutritional Therapies Zatuchni G.I. *et al.* "Bromelain therapy for the prevention of episiotomy pain" *Obstetrics and Gynecology* 1967, 29(2):275–78

Acupuncture De Aloysio D., Penacchioni P. "Morning sickness control in early pregnancy by Neiguan point acupressure" *Obstetrics and Gynecology* 1992, 80:852–54 Cardini F. *et al.* "Moxibustion for correction of breech presentation: a randomised controlled trial" *J. of the American Medical Association* 1998, 280:1580–84

Visualization Feher S.D.K. *et al.* "Increasing breast-milk production for premature infants with a relaxation/imagery audiotape" *Pediatrics* 1989, 83(1):57–60

(**Chiropractic** and **Osteopathy** *see* **Back & Neck Pain**)

MENOPAUSE

Western Herbalism Linde K. *et al.* "St John's wort for depression: an overview and meta-analysis of randomised clinical trials" *British Medical J.* 1996, 313:253–58

Nutritional Therapies Adlercreutz H. *et al.* "Dietary phytoestrogens and the menopause in Japan" *Lancet* 1992, 339:1233 Chow R. *et al.* "Effect of two randomised exercise programmes on bone mass of healthy post-menopausal women" *British Medical J.* 1987, 295:1441–44

VAGINAL THRUSH

Nutritional Therapies Collins E. "Inhibition of *candida albicans* by *L acidophilus* – experimental study" *J. of Dairy Sciences* 1980, 63:830–32

Aromatherapy Belaiche P. "Treatment of vaginal infections of *Candida albicans* with essential oil of *Melaleuca alternifolia*" *Phytotherapie* 1985, 15

CYSTITIS

Western Herbalism Avorn J. *et al.* "Reduction of bacteriuria and pyuria after ingestion of cranberry juice" *J. of the American Medical Association* 1994, 271(10):751–54

Acupuncture Aune A. *et al.* "Acupuncture in the prophylaxis of recurrent lower urinary tract infection in adult women" *Scandinavian J. of Primary Health Care* 1998, 16:37–39

PROSTATE PROBLEMS

Western Herbalism Wilt T. J. *et al.* "Saw palmetto extracts for treatment of benign prostatic hyperplasia: a systematic review" *J. of the American Medical Association* 1998, 280:1604–609 Shah P.J.R. "The treatment of disorders of the prostate with the rye-grass extract" *Complementary Therapies in Medicine* 1996, 4:21–25

MALE SEXUAL DYSFUNCTION

Western Herbalism Sikora R. *et al.* "Ginkgo biloba extract in the therapy of erectile dysfunction" *J. of Urology* 1989, 141:188

STRESS

Western Herbalism D'Angelo L. *et al.* "Double-blind controlled clinical study of the effect of standardized ginseng extract on psychomotor performance in healthy volunteers" *J. of Ethnopharmacology* 1986, 16:15–22

Aromatherapy Stevenson C. "The psycho-physiological effects of aromatherapy massage following cardiac surgery" *Complementary Therapies in Medicine* 1994, 2(1):27–35

T'ai Chi Jin P. "Efficacy of T'ai Chi, brisk walking, meditation and reading in reducing mental and emotional stress" *J. of Psychosomatic Research* 1992, 36(4):361–70

Meditation Janowiak J.J. *et al.* "Meditation and college students' self-actualization and rated stress" *Psychological Reports* 1994, 75(2):1007–10 Dillbeck M.C. "The effect of the Transcendental Meditation technique on anxiety levels" *J. of Clinical Psychology* 1977, 33(4):1076–78

ANXIETY & PANIC ATTACKS

Western Herbalism Kinszler E. *et al.* "Effect of kava extract in patients with anxiety, tension and excitation states of non-psychotic genesis: a double-blind study with placebos" *Arzneim Forsch* 1991, 41(6):584–88

Nutritional Therapies King D. "Can allergic exposure provoke psychological symptoms? A double-blind test" *Biological Psychiatry* 1981, 16(1):3–19

Massage Field T. *et al.* "Massage reduces anxiety in child and adolescent psychiatric patients" *J. of the American Academy of Child and Adolescent Psychiatry* 1992, (1):125–31

Therapeutic Touch Simington J.A., Laing G.P. "Effects of therapeutic touch on anxiety in the institutionalized elderly" *Clinical Nursing Research* 1993, 2(4):438–50

Psychotherapy & Counselling Clark D.M. *et al.* "A comparison of cognitive therapy, applied relaxation and imipramine in the treatment of panic disorder" *British J. of Psychiatry* 1994, 164(6):759–69

Meditation Miller J.J. *et al.* "Three year follow up and clinical implications of a mindfulness meditation-based stress reduction intervention in the treatment of anxiety disorders" *General Hospital Psychiatry* 1995, 17:192–200

Hypnotherapy Scott J.A. "A comparison of medical hypnoanalysis and cognitive hypnotherapy for the treatment of anxiety disorders" *Medical Hypnoanalysis J.* 1995 Dec., 10(4):355–81

Visualization Stanton H.E. "Using hypnotic success imagery to reduce test anxiety" *Australian J. of Clinical and Experimental Hypnosis* 1992 May, 20(1):31–37

DEPRESSION

Western Herbalism Linde K. *et al.* "St John's wort for depression: an overview and meta-analysis of randomised clinical trials" *British Medical J.* 1996, 313:253–58

Nutritional Therapies, Massage and **Aromatherapy** Wallcraft J. *Healing Minds* Mental Health Foundation jwallcraft@mentalhealth.org.uk

Acupuncture Luo H. *et al.* "Electro-acupuncture in the treatment of depressive psychosis: a controlled prospective randomised trial using electro-acupuncture and amitriptyline in 241 patients" *International J. of Clinical Acupuncture* 1990, I(I):7–13

Exercise Klein M.H. *et al.* "A comparative outcome study of group psychotherapy vs. exercise treatments for depression" *International J. of Mental Health* 1985, 13(3–4):148–77

Psychotherapy & Counselling Murphy G.E. *et al.* "Cognitive behavior therapy, relaxation training, and tricyclic antidepressant medication in the treatment of depression" *Psychological Reports* 1995, 77(2):403–20

Meditation Smith W.P. *et al.* "Meditation as an adjunct to a happiness enhancement program" *J. of Clinical Psychology* 1995, 51(2):269–73

INSOMNIA

Western Herbalism Lindahl O. *et al.* "Double-blind study of a valerian preparation" *Pharmacology, Biochemistry and Behavior* 1989, 32:1065–66

Nutritional Therapies Garfinkel D. *et al.* "Improvement of sleep quality in elderly people by controlled-release melatonin" *Lancet* 1995, 346:541–44 Petrie K. *et al.* "A double-blind trial of melatonin as a treatment for jet lag in international cabin crew" *Biological Psychiatry* 1993, 33(7):526–30

Hypnotherapy Morin C.M. *et al.*

"Nonpharmacological interventions for insomnia: a meta-analysis of treatment efficacy" *American J. of Psychiatry* 1994, 151:1172–80
Meditation "Integration of behavioural and relaxation approaches into the treatment of chronic pain and insomnia" *J. of the American Medical Association* 1996, 276:313–18

FOOD SENSITIVITIES
Nutritional Therapies Nanda R. *et al.* "Food intolerance and the irritable bowel syndrome" *Gut* 1989, 30(8):1099–104
Environmental Medicine McEwan L.M. *et al.* "Enzyme-potentiated desensitisation: the effect of pretreatment with glucuronidase, hyaluronidase and antigen on anaphylactic sensitivity of guinea-pigs, rats and mice" *International Archive of Allergy* 1972, 42:152–58

RHINITIS & HAY FEVER
Western Herbalism Bellussi L. *et al.* "Evaluation of the efficacy and safety of sobrerol granules in patients suffering from chronic rhinosinusitis" *J. of International Medical Research* 1990, 18:454–59
Homeopathy Taylor Reilly D. *et al.* "Is homoeopathy a placebo response? Controlled trial of homoeopathic potency, with pollen in hayfever as a model" *Lancet* 1986 II(8512):881–85
Wiesenauer M. *et al.* "The treatment of pollinosis with Galphimia glauca D4: a randomized placebo-controlled double-blind clinical trial" *Phytomedicine* 1995, 2(1):3–6
Acupuncture Davies A. *et al.* "The effect of acupuncture on nonallergic rhinitis: a controlled pilot study" *Alternative Therapies* Jan 1988, 4(1):70–74
Hypnotherapy Fry L. *et al.* "Effect of hypnosis on allergic skin responses in asthma and hayfever" *British Medical J.* 1964, i.1145–48

ASTHMA
Homeopathy Reilly, D. *et al.* "Is evidence for homeopathy reproducible?" *Lancet* 1994, 344:1601–06
Nutritional Therapies Lindahl O. *et al.* "Vegan diet regimen with reduced medication in the treatment of bronchial asthma" *J. of Asthma* 1985, 22(1):45–55
Skobeloff E.M. *et al.* "Intravenous magnesium sulfate for the treatment of acute asthma in the emergency department" *J. of the American Medical Association* 1989, 262:1210–13
Chiropractic Nielsen N.H. *et al.* "Chronic asthma and chiropractic spinal manipulation: a randomized clinical trial" *Clinical & Experimental Allergy* 1995, 25(1):80–88
Acupuncture Linde, K. *et al.* "Evaluation of the effectiveness of acupuncture for the treatment of asthma bronchiale" *The Cochrane Library* 1997, 2
Yoga Nagarathna R., Nagendra H.R. "Yoga for bronchial asthma: a controlled study" *British Medical J.* (Clinical Research) 1985 Oct 19, 291(6502):1077–79
Hypnotherapy Ewer T.C., Stewart D.E. "Improvement in bronchial hyper-responsiveness in patients with moderate asthma after treatment with a hypnotic technique: a randomised controlled trial" *British Medical J.* (Clinical Research) 1986 Nov 1, 293(6555):1129–32

Meditation Wilson A.F. *et al.* "Transcendental meditation and asthma" *Respiration* 1975, 32(1):74–80
Relaxation & Breathing Henry M. *et al.* "Improvement of respiratory function in chronic asthmatic patients with autogenic therapy" *J. of Psychosomatic Research* 1993, 37(3):265–70

CANCER
Massage
Corner J. *et al.* "An evaluation of the use of massage and essential oils on the well-being of cancer patients" *International J. of Palliative Nursing* 1995, 1(2):67–73
Zanolla R. *et al.* "Evaluation of the results of three different methods of postmastectomy lymphedema treatment" *J. of Surgical Oncology* 1984, 26:210–13
Acupuncture Vickers A.J. "Can acupuncture have specific effects on health? A systematic literature review of acupuncture antiemesis trials" *J. of the Royal Society of Medicine* 1996, 89:303–11
Psychotherapy & Counselling
Spiegel D. *et al.* "Effect of psychosocial treatment on survival of patients with metastatic breast cancer" *Lancet* 1989, 2: 888–91
Greer S. *et al.* "Adjuvant psychosocial therapy for patients with cancer: a prospective randomised trial" *British Medical J.* 1992, 304:675–80
Hypnotherapy Spiegel D. *et al.* "Group therapy and hypnosis reduce metastatic breast carcinoma pain" *Psychosomatic Medicine* 1982, 45:333–39

CHRONIC FATIGUE SYNDROME
Psychotherapy & Counselling Deale A. *et al.* "Cognitive behavior therapy for chronic fatigue syndrome: a randomized controlled trial" *American J. of Psychiatry* 1997, 154:408–14

PERSISTENT PAIN
Western Herbalism Watson C.P.N. *et al.* "Post-herpetic neuralgia and topical capsaicin" *Pain* 1988; 33:333–40
Massage Ferrell-Torry A.T. *et al.* "The use of therapeutic massage as a nursing intervention to modify anxiety and the perception of cancer pain" *Cancer Nursing* 1993, 16(2):93–101
Acupuncture Ter Riet G. *et al.* "Acupuncture and chronic pain: A criteria-based meta-analysis" *J. of Clinical Epidemiology* 1990, 43(11):1191–99
Psychotherapy & Counselling "Treatment of chronic pain and insomnia: integration of behavioural and relaxation approaches into the treatment of chronic pain and insomnia" *J. of the American Medical Association* 1996, 276:313–38
Visualization Albright G.L. *et al.* "Effects of warming imagery aimed at trigger-point sites on tissue compliance, skin temperature, and pain sensitivity in biofeedback-trained patients with chronic pain: a preliminary study" *Perceptual and Motor Skills* 1990, 71:1163–70
Biofeedback Stuckey S.J. *et al.* "EMG biofeedback training, relaxation training and placebo for the relief of chronic back pain" *Perceptual and Motor Skills* 1986, 63:1023–36
Meditation Kabat-zinn J. "Four year follow-up of a meditation-based program for the self-regulation of chronic pain: treatment

outcomes and compliance" *Clinical J. of Pain* 1986, 2:159–73
Relaxation & Breathing Cappo B. *et al.* "Utility of prolonged respiratory exhalation for reducing physiological and psychological arousal in non-threatening and threatening situations" *J. of Psychosomatic Research* 1984, 28(4):265–73
Healing Sundblom D.M. *et al.* "Effect of spiritual healing on chronic idiopathic pain: a medical and psychological study" *Clinical J. of Pain* 1994, 10(4):296–302

HIV & AIDS
Nutritional Therapies Allard J.P. *et al.* "Effects of vitamin E and C supplementation on oxidative stress and viral load in HIV-infected subjects" *AIDS* 1998, 12(13):1653–59
Massage Scafidi F. *et al.* "Massage therapy improves behaviour in neonates born to HIV-positive mothers" *J. of Pediatric Psychology* 1996, 21(6):889–97
Acupuncture Tindall J. *Complementary Medicine Bulletin* vol. 1 (10):4
Stress Management Coates T.J. *et al.* "Stress reduction training in men with HIV" *American J. of Public Health* 1989, 79:885–87
Taylor D.N. "Effects of a behavioral stress-management program on anxiety, mood, self-esteem, and T-cell count in HIV positive men" *Psychological Reports* 1995, 76(2):451–57
McCain N.L. *et al.* "The influence of stress management training in HIV disease" *Nursing Research* 1996, 45(4):246–53
Healing & Therapeutic Touch Sicher F. *et al.* "A randomized double-blind study of the effect of distant healing in a population with advanced AIDS. Report of a small scale study" *Western J. of Medicine* 1998, 169(6):356–63
Ireland M. "Therapeutic touch with HIV-infected children: a pilot study" *J. of the Association of Nurses in AIDS Care* 1998, 9(4):68–77

INCONCLUSIVE TESTS
In the following studies the relevent therapies proved ineffective or inconclusive:

Iridology Diagnosis Knipschild P. "Looking for gall bladder disease in the patient's iris" *British Medical J.* 1988, 297(6663):1578–81
Simon A. *et al.* "An evaluation of iridology" *J. of the American Medical Association* 1979, 242(13):1385–89
Hair Testing Sethi T.J. *et al.* "How reliable are commercial allergy tests?" *Lancet* 1987, 1:92–94
Muscle Testing for Intolerances Rybeck C.H. *et al.* "The effect of oral administration of refined sugar on muscle strength" *J. of Manipulative and Physiological Therapeutics* 1980, 3(3):155–61
Triano J.J. "Muscle-strength testing as a diagnostic screen for supplement nutrition therapy: a blind study" *J. of Manipulative and Physiological Therapeutics* 1982, 5(4):179–87
Skin Testing for Food Allergies Jewett D.L. *et al.* "A double-blind study of symptom provocation to determine food sensitivity" *New England J. of Medicine* 1990, 323(7):429–33

USEFUL ADDRESSES

THE ORGANIZATIONS LISTED BELOW range from professional bodies whose members include conventional doctors, to those run on a voluntary basis with relatively few members. It is advisable to send a stamped, self-addressed envelope with your enquiry.

Always bear in mind the guidelines suggested for finding a practitioner (*see pages 180–81*).

ACUPUNCTURE
British Acupuncture Council
63 Jeddo Road, London W12 9HQ
0208 735 0400
Regulates standards of training and codes of practice, and maintains a register of UK practitioners.
www.tcm.org.uk/assoc/ba.htm
British Medical Acupuncture Society
Newton House, Newton Lane, Whitley, Warrington, Cheshire WA4 4JA
Represents doctors who have trained in acupuncture techniques.
www.medical-acupuncture.co.uk

ALEXANDER TECHNIQUE
The Society of Teachers of Alexander Technique
20 London House, 266 Fulham Road, London SW10 9EL
0207 351 0828
Most Alexander teachers are registered with the Society. Members have completed three-years' full-time study and hold the title MSTAT.
www.university-of-life.com/ip000963.htm

AROMATHERAPY
Aromatherapy Organizations Council
P. O. Box 19834, London SE25 6WF
0208 251 7912
Provides a list of member associations and training establishments.

ART THERAPY
British Association of Art Therapists
11a Richmond Road, Brighton BN2 3RL
All practitioners undertake a two-year full-time postgraduate diploma course.

AUTOGENIC TRAINING
British Association for Autogenic Training and Therapy (BAFATT)
c/o Royal London Homeopathic Hospital, Great Ormond Street, London WC1N 3HR
0207 837 8833
Members are health professionals who have completed three years' part-time training.

AYURVEDA
Ayurvedic Medical Association UK
Eastern Clinic, 1079 Garrett Lane, London SW17 0LN
0208 682 3876
www.ayurveda.demon.co.uk

Fully qualified Ayurvedic physicians complete a five-year degree course at Indian or Sri Lankan universities.

BIOFEEDBACK
Most biofeedback devices are to be found in hospitals and universities.
Ultramind Ltd.
2 Lindsey Street, London EC1A 9HP
Supplies portable machines and computer programs for home use.
www.ultramind.com

CHIROPRACTIC
The British Chiropractic Association
Blagrave House, 17 Blagrave Street, Reading, Berkshire RG1 1QB
0118 950 5950
Maintains a register of practitioners. Members have completed a five-year full-time BSc (Hons) degree course and a further one year's postgraduate study leading to the Diploma in Chiropractic.

HEALING
The Confederation of Healing Organizations
113 High Street, Berkhamstead, Hertfordshire HP4 2DJ
National Federation of Spiritual Healers
Old Manor Farm Studio, Church Street, Sunbury-on-Thames, Middlesex TW16 6RG
Members complete a probationary period of 18–24 months, followed by an assessment.
www.nfsh.org.uk

HERBALISM
Information on finding a practitioner can be obtained from:
National Institute of Medical Herbalists
56 Longbrook Street, Exeter, Devon EX4 6AH
01392 426022
Accredits four-year full-time clinical training courses. Members with at least ten years' experience may apply to become fellows (FNIMH).
www.btinternet.com/~nimh/

HOMEOPATHY
The Faculty of Homoeopathy
15 Clerkenwell Close, London EC1 0AA
0207 566 7810
Members are medically qualified homeopaths.
The Society of Homoeopaths
2 Artizan Road, Northampton NN1 4HU
01604 621400
Members are not doctors but have completed a three-year full-time or four-year part-time course, and a year in supervised practice.

HYPNOTHERAPY
Some psychologists working within the National Health Service practise hypnosis;

your doctor may be able to give a referral. The following organizations can refer you to members of professional bodies whose training complies to certain standards:
British Society of Experimental and Clinical Hypnosis
c/o Phyllis Alden, Department of Psychology, Grimsby General Hospital, Scartho Road, Grimsby, South Humberside DN33 2BA
Members are doctors and psychologists practising hypnosis.
British Society of Medical and Dental Hypnosis
National Office, 17 Keppel View Road, Kimberworth, Rotherham, South Yorkshire S61 2AR
Members are doctors and dentists practising hypnosis.
www.bsmdh.org
Central Register of Advanced Hypnotherapists
P. O. Box 14526, London N4 2WG
Members have completed a one year part-time diploma course followed by two years' supervision.
The National College of Hypnosis and Psychotherapy
12 Cross Street, Nelson, Lancashire BB9 7EN
Member organization of the UK Council of Psychotherapy. Maintains the National Register of Hypnotherapists and Psychotherapists. Members have completed a two-year part-time course.

MASSAGE THERAPY
Your doctor may be able to recommend a massage therapist. Health farms and clubs, sports centres and beauty clinics routinely offer massage. Professional therapists should have attended an accredited college, and have received some training in anatomy and physiology. For information:
British Federation of Massage Practitioners
78 Meadow Street, Preston, Lancashire PR1 1TS
01772 881063
Represents a number of professional organizations covering all forms of Eastern and Western massage.

MUSIC THERAPY
Most music therapists work within the National Health Service or in state education, with a few in private practice. All are trained musicians who have completed a degree or diploma course at a recognized college, followed by a year's postgraduate training.
Association of Professional Music Therapists
26 Hamlyn Road, Glastonbury BA66 8HT

The Nordoff-Robbins Music Therapy Centre
2 Lissendon Gardens, London NW5
0207 371 8404
www.nyu.edu/education/music/nrobbins/

NATUROPATHY
The British College of Naturopathy and Osteopathy offers a four-year full-time BSc degree course in osteopathy, which incorporates a diploma in naturopathy. All qualified naturopaths hold the title Registered Naturopath. For information:
General Council and Register of Naturopaths
Goswell House, 2 Goswell Road, Street, Somerset BA16 0JG
01458 840072
www.naturopathy.org.uk/gcrn.htm

NUTRITIONAL THERAPY
The British Society for Allergy, Environmental and Nutritional Medicine
P. O. Box 28, Totton,
Southampton SO40 2ZA
Only accepts patients with a doctor's referral. Members are medically qualified doctors.
British Association of Nutritional Therapy (BANT)
P. O. Box 17436, London SE13 7WT
Institute of Optimum Therapy
13 Blades Court, Deodar Road,
London SW15 2NU
0208 877 9993
Society for the Promotion of Nutritional Therapy
P. O. Box 47, Heathfield,
East Sussex TN21 8ZX
01825 872921

OSTEOPATHY
The first UK State Register of Osteopaths was established in 1998. All qualified osteopaths have completed a four-year full-time BSc degree course, run by several schools accredited by the General Osteopathic Council. Further information on finding a practitioner can be obtained from:
Osteopathic Information Service
Osteopathy House, 176 Tower Bridge Road, London SE1 3LU
0207 357 655

PSYCHOTHERAPY & COUNSELLING
Anyone can call themselves a counsellor or psychotherapist. Information on finding a qualified practitioner can be obtained from:
British Association of Counselling
1 Regent Place, Rugby,
Warwickshire CV21 2PJ
01788 550899
UK Council for Psychotherapy (UKCP)
167–169 Great Portland Street,
London W1N 5FB
0207 436 3002
Represents all forms of psychotherapy and maintains a national register of practitioners.

British Confederation of Psychotherapists
37 Mapesbury Road, London NW2 4HJ
Maintains a national register of psychoanalytic psychotherapists.
www.bcp.org.uk

QIGONG
Qualified teachers should have at least five years' experience
Tse Qigong Centre
P. O. Box 116, Manchester M20 3YN
www.michaeltse.u-net.com/centre/index.htm

REFLEXOLOGY
Reflexologists must be registered with one of the associations listed below, which have a code of practice and training standards.
Association of Reflexologists
Katepwa House, Ashfield Park Avenue,
Ross-on-Wye, Herefordshire HR9 5AX
08705 673320
International Federation of Reflexologists
76 Edridge Road, Croydon, Surrey CR0 1EF
0208 667 9458
Reflexologists Society
249 Fosse Road South, Leicester LE3 1AF
0116 282 5511

REIKI
The Reiki Association
Cornbrook Bridge House,
Clee Hill, Ludlow, Shropshire SY8 3QQ
01981 550829

SHIATSU
All practitioners undertake a minimum of three years' part-time study and must satisfy the Shiatsu Society's assessment panel.
The Shiatsu Society
Barber House, Storeys Bar Road,
Sengate, Peterborough PE1 5YS
01733 758333
www.shiatsu.org

T'AI CHI
UK T'ai Chi Association
P. O. Box 157, Bromley, Kent BR1 3XX
0208 289 5166
Provides a list of local teachers and further information.
The T'ai Chi Union for Great Britain
9 Ashfield Road, London N14 7LA
0208 368 6815

THERAPEUTIC TOUCH
The Sacred Space Foundation
Redmire, Mungrisdale, Cumbria CA11 0TB
017687 79000
www.cumbria.com/sacredspace

TRADITIONAL CHINESE MEDICINE
Register of Chinese Herbal Medicine
P. O. Box 400, Wembley,
Middlesex HA9 9NZ
0207 470 8740
www.rchm.co.uk
Maintains a register of practitioners who have trained with reputable colleges.

YOGA THERAPY
Qualified teachers will have trained with one of a number of recognized organizations, such as the following:
British Wheel of Yoga
Central Office, 1 Hamilton Place,
Boston Road, Sleaford,
Lincolnshire NG34 7ES
www.members.aol.com/wheelyoga
Iyengar Yoga Institute
223a Randolph Avenue, London W9 1NL
www.iyi.org.uk
Yoga for Health Foundation
Ickwell Bury, Biggleswade,
Bedfordshire SG18 9EF
Yoga Therapy Centre
Royal Homeopathic Hospital,
60 Great Ormond Street,
London WC1N 3HR
0207 419 7195
Runs clinics for patients with asthma, diabetes, hypertension and back pain, and maintains a register of trained therapists who have completed a two-year course.

GENERAL ORGANIZATIONS
British Complementary Medicine Association
249 Fosse Road, Leicester LE3 1AE
Encourages communication between existing organizations to establish codes of conduct and ethics.
British Holistic Medical Association
59 Lansdowne Place, Hove,
East Sussex BN3 1FL
01273 725951
Links health professionals and laypeople interested in developing holistic healthcare.
The Foundation for Integrated Medicine
International House, 59 Compton Road,
London N1 2YT
0207 688 1881
www.fimed.org
Encourages the development of safe, effective and efficient integrated healthcare by encouraging greater collaboration between conventional and non-conventional practitioners.

INDEX

A page number in **bold** indicates the main entry on a topic. A main entry for an ailment includes details of the ailment, the factors causing it, the treatment options, and relevant case studies and precautions. A main entry for a therapy includes details of its effects, its history and main principles, its main uses and a description of what is involved in a treatment session.

ACKNOWLEDGMENTS

Authors' Acknowledgements
We are extremely grateful to those who helped us in various ways with
this book. For their professional advice and wisdom, we would like to
thank psychologist Ashley Conway, acupuncturist Gerry Harris,
osteopath Mark Kane, nutritional therapist Kate Neil, naturopaths Leon
Chaitow and Roger Newman Turner, homeopath Gabrielle Pinto and
medical herbalist Julie Whitehouse.
    Many thanks for practical support and general hand-holding to Debbie
Cole and Karen Mayze, and to Mary Bredin and Stephen Claypole for
their considerable qualities of patience, tolerance and encouragement.
    None of this could be achieved without the good humour, creative
ingenuity and fortitude of the team at Dorling Kindersley, for which an
enormous thank you to Daphne Razazan and Susannah Marriott, and
especially to David Summers and Penny Warren.

Publisher's Acknowledgements
Dorling Kindersley would like to thank Monica Chakraverty and Tracey
Beresford for editorial assistance, Carol McGlynn and Christa Weil for proof-
reading, Alison Verity for design assistance and Sue Bosanko for the index.

Picture Credits
Picture research: Anna Grapes
Picture library: Melanie Simmonds, Denise O'Brien, Charlotte Oster
The publisher would like to thank the following for their kind
permission to reproduce their photographs: (Abbreviations key: t=top,
b=below, r=right, l=left, c=centre, a=above.)
AKG London: 148–49
Science Photo Library: Alfred Pasieka 11tr; Don Fawcett 167; Ed
Young/Agstock 166c
Tony Stone Images: G W Willis/BPS 158-159; Ken Fisher 168–69; Vince
Michaels 148cr.